UP FROM HESTER STREET

JANIECE S. NOLAN AND ROBERT L. NOLAN

WITH Mollie Flaumenhaft Nolan

ISBN: 1479142069
ISBN 13: 9781479142064

Cover Photograph: Mollie Flaumenhaft at about age three, Lower East Side, New York, circa 1897

We dedicate this book to our six children:
Douglas, Patricia, Nancy, Margaret, Sheffield, and Gemini,
as well as to the memory of Mollie F. Nolan

CONTENTS

ACKNOWLEDGMENTS

We thank Patricia Nolan Suskin for asking Mollie to write her memoirs and thank Mollie for writing them. The Berkeley Writers' workshop reviewed and made many suggestions for this book, with special thanks to Doris Fine and Sally Tubach as well as the Non-Fiction Section: Virginia Foote Anderson, Ruth Hanham, Joanne Lagerstrom, Lynn De Jonghe, and Ione Elioff. Susan Austin gave us great ideas for publishing. Thank you to Rabbi Judy Shanks of Temple Isaiah (Lafayette, California) who edited the section on Galicia and Jewish history. Thank you to Rabbi Ruth Adar (Berkeley, California) for help with Jewish history and Hebrew translations. We are grateful to Kim Formica who provided valuable genealogy information and documents. We appreciate our copy editor, Sue Mann, and Denny Weigand of Digital Whims, who restored the old photos and digitized the rest. Thank you to Nancy Peterson who typed Mollie's autobiography into electronic format. Thanks to our six children who encouraged us and to Mollie, without whom there would have been no book.

INTRODUCTION

Mollie Flaumenhaft was born in 1893 in New York City's Lower East Side, in the heart of the ghetto. Her parents were Yiddish-speaking immigrants, Orthodox Jews who eked out a living by first working in garment factories, then by starting a number of ill-fated businesses that ranged from pushcarts to candy stores. When Mollie was a toddler, she witnessed a horrific accident in her home during a Jewish ritual that left her mother dead within a week. Additional tragedies almost devastated Mollie later in life. Overcoming many barriers, Mollie managed to graduate from high school. After two years of full-time teacher training, she graduated with a public school teaching credential in 1912. She taught school for about twelve years. More than a decade later she returned to teaching and completed studies for a bachelor's degree equivalency.

During high school Mollie turned away from the practice of Judaism to participate in meetings of the Brooklyn Society for Ethical Culture, a nondeistic congregation for humanists founded by Felix Adler in 1876. There she met her future husband, John Nolan, the son of Irish immigrants who was raised a Roman Catholic but as a youth rejected that religion and later chose Ethical Culture.

Mollie was always an advocate for the poor and the handicapped. She was passionately involved in civic affairs, speaking out against social injustices until her death in Walnut Creek, California, in 1980 at age 86.

After Mollie died, we found the autobiography she had written covering the years from her birth until 1924. She discussed her Jewish upbringing and her husband's Irish immigrant background, as well as the years of their courtship, marriage, and birth of their first child. We printed her manuscript just as she wrote it, transferring her longhand into an electronic handwriting font, adding section headings for ease of reading, and inserting occasional clarifications. We added comments in a prologue that covers the years that Janiece knew her, from 1972 to 1980. We also added a continuation biography encompassing the years from 1924 to 1980, consisting of short vignettes about Mollie. The Afterword contains updated information about Mollie's siblings and their children, and the Notes section contains our conclusions about Mollie and her heritage. Throughout *Up from Hester Street* you will hear the voices of Mollie, Janiece, and Robert.

As a first-generation American, Mollie Flaumenhaft Nolan rose from 3 Hester Street to live a life of courage, conviction, and social activism. Her son Robert is a physician and attorney, and he carries on his mother's tradition of advocating for social justice. Mollie's grandchildren — Douglas, Patricia, Nancy, Margaret, Sheffield and Gemini — are very successful, and they, too, are staunch advocates for social justice and civil rights. Mollie's legacy continues.

PROLOGUE

1972–1980

JANIECE: MEETING MOLLIE

I first met Mollie at the entrance to her apartment on MacArthur Boulevard in Oakland, California. The year was 1972 and she was seventy-nine years old. I noticed right away that she was short, not more than four foot ten inches. Her long gray-black hair was in a braided twist piled atop her head, which gave her some added height. She wore a blue flowered housedress, heavy beige hose, and black laced shoes that were oddly shaped and square. I found out later that they were Earth Shoes, custom fit to accommodate her arthritic feet. Her hands were twisted with arthritis. She had huge knuckles lined with veins. She wore no rings. Her face was smooth and pink as a flower and appeared to be freshly washed and powdered, her large eyes a faded shade of brown. She looked up at me expectantly through thick glasses set in light-colored plastic frames, giving me a very toothy smile. Her jaw line was strong and jutted out at a determined angle. As she extended her hand and gave me a firm handshake and hearty welcome, I was startled by her deep and powerful voice; how could such a big voice be coming from such a tiny person?

I had not known what to expect. Her son Robert and I were in love and involved in a whirlwind romance that was very secret because we both were married to others. Robert had a wife and four children (ages ten through nineteen). He and his family had left the Bay Area for three years to live in West Virginia while he was on the faculty of the medical school there. He had moved back to the Bay Area several months ahead of his family, who would soon be on the way. He and I met at the VA Hospital in Martinez, California, where we both worked. I had a husband and four-year-old son. It was complicated. We worried about the impact our marriage plans would have on our respective families, especially on the children. My parents were in Texas and his mother, a widow, was in Oakland. We were unsure of their reactions. It was time to find out.

Robert was very devoted to his mother, and she to him. I would overhear him having long telephone conversations with her that included friendly arguments. He had wanted me to meet her right away, so he called her one afternoon and asked if he could drop by her apartment to introduce her to a colleague. Despite the lack of notice, Mollie graciously received us. Although it was the free-wheeling 1970s, Mollie, someone who was born in the nineteenth century, could well have been shocked by our relationship and reject me. Instead, she embraced me. Yes, she immediately determined that I was more than a colleague, as she told Robert on the telephone that night. He admitted it. Mollie enjoyed being in on our secret romance and endorsed our plan to marry as soon as we were free to do so. It was clear she was devoted to her son and wanted whatever would make him happy. I was thrilled with the idea that she wanted me as her daughter-in-law.

Mollie lived in a small one-bedroom apartment cluttered with photos of Robert and her grandchildren as well as with books, magazines, and piles of newspapers. As she brought out some refreshments for us, she looked sturdier than I had anticipated. She walked quickly and confidently, with a wide gait. She immediately engaged in some friendly bickering with Robert about topics that were not clear to me. Robert had told me that she fit the stereotype of a Jewish mother, and their back-and-forth conversation that day seemed to bear out the description. She seemed overly concerned about details of Robert's shipment of his belongings from West Virginia, about his job and his health and general welfare. He seemed to resist answering many of her questions and attempted to turn the conversation to me and my accomplishments.

Mollie was obviously delighted with Robert's recent return from West Virginia. After she became a widow in 1959, she soon moved from New York to Oakland to be close to Robert and his family. She had remained in Oakland while Robert and his family were in West Virginia, hoping for their return.

As Robert and his mother talked that afternoon, I absorbed the atmosphere of her apartment. It was summer and the air was rather warm inside but not uncomfortable. A dark wooden bookcase with glass doors dominated the living room, a decal from NYU on one door. Books were packed into the bookcase, with some turned on their sides for better fit. I saw all types of textbooks on the shelves, probably accumulated from her years as a public school teacher in New York. Crochet work was on every armchair. A very big radio and a small TV fit in the room. From my chair in the living room, I could see into the kitchen alcove with its blue Formica table and three white wooden chairs. I thought I detected the smell of roasted onions drifting out from the kitchen. When I entered her bedroom during another visit, I found a single wooden bed covered with a crocheted blanket, and a plain wooden dresser and mirror. Framed family photos filled every surface.

ROBERT: WHEN JANIECE MET MY MOTHER

It was a sunny day in the summer of 1972. Janiece and I were enjoying lunch together at Jack London Square and preparing to return to work in Martinez. I suggested we swing by my mother's apartment on the way. Then I went to a phone booth and phoned Mom. I told her I was bringing a colleague and that we would stay only briefly, and she responded saying that was fine.

Fifteen minutes later we were at her apartment door on MacArthur Boulevard in Oakland, opposite the Altenheim Home for the Aged. At age seventy-nine she was in good health and had lived independently following my father's death in Brooklyn in 1959.

Standing erect and not quite five feet tall, Mom promptly welcomed us at the door and led us into her living room. She wore a flowery one-piece dress and smiled graciously as she spoke to us. Her gray-black hair was in a bun. Her brown eyes were warm and alert.

Janiece wore a plain skirt and blouse in bright primary colors that complemented her naturally curly blonde hair. She was thirty-three years old, five-foot-five-inches tall, slim, with hazel eyes and a friendly smile that lit up her pretty face. We were in our work clothes. I was in a short-sleeve shirt and tie, slacks, and seersucker jacket. I was forty-six years old with brown eyes and black hair, about three inches taller than Janiece, euphoric and healthy.

Mom had a tray of iced tea ready for us. Our conversation focused mostly on her questions and on events at the hospital where Janiece and I worked. I urged Janiece to describe her position there and her outstanding professional background. At the time Janiece was acting associate chief of staff for research and director of a research lab, and I was chief of staff, although she did not report to me.

This visit marked the first time I had brought a woman friend to meet a parent. (I had married my first wife secretly during medical school and did not first introduce her to my parents.) Mom had not heard of Janiece, but she was engaged, interested, and welcoming. They related well instantly. After an animated conversation of about twenty minutes, Janiece and I left to return to work.

We all enjoyed the visit. For Janiece and my mother, it was the beginning of a deep relationship that evolved and endured until Mom's death in 1980.

JANIECE: MOLLIE SUPPORTS OUR MARRIAGE PLANS

Several months after I met Mollie, Robert and I married in Mexico and again in Nevada (after our Haitian divorces) so we could live together as an honorable couple before our California divorces were finalized. Mollie was very supportive of our plans to marry and was not at all disturbed by our unusual situation. We lived on Warren Road in Walnut Creek, California, with two of our children: my son, Sheffield and his daughter Nancy (Margaret was living with her mother in Walnut Creek, Patricia was in college, and Douglas was in the navy on Midway Island).

On May 7, 1973, when our California divorces were final, we were able to get married in California. Mollie attended our simple home wedding ceremony and there met my mother, who had flown from Texas for the occasion. They got along very well. My father very much supported our marriage, but was unable to attend the ceremony. He later came out to visit us in 1974.

After the marriage ceremony Mollie slyly pulled me aside and with a big grin began to tell me (in whispered confidence) how we could go about having only sons. She and her husband had been successfully instructed by their kosher butcher who knew a man who was able to get bulls every time. After hearing her earnest advice, I laughed out loud. I was quick to tell her that I wanted a daughter, since I already had a son by my first marriage. And indeed, we were blessed with our daughter, Gemini Janiece Nolan, born September 8, 1974. I later told Mollie we followed the converse of the butcher's advice, and she blushed. That advice is covered in her autobiography.

Mollie was a wonderful grandmother to my four-year-old son, Sheffield, who was more than a handful. She said he reminded her of her firstborn, Bernard, with his high energy, ready smile, and platinum blonde hair and blue eyes. Although Mollie was eighty years old with developing health problems, she babysat rambunctious Sheffield with great skill at her apartment, sometimes giving him boards to nail with a real hammer. He loved visiting Mollie. It was also obvious that the older children—Douglas, Patricia, Nancy, and Margaret—all adored her as well. We often had family dinners that included Mollie. I have a photo of Thanksgiving 1974 showing Mollie posing proudly with all six grandchildren. From the beginning Mollie never made any status difference when she proudly discussed her grandchildren (Robert later adopted my son, Sheffield).

I continue to feel so fortunate to have four additional children and love them all. We purchased our large home in 1974 so each of our children would have a place to stay whether they lived with us or visited us. The four older children have always been close to their mother, Virginia. In recent years she has been included in family events we have organized and we are all very cordial. Mollie was a connecting link for all of us.

Although Mollie was short in stature, she rose above all others in her intellect, compassion for worthy causes, and devotion to family. She advocated for the disadvantaged and aging populations and kept up with current events much better than I did. After our daughter, Gemini, was born, I remember times at our house when Mollie suddenly would become very passionate about an injustice in another part of the world, yelling out what concerned her with her big deep voice. I often could not follow the thread of her tirades. When I was nursing the baby, I had to ask her to stop because the level of her anger was inhibiting my milk. Although she would quickly comply, she would look slightly bewildered, not understanding why her ranting against social injustices would bother me.

In 1975 Mollie broke her hip, and then suffered a terrible infection in the hospital that caused her to lose the use of both her shoulders. She refused to give up, went through extensive inpatient rehabilitation, and managed to stay in her apartment for four more years with the help of people she hired to do chores. I helped her figure out how to dress without using her shoulders. I suggested she drape her blouse over the back of a chair so she could sit and slide her arms into the sleeves and then stand up. Mollie was most grateful, stating that the therapists had never come up with such a solution. I felt proud to have helped her gain more independence.

Toward the end she hired a young neighbor girl to stay overnight with her. She continued to come to our house in Lafayette where we moved in 1974, and for a couple of years we were able to drop off our two youngest at her apartment for occasional babysitting. She called us at least once a day. One day in 1979 we became alarmed when she had not telephoned, and she did not answer her telephone that evening. We went to her apartment and found her on the floor, disoriented. We called an ambulance that took her to Kaiser Hospital in Oakland. They found that she had a serious electrolyte imbalance, the cause of which could not be determined. After a few days, we became dissatisfied with her care at Kaiser; for example, once we found her oxygen tube disconnected and no staff in attendance. We had her transferred to a pulmonologist colleague at John Muir Medical Center in Walnut Creek. There she became somewhat stronger, but it was obvious she could not return to her apartment when she no longer needed inpatient care. She agreed to be admitted to Rossmoor Convalescent Hospital in Walnut Creek for what we hoped would be a temporary stay. There she continued to experience falls for no apparent reason, and on September 6, 1980, she died of a cardiac arrest at the age of 86.

After she died we were faced with clearing out her apartment, which she had left abruptly the night she was taken away in an ambulance. We had been aware that she was writing her recollections after she broke her hip in 1975, but she never showed them to us. (Our daughter Patricia had suggested that she write them.) I made it my mission to find those writings, and I did. They were written on lined notebook paper in her beautiful teacher's cursive writing. They were scattered about the apartment, but I was able to put them together, along with the photos she had amassed. Unfortunately, the writings did not go past 1924. She had told us that she stopped there and was unable to continue because of profound sadness around an event in her life that occurred in 1924. In 1983 I put the handwritten papers and photos together and had them copied and put into spiral booklets as gifts for my husband and each of her grandchildren.

It has been more than thirty years since Mollie's death. Now that Robert and I are aging, the need to celebrate Mollie's life has become more acute for us. With the help of Robert, I resolved to complete Mollie's story, taking up where she left off in 1924. The first step was to type her handwritten recollections into electronic format in a handwriting font. The second step was to write what I remember about Mollie and the facts that emerged in our genealogy research after her death. The third step was to have Robert write about events in their shared lives.

RECOLLECTIONS OF MOLLIE F. NOLAN

(Nee Flaumenhaft) [Written in 1975]

From information obtained from my father, Louis Flaumenhaft, and his two sisters, Sarah and Dora, I was born in New York City on Ludlow Street in the heart of the ghetto on December 25, 1893. The year I was born the day coincided with the first day of Chanukah.

My father was the son of Reb Zezil Flaumenhaft and Malka Asher Flaumenhaft for whom I was named. Malka, in Yiddish, means queen. My husband, John Nolan, nicknamed me Malkela, meaning little queen. My father was one of 13 children. Reb is the abbreviation for rabbi. I do not know whether my grandfather was a practicing rabbi. All 13 children were afflicted with smallpox. The family was living on a small farm in Austria. The children lay on beds in the width. One by one they died. My grandmother, Malka, was so overcome with grief, that she became blind and passed away. Only my father and his two sisters, Dora and Sarah, survived this awful scourge.

My grandfather, <u>Reb Zezil Flaumenhaft</u>, circa 1892. He and his wife, Malka Asher Flaumenhaft, had 13 children. They lived on a small farm in Austria. Only 3 children survived after a small pox epidemic. This picture was taken in Austria during a visit of my aunt Dora Flaumenhaft Berger.

<u>Dora Flaumenhaft Berger</u> *my father's older sister, the "brains" of the family, circa 1892. She and her husband, David, ran a restaurant in the Williamsburgh section of Brooklyn. They had no children, but adopted the second daughter, Rose Bisgyer, of Dora's younger sister, Sarah Flaumenhaft Bisgyer [other family members say that Rose was not formally adopted but lived with Dora and her husband for some time, as census records show].*

In his youth, my father, jumping over a fence, broke his right arm at the elbow. At that time, all males were drafted into the Austrian army at 18. My grandparents did not have his arm set because the square elbow (as a result of the injury) would make my father ineligible for army service. At that point, my father came to U.S. thru the efforts of his sister, Dora, who was already here.

JANIECE: DORA FLAUMENHAFT

Dora and her sister, Sarah, came to the United States in 1883 (as indicated in the 1910 census records). Their brother Louis arrived five years later in 1888. Dora was known as the brains of the family who married "well" to David Berger, who ran a success-ful restaurant in the Williamsburg section of Brooklyn. The photo of Reb Zezil Flaumenhaft was taken in 1892 when Dora and her hus-band went back to Europe to visit her father (returning to New York on the *Furst Bismark*). They had tried to convince Zezil to come to New York to be with his three children, but he did not agree. Dora and David had no children, but Sarah's second daughter, Rose Bisgyer, lived with them for years. Sarah had a total of five children.

MOLLIE:

My father went to work in a garment factory and met (I do not know where) Breindel Feier, my mother, whom he married on June 15, 1890. Years later (in 1947) when I sought to get a copy of my birth certificate for Social Security reasons, mine could not be found. A lady working in the health department became interested in my case, made a search through marriage records and found a record of the marriage of my parents to corroborate this information. She wrote to the Census Bureau and the Department of Commerce in Washington, D.C. She furnished me with the documents to prove my birth in New York City.

At the time tragedy came to my parents when I was about one year of age. We were living in the ghetto at 3 Hester Street, New York City. A three-flight walk up tenement, stores on the street level. I do not know the floor upon which we lived. There were other families on each level. One cold water faucet in the main hall supplied all tenants of that floor with cold water. There was none in any of the flats, no bath tubs. Toilets were in the yard, no indoor toilet *facilities. Note that I was born 3-1/2 years after their marriage. My arrival was hailed with great joy. My father worked as an operator in a factory. <u>Hester Street</u>, circa 1900. On this street at number three, I lived for the first year of my life. My mother died in 1896 when we were living here.*

My parents were Orthodox Jews. I can still see in my mind's eye my father's wearing his phylacteries (twilled two little leather boxes containing bits of paper containing scriptural passages). One little box is on top of a Jew's head, the other on the left arm connected by a narrow leather strap bound around the left arm while the wearer is at prayer in his prayer shawl. My father possessed a very ornate prayer shawl, adorned by a lovely brass thread design. When he passed away he was attired in this prayer shawl (tallis) with his phylacteries (twillem) on his head and left arm and a skull cap on top of his head. My father came here at about 18 years of age, lived to about 81 or 82, never learned to read English, or learned to speak the language. He was literate in Jewish (Yiddish), could read a Jewish (Yiddish) newspaper. I know nothing about my mother except what my Aunt Dora told me about her. I understand my mother was a very attractive red head, about a head taller than my father who was barely 5 feet tall with coal black hair and brown eyes.

It is the ritual custom for devout Jewish women to light a set of candles at dusk Friday evenings to hail the Sabbath (Saturday, Shabis) and to wear a covering over the head to say a prayer to bless the candles. This was my mother's practice. After lighting the candles, my mother threw down the match stick, warm, probably still smoldering. Probably the smoldering match stick ignited my mother's long skirt. Instead of trying to smother the burning skirt, she took me up in her arms and ran to the nearest neighbor on the floor. Undoubtedly, by this time, she was ablaze. The neighbors sent for the fire engines. By the time the fire engines arrived, all my mother's clothing had gone up in a fiery blaze. As my aunts told me, even the beautiful red hair on my mother's head had been burned. She was taken to the hospital. The neighbors kept me until my father came home from his job in the garment factory. Years later, when I visited the family, he remarked, "When I was young, I left my wife and child (me) to go to work. When I came home, nobody was there."

I do not need to relate the agony that was his and the suffering my mother endured as the result of the burns. She spent a week in the hospital. Then she begged my father to take her home. He did. She died a week later at our home on Hester Street.

JANIECE: RECENTLY DISCOVERED DOCUMENTATION OF THE FIRE

On the day after the fire (Saturday, January 18, 1896), the *New York Sun* published on its front page a gripping account of the terrible scene of the fire:

ALTAR CANDLE FIRED HER GOWN
*Mrs. Flaumenhaft Saved Her Child
at Perhaps the Cost of her Own Life*

At the sunset hour on Friday, when the Jewish Sabbath begins, the wife or mother of every Orthodox home lights the candles on the family altar and says a prayer for the household. While performing that office last night, Mrs. Flaumenhaft of 3 Hester Street in some way set fire to her dress. She had her baby in her arms and holding it out at arm's length before her; she dashed into an adjoining room and placed it on a couch. The child was saved, but the mother's swift movement caused the fire in her clothing to spread beyond her power of extinguishing it. Her screams brought to her assistance Samuel Burrows of 7 Hester Street and Louis Singer, whom he was visiting, on the floor above. The men threw the victim down and tore off her burning garments, but not before Mrs. Flaumenhaft was badly burned from head to foot.

When Burrows ran out to summon a doctor, he found the other people in the house rushing through the halls

dragging screaming children, trunks, and pieces of furniture with them. Someone rang an alarm of fire, and
the arrival of the firemen added to the excitement. When
the police had restored order they called an ambulance from Governor Hospital. Dr. O'Mara swathed
the injured woman in bandages and hurried her to the
hospital, where it was said she might die. The hands of
Burrows and Singer were badly burned in divesting the
woman of her garments.

JANIECE: MOLLIE SPOKE OF HER MOTHER

Mollie often spoke to us about the death of her mother,
Breindel Feier Flaumenhaft, but was not aware of the front-page
story noted above. It was not until after Mollie died that we found
a large framed photo of Breindel; Mollie had inscribed on the back
of the photo the following comment:

*Robert, this is a photo of your maternal grandmother, Breindel
Feier married to Louis Flaumenhaft on June 15, 1890 in New York
City. I am their first and only child. My mother died about one year
after my birth in a fire.*

M. Nolan

My mother, Breindel Feier Flaumenhaft, circa 1895, born 1870, died 1896 at age 26.

Breindel was just twenty-six years old at the time of her death. Calculating from Mollie's birth date (December 25, 1893) and the death date (January 25, 1896) of her mother, Mollie was actually two years old at the time of the tragedy, a toddler who may or may· not have had memories of the fateful fire. Mollie never told us if she remembered the accident. We now have Breindel's death certificate, corroborating that she died at home, 3 Hester Street, at 6:00 p.m. on January 25, 1896. She was buried the day after her death in Silver Lake Cemetery, Staten Island, a site run by the Hebrew Free Burial Association. Thousands of Jews from the Lower East Side were buried there until 1909, when it was filled. Breindel's parents are listed as Solomon Feier and Sarah Feier, whose birthplaces are listed as Austria. Breindel had been in the United States for ten years, which would have made her immigration at the age 16 in 1886, two years before Louis arrived.

Breindel's death certificate states that the cause of her death was from "shock after third degree burns by having a lighted match ignite her dress…accident." Of course, we now know that a victim in burning clothes should be rolled in a blanket or rug to starve the flames of oxygen. Apparently, that was not known in 1896. Her well-meaning neighbors' attempts to remove her burning garments probably contributed to the severity of her burns. It also seems that order was restored by the police before an ambulance or doctor was called to the scene. That would not be the priority today. Such a horrible, tragic accident, but thanks to her mother's selfless actions, Mollie was not harmed in the fire.

MOLLIE:

After my mother's death then began a series of shuttles of me between aunts (my father's sisters). This lasted about a year. Then my father met and married Rachel Eisler. At the time of their marriage, my second mother was working as a domestic for a family named Marcus. These workers at that time were called servants. My mother [second mother

Rachel] received $5.00 per month for all the household work, just every bit of work, plus her food and lodging. She was newly arrived from Austria. Rachel had two brothers and one sister. The two brothers, Sam and Don Eisler, were butchers and each had a butcher shop with a huge painted word (in Yiddish) on their store windows to signify that the meat was Kosher. However, the family knew that the signs were not true, for the brothers bought (treff Christian) meat at a lower cost and then sold it as Kosher and thus made great profits. They invested their savings in real estate and became quite wealthy as a result.

I'd like to digress for a moment. From the time of my mother's experience in the hospital, my father had a tremendous fear of hospitals and through my lifetime I have experienced the same. I suppose the conversations I heard about the tragedy in my early childhood left its indelible impression upon my mind.

My father and second mother (Rachel) took up residence with me in a small flat in the ghetto, similar to the one in which my parents, Louis and Breindel, and I had lived on Ludlow Street, where I was born. They must have wanted to get away from Hester Street where my mother was so badly burned. About a year after the marriage of my father and Rachel, my sister, Sadie, was born in January 1897. She is three years younger than I.

JANIECE: MOLLIE'S SISTER SADIE

We were aware that Mollie had been estranged from Sadie for years. Nevertheless, on the day Mollie died we thought it best to call Sadie, who lived in New York. She was most gracious and thankful that we had notified her. A short time later we received the following letter from her:

September 7, 1980

Dear Robert,

I am saddened by the death of your mother. She was one of the lessening number of stalwart souls, as I need not tell you.

We grew up together in stark poverty, she scrubbing our floors and I ironing the family clothes at the mature ages of say 12 and 9, while our unhappy parents were trying to eke out a living in a small grocery or fruit store.

In those distant days teaching was one of the most honored professions and Mollie decided that that was for her. Our father hoped that as his children grew up they would get jobs and help get food for the family. Mollie endured.

Her ideas were often less than conformist but she did do it her way.

I am sorry she suffered so much illness in her last years, but she seemed always to snap back.

I regret that we were estranged all the years, and did not know what it was all about.

I'm sure you will miss her devotion- and worry.

Sincerely,

Sadie

MOLLIE:

My own earliest recollection of life in the ghetto is of Division Street. I recall sitting on the doorstep at the entrance to the building. Rachel had engaged a young girl to teach me to crochet! I understand my own mother had great skill in handiwork for all over the flat was evidence of her handiwork – tidies for couch, mantel, etc. Rachel's interest in my learning this skill enabled me in later years to make many articles for my family.

JANIECE: CROCHETING

Despite her arthritic hands, Mollie continued to crochet items for the family until her death. She made us an enormous green and gold crocheted king-size blanket for our bed. She made many articles of clothing for her grandchildren. The plethora of the crocheted items in her apartment spoke of her love of the craft.

MOLLIE:

My father had no skills. He was a devoted family man and used his brawn to make a living. In my mind's eye, I can see him coming down the tenement steps with a huge iron kitchen stove strapped to his back. He was a helper in the moving business. This was far too strenuous a job for a man of his physical stature – only five feet in height and slender build. The iron stove mentioned above, belonged to the individual tenant. It burned coal, provided heat for the flat, baked and the tenant cooked the meal on the top of the stove.

I believe I was less than six years of age when I became very ill. The doctor said I had a combination of diphtheria and scarlet fever. He recommended my being sent to the hospital as these are very contagious diseases and dangerous for the other children of the family. At the time there were two additional children, Sadie, and my first brother whose name I no longer remember. These children were sent to relatives. My father refused to send me to a hospital. The flat was quarantined with a sign on the outside door. No one was to enter. I have a recollection of my father and Rachel sitting on the edge of the bed all of one night to watch me. I wasn't expected to survive. I did. During my illness, I remember my mother's (Breindel's) first cousin's coming to visit me. She brought me a doll. It was the only one I ever had. I prized it a lot.

THE MOVE TO BROOKLYN AND DEATH OF MY INFANT BROTHER

When I had fully recovered, the family decided to move to Brooklyn. At the time of my illness, we lived in Manhattan. My infant brother, only a few months old (his name I no longer remember), passed away before we moved. I heard it said he had suffered brain inflammation. My memory of this is very dim.

To facilitate the family's move to Brooklyn, my aunt, Dora Berger, whose photograph appears in this story, came to our house to take me over to her home in Brooklyn until my family could move. I remember she had me swaddled in blankets covered from head to foot. It must have been winter. I could see nothing until we reached the ferry when my aunt removed my head covering. I remember seeing the ferry lights on the walls of the ferry cabin.

The family finally arrived and went into business. Of all things we were proprietors of a candy store in another ghetto in Brooklyn on Moore Street. There were push carts on both sides of the street with all sorts of things for sale — food, clothing, secondhand, etc. We lived in a couple of rooms behind the store. I do not know whether my father had an extra job. The candy store proved to be a fiasco. Then followed a series of ventures in business, a small restaurant or lunchroom, fruit or vegetable store, or fish market.

Always, the family lived in a couple of rooms in back of the stores. From time to time a new baby arrived. By that time I was enrolled in school and old enough to help care for the younger children and do chores around the crowded quarters. To do any chores around such crowded quarters was no easy matter. There were no mops, vacuum cleaners. All we had was a hand scrubbing brush, a hand wash board and our willingness to cooperate. There was no linoleum on our floors - just white boards. Down on your knees, you scrubbed these boards with hot water and soap until the boards became white. At one time, when my parents were running a small grocery store, we had a visiting rabbi who came several times a week to teach my two oldest brothers to prepare them for their bar mitzvahs when they became 13 years of age.

FRUIT AND VEGETABLE STORE

Before we moved into the Wallabout Street property owned by the Eisler brothers, our mother's brothers, we had a fruit and vegetable store on Cook Street in Brooklyn. The store had one large window in front of which was a huge wooden bin with a lock on it. Here was stored coal for sale by the scuttle. The inhabitants here had these old iron stoves in which they used coal to heat their homes and upon which they cooked. My father had a horse and wagon, sold fruits and vegetables to various customers. Any produce that he didn't sell, he brought back to the store.

Our mother was bearing Al. She seemed radiant so it seemed. I recall her being upon a ladder white washing the ceiling and sidewalls of our *quarters behind the store. It was the winter of 1902 and very cold it was. In addition, times were indeed bad. Coal was in short supply. I do not remember why.*

During the wee hours of one night, there was a terrific banging on the store door. Our father hastened to the store door to see what was the trouble. A man with a coal scuttle was there. The man pleaded for some coal. His family had run out of a supply. Their rooms were so cold. Besides his wife was about to have a baby. My father handed the man the key to the bin and a shovel; told him to take all he needed, lock the bin and return when he had to have more. The man was very agitated, offered to pay my father but my father refused to take the money. We were awake for quite a while after this incident. We were glad we were warm in our rooms behind the store.

YIDDISH / THE RABBI VISIT

I, too, received instruction for a while in reading a Yiddish prayer book. I never understood what I was learning so I gave it up. The rabbi was a tall, slender man attired in the traditional caftan broad brimmed black felt hat from which protruded a short gray curl from his hair. He also had a long gray beard. Beneath his hat, there was his yarmulke, a little round skull cap. Orthodox Jews are never bare headed. On one occasion, the rabbi happened to come while I was on my knees scrubbing the room that served as a combination living room, kitchen, and part bedroom. Remarked the rabbi, "With your brains you must lay on the floor scrubbing?" Not until I grew older did I fully realize the compliment he was paying me. Without their knowing it, our parents were training us in the "work" ethic. No one of us seemed to object to chores assigned to us. The goal was to do the things we were asked to do so that our parents could give all their working hours to making a living for an ever growing family.

THE HOUSE ON WALLABOUT STREET, BROOKLYN

We were living in Wallabout Street in Brooklyn in a house which belonged to the Eisler brothers, the brothers of my second mother, Rachel.

The house was at the back of the lot which was between a brewery on one side and a wooden three-story tenement on the other. The latter was completely occupied by Negro families. Across the street were some factories, the lower windows of which had heavy wire screens over them with wide meshes. At the front and to one side of the lot was a one-story wooden structure where mattresses were made. Beyond this was a closed in structure for a number of horses.

My father had become a peddler of produce and owned an open wagon and a horse. Within this structure was the family toilet and in front of all this, covered by long planks of wood, was a manure pit. You had to be careful when you used the toilet not to dislodge the planks that covered the manure pit. As I said above, the house was at the end of the lot. At least we had more living room. There was a wide area from the street to allow the entry of the wagon and the horse. The house had one huge iron stove for cooking and heating. One of the bedrooms faced a small courtyard with the brick wall of the brewery for a boundary.

It was while living here that our father bought a billy goat, a small cart and a harness for the goat. Where he obtained it, I do not know. The cart had a seat on each side from front to back upon which children could sit. What his idea was, I do not know, but I do recollect that Sadie and I took kids for a ride in this cart drawn by the goat for two cents each. I drove the cart and Sadie looked after the children. We drove them all around the block. One particular time stands out in my memory. We made two dollars in pennies. This we turned over to our father!

It was in this house that my brother, Al, as born on December 16, 1902. It was a terribly rainy day. The doctor, Dr. Glasgow, was on his way home from New York City. My mother, Rachel, liked him. He had delivered her of my sister, Sadie, and a brother (whose name I no longer remember). I happened to be in the toilet, but I could see through the cracks the doctor approaching. Within the house was my grandmother (Rachel's mother) who had come over from one of the Eisler brothers with whom she lived. She was a small squat person, very vigorous for her more than 80 years. She took care of all of us, the new baby and the mother. She wore a wig. Some old women had their heads shaven. The wig was called a sheitel (wig). She was very particular about having the house very warm for the new baby. If you dared open the house door to go out, she would give you a hard slap on the face. The reason was that the gust of cold air could endanger the baby's health. I was nine years old at that time.

THE PIANO

One day I was out on an errand near Harrison Avenue, when I learned that a family on my street had a square piano for sale for $5. I told my parents about it and begged them to buy it for me. I wanted to learn to play the piano. They didn't buy it. Of course they had very little money for a luxury and I do not know whether the matter of the space in the house was another reason. I remember I lay on the floor crying to no avail. A few days later, when I was walking down the street, I saw the piano chopped up and lying in front of the house. It had been put there for the garbage wagon. I felt terribly frustrated.

THE CHICKEN AND HER EGGS

I might mention that my mother had a few chickens. She had set a hen on some eggs for hatching on some hay in a small crate in the cellar of the house. During a heavy rainstorm, the cellar below the house became filled with water. The hen sitting on the eggs in the crate came floating out into the small courtyard between our house and brick wall of the brewery. Everyone was excited and worried about the hen and her eggs. My father lowered a ladder from the bedroom window, held it in position while my mother descended into the water and safely pulled the crate over to the ladder and handed it to my father. We were so happy that the hen and her eggs had been rescued. I do not remember whether we had any baby chicks.

MOVING TO ANOTHER HOUSE ON WALLABOUT STREET

My parents were paying the Eisler brothers a small rental for the house in which we were living. The Eislers felt this property was a white elephant and wanted to unload it. They offered it to my parents at the price they had paid for it and to use the rents as payment for the property. My parents did not take advantage of the offer. Soon thereafter, Kissel, who owned the adjoining brewery, wanted to expand his business and bought it at a good price. Had my folks agreed to buy it, they would have made quite a sum of money. The result – soon we had to move. Now there were four children. Sadie, Max, Al, and me.

RACHEL'S SODA WATER STAND

Before I close this part, I want to relate another matter. You will recall the factory across the street from the house. To supplement the family income, my mother set up a little soda water stand at the front of the yard facing the factory. When any worker in the factory (during the hot summer days) wanted a cold drink, he appeared behind the open screened window and signaled my mother. She would take a funnel and bottle of cold soda over to the man behind the screen. He had a container into which my mother poured the cold soda thru a funnel. He would hand her the money through the screen. The problem was what to do with Al who was an infant. There was a middle-aged Negro woman in the tenement next to the house. She was as black as could be. I remember so well she had a white spot (a cast) over one of her eyes. I imagine there was no sight in that eye. Her hair was pretty gray. She took care of Al during the day while my mother tended to the soda stand. This lady gave Al all the loving care and attention a devoted mother would give to her very own. Al thrived.

RACHEL'S SISTER

Before I proceed with the next episode, I shall relate what I remember of Rachel's sister and family. All I can recall is that their name was Lewis. There were two children – Charles and a sister whose name I think was Rose. If we lived in squalor, their home was even worse. In those days, there were two houses on a lot. One faced the street. The other house was at the back of the yard with a small yard between. This was called the rear house. It was this kind of house in which the Lewis family lived in two rooms in a Brooklyn ghetto. The father seemed quite old and bent. All over one room there were stacks of men's trousers which both parents were finishing by hand. This is how they supported themselves and their children. Charles was a slight short person. He was very ambitious, did very well in school. To make some extra money, he sold newspapers and shoe laces in front of City Hall in Brooklyn. Many of his customers felt sorry for this young boy and gave him extra money. Charles saved, went to college, and became a chemist and ran a very successful business. Years later, when I saw him at Rachel's funeral, he had become old, bent "squat", and looked just like his father. I hardly recognized him. His sister, a very attractive woman, had come to no good end.

OUR GROCERY STORE

When the Eisler brothers sold the property where Al was born, we had to move. A block away on the same street, Wallabout Street, in Brooklyn, my parents started a small grocery store. Again, we lived behind the store. I do not remember whether my father supplemented the family income with an outside job. Ours was the only grocery store in that area. It seemed to prosper.

GRADUATION FROM ELEMENTARY SCHOOL, AND ON TO HIGH SCHOOL

At this time I graduated from an all girls' school. The elementary schools in those days had an eight year curriculum; since I had skipped twice, I graduated at age 13. The question on what I was to do at graduation arose. At that time, a child could get working papers at age 14. My father thought I ought to get "working papers". My mother, Rachel, disagreed. Her attitude was "Malka is very small. She would earn very little. She loves school and does good. So why don't we let her go to high school? Later, she could earn more!" I was delighted with their decision. However, there was a problem. There was a high school within walking distance. It was coeducational. I was afraid of boys;

felt I wouldn't learn as well in that kind of setting. There was another high school about 1-1/2 miles away. This was an all-girls school which I wanted to attend. There was the question about car fare — 5 cents each way. Since the family income was so limited, my parents told me they would agree to my attendance at Girls' High School if I agreed to walk to and fro. I did. For four years I did just that — rain or shine. A number of times my teacher would send me home (giving me the car fare when my feet were wet).

MY ELEMENTARY SCHOOL GRADUATION CHALLENGE

When children graduated, it was the custom to have graduation exercises in the school. Each pupil would get two tickets for the parents. The all girls elementary school was situated in a predominately Jewish neighborhood. Hence, most of the girls were Jewish. Graduation took place in January and June since at that time promotions occurred twice a year. My class was to graduate in January 1907. It was the Christmas season before graduation. We were being taught to sing holy Christmas carols. Since most of the girls came from Orthodox Jewish homes, they refused to sing! Miss Anna M. Olson, the principal, appeared in the auditorium and asked the assembled girls to sing. Not a musical note was heard. Thereupon she told us that there would be no graduation exercises in January. Still no one sang.

In my class, there was a pair of twins, Davidson. They had an older brother much older than they. He took over the matter. A large hall was rented not far from the school where we would have our graduation exercises. We rehearsed under Mr. Davidson's direction. We were to give a scene from Julius Caesar which we had studied. The scene was the argument between Brutus and Cassius and their reconciliation. I was to take the part of Brutus. My voice carried well. The hall was crowded. There was thunderous applause. The following week we got our diplomas. We had won our point.

My elementary school graduation. I am the one standing, 1907.

JANIECE: MOLLIE'S SPEAKING VOICE

Mollie often spoke with pride of her role as Brutus in the school play. She knew she had a big, deep voice and would speak a few lines from the play to illustrate how well her performance went, and then she would laugh with pleasure. Robert and at least one of her great-granddaughters have the same bold speaking voice.

MOLLIE:

FAMILY PROBLEMS

Our grocery store was doing well. During that time a baby girl was born. I think her name was Rose. She lived only a few months. Some sort of skin disease afflicted her. My parents called a specialist. A house fee was $25. A Dr. Lourie. That was a fortune in those days. He told them what the family doctor had said. No hope. All of us felt pretty bad about this.

As if the family problems weren't enormous enough, Al became very sick. He had some contagious disease, the name of which I no longer can recall. The doctor told the parents that Al would have to go to the hospital. My father refused. As a result, our grocery store was closed. The children were sent to different relatives. Since I had already had the contagious diseases, I was permitted to remain at home. Newspapers were posted all over the store windows. One of the beds was moved into the store. This was where I slept. Al was sick for a long time, but finally recovered. When Al became well, the other children came home. My parents decided against reopening the store. They would have had to buy all new stock. During the time the store was closed, they had lost all of their customers.

ELIZABETH SEELMAN, MY TEACHER

I believe I was attending high school at this time. As I mentioned earlier, Girls' High School was a long way from home. I thoroughly enjoyed my four years there. I think the main reason was the good fortune I had in having Elizabeth Seelman as home room teacher and my first teacher of English. She and I became fast friends. I became acquainted with all her large family, visited there often. She often gave me dresses that her younger sisters discarded. This friendship lasted until her death. At that time, I was a grown woman, happily married to John Nolan and the mother of two fine boys — Robert and Jerry. I shall digress here and relate some highlights of my high school days. I took the regular academic course, since I thought I might go to college and become a teacher — Latin, science, English, mathematics, etc. I seemed to be doing well and was elected to the Arista, an honor society for excellence in scholarship. My name was inscribed on a huge wooden bulletin board in the foyer of the school with the names of other honor students. Subsequently, the names of my two sisters, Sadie and Cecile, were also added to the Honor Roll.

MOVE TO FLUSHING AVENUE

After leaving the grocery store on Wallabout Street, we moved to Flushing Avenue. Here we had another grocery store and a candy counter. Again we lived behind the store. I cannot remember at which point Cecile arrived. However, I distinctly recall that Cecile was part of the family when we had this store. She was at the time a nursing infant. When there was no customer to wait on, my mother was in the back of the store in the family quarters. There was a little bell on the inside of the store door. When someone would enter the store, the little bell tingled and my mother would hurry out. Sometimes she would be nursing the baby when the bell rang. Hastily she placed Cecile on a pillow on the floor (so she wouldn't fall off the bed) and went into the store only to find a child who wanted a penny's worth of candy. I believe my father had a horse and wagon and had a number of customers to whom he sold fruits and vegetables.

MY FATHER'S ILLNESS

It was during this time that my father became quite ill. I do not know the nature of his illness. However, I know he was afflicted with awful headaches and various body pains. He was unable to work. It was during this time that my Aunt Dora, my father's older sister, came to visit him. We called her Tanta Dora. Tanta is the German word for aunt. We all dearly loved her. She told him the following story which made an indelible impression on my memory. Here is the story she told my father:

"A king was on his sick bed unable to move. A messenger came to tell the king that the enemy was at the 'gates' of the kingdom to invade and seize the kingdom Upon hearing this, the king quickly arose from his sick bed, summoned his aides, ordered them to muster the army and he'd be there. The kingdom was saved. The king had recovered."

Soon thereafter my father also improved. My Aunt Dora, you can see, although self-taught, was a real psychologist.

As I jot down my recollections they may not be in chronological order. However, I put them down as I recall them.

INTERMARRIAGE?

During my first year at high school, we studied Ivanhoe in our English class. In that story, the Templar falls in love with a Jewess, Rebecca. The advisability of their marriage was a point of discussion in our English class. Frances Carrington, a staunch Catholic, a girl in my class and I were very good friends. One day she asked me, "Would you, Mollie, marry a Christian if you were in love with him?" My response was: "I never shall need to make that decision." Of course later on I did have to decide this very issue when I met and was captivated by John Nolan.

One of my good fortunes in high school was having Miss Elizabeth Seelman, my teacher and dear friend through not only my high school days but also until I was married. Elizabeth Seelman, along with three brothers and four sisters, were the children of Maurice Seelman and his wife. Maurice Seelman and his wife were German born Jews who had emigrated to England and lived in London. All their children were American born and educated here. The parents were educated in

London. All five girls became teachers in Brooklyn. One of the boys, Ernest, became a well-known attorney.

Maurice, the father, sold sponges and chamois. He was a traveling salesman. He always came to my husband for his dental work. They liked each other and enjoyed each other's company. There was a real charm about Maurice Seelman, with his spotless white shirt cuffs protruding from his dark sleeves of his jacket, his little black bow tie. He loved to talk. His short gray, well-groomed beard, lent him real distinction. He was a slender man of average height. Once he told John: "I hated sponges and chamois and riding all over the country to sell them but I had to make a living. So I mixed my sales talk with philosophy. My customers loved this. My sales surpassed those of men half my age." Actually he was selling sponges and chamois after he was 90 years of age. He never retired. We always enjoyed his visits.

CARRIAGE WITH A SURREY ON TOP

During our time in the grocery store, my father had bought a second hand carriage with a surrey on top. On Sundays he would often "hitch up" his horse and drive us all out to Coney Island. We'd sing the songs of the time. We felt very elegant.

WORK DURING THE SUMMERS AND SATURDAYS

From the time I was 14 or 15, I worked during the summers. One job I had was being an errand girl for a mercantile house in New York. The job was to deliver small articles such as samples, etc. to nearby offices. If the delivery place were less than ten blocks, you walked. If you had to travel more than ten blocks, you received ten cents in fare, five cents each way. Very often I walked the extra areas to keep the dimes. The salary for the week was $3.00.

While in elementary school, a few of my classmates and I worked on Saturdays in a department store in New York City, Siegel & Cooper, on 18th Street. We'd walk down to the Willamsburgh Bridge and then take a trolley which brought us to the store. We sold sheet music. There was a piano in the department and a pianist who played the selections for the customers. All of us brought our lunches. Hence, we had the entire one dollar, the pay for the day. All the girls and I enjoyed our Saturdays in Siegel & Cooper.

During my high school days, through the influence of Elizabeth Seelman, I had a summer job with a family of school teachers, the Goodrich ladies. They were spinsters – five of them who had built a summer home in the Berkshires. This home was opposite a farm of their brother who had a houseful of children and a charming wife. I was to do all the light housework – dishes, beds, and dusting. I was to receive $25 for the summer plus my food and lodging. It was a beautiful place with all conveniences except electric lights. I had my own room. The work was not arduous. However, there was a fly in the ointment. After a few days, I became very lonely. I wanted to go home. Since the ladies had paid for my transportation, they said I could leave if my parents sent me the fare for the return trip. My parents were so short of money they didn't send the fare. I stuck it out. The children from the farm came up often to visit their aunts. That alleviated my loneliness!

Another job that I held another summer was one on Block Island off the coast of Rhode Island. The family's name was Barlow. The father was a lawyer in New York City. It was his daughter who taught at Girls' High School. That summer I was more mature and enjoyed the ocean bathing and the rugged scenery. The family was very kind. The work was not hard.

I do not recall exactly where we moved after the grocery store on Flushing Avenue. However, my memory is very clear about our fruit and vegetable store on Ten Eyck Street in the middle of the block near Graham Avenue. My father had a horse and wagon in which he brought the produce to the store. My mother tended to the store while my father sold produce to his customers using his rig. At this time I was attending the Brooklyn Training School for Teachers.

PLANS FOR AFTER HIGH SCHOOL

Upon graduation from high school, it was my ambition to attend college. I had an idea that I might get a scholarship for Mount Holyoke College, an all girl institution. Incidentally, it was a Catholic institution. My teacher, Elizabeth Seelman, discouraged this because, as she pointed out, my parents would be unable to maintain me there. How right she was. While attending the training school for teachers, I had a job in the summer playgrounds run by the New York City Board of Education. The pay was one dollar per session payable at the end of each month. Hence I earned about $50 per summer, a huge sum in those days. At this store we occupied a flat above the store. We felt we really were improving, we had more room.

MY FATHER'S ARREST

This incident I relate occurred during one summer while I was in attendance at the training school. My father was distributing produce to his customers. He was using his horse and wagon. Suddenly we learned that my father was under arrest for driving a lame horse. I do not remember how we got this news. We had no telephone. It probably was a policeman. My father was being held in jail. There would be a $25 fine to have him released. I had a $25 check for one month's work in the playground. I was determined to have my father out of jail. We contacted, I think it was Don Eisler, one of my mother's brothers. Recall he was a butcher. He accompanied me to the jail. We interviewed one of the court attendants to find out just what the judge's verdict was. It was $25 fine or ten days in jail.

My uncle and I went out and brought in some coffee and sandwich for my father. I told my father I had the money for his release. He told me that under no circumstances was I to pay that fine. He said he'd rather spend the ten days in jail because, as he said, he couldn't earn $25 in ten days. My uncle and I waited for an interview with the judge. My uncle warned me that the judge would fine me for contempt of court if I weren't very careful of what I said. Finally we reached the judge for an interview. He informed us that my father was driving a lame horse.

I do not know what prompted my giving the judge an argument. I told the judge that my father loved horses and would not have started out had the horse been lame at that time. My father was a poor man trying to support a large family by selling produce from door to door. Still the judge would not relent. I continued by telling him that if he kept my father in jail, we'd be hungry. The judge countered that he would send food to our family. I thanked the judge but told him this would not be the same as having our father at home. As the interview was proceeding, my uncle was nudging me lest I become too argumentative.

At this point, the judge announced he was going out to lunch and would see us upon his return. So we waited. It seemed as though the lunch hour would never end. It did. The judge called my uncle and me into his chambers. He said, "Case against Louis Flaumenhaft dismissed." I was so excited all I could utter was "Thank you." My father was released and very proud of his oldest daughter.

RELIGIOUS ISSUES

At this time I had already joined the Brooklyn Ethical Society. Elizabeth Seelman was the secretary. This was no hasty decision. From my earliest days, even when I attended the synagogue to which my father belonged (Congregation Yoches, Lesher on Wallabout Street) I realized the iniquity of things. In the orthodox synagogues, the men sat downstairs and the women in this particular one sat in the balcony upstairs. The wives of the two wealthy Eisler brothers occupied seats in the front row of the balcony. They made it a practice to hold their bediamonded hands over the edge of the balcony so everyone could behold their affluence. I resented this because I felt my mother, Rachel, was just as good as they but had to sit in a seat far behind the front row. Also, daily I saw my father in his prayer shawl and phylacteries (twillem) beseeching God for a better lot to no avail. These things shook my faith to which I had been born.

One of the reasons for this change was due to my Aunt Dora's influence. She was an agnostic. I recall that when my father would call upon her after services on a holy day, she would say, "Well, Louis, did you pray for a good year?" As I think of it now, I feel she was being a little sarcastic but my father never realized it. Besides, while I attended high school, most of my teachers were Christians whom I admired and who were very kind and helpful to me.

I enjoyed attending the Sunday morning platform addresses of the Ethical Culture Society for Elizabeth Seelman was always there and her friend, Clarence Kingsley, whom late in life she married. The speakers were learned people. Their talk was devoid of creed or dogmas of any kind. The audience comprised people of various denominations who, for the most part, had abandoned their original religions. This appealed to me.

TAKING CARE OF BABY CECILE / RACHEL CLEANING FISH

We also had a fruit and vegetable store on Lorimer Street, where we lived behind the store.

Cecile was an infant. It was my duty to wheel her about in a carriage when I was not doing anything else. Also, my sister Sadie and I, were required to deliver a piece of ice in a dish pan to nearby customers. This was quite a heavy job for two children. The cube of ice must have been 12 or 15 inches and we'd deliver 10 or 15 cents to our parents for it.

From Lorimer Street, we moved across to a corner store where my parents opened a fish store. I recall my mother's being behind the counter cleaning the fish for the customers. In the cold weather her hands would be very red from the icy fish.

We were not in the fish business very long. The next move was out to East New York – another fruit and vegetable store. As in the past, my father had a number of customers to whom he delivered both fruit and vegetables. My mother took care of the store. Here we occupied a flat above the store. We felt less crowded.

Later Miss Seelman visited us and advised my attending the Brooklyn Training School for Teachers. This store was on Atlantic Avenue at the corner of Sheffield Avenue where the elevated trains rumbled by right in front of our flat. Here, also, my best friend of high school days and her brother, Leon, visited us. He was younger than my friend Edna. I thought he was just a very handsome young man. I believe I had what the girls called a "crush". Edna and Leon were the two only children of Isaac and Minnie Sternberger. Minnie was a Christian, Isaac, a Jew. They were a wonderful family, occupied a beautiful two-story cottage in Flatbush. I visited there often and stayed over night sometimes. I thought they were very rich. Isaac S. had an executive position with a large life insurance company. Minnie did the housework, the cooking and other household chores. They seemed a very happy family, also members of the Brooklyn Ethical Society.

Just as the other businesses proved unlucrative, so did this one. We moved up the street to a corner flat — lots of rooms, a private hall, a bathroom there, too. Since it was a corner building, there were many windows. One handicap — only a coal stove in the kitchen to heat the whole flat. This was no easy matter in the winter. To add to all our problems, so it seemed at the time, our mother was pregnant. Cecile was the youngest, six years of age. The Eisler aunts were willing to give our mother money so she might get an abortion. My mother would not accept the offer. She figured that it was safer to have the baby than to submit to an abortion.

It was winter. Winters in New York were very cold. One morning we awoke to find an ice skating rink in the private hall of our flat. One of the pipes had burst and flooded the whole area.

ANOTHER BABY

Our parents were expecting the baby any day. Since the baby was to be born at home, this was not the place. My father went into the Williamsburgh section of Brooklyn and rented the first available place.

It was a five-room railroad flat, toilet in the main hall. This was used by two families. At least it wasn't in the yard.

He made the move in the nick of time, for Richard arrived a few days later on a cold January afternoon in 1914. I had been appointed to my first school the previous November 1913. The school was within walking distance of our new home 252 Heyward Street. Well do I remember it. Upon my arrival from school, I found Dr. Margolies' sleeves rolled up helping my mother. She was in labor and in great pain. The children were with neighbors I think. At least they weren't present. Dr. Margolies greeted me by saying, "Why don't you take a walk around the block? Then you can come back and kiss the baby." I was 20 years of age!!

Cecile was six years of age at the time. None of us seemed excited about Richard's arrival. I cannot remember who helped with the household work. Sadie was 17 and was attending a business school on Fulton Street in Brooklyn. She had no desire to become a teacher. Max, my oldest brother was 13; Al was 11 years of age.

CECILE AND THE BLACK GIRL

One incident of our life at this address stands out in bold relief. There were a few black people in this neighborhood. One day Cecile brought in a little black girl with whom she played. Al didn't want this little girl in the house and told Cecile to take her out. Cecile refused and remarked, "She is as good as you are even if she is a Negro." When Cecile became a teacher, she spent her entire time in Negro schools. She learned to understand these children and did very effective work with them. Of course Al's attitude changed, too.

MY LIFE AS A SCHOOL TEACHER

When I was appointed to my first school in November 3, 1913, the salary was $720 per annum. For three years, the salary remained stationary. Each year a teacher was examined while at work with the children. If approved each year for three years, the teacher received a $60 yearly increase. This came to $5 more per month. There was a teacher's pension system for which one percent of the salary was deducted. This meant that the take home monthly pay for three years was $59.40. There was a tacit understanding that as we earned, we would contribute to the family coffers. Hence, I gave my parents $40 every month. That left me $19.40 for clothes, any lunches I bought or any incidentals. I learned to make my own clothes. It was possible to get a good woolen overcoat in the New York City East Side for $10. Money was worth something in those days. Actually, I was able to save some money. At the end of three years, I had saved almost $400.

I shall digress here for a few lines to tell something about my first teaching assignment. I was appointed to an all boys school in Williamsburgh. The class was a first grade. The neighborhood from which the children came was an immigrant ghetto. They and their parents were newly arrived in the U.S. Most of them were of Jewish origin. There were a few from Italy. These children did not know a word of English. The attitude of the parents, who often brought them right into the classroom, was very unusual. They would say in Yiddish: "Teacher, you may kill him, murder him, but make him smart." What they really meant, be strict so that they will pay attention and learn. Learn they did. We would start with a class of 50 boys in September. About October 1, ten children were transferred from each first grade to form a new class of 40.

Three brothers from Russia were in one of my first classes. Their ages varied by one year. They learned English quickly. One by one they were sent to the next grade. The oldest brother had a finger deformity. His fingers looked like claws. Years later I had occasion to go to the Brooklyn City Hall to file some documents. As I handed the papers to the clerk behind the counter, there were those fingers. There was my pupil, a young man holding a civil service job. He remembered me and called me his first teacher.

Mollie Flaumenhaft, circa 1913

BABY RICHARD

Often when I returned from school, I took Richard out in his second-hand carriage. It was a huge one on big wheels. I did this for a while until one day, while I had Richard out, someone in passing remarked: "So young to have a baby!" This person thought I was the mother. I was so embarrassed; I never took him out again!

One problem was troubling me. I had met and seen John Nolan a number of times at the Sunday morning platform addresses at the Ethical Culture Society. He was to call for me to take me to a dance for young people of the Society. I was ashamed to tell him there was a young baby at our house. When I finally told him, his remark was: "What's so bad about having a young baby?" Actually, as Richard grew a little older, John would bounce Richard on his knee. He often gave Cecile a ride on his knee and sang "A penny for a cotton ball, a half penny for a needle, pop goes the weasel."

Here are the exact words of the ditty John would sing to Cecile and Richard:

"A penny for a cotton ball
A hae penny (half penny) for a needle
That's the way the money goes
Pop goes the weasel."

As he'd say the last line, he'd toss the child up in the air. The kids loved this.

MY HUSBAND –TO-BE: JOHN LOUIS LEO NOLAN

John escorted me to the Ethical Culture dance. Actually, we did very little dancing. We sat on the side lines talking. It seemed we had so much in common to talk about. John was 31 at the time, I was 20. He had returned to the U.S. from Panama where he had been storekeeper for the Isthmian Canal Commission from August 1904 to May 1911. All his family, mother, brother Joe, sisters Ruth and Anna, were there with him. Their father had passed away a number of years before. Joe had started out as a printer. Then John got Joe a job on a steam shovel as crane man and, finally, Joe became a steam shovel engineer and helped dig the Panama Canal.

JANIECE: PRESIDENT ROOSEVELT PAYS A VISIT

A famous photo of President Teddy Roosevelt operating an American steam shovel at the Culebra Cut, Panama Canal, appeared in various United States newspapers in 1906. Joe Nolan had been operating that particular piece of equipment when a photo opportunity was requested for the president. In the photo just to the right and above the president, Joe Nolan sits holding a cable, possibly to provide a better view of the distinguished guest.

John Nolan (with straw hat in middle) with co workers in 1904 in Panama — 21 years of age in charge of a government warehouse. He remained there seven years until 1911 when he returned to the U.S. to pursue his education.

John Nolan (with straw hat in middle) in Panama, 1904

Joe Nolan to the right and above President Teddy Roosevelt, Panama Canal, 1906.

MOLLIE:

JOHN NOLAN AND THE CATHOLIC CHURCH

The information I put down now I did not learn all at one time. John revealed it from time to time during our visits. As a child, he and his brother Joe and his two sisters attended the parochial school in Brooklyn, Sacred Heart. John maintained it was a place where one's brains were "dug out". So much time was given over to endless prayers. Later he served as an altar boy. In this capacity he had an opportunity to be very close to the priests. Here he often worked with the priests who were drunk as they uttered their chants in Latin. This caused John ultimately to leave the Roman Catholic Church. Not only did he sever his relationship with the church, but prevailed upon his mother to do the same. Only Ruth, the older sister, retained her connection with the church and later married William Dorsey, a fine fellow, a Catholic, whom she met while all of them were living in Panama. Joe and sister Anna both married Protestants.

Another incident John related I shall state here. As young boys, John and Joe were sent to church Sunday mornings. They didn't attend. They knew their mother would ask them what the pastor had said. They would walk around and wait outside the church until the service was over. Then they would ask one of the parishioners what the pastor had preached. This they told their mother. It's easy to see that although born in entirely different settings, we were of the same religious points of view. Both of us had attended Ethical Culture meetings, both in Brooklyn and in the New York Ethical Society in Manhattan.

MEETINGS WITH JOHN NOLAN

Most of the times we met at the Academy of Music in Brooklyn where the Sunday morning platform addresses of the Ethical Culture Society were held. John was an usher there. He and others collected the offering after the address. He looked very handsome – 6 feet tall. Our friendship seemed to grow.

We'd meet at the L.I. [Long Island Railroad in Brooklyn] waiting room. We'd take a ride out to Shore Road, walk along the shore line. Then we would go out to dinner and John would ride back with me to a nearby stop — never all the way home. Why? I feared my parents would put a stop to my seeing him. All the time, I was becoming more interested in him, his charm, his wit, and his being so knowledgeable. Later, he invited me to accompany him to a Carnegie Hall Sunday afternoon concert of the Philharmonic Orchestra under Joseph Stransky. I had never before been to a concert. Just sitting next to him was a thrill. I did not understand the music. It was easy to see how absorbed he was in the music and how much he enjoyed it. These concerts taught me to appreciate great music and made these events very pleasurable.

I do not know now whether I have mentioned the fact that at the time of our becoming acquainted, John was attending Columbia University in New York City to obtain the requisites for admission to the College of Physicians and Surgeons.

As I sit here in my hospital bed, recovering from a broken hip, this writing reminds me of Mark Twain's engaging in his literary pursuits from his sick bed at his home. I am not trying to compare myself to him.

I am overlooking the beautiful Oakland hills. It is 5:30 a.m. Daylight is appearing over their tops. Through the greenery, the lights are blinking; one by one they are disappearing. It is a refreshing sight.

JOHN NOLAN AND STUDIES AT COLUMBIA

To get back to my narrative, John was taking a course in English literature. The text was Representative Essays in Modern Thought. This book is still in the bookcase. Professor John Erskine was the lecturer. During one of the classes, Professor Erskine made the statement that the Socialists were immoral. This aroused John because he had met and known many fine people interested in a different order of society and who had very high moral standards. He opened fire on the professor and made him look ridiculous. Even late in life, John regretted he had spoken out and that things had not gone well with him at Columbia after gaining admission to the Medical College.

THE NOLANS WERE IRISH IMMIGRANTS

Perhaps at this point, I should relate the facts about the Nolan family. My husband John Louis Leo Nolan was the oldest of four children born to Catherine Normoyle Nolan and John Joseph Nolan. Catherine was the daughter of Patrick and Johanna Fitzgerald Nolan. Catherine Normoyle was one of 17 children born to them in Limerick, Ireland. John Joseph Nolan came from Kilkenny Ireland.

JANIECE: JOHN JOSEPH NOLAN'S BAPTISMAL RECORD AND HIS PARENTS' MARRIAGE

On a visit to Ireland in 2006, Robert and I visited Kilkinney and with the help of the Paulstown parish priest found the original baptismal record for Robert's grandfather, John Joseph Nolan. We saw the actual Church of Paulstown and the baptismal font where the baptism had taken place on February 1, 1846. The parish priest told us that baptisms during that period usually took place the day the baby was born, so we are taking that date as the birth date. John Joseph Nolan's parents, Peter Nolan and Catherine Walsh, had been married in the same church January 9, 1831. The parish priest issued us certificates for both of these events.

MOLLIE:

John Joseph Nolan and Catherine Normoyle were married in New York. They were the parents of four children: John Louis Leo, Joseph James, Catherine (Ruth) and Anna Agatha. Catherine called herself Ruth because the children had nicknamed her "Kitty Cat". All the children were born in Brooklyn, N.Y.

John Joseph Nolan (the father) sold Singer sewing machines. He had a horse and wagon, plied his trade through the small towns of Connecticut. They were a happy family. Their happiness didn't last very long. John, the father, met with an accident. The exact nature of the accident, I do not know. However, my recollection is that the accident was related to the horse. This led soon thereafter to his death.

JANIECE: NO RECORD OF JOHN JOSEPH NOLAN'S DEATH

Try as we might, and even with the help of a professional gene-alogist, we were unable to find the death certificate or grave loca-tion for John Joseph Nolan. Because their youngest child, Ana, was born in January 1892 and the census record of February 1892 shows Catherine a widow with four children, we were able to determine that her husband must have died between May 1891 and February 1892. The Connecticut death index begins in 1897, so it was no help. Other relatives think he died in Boston. That search was also fruitless. Nevertheless, his death left the family in a bad situation.

MOLLIE:

CATHERINE'S DECISION

Here was a young mother with four children and no means of sup-port. Catherine Nolan's father, Patrick Normoyle, sent her money for the family's trip to Limerick, Ireland. John used to relate how they drove out to the farm in Limerick in a two-wheeled cart drawn by a pair of oxen. At the farm, Uncle Mike, a bachelor, and Aunt Mary, Catherine's brother and sister, ran the farm under the supervi-sion of Patrick Normoyle, the father, also grandfather of the Nolan children. John was ten years of age, Joe, eight, Ruth about four and Anna about two. Everyone loved the Yankees. Their living quar-ters by today's standards were almost primitive. The floors were of pounded earth. There was a huge fireplace in the combination kitchen

Catherine Normoyle Nolan, circa 1882

John Joseph Nolan, circa 1882

Children of Catherine Normoyle Nolan and John Joseph Nolan circa 1892

Top row – John (Louis Leo) Nolan about 10 years old
Bottom row-left – Ruth Nolan, 4 years old
Bottom row-right – Anna Nolan, 2 years old
Joe Nolan was hiding behind the door.
Photographed at 330 Bergen Street, Brooklyn, their home

and living room. Here, the meals were cooked in the fireplace which also heated the place. John often related that deference and respect for parents were different in those days in Ireland. For example, Mike, who was 45 years of age at the time, ran the farm with the help of Mary, who had never married.

As I mentioned before, there were 17 children born to Patrick and Johanna Fitzgerald Normoyle. The other 14 children had left the farm and made their homes in Canada, U.S., and Australia, and even New Zealand. When they were home, and the children became too noisy at meal time, all Patrick would have to do was look over his eye glasses at the assembled family and all would be quiet. When Mike needed to go to town to get a pair of shoes or some other time he'd go to his father and say: "I need a pair of shoes, father. May I have a horse?" Patrick always responded positively, gave him money and permission to use the horse.

It was in this atmosphere that Catherine and her four children lived for one year in Limerick, Ireland. One day, her father, Patrick, said to her: "Kate, you do not need to worry. We'll build you a cabin here where we'll all help you to raise the children." Catherine became very excited. "Oh no," she said. "My children are Americans. When they grow up, they will go back to America and I'll be here alone. So, I am going back with them now." Soon thereafter, they all left for the U.S.

JANIECE: CATHERINE'S RETURN FROM IRELAND

We found documentation of that return voyage from Ireland. Catherine and her four children are listed on the manifest of the *Tutonic* from Liverpool, England, arriving at Ellis Island on September 12, 1894. What a brave woman she must have been to have made two crossings of the Atlantic as a young widow with four children.

MOLLIE:

The following incidents related here give you some idea of Patrick Normoyle's character.

During Catherine's childhood in Ireland, she was very, very ill. Her life was in the balance. As in all Catholic families, the priest visits to console the family. During the conversation, the priest said to Patrick: "Do you begrudge her to God?" Patrick was ready with an answer: "Yes I do. I want her for me self!" Catherine recovered.

IRISH TENANT FARMER

In Ireland the farms belonged to British landowners. The tenant rents the farm and develops it. Patrick Normoyle also had a farm in an area adjacent to Limerick. I do not recall the name of the place. The adjacent farm was is disrepair. I do not know the reason for this. At any rate, Patrick thought he had a case against the British landowners. He brought suit against the British owner. This was costly. After considerable litigation, the case was settled. Patrick Normoyle was the first Irish tenant farmer to win a case in the courts of Ireland against a British landowner.

When the news of Patrick's victory reached Limerick, the other tenant farmers had bonfires on all the surrounding hills to celebrate this victory. It was a moral victory, but much had been destroyed at this farm.

After our marriage and since coming to Oakland, I tried to obtain transcript of this lawsuit without success. I even wrote to Dublin and learned that a fire had destroyed the records of that time.

I have just been able to recall that the name of the adjacent farm was in Tipperary. The Normoyle original farm was in Limerick.

JOHN NOLAN'S LIFE AS A CHILD IN NEW JERSEY

They went to live for a while in Jersey City, New Jersey, near Catherine's sister. In those days, there was no outside help. You had to make it on your own. Catherine went to work in a factory. I believe she worked on wrappers. After a short time, the family went to live in Brooklyn, near some of John Nolan's relatives. I believe their name was Brennan. She had arranged with the factory to take the wrappers home to Brooklyn to finish.

One day, when Catherine was returning her bundle of wrappers, she was told that she no longer would be permitted to take wrappers back to Brooklyn for completion. A new inter-state commerce law forbade it. She was so overwhelmed by this, that she sat down and cried. A little man came by and spoke to her. "Why are you crying?" he asked. Catherine related her tale. He said, "Come with me." Together they went to the office. The man said to the clerk, "What kind of work does Mrs. Nolan do? Is it satisfactory? Does she return the work on time?" He received affirmative answers to all these questions. The man turned to the clerk and gave the following orders: "For as long as we have wrappers to complete, Mrs. Nolan is to have the work. Further, we shall deliver them to her and pick them up when ready!" Imagine Catherine's relief. This gentleman happened to be the owner of the factory and also happened to be a Jew. So life went on for a while.

Catherine's nephew, Jim Brennan, owned a hand laundry nearby in Brooklyn. It wasn't doing too well. In exchange for a small life insurance policy, Catherine became the owner of this hand laundry. The family lived behind the store. Catherine had a couple of girls working for her. This was the best situation for them, for now she and the children were together. This store was on Park Avenue in Brooklyn near Fort Greene Park. Once John and I went there to see the old neighborhood.

It was while they lived here that John became very ill. The doctor who attended almost despaired of his recovery. He told Catherine that he believed John had diphtheria and that the last resort was the new anti-toxin which had just been developed. It was very expensive the doctor said and because he had had his own family to maintain, he couldn't donate the anti-toxin free. "Oh", said Catherine. "I have the money for it. Try to save him." She pulled the money from her bosom! John recovered, but was very weak for a long time after. The doctor suggested some outdoor exercise. Catherine bought John one of those two-wheeled bicycles – the huge wheel in front and the little tiny wheel behind. This seemed to do him good. He grew stronger and regained his health.

Another incident occurred when the family had the laundry. One of Catherine's customers was a rather elderly gentleman whose name was Dann. He owned a bakery and had a fleet of horses and wagons which delivered his bread. Catherine's laundry did his shirts. I remember from a photograph that she was a very attractive woman. Across the counter, he proposed to her and offered his hand in marriage. She thanked the gentleman for the compliment of the proposal. She said, "I have my children. I would not want them to have a stepfather."

They kept the laundry until John left New York to accept a position in Panama. He was either 20 or 21 years old. Catherine never had to make a living after that. John and Joe provided for her and their two sisters. Joe worked on a printing press. John was working for a William K. Peters for whom John collected rents. Mr. Peters was very pleased with John's work. He was the man who designed and made the all brass candlesticks which hang in my living room. There are probably very few of them around in the whole U.S.A. Mr. Peters gave these beautiful all brass items to John in appreciation of his good work. I have always cherished them.

BETTER HOUSING FOR THE FLAUMENHAFTS

As soon as Sadie and I began working and contributing to the family, we began thinking of embellishing the home. In those days we had parlors or front rooms reserved for special company. The family spent most of its time in the large kitchen of the flat. It really served as a family room.

We bought a three-piece set of furniture and an upright phonograph and a few records. Although we had no rug on the floor of the parlor, we felt quite elegant. How did we get these things on such limited incomes? Time payments – so much a week. In this way, the items cost more but there was no other way we could have had them.

We lived on Heyward Street for about three years and then moved to a three-flight walk up brick building at 734 DeKalb Avenue in Brooklyn. We had a top floor flat, six rooms – a complete bathroom. This certainly was a big improvement for us. Furthermore, the houses which abutted each other were built in the bedroom section around a small courtyard. Since we were on the top floor, all the rooms were light.

TIME APART FROM JOHN NOLAN

During all this time, John and I were meeting from time to time without the knowledge of my parents. Somehow I felt it would not work out and I did not see John again for about two years. He was always in my thoughts. Since I was teaching, I went for vacation a couple of summers in Mountainville, N.Y.

It was a girls camp run by the downtown Ethical Culture Society. They ran a settlement house at 216 Madison Street where young people met and enjoyed various kinds of entertainment. The vacation rates were very low. The set up of the camp was most unusual. It consisted of old horse drawn trolley cars. The seats had been taken out and four cots installed in each car so that four girls occupied each car. There were about ten of these old trolleys. In front of the cars was a fresh water creek surrounded by beautiful trees. Here we went swimming. All the girls seemed to enjoy themselves. Ten miles away was a boys camp run by the same society. Sometimes the boys would hike down to visit the girls for a day. Occasionally, some of the girls would hike up there. It was a lot of walking for a day – ten miles each way.

So time passed. During all this time passed, I felt incomplete and missed John so much. I recall meeting Joe Nolan. He told me John had left the College of Physicians and Surgeons where he had been enrolled and used his Medical college qualifying certificate as admission to the College of Dental and Oral Surgery. This college was on East 35th Street in New York City. Later, it was to become a part of Columbia University. I felt sorry that John had had to make a change in his career for I knew medicine was his first love.

ROBERT: SPECULATIONS ON WHY MY FATHER LEFT MEDICINE, HIS FIRST LOVE

As a youth I was always aware of what Mom wrote about my father switching to dentistry during the interval before they were married. I do not recall that he ever discussed the decision in my presence. Dad completed two years of undergraduate studies at Columbia College in 1915 and received his Qualifying Certificate for Admission to Medical School issued by the state. When he retuned from working on the Panama Canal to support his family, he received permission to enter Columbia with the understanding that he would complete his missing high school courses while enrolled in college. In 1915 he was 32 and fully supporting himself with very hard work, including employment as a fireman on the NYC ferryboats at the same time he was in school. Medical schools at that time required only the Qualifying Certificate. There was no undergraduate degree required and Dad never had one, nor for that matter a high school diploma. Medical schools for the first half of the 20th century typically enrolled more students in the first year than they had room for in subsequent years, so many good people were eliminated arbitrarily. Dad had a grueling schedule of employment to follow as well as medical school and later dental school studies. I can only surmise that these could have been factors in his switch to dental studies. We probably will never know. But we do know that Dad received his D.D.S. degree in 1920, at the age of thirty-seven. The certificate for John Louis Leo Nolan hangs in our dining room.

When Dad was born in 1883 and for years thereafter, Nolan was a very common surname in New York as was the name John L. Nolan. In order to distinguish himself from other John L. Nolans, Dad added a second middle name, Leo, and by 1915 and thereafter he was known as John Louis Leo Nolan, and for the rest of his life all his documents reflected this change. I do not know why he selected Leo for his additional middle name.

MOLLIE:

DECISION TO MARRY JOHN LOUIS LEO NOLAN

Somehow, after being apart for two years, John and I met again. We felt we just had to be together and decided to marry, just when, we did not settle. John decided he would go to see my parents and tell them of our decision and ask my father for my hand. My father's reaction was: "Why don't you get a nice Christian girl and marry her?" John responded, "I have a girl, your daughter." Then my father looked up at him and said: "Do you have to marry her?" "Oh, no," said John, "but I'd like to." I was so angry at my father's remark. I felt it was an insult to us both.

Now, as I have grown older, I realize the anguish which was his.

At the time we were contemplating our marriage, for people to inter-marry was a dreadful thing. As far as an Orthodox Jewish family was concerned, a son or daughter who married a Christian was considered dead and mourned as such. My sister Sadie thought violence might follow when I announced my intention to marry John. She remained awake most of one night to watch over me. I realized I could not stay at home under such conditions and went out to the home of a cousin, Niomie Franklin, and her husband, Irving. John came with me. They were very impressed with John.

Later, I visited my Aunt Dora, my father's sister. She, too, took quite a fancy to John. Both of these people visited my father and tried to intercede in my behalf and mollify him. I returned home. This was in the fall and early winter in 1916. Just before Christmas, I announced to the teachers with whom I worked that I was engaged to be married. When we decided to marry, John said: "We'll go to Tiffany in New York and we'll select the nicest diamond I can afford." I became quite excited about that and exclaimed: "Oh, no, please don't. That isn't necessary. I want you to save the money for your tuitions." I meant it. Why? Because John had practically three years of study before him, had his tuitions and dental instruments to buy, and he had insisted that he pay half the cost of running our apartment.

Well, when I announced to the teachers that I was engaged to be married, the first thing they said: "Where's your diamond?" I was sort of "flabbergasted" at the question. My reply was "Well, my diamond is so heavy I can't carry it. He weighs 200 pounds more or less. You will meet him!" They had their answer. Aren't women funny. The faculty did meet John and were very much impressed with him and why not.

As I said this was about Christmas 1916. War was declared April 5, 1917. John was 34, I was 23. Of course, I feared he might be drafted, but not likely because of his age. However, were that contingency to arise, we thought it might be better to be listed a married man. We decided to be married on Easter Saturday, April 7, 1917. Joe Nolan and Sadie Flaumenhaft went with us to the City Hall where we were married by the City Clerk. Because of my family, Sadie's name was entered as a witness.

John Louis Leo Nolan and Mollie F. Nolan married 1917.

MOLLIE F. NOLAN

When John and I were married, I announced: "Now I am Mollie Nolan." "Yes," he said, "but I want you to retain the F – the first initial of your former name as your middle name. Mollie F. Nolan. You are not giving up your identity for me!" And so it was and has continued to be ever since that day.

In connection with my name, I have experienced some interesting episodes. Years later, as a member of the Alameda County Democratic Women's Study Club, Lillian W. Thomas asked me what the F in my name was. Now I had never asked her what the W in her name meant. I felt the question was rude. So, in a somewhat flippant manner I replied, "It stands for Firebrand. That's an Indian name. I am descended from the Indians." Of course I do not look like a product of the Emerald Isle.

On another occasion, when I was substituting in a junior high school, the assistant principal came in to interview me. Said she: "Mrs. Nolan?" "Yes," I replied. She went on: "That is not your name." "Indeed it is," I said. " Furthermore, I have embellished it since I have had the name." Some people are very impolite.

JANIECE: THE NAME MOLLIE F. NOLAN

Mollie related these stories about her name to me several times. I believe she felt an inquiry about whether her name was really Nolan smacked of anti-Semitism and that the point of the question was to force her to admit she was Jewish by birth. She never denied being Jewish, but of course she did not look Irish. She always wrote her name Mollie F. Nolan, just as her husband had asked. We put that name on her tombstone.

MOLLIE:

After our marriage, we stayed for awhile in Joe Nolan's house in Bay Ridge, Brooklyn – 8414 -7ᵗʰ Avenue. It was a large, one family frame house with three bedrooms and bath upstairs, spacious parlor, dining room and kitchen on the first floor. John had a large room. The house was bounded by a few lots which Joe owned. These he later sold to a builder.

At this time, there was some sort of regulation (if I recall correctly) that stipulated that all males in a certain age group at a certain time would have to join the National Guard for New York State. Since we were opposed to become involved militarily unless absolutely necessary, we decided to move over to Jersey City, New Jersey. We took a trip over there and found a very pleasant three-room apartment near a small park at 260 Jewett Avenue. From here we commuted to our schools. It was quite a distance from the apartment to the Hudson tubes. We walked together but instead of just chatting, John would recite the items he had to memorize for his dental assignments such as the time of eruption of the temporary and permanent teeth. I had the dates on a piece of paper and checked for accuracy.

MARRIED LIFE

When John and I returned from our respective schools, he'd do his homework while I got the supper ready. After that there was more studying he had to do. He scored his texts and after doing a few pages, he would ask me to follow the scored tests to see if he was reciting correctly. Nothing seemed difficult to us. Things don't if you care very much for one another.

When we set up house-keeping in Jersey City, John brought with him some of the things he had had in Brooklyn. One of these was a hand-powered wooden washing machine. He had a light-colored tan linen summer suit. He had asked me to wash it in the washing machine. This I did and hung it up on the roof to dry. It was a weekend. When John came home, he asked me if I had taken the money out of the trousers. I had not. Both of us hurried up to the roof. There was his suit and three paper folded dollars in the little watch pocket thoroughly washed. We both laughed. After that, I always went through the pockets.

A JEWISH WEDDING

Gradually my parents accepted the fact that we had married. However, they were dissatisfied because we were married in what they called the "court". They wanted us to have a Jewish wedding and have a rabbi perform the marriage rites. I was very loathe to comply with this request. Much to my astonishment, John was ready to comply. We went to a rabbi in a neighboring area. The marriage was performed by the rabbi who issued us a marriage certificate written by him in long hand Jewish script. We preserved this in John's steamer trunk after we showed it to my parents. This was in late August 1917.

When I was getting ready to come to California and was clearing out some items in the trunk, unfortunately this document was lost in the shuffle. This I have regretted so much.

Had John asked me at the time to accompany him to the Rectory of the Catholic Church to have our marriage validated (?), I doubt I could have agreed.

BROTHER AL'S ILLNESS

It was while the family were living at the DeKalb Avenue address, that Al became very ill. He was about 14 years of age. It was the time of the First World War. There was a flu epidemic. Even the family doctor, Breitzer, had had the flu, but was too weak to mount the three fights to take care of Al. He did come for one visit and said Al was so ill that he needed expert nursing care because of the injections Al would need. He said he'd keep the case if John would agree to nurse Al and give him the necessary medication. Of course John readily agreed. Both he and I went to DeKalb Avenue and remained here for the best part of a week.

Long after Al recovered, John revealed that after he gave Al the injection of (I believe) camphor, he found that his heart beat was far worse. John took it upon himself to stop the medication and give nature a chance. We watched him thru a few harrowing nights and finally Al was on the mend. Everyone was happy.

MOVE TO BAY RIDGE, BROOKLYN

After about a year's residence in Jersey City, we decided to set up an apartment in Brooklyn, Bay Ridge area. We found a four-room, box *arrangement apartment at 453 – 68th Street. It was a pleasant place near to the Nolan home on 7th Avenue and not too far from my folks whom now we visited often for Friday night suppers. The family was growing more and more fond of John. This pleased us a lot. The apartment's living room and bedroom faced the street, the dining room and kitchen faced a large inside court. There was steam heat in the halls of the building but none in the apartment. Each tenant supplied his own coal to heat the place – an iron stove and a two-burner gas stove came with the place. The rent was $27 a month.*

We had a novel way of keeping house and records, a system of envelopes. John supplied his half from his savings and I the other half - rent food, electric lights, coal. I do not recall whether we had a telephone. I do remember that it was while we lived here that we bought our cabinet foot pedal Singer sewing machine. I believe it was under $50 – time payments. The reason for this purchase was to enable me to make my own clothes. Teachers' salaries were extremely low. With the help of a dress pattern and a little know-how, I could make a dress for $3.00.

So life went on. John was in attendance at the College of Dental and Oral Surgery. Our schedule after school was getting the supper ready, building a coal fire in the winter to heat the apartment, and then his studies. I would follow the recitations by the parts he had scored in his texts. On the weekends, there was the grocery shopping, doing the washing, house cleaning. It was a full schedule. Occasionally, we went to my family for a Friday night supper or to a Sunday dinner at the Nolan home.

One Friday night, my father remarked, "Your husband knows more in his one little finger than my three sons know in all their heads." It was a queer way to put it, but it did show the high regard my folks had for John. Then my father said: "Have John call me "Pop," not "Mr. Flaumenhaft."

JOHN BECOMES A DENTIST

The time just flew, we were so busy. The dental college and New York State licensing exams were to take place in the spring of 1920.

Naturally we were excited about the results. We knew we had worked hard and been very conscientious and that the results should come out in John's favor. They did. Now John had his degree Doctor of Dental Surgery and licensed to practice in New York State. We were very happy.

John had bought no new clothes in all the time he was at college. His trousers were so thin that the white of his underwear showed. One day Joe Nolan came to visit us and jokingly said: "You should throw a bottle of ink in there. Then it won't show." I didn't think it was a joke, especially since John had helped him to get the good job in Panama which had brought him an excellent income. It's the old adage: "The prick of a thorn is remembered longer than the scent of a thousand roses." Joe had married Anna Arbia, a school teacher, either in 1919 or 1920. She went to live in the big house on 7ᵗʰ Avenue.

ROBERT: MY FATHER'S SIBLINGS

When my father died at age 76, Joe Nolan did not attend the services in New York, nor did his sister Ruth, despite notification by my mother. At the time both were in their 70's, but lived far away in St. Petersburg, Florida, and St. Louis, respectively. Anna did not survive my father; she died in Los Angeles in 1956. I visited her in a hospital there when she was quite ill. Mom often bitterly retold the story of Joe Nolan's inappropriate joke to throw a bottle of ink on Dad's trousers where they were worn through. When my father could have used financial help, that was Joe's response.

MOLLIE:

THE NORMOYLE HOUSE IN BROOKLYN

In the early days of their marriage, Catherine Normoyle Nolan and John Joseph Nolan bought a little house as a kind of summer resort for all of them at 174 Battery Avenue, Brooklyn. At the time of the purchase, this area was a small town and very rural, not far from the beach. When Joe Nolan bought the house on 7th Avenue, the Battery Avenue property became part of the down payment on 8414 - 7th Avenue. Because 174 belonged to Catherine Nolan after John Nolan's death and she did not get any money for it, it was agreed that she would have a home at 8414 - 7th Avenue for the rest of her life. When Joe Nolan was courting Anna Arbia, he prevailed upon her to agree to this. It was a marriage prerequisite.

JOHN'S CLOTHES AS A DENTIST

Now back to John's clothes following his graduation from dental college. He had just enough money left in the bank to invest in two new suits of clothes. This was really imperative as he was seeking employment in a dental office before embarking on his private practice.

JOHN BEGINS TO PRACTICE DENTISTRY

John went into the practice of dentistry with a dentist in the Bronx. The salary was low but it was a busy office so he had lots of practical experience. He did not remain very long with the Bronx dentist. From there he took a position with a dentist on Fulton Street, Brooklyn. All in all, he worked in these two locations about one year. We began looking about for a location in Bay Ridge, Brooklyn, not far from where we were living. We decided John would start in private practice.

While shopping on 5th Avenue in Bay Ridge, I noted what looked like a good location in a fine -looking building. The quarters were above a music shop. This place had been occupied by a beauty shop. Many of the walls had been torn down to make ample room for the beauty booths. These walls had to be rebuilt to provide reception room, operating room, and bedroom. There were large office windows facing both on 72 Street and 5th Avenue. John and I went to inspect the place and agreed to take it at $120 per month and a three-year lease. This was a large sum of money in those days. It was 1921. We spent the next 26 years there.

In this building at 484 – 72ⁿᵈ Street, corner of 5th Avenue in the Bay Ridge Section of Brooklyn, our happiest and saddest times occurred. It was a big, big undertaking for two people to establish a dental office. There was the rebuilding of walls to set up two dental booths for two dental chairs and a small area for laboratory work. There was the matter of extensive and approved plumbing, dental chairs, cuspidors to be purchased and reception furniture, curtains for the office windows, shades and drapes. All this would take considerable money. While John was in attendance at the dental college, teachers' salaries had increased, and I was able to save.

One day Joe Nolan dropped in to visit us in the midst of all the preparation. He wanted to know whether we needed any money. Said Joe, "If you need any money, you can borrow from Mother." We had not asked anyone for anything. Joe got his answer from John: "We shall not need to borrow from anyone. Mollie has saved some money, and we shall use that to get started!"

It was the summer of 1921. There was painting, purchases, all sorts of work to get ready. John bought two S. S. White Manufacturing Company white enameled dental chairs, two cuspidors, electric dental engine, overhead lighting, reception room furniture. Our white dental office freshly painted was ready about August 1, 1921. It looked good. All the above purchases were made with down payments (the plumbing bill had to be paid in full) with interest at the rate of 6%. When we were ready to open our office, we had exhausted all our savings for the initial expenses. We had one $50 Liberty Bond, my job and John's insurance on his hands – nothing more. We sent out announcements to the citizens of the area.

John was competent and very conscientious, had a real sense of humor. In his hey-day, his laughter would "rock the rafters". We made our expenses, met our notes from the very first day. We were greatly encouraged.

ROBERT: MEMORIES OF MOM AND THE DENTAL OFFICE

A heavy brown corduroy curtain and a door in the wall separated my father's dental office in the front from our living quarters behind it. I can still visualize Mom emerging through that curtain and door to attend to something prompted by me or initiated by her or my father. She would be dressed in a wrap-around white smock she wore while helping in the office. Her shoes were black and stockings light brown. She had her black hair in a bun at the back of her head with a comb in it. With her brown eyes and earnest smile, she proceeded confidently and directly to the task at hand. If I called her to do something she would do it efficiently and then return to the office area.

In the office was a waiting room. Walking through that area would bring you to the first dental chair; a second dental chair was behind an adjoining partition, and another partition separated that area from a small dental laboratory.

Mom greeted patients in the waiting room, led them to the dental chairs, and handled the paperwork. She also served as dental assistant to my father, providing needed instruments or medications or bringing sterile supplies from the laboratory. I often overheard parts of these transactions from the other side of the wall. Mom had a very strong, resonant voice that projected well through the wall and curtain barrier, but it never seemed loud. During this period I rarely heard my father's voice from the office. (A later exception arose when I took piano lessons and he called out corrections to me as he worked on patients.) Although tooth extractions were a significant part of his practice, I never heard sounds of patients in pain.

My father had a great love of classical music, especially opera, so other sounds from the office often included operatic or symphonic music on the radio, especially from station WQXR, New

York. Mom did not have that same attraction to music, although she never expressed any displeasure toward hearing it. Decades later I learned that as a child my mother's parents could not afford to acquire an old discarded piano she wanted, so she never had the music lessons she had sought. However, my father had a brief exposure to violin lessons when he was very young, before the sudden death of his father and loss of family income.

Our first room behind the dental office was a combined daytime living room and nighttime bedroom. Against the far wall away from the windows facing the street was a roll-out daybed that functioned as a couch. At night it became a large bed in which everyone slept. It may have been the same bed in which I was born, there behind the office, on February 12, 1926. I was told that I first walked in a playpen on top of that couch and that I would express a need for a parent by shaking the playpen, which could be easily heard in the office. My mother would be the one to respond.

I do remember the family ritual regarding parental inspection of stools. After a bowel movement I was expected to stay on the toilet until one of them checked the toilet contents. They thought of this as a health measure. It was a logistic problem if both of them were in the dental office. I could not call out and disturb everyone in the office, even though the only bathroom was at the end of the apartment and farthest from the office, so I developed my own signal system: With my fist I would pound the plaster wall next to the toilet to give notice that it was time to check. Usually it was my mother who responded to the pounding, walking from the office through the living room, then the kitchen to that remote site. By the time the ritual was abandoned somewhere before school age, I had left a deep hollow in the wall that required repair.

My mother's role in the office changed abruptly after my younger brother Jerry's death in December 1935. He was seven-and-a-half years old. Grieving and depressed by his loss, and to get involved out of the house, in early 1936 she returned to teaching as a substitute teacher. I remember the three of us discussed this decision and were in agreement. Later that year when assisting as a messenger at my school, Public School 170 (P.S. 170), I found to my surprise and embarrassment that it was my mother at the teacher's desk when I entered the classroom to deliver some documents.

Mom's absence meant that my father practiced alone, without any office assistance. Years later I realized that her departure from the office coincided with the gradual decline of his practice.

We remained on the second floor of 484-72nd Street, Brooklyn, until about 1946, when we purchased a house at 361 Bay Ridge Avenue, a few blocks away. We established a small dental office on the first floor with a small rental apartment behind. The second floor was entirely our living quarters. I lived there for almost two years, until 1948, while finishing pre-med. After June 1959, when my father died, Mom came to live near us in Oakland, California.

MOLLIE:

JOHN HAS A PROBLEM

Since it was summer (1921), and we were not planning any vacation because we had just opened our office, we decided we would open an hour later and go for an early morning swim at Manhattan Beach just beyond Coney Island. We did this for a while. One morning, I kept waiting for John to appear after the swim. He was so long in coming that I began to worry about the delay. When he finally came, he was greatly distressed by a pain in his left ear and was letting the cold water spray over it as it gave him relief. He had swum under water and then snorted some of the salt water through his mouth into the middle ear. That day we went to an ear specialist. He told us that John had an infection in the middle ear. I do not recall the exact nature of the treatment the doctor ordered. I believe it was hot salt packs. In a few days a serous discharge came from the ear. We were visiting the ear specialist twice daily. John had difficulty mounting the steps to the doctor's office. It wasn't long before the doctor began talking about an x-ray and an operation on the middle ear. John felt that after such a short interval the x-ray would reveal nothing and decided to leave this doctor.

We arranged with John's mother to man the office as we hadn't had time to notify the patients of the cancellation. John and I went to the Hoeber's Book Store in Manhattan to find a book on the ear written by a doctor nearby. We did find a book called Otology by a Dr. Perkins of St. Luke's Hospital in New York and John decided to see him. We looked him up in the telephone book and found Dr. Perkins was not far away in mid-town Manhattan. He had his office in a medical building where we learned that Dr. P was out getting ready to leave on his vacation but would come to pick up his mail. His Ford car, somewhat dilapidated, was parked nearby. I asked the doorman if John might wait in the doctor's office as he felt weak. I would watch out for Dr. Perkins. The wait was not long. A tall, slender man, who looked like a farmer and was accompanied by his wife, approached the old Ford. At this point, I went over and told him John's plight. "Would he please see John?" Dr. P readily agreed, and the three of us went up to the doctor's office.

Dr. Perkins examined John's ear as his diminutive wife on her toes kept peeking. Dr. P turned to us and said: "I have seen worse ears get better without the knife. If the discharge lessens and the temperature goes down, you will not need to see my assistant, Dr. Mac Isaacs, for two weeks. If, on the other hand, the reverse is true, consult Dr. Mac Isaacs at once." He wrote a note to Dr. Mac Isaacs to charge $5.00 per visit. Luckily for us, John's ear mended. We went to Dr. Mac Isaacs a few times. When John felt stronger, we took a vacation at Haddam Neck, Connecticut, where our friends, Emil and Gertrude Peterson, had a cottage which we rented from them for two weeks.

So life went on. The practice was flourishing. We were meeting our notes, earning a living and everything was going all right at school. Since John's income was proving adequate, he insisted that my school check be banked in full. In this way, we built up a financial reserve.

JOHN AND THE YIDDISH THEATRE

One humorous incident during this time comes to mind. On 2nd Avenue, in the borough of Manhattan, there was a Yiddish theatre where plays were given in Yiddish. One day John remarked: "I'd like to see a play in Yiddish in the Yiddish theatre on 2nd Avenue." I looked at him in amazement. "Why would you care to see a play in a language you do not understand?" I asked. "Never mind," he replied, "I can understand the motions." We went, sat in the balcony with an all Jewish population. As I mentioned earlier, John had a keen sense of humor and his hearty laughter would "rock the rafters". This was exactly what happened. He was laughing with the actors, not against them. The people around us began laughing and applauding. It was an event I never forgot.

Our office was within walking distance of the Nolan home on 7th Avenue. Quite often John's mother would walk over, stay in our quarters until he had a little time to visit with her. From time to time, I'd find her there when I returned from school. She and I had a good relationship. We'd visit.

FOREGOING AN ART WORK

John and I happened to be walking along Fulton Street, Brooklyn, one day during the early days of our marriage when we passed a second-hand store. In the window was the most beautiful ornate reproduction in color of a Petition to the Doge. The beautiful white marble entrance with its arches showed the Doge descending the carpeted stairway, as a lady clad in the costume of the day and holding a letter to the Doge was approaching. The picture was about four feet plus by three and one-half feet in a scroll-like quilt frame. John was entranced by this picture.

We asked the storekeeper what he wanted for it. The selling price $5.00. That was a great deal of money to us in 1918 or 1919 and John at college. We did not buy it. Upon thinking it over, we decided we'd go back to the store and purchase it. Alas, it had been sold! We regretted this for a long time.

WANTING A BABY

Working with the children at school gave me a feeling of satisfaction and achievement, while John enjoyed his work with his adult patients and children patients. However, I felt the need of a child of our own. We had been married for more than five years. Somehow I felt we ought to have our first before my 30th birthday. One Sunday afternoon we were walking along 5th Avenue in Manhattan and window shopping. I do not know what prompted my giving John a slight kick in his lower leg. He turned to me, laughed and said "What's this all about?" "Well, don't you think it's time we had a baby?" I asked. "OK, you send me a registered letter and we'll see!" was his answer. He took it very well!

Not long after, while in New York, we entered a professional building. John said "I want to see a friend of mine." I wondered what it was all about. We entered the medical office of Dr. Anthony Hart Harrington. Why: Before much ado, John blurted out "My wife wants to have a baby. Do you think it would be safe for her?" I didn't expect this kind of unexpected examination. Naturally I submitted. Dr. H said: "She's fine, was made to have babies!"

John wanted a son. He would joke and say: "It's enough to buy stockings for one female (me)." I am sure he'd have loved a daughter if he had one, for well do I remember how much he loved all his grandchildren. One of our patients' families was the Kosher butcher, Irving Kantor, who had his shop across from our office. During one of his visits, John happened to ask him how it happened that their three children were boys. He told John that it's all contained in the Old Testament. The ancient Jews wanted warriors to protect themselves. Hence, they set up some rules from experience and advised the husbands when to be with their wives.

Prior to this, we had come across an article in the Physical Culture magazine by a Dr. Reeder, a physician who had five sons and wanted more bulls on his ranch. He followed the rule set up and was successful. I shall try to attach this article to these pages.

JANIECE: HOW TO HAVE SONS

Mollie did not attach the article about how to have boys. The concept as we understand it was for a man to be with his wife only during the few days she was most fertile and not other times during her cycle. Mollie and John had three sons, so apparently they were most successful in this practice.

MOLLIE:

OUR FIRST BORN

We had our first born, a son, born in my family's home at 130 Howard Avenue, Brooklyn, on September 14, 1923, six and a half years after our marriage. I was dreadfully afraid of the hospital, the surgeon would not travel out to Bay Ridge, and so we arranged it this way. Bernard Donald Nolan died December 25, 1924.

In the fall of 1924, aboard the S. S. Richard Peck, en route on Long Island Sound to New Haven, Connecticut, Bernard Donald Nolan and his mother. His father is at the end of the deck. Bernard is about one year of age. He died December 25, 1924.

THE YEARS 1924–1935

JANIECE: CONTINUING MOLLIE'S BIOGRAPHY

In 1975 Mollie told us she had been writing her memoirs, but we did not realize she had terminated the effort after writing about the death of her firstborn in 1924. We regret that she was unable to go on with an account of her life after that. The last entry was dated July, 1975; she died five years later on September 6, 1980. We will attempt to provide an account of Mollie's life for the almost half-century between 1924 and her death.

Bernard died in 1924 during the medical treatment received for his pneumonia in a hospital, the very place Mollie and John dreaded. They had taken him to the hospital when he became worse and agreed to treatment with pneumococcal antiserum, which was experimental. Bernard died shortly afterward, at the age of fifteen months and on Mollie's birthday, which was also Christmas Day. No one can imagine the horror the family endured.

Somehow the couple survived and fourteen months after the death of Bernard, Mollie and John had a second child named Robert Lincoln Nolan, who became my husband in 1972. Mollie told me she wanted Robert to be born on Lincoln's birthday, which

A recent photo (2006) of 484-72nd Street, corner of 5th Avenue in the Bay Ridge section of Brooklyn, which was the family home and dental office on the second floor, from 1921 to about 1946.

was near her due day, so she ate a lot of figs the night before to stimulate delivery. And indeed she did deliver Robert on Lincoln's birthday, February 12, 1926, giving him Lincoln as his middle name. He was born at home on 72nd Street in Brooklyn.

When Bernard was born, Mollie stopped teaching because she wanted to stay home with her son and help in the dental office. That practice continued after Bernard's death and after Robert's birth. They were so relieved to have a healthy little boy, but worry about sickness was ever-present. They lived behind the dental office, so she could tend to domestic duties as well as help her husband.

According to Mollie, they were so careful of Robert—worrying that he might catch germs—that they kept him off the floor well past the time he could walk. He learned to walk in his crib, and since the mattress was bouncy, Mollie said that when they finally put him on the floor he walked like a sailor, swaying to and fro.

Two years after Robert's birth Mollie and John had their third son, Jerome Tilden Nolan, born May 19, 1928. The family of four—Mollie, John, Robert, and Jerry—had a happy life, with time spent in their country place near Allamuchy, New Jersey. The boys were close and played well together. The family continued to live behind the dental office in one large room with a kitchen and one fold-out bed, where all four slept together.

Despite all their caution, sickness came into their lives again. At the age of seven, Jerry contracted diphtheria. He was cared for at home and not at a hospital, perhaps due to the family's fear of hospitals and what had happened with their firstborn.

Jerome Tilden Nolan (in front) and Robert Lincoln Nolan outside their home on 72nd Street, circa 1934.

Jerome Tilden Nolan (left) and Robert Lincoln Nolan, at their country place near Allamuchy, New Jersey, circa 1934.

THE YEARS 1935–1980

ROBERT: MY BROTHER'S DEATH

When I awoke on the morning of December 6, 1935, I noticed that my brother, Jerome Tilden Nolan, age seven-and-one half, was motionless next to me. My parents said nothing and appeared somber. Jerry had been ill briefly; that's all I remember. I walked to school, P.S. 170, about a block away from our combined apartment and my father's dental office at 484-72nd Street, Brooklyn. That morning it was the longest block I had ever walked.

As I entered the school yard I broke down and cried and cried. Some teachers and students came to talk to me, and I told them my brother had died. I do not know how I managed to get through the school day. When I returned home, my parents, who were very distressed, told me what I already knew. Sometime later I learned that Jerry had died of diphtheria. There were no DPT shots available in those years. Jerry's open casket was in our waiting room, next to our bedroom/living room, for a day or two. Some came to say farewell. I was too upset to go to the burial, and Harry Cody, my father's old friend from the Panama Canal Zone, came to stay with me while my parents were away for the burial.

Tilden, Jerry's middle name, was to honor John Henry Tilden, M.D., a Denver physician who preached among other things avoidance of processed foods, emphasis upon fresh fruits and vegetables, and whole grains, and limitation on meats in the diet. He published a periodical called *The Stuffed Club* and other works setting forth his views, many of which my parents supported.

At the time of Jerry's death, Mom was at home taking care of us and helping out in the dental office. Then, in the early part of 1936, still depressed from the death, she decided she needed to get out of the house and returned to teaching as a substitute teacher. Initially it was part time, but she was in great demand and wound up teaching virtually full time in the substitute capacity.

Formerly, Mom had been a permanent tenured teacher after she graduated from the Brooklyn Training School for Teachers at age 19. She resigned the position to stay home in the dual capacity of homemaker and dental office assistant. However, in 1936 the standards for permanent appointment required a minimum of a bachelor's degree or the equivalent, essentially two additional years of college training than she had when she entered public school teaching in 1913.

While she continued teaching full time she undertook the additional two years of college part time, mostly at the College of the City of New York (CCNY) at night, completing the equivalency around 1941 and thereby earning regular permanent status. She taught elementary grades in Brooklyn schools and finally retired around 1958.

ROBERT: TRIP TO DENVER

In early 1936, when I was approaching age 10, my parents were talking about a trip to Denver for me to see Dr. Tilden. I was not ill. Their purpose was to have me evaluated from a preventive standpoint by this M.D. to see if he had any suggestions regarding promoting my health. They had lost two sons to infectious disease and sought advice about avoiding a repetition. Mom never forgot those December death dates and always grieved every December. By Easter 1936 the trip to Denver was agreed upon and reservations for the train and hotel were being made. My father was to stay at home to keep his dental office open.

School closed for the summer in June and the next month Mom and I took the train to Denver. We left from Grand Central station on the New York Central, which traveled through upstate New York then westward to Chicago. There we connected with the Union Pacific, which took us in a sleek train, the City of Denver. We were in coach the whole time from New York to Denver, which meant sleeping in our chairs for at least two nights.

After resting in our Denver hotel overnight, we found our way to Dr. Tilden's office, which seemed to me to be in a suburb of Denver. Going to the doctor was always a dress-up occasion in those days. This was a very special appointment, so we were both in our best clothes. I remember that Dr. Tilden was a white-haired, friendly man who shook hands with me in his relatively large, wood- paneled office. After he examined me, he told my mother that I had a somewhat fast pulse and recommended avoidance of white bread. I don't think I ever saw white bread at home after that, but I do not recall if there were any other changes in the family diet.

From almost everywhere in Denver it seemed I could see Pikes Peak high in the distance, covered with snow. We did not go there nor do other sightseeing. I was a little disappointed but didn't complain. Having completed our objective, we retraced our trip home by train. The whole adventure took a little over a week.

After the summer, in September 1936, I returned to school in the 6th grade. I was ten. On one occasion that semester we were asked to write essays about something we did the preceding summer. I wrote about Pikes Peak and described in detail the trip to the summit that I had not taken, facts supplied by my imagination. I was one of the few who received an A for that assignment.

ROBERT: MOM'S ROLE IN MY HIGH SCHOOL SELECTION

In the summer of 1939, following my elementary school graduation, we learned that Jack Monderer, one of my classmates at school, had been admitted to Townsend Harris High School (THHS), the Preparatory School of CCNY. Jack decided he wanted to go to Brooklyn Technical High School instead, where he had also been accepted. I had not previously known of THHS. One advantage that seemed appealing was that the school completed four years of high school in three years and all graduates were guaranteed admission to college at CCNY, then a distinguished school.

My mother and I went up to 77th Street and Fifth Avenue in Brooklyn and talked with Jack's parents at their candy store. I think my mother got something in writing that said Jack was going to Brooklyn Tech, not THHS, and that the Monderers were fine with my applying for the place Jack was giving up. Mom arranged for us to go to THHS, which was at Lexington Ave. and 23rd Street in Manhattan. She had my records from P.S. 170, including the graduation program showing my many academic awards and special recognitions. We met with Dr. Morton Gottschalk, the acting dean of CCNY and the acting director of the high school during the summer when the school was closed. He seemed quite tall to me (I was quite short at age 13). After my mother's presentation and after I had answered some questions assuring him I really wanted to go there, Gottschalk turned to Mom and asked, "Mrs. Nolan, is there anyone else who went to that elementary school?" Mom beamed, and then he told me I was accepted at THHS. We went home on the subway. I never forgot how my mother had successfully advocated for my THHS admission and the Dean's humorous question.

ROBERT: TRANSITION TO WAR: PARENTS FEAR THE OUTCOME BUT HELP ME ENLIST

When Pearl Harbor was attacked on December 7, 1941, I was fifteen and would be sixteen in two months. My parents were grim. I overheard concerned conversations about the possibility of my entering the war at eighteen, when I would have to register for the draft. When the United States declared war, I was a junior in high school. Soon after graduation from THHS in June 1942, I started college at New York University in the Bronx because this was the only university on the East Coast with an aeronautical engineering program. I was sixteen. The country was mobilized, patriotism was everywhere, and people supported the war with their lives.

In December 1943 I was nearing eighteen, almost a junior in college and eager to get in the fight. When I brought home papers to enlist in the navy's Eddy program (electronic training, named after a Captain Eddy), my parents, though worried, signed without hesitation. I decided against that program and tried to enroll in navy officer programs, including V-12 (the navy's college training program for officers) and then the U.S. Merchant Marine Academy. These programs all required the same naval officer physical exam, which I failed twice for being underweight. My family would not accept this result. Mom promptly contacted a congressman so I could be reexamined. Our family physician recommended that I eat bananas and drink lots of water just before being weighed. I did so, and finally I was able to overcome the weight hurdle. In May 1944 I was a junior, left college, and went to the U.S. Merchant Marine Academy at Kings Point, New York, for basic training as a cadet midshipman. If I survived the training, in about two years I would complete the program and also be commissioned in the navy. Now Mom and Dad were alone at home, and their only surviving child was in the war.

ROBERT: SEA DUTY

After completing basic training at Kings Point, in August 1944, I was assigned to sea duty in the merchant marine on a T-2 tanker loaded with high-octane gasoline preparing to leave for England.

We still lived at 484-72nd Street in Brooklyn. I had been on leave at home for about a week before I was to join the ship, the *S.S. Whitehorse*. During the leave I was busy at home gathering things to take on my first ship assignment. My parents helped getting things I needed. Eventually I wound up with a foot locker and a heavy, tightly packed seabag. One item was a portable Hermes typewriter Mom had bought for me to use in completing a detailed written sea project required by the merchant marine academy. Everything was stuffed into my seabag, which was made of heavy white canvas and shaped like a cylinder three feet high. In retrospect it seems surprising that during that week neither Mom nor Dad were kvetching (complaining) about the dangers before me. I knew they must be worried, but they tried not to show it and did not speak about their concerns.

Late one Sunday afternoon my parents got in the front seat of their 1932 Model B Ford. I sat in the back seat with my gear, and they drove me to Bay Way, New Jersey, where the *S.S. Whitehorse* was tied up. We drove more than an hour to reach the ship at a fuel port next to a refinery, across from Staten Island, New York. There wasn't much talk. I was nervous but also fearless and naïve. We reached a parking area near the ship's dock. There was an acrid smell of crude oil. I unloaded my foot locker and seabag. We hugged and said good-bye. Then I hauled my way across the planks to the ship about 300 yards away. I went up the gangplank and a crewman directed me to the room amidships for the cadets.

There was no looking back. The next morning we were at sea, joining a convoy headed across the Atlantic. We did not know that a week later our convoy would be attacked and some of us would never return. Neither my mother nor my father ever discussed my close call with death, although they knew about it.

ROBERT: THE WAR IS OVER

On August 5, 1945, the superintendent of the academy announced at our dinner in the mess hall that Japan had surrendered—the war was over. I was a second classman at the time and on the accelerated program scheduled to graduate in less than a year. However, although I had been on an engineering track, I had already decided that I wanted to pursue a career in medicine, not engineering.

ROBERT: WHY I CHANGED CAREER PLANS

In 1942, at sixteen years of age and based upon my assessment of future needs for engineering, it had been my career choice. In April 1944 I had taken a leave of absence from my junior year at New York University's College of Engineering and entered the U.S. Merchant Marine Academy. While at sea during the war from 1944 to 1945, I had a chance to reflect further on this choice. It had become apparent to me that an engineering career probably meant work that did not directly involve working with and helping people, but serving the needs of companies to advance their businesses. I also knew I wanted to be active in causes I believed in and insulated to the extent possible from pressures limiting freedom of expression. I also wanted to make a career choice that involved very high standards of ethical behavior and loyalty to one's beliefs that did not have to be sacrificed in order to make a living. Although I was also interested in law, medicine won out as the profession that offered the best opportunity to follow my ideals.

A change to pre-med had enormous implications. I would get only limited credit from engineering studies toward my A.B., would have to return to NYU from the academy to do that. I faced a long and very expensive training period at medical school and postgraduate residencies. I told my parents about my change in career plans when I returned from the South Pacific in April 1945. There was no challenge, and they were always supportive.

ROBERT: ADMISSION TO NYU

Soon after VJ day (August 14, 1945) the academy announced that the accelerated program was being abandoned in favor of the original four-year program. That meant almost two years to graduation and further delay in switching to pre-med. I kept my parents informed of my thinking but spoke mostly with Mom. My parents said they would support whatever plan I wanted to follow. I was relieved.

Since I was on leave from the NYU College of Engineering in order to study pre-med, I planned to transfer to the NYU College of Arts and Sciences on the same campus in the Bronx. They had a big pre-med program, and I expected to get the best break there for admission and transfer of my unit credits from their engineering school. There was some urgency because of the expected surge in college applications from returning veterans. Within a few weeks I got word of their approval of my college transfer, and I resigned from the academy. My parents were very happy. It meant I was coming home, for I planned to live at home and commute to college to save money.

Although the war was over, Selective Service was still inducting young men for Army of Occupation duties. This included individuals who had served in the merchant marine. So after no more than two months I had to leave college again and return to sea in the merchant marine until my status was resolved. During this whole period I never heard one word of opposition from my parents. They had confidence in my judgment and were totally supportive.

ROBERT: FACE IN THE WINDOW, 1946–48

It was about 2 a.m. on a Sunday morning in 1947 when I emerged from the subway close to our home at 361 Bay Ridge Avenue, Brooklyn. I had been dozing and awakened as the train entered the station. It had been a long ride from Sunnyside Queens, where I had returned Helen, my date, to her home. We had been to the symphony at Carnegie Hall; then, after stopping for a snack nearby, we had taken the subway to Long Island City. After walking her home, I rode the subway back to Bay Ridge. After climbing the stairs, I was out on the street and turned the corner to walk down Bay Ridge Avenue. Halfway down the street to our house, I was startled to see a face in our window peering down toward me. In an instant the face disappeared. It was Mom—the champion worrier, staying up and watching for my safe return.

I was 21 years old, a survivor of wartime combat, a pre-med in my junior year, capable of taking care of myself, and I was furious. When I went upstairs to our second- floor home, all was quiet. Mom had apparently gone to bed and seemed to be pretending to be asleep. So I waited until later that Sunday to confront her. Mom denied that she had been up waiting for me. Of course that was not true. I also complained to my father, who referred me back to her. Despite my complaints the face in the window pattern continued. It was like a cat-and-mouse game. Although I tried to catch her looking for me, she perfected her fast disappearance from the window. At one point she admitted it, but she continued worrying and watching despite promises to desist. Only when I moved to New Haven to go to medical school did her oversight of my activities become impossible for her. Now that I have been a parent and grandparent for many years, I have become more understanding of such parental anxiety.

However, Mom, with the apparent support from my father even before the face in the window appeared, had been overly intrusive regarding my dating activities. In 1944 shortly before heading across the North Atlantic, I had met Connie at a college dance and had gone out with her while on leave. I had become infatuated with her and wrote to my parents about my feelings. When I returned from England about a month later, I was flabbergasted to learn that my parents had gone out to her home in New Jersey to meet her. I was mortified, angry, and incredulous. After another brief leave I was on my way to the South Pacific and never contacted Connie again.

In my last year in the merchant marine (1945-46), I was dating a girl named Debbie from Barnard whose parents lived in New Haven. We were getting engaged and both Mom and Dad had expressed opposition. I found out that they had even met with Debbie's mother, who commuted to Manhattan to practice law. Debbie and I broke up later that summer.

By the time I returned to NYU in September 1946, I was determined not to tell my parents anything about the girls I met that could enable similar interventions. Therefore, the face in the window had never met Helen, knew little about her, and had no opportunity to intrude into the relationship. Nevertheless, the relationship ended for other reasons before I graduated from NYU.

ROBERT: ON TO YALE AND NEW HAVEN

In my senior year at NYU (1947-48) I concentrated on applying to medical school with the strong support of my parents. I was still commuting daily to school in the Bronx via a one-and-a-half-hour subway ride plus a twenty-minute walk to campus. My small study at home was like a busy political campaign office. Medical school catalogs, envelopes, and application forms were stacked all over my desk and the room. My Underwood typewriter was clicking constantly. Mom would stop in to see if I needed anything, including something to eat. She helped me pick out the clothes I needed for interviews, ran many errands getting documents and letters copied, and supplied additional copies of application photos and mailing materials.

My first interviews occurred in November 1947, and by the end of December I had achieved my goal: admission to the NYU School of Medicine in Manhattan. That meant I could continue to live at home, which seemed a financial necessity.

Unexpectedly, early in January 1948 I received a special delivery letter inviting me to interview for admission to the Yale School of Medicine. My parents and I were happily settled on NYU but decided it was worth going to take a look. So one morning I took the train up to New Haven, was interviewed by two professors—one was also the assistant dean—toured the campus, and returned home that evening. It was hard not to be impressed by the small, friendly school with the noncompetitive atmosphere. Soon I received my letter of acceptance. Mom went into a huddle with Dad and then told me that if I wanted to go to Yale they could handle the expense.

I never knew much about their finances or details of what a struggle it must have been for me to go away to medical school. I was thrilled with the idea of going to medical school at Yale and never regretted the decision. Of course there was an added benefit: I didn't have to watch for the face in the window. Although I was very busy with studies, almost everyone went out on Saturday nights, often including me.

In 1949 I met Virginia Reynolds in the Yale medical library. A graduate of Texas Christian University in Fort Worth, Texas, she was enrolled in the Yale School of Nursing as a master of nursing candidate. Soon we were dating regularly. My family did not know about it. In April 1950 we were secretly married in New Haven by a judge at New Haven City Hall. Neither family was informed. About a year later when we set up housekeeping, I told my parents. They were surprised and shocked but seemed supportive. Only some twenty-five years later when Mom was living in Oakland did she reveal what their true thoughts had been at the time.

ROBERT: MY FATHER IS DEAD

Early on Monday morning, June 15, 1959, I was in the newborn nursery at Kaiser Hospital Oakland. As another pediatrician and I neared completion of an emergency exchange transfusion on a newborn, I received a phone call. I went outside to the nurse's station to suddenly and unexpectedly hear my mother calling from Brooklyn. She told me that my father had died at home the previous night. I was shocked. I had not known he was ill. We spoke very briefly. I told her I would come to Brooklyn as soon as I could. I called my home in Oakland to pass on the sad news. I went to see the department chief, Dr. Alex King, to tell him why I had to leave. Since I was scheduled to take my pediatric oral board exams the next day in San Francisco, I phoned the board to explain my absence. Instead, on that day I was on a flight to Idlewild Airport in New York and then drove a rental car to Bay Ridge.

At one point Mom told me that she and my father decided not to tell me about his illness so as not to worry my family or me. It had been about eighteen months since Virginia and I had moved with our three children from Long Island to Oakland for me to take the job with Kaiser. Before we left, there had not even been a hint of illness in my father. In the remaining twenty-plus years of Mollie's life, we never talked again about Dad's final illness. It always remained painful for me to contemplate discussing it. Now I will never know what had happened. I wish I had found a way to discuss it with her.

JANIECE: JOHN'S ILLNESS

Mollie and I were once talking about the chores at home the working woman has to do in addition to her job. I was probably lamenting all my duties. Mollie may have wished to put those issues in perspective for me. She told me that her husband, John, was ill for many months preceding his death. She said she had to come home after her days teaching school to do everything around the home that John had once done. She recalled, for example, that he became too weak to shovel coal in the basement for their furnace, so she did it. It was hard for me to imagine such a tiny woman doing such heavy labor. But she smiled when she spoke proudly of keeping up the house and not bothering Robert with what was going on with his father. She failed to understand how that upset Robert, who as a physician felt he could have intervened and helped direct the medical care of his father. To this day Robert still regrets he did not know and could not help. When any family member (or friend, for that matter) is ill, Robert now always offers to help and act as a patient advocate, advisor, or both, linking the patient to second opinions and advice.

ROBERT: MOM AND HER GRANDCHILDREN

During the Oakland years of Mollie's life, her grandchildren became an even greater source of joy and happiness and a major focus of her life. When she arrived to live in Oakland in 1960, Douglas was six, Patty was four, and Nancy was two. Her apartment near the Fruitvale section was only minutes away from us in the Montclair section. Mom was a frequent source of baby sitting. The children all enjoyed her.

On April 1, 1962, Margaret was born, and now Mom had four grandchildren to lavish her attention upon. Sheff arrived as a part of our blended family at age four in 1972, followed by Gemini in 1974. Mom gave them all her attention and affection, bought them clothes, books, and toys. She attended all their birthday parties, which she often hosted in her apartment. Excursions to Diamond Park and the Oakland Zoo were highlights for the four older grandchildren as was the *Nutcracker* at the San Francisco Ballet every Christmas season.

Douglas, Patricia, Grandma Mollie, Nancy, and (front) Margaret Nolan, 1970.

Margaret and Grandma Nolan, circa 1968.

Grandma Nolan (back shown) giving a birthday party for Margaret (glass raised), with Patricia and Robert in the background, Oakland, California, 1969.

Despite increasingly arthritic hands, Mom crocheted numerous items for the grandchildren, including hats, sweaters, and blankets they much enjoyed. One of her biggest crocheting projects was a large, colorful, woolen king-size bedspread she made for Janiece and me. Even when her mobility was limited after her complicated hip fracture in 1975, she maintained a continuing interest in all of us. In 1977, with great effort, she was able to attend Patty's graduation from college at UC Davis.

A champion worrier, she always had on her worry cap, but more important, she remained encouraging, supportive, and loving of all six grandchildren. To her last day she strived to treat each of them equally. She is remembered by all of us as a model grandmother whom we try to emulate.

JANIECE: MOLLIE AND HER GRANDCHILDREN

I remember how grateful I was to Mollie in the way she welcomed Sheff into her life as her fifth grandchild. Sheff carried the Nolan name from the time he was four. We have a photo of his ninth birthday party at her apartment. Sheff is smiling broadly, sitting next to her and holding up the birthday cake she had made for him. Mollie's school teacher background may have contributed to the way she was able to command this rambunctious boy's respect and cooperation, seemingly without effort. Finally, five years after Mollie's death, Robert was able to adopt Sheff as his son, making him "official." There is and was no step status in our vocabulary or Mollie's. All six grandchildren by name were listed in Mollie's obituary.

Grandma Nolan and Sheffield at his 9th birthday party at her apartment in Oakland, California, 1977.

Mollie was ecstatic when Gemini Janiece arrived on September 8, 1974, to become her sixth grandchild. She wrote poems to Gemini on the occasion of her birth. We remember Mollie and Gemini doing "This Little Piggy" with Gemini's toes, an all-time favorite. Mollie always read to the children and instilled in them a great love of books.

Grandma Nolan with her sixth grandchild, Gemini Janiece, 1974.

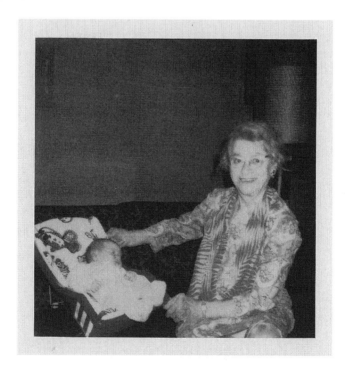

Grandma Nolan teaching Gemini how to read, circa 1979.

Mollie was always so supportive of her grandchildren. I remember one evening when Doug was staying with us, Mollie was cooking for the children so Robert and I could go out on a date. As we left, Mollie exclaimed to me proudly, "Doug thinks we should put some of the raw spinach in our salad," as if that was the most original idea anyone ever had. Doug, of course, was beaming.

On that occasion and others, as soon as Mollie walked in our front door she would start dusting our furniture, making me feel embarrassed rather than grateful. If I complained to Mollie about the household chores with my working full time while pregnant and later with two children under age seven, Mollie would always say, "You have those daughters; put them to work." Mollie would recall with pride how as a child she scrubbed the wooden floors while on her hands and knees. Growing up as an only child with a stay-at-home mother who had a maid, I was told just to study and have fun, and I was not allowed to do housework while growing up. I was surprised that Mollie made the solution to my overwork so simple. I asked Nancy and Margaret to do after-school baby sitting with Gemini and Sheff, their laundry, and dinner preparations. At that time we could not afford household help. (Patty was away at college and Doug was living on his own.) Years later I came to realize that Nancy and Margaret, who had a stay-at-home mother, had probably never done many household chores before they met me. They were very helpful, but I regret that I put them to work, as Mollie so helpfully instructed, which probably added to the stresses they were experiencing at that time.

Mollie and I often discussed Doug as well as her three older granddaughters. We talked about how Margaret was reacting to her parents' divorce and then to her new living situation with us. Mollie expressed concern when right after high school Nancy abruptly moved to Colorado. When Patty was away at her internship in dietetics in St. Louis, Mollie, the consummate worrier, often called us to see if we had heard from Patty and then kvetched about Patty being so far away and alone. Our finances were such at the time that we could not bring Patty back for visits during her year away. Mollie was unable to attend Patty's wedding, which occurred just four months before Mollie died.

In addition to worrying about the grandchildren, Mollie maintained a special set of civic worries about the direction our local and national governments were heading.

ROBERT: MOM'S CIVIC CONTRIBUTIONS

In 1960, shortly after Mom moved to Oakland, she became active in local politics. She joined the Democratic Women's Study Club in Oakland and soon was elected secretary. At that time the local Democratic Party had a storefront office on MacArthur Boulevard, not more than a block from her home. This group was one of several Democratic clubs in Oakland that played an active role considering issues, candidates, and other concerns. Mom's club was composed primarily of senior ladies who had been involved in the local political scene for many years. Although a newcomer, Mom dived into the work of the club and soon played a leadership role in all their activities.

She was busy with the mundane tasks, such as preparing agendas and addressing envelopes. She also was involved in policy-making activities such as drafting resolutions on varied subjects—from local elections, to needs of seniors, to school board issues, to civil rights, to opposition to the Vietnam War. She was passionate about correcting all the world's ills; this passion expressed itself in the club's resolutions, which were often published in the political columns of the *Oakland Tribune* and other local newspapers.

My mother was an avid follower of current events. She read the local papers and listened to both radio and television news reports and commentaries. Although I thought myself well read on current events, Mom often mentioned news items I had never heard of. She was always on the side of the downtrodden. We often had brief skirmishes in which she asserted that socialism was the answer and I objected that it was not a practical solution. We never convinced each other.

Mom worked hard in Democratic campaigns. In the course of her duties at the Alameda County headquarters, she became well known to many locally elected officials, including State Senator Nick Petris and Alameda County Supervisor John George. She mobilized her club to support my election to the Oakland Board of Education. When Martin Luther King, Jr. came to town in 1961, she was at the Oakland Auditorium handing out leaflets supporting my school board election. Mom's club continued their support during my four years on the board while we were in the contentious process of many reforms including integrating Skyline High School.

Mollie F. Nolan, circa 1961.

Mom remained active and involved in civic affairs until her hip fracture and sepsis complications, which resulted in confining her to a wheelchair. Nevertheless, she continued to write letters to officials on local and national matters. In 1979, the year before her death, she appeared before the Alameda County Board of Supervisors to testify in support of continued funding for the Center for Independent Living. She delivered a compelling and articulate statement; Supervisor John George left the dais and went down to personally congratulate her. *Roots*, Berkeley's community newspaper, published her letter to the editor about the services offered by the Center for Independent Living, urging funding support. It took another year of illness before her strong voice was silenced as she approached age 87.

ROBERT: MOM'S FAVORITE SAYINGS

Mom had at least three favorite sayings she would quote at the appropriate times to impart advice to the family:

·   Don't bite the hand that feeds you!
·   Live and let live
·   "How sharper than a serpent's tooth it is to have a thankless child" (from Shakespeare's *King Lear*)

JANIECE: MOLLIE IS DEAD

On Thursday, September 4, 1980, shortly after noon, I was in my office at John Muir Medical Center in Walnut Creek when I received the call from the nursing supervisor at Rossmoor Manor. She told me they were trying to reach Robert because Mollie had slumped over in her wheelchair and was dead. I immediately called Robert at his office in Sacramento, and he hurried home. Although we knew she was not doing well and was suspected of having cardiac arrhythmias after a fall the previous week, the news of her death was very difficult to hear. Robert had just visited his mother the previous night and had told me that the last thing Mollie the worrier said to him was about her concern for his long daily commute to Sacramento. Robert came to my office and we went together to the center to pay our final respects. I watched her leave in a hearse. We made all the calls to family and planned to hold a service as soon as possible. Although Mollie was not a practicing Jew, I knew that prompt burial was important to those of Jewish faith.

We planned a funeral at the Chapel of the Chimes in Oakland, a favorite place for Mollie because of its peaceful surroundings. We decided she should be buried in Lafayette (near Oakland) so family could visit the gravesite, rather than take her to New York to be buried alongside her husband. We thought she would have agreed. We had never discussed such things with her. Years later Robert learned from Mollie's younger sister Cecile that Mollie had talked about being buried in New York next to her husband.

We picked a tree-shaded gravesite in the Garden of Hope at Oakmont Cemetery in Lafayette. The cemetery office agreed to make an exception and allowed us to hold the service on a Sunday. So three days after her death we had a lovely service the afternoon of Sunday, September 7, 1980, followed by burial at Oakmont. Many of her friends from the Fruitvale neighborhood and Humanist society attended the funeral. All her grandchildren were present as well as Virginia Nolan, the mother of Mollie's four older grandchildren. I was able to find a leader from the Fellowship for the Humanities in Oakland to conduct the funeral. Reverend Guy Meyer gave a moving eulogy, carefully omitting any reference to deities or afterlife in accordance with Mollie's philosophy. After the service, we had a reception at our home for family and friends.

As a poignant footnote, I should add that as I was clearing out and closing her apartment, the landlord informed me that Mollie had had on-site storage for almost twenty years, since her move from New York. I protested that we knew nothing about a storage unit, that there must be some mistake. When he took me to it, I found her mother's photograph in a large frame as well as many vinyl chairs and other pieces of inexpensive period furniture from the 1950s or earlier. I was very puzzled about these items and wondered if the furniture belonged to someone else. Robert had been unable to deal with cleaning out her apartment and had left the chore to me. Nevertheless, I urged him to take a look at the storage items that I was sure did not belong to her. Robert immediately recognized the furniture as items from the waiting room of the Brooklyn dental office. Mollie had never revealed that she had paid to move those items across the country. She must have been too sentimental to discard them and too embarrassed to disclose the fact to us. We were touched and flabbergasted—she was a very practical and frugal person to have spent so much money over the years to preserve this important part of her life with John.

AFTERWORD

Janiece's Notes on Mollie's Parents and Siblings

Mollie's parents died in the 1950's. They are buried in Washington Cemetery, on Ocean Parkway in Brooklyn. We have a photograph of their joint gravestone, inscribed in English and in Hebrew. Mollie's father Louis died at the age of 81 on January 10, 1951. His obituary was in the New York Times on January 14, 1951. Louis's Hebrew name is inscribed as Leyzer ben Zissel. Rabbi Adar, who provided us a translation told us that the name Zessel (Zezil) is Yiddish, meaning "sweet". Mollie believed that her paternal grandfather was a rabbi because his name was always written Reb Zezil Flaumenhaft. Mollie's second mother, Rachel, died at the age of 84 on December 5, 1959. According to the gravestone, Rachel's father was a rabbi.

Throughout Mollie's autobiography she discussed the births, deaths, and lives of her siblings who were the children of her father and his second wife, Rachel. Only five of her siblings survived to adulthood, but they all lived long lives. Max died in 1973 at the age of 72, predeceasing Mollie by seven years. The others died after Mollie. Al died in 1984 at the age of 81, Sadie in 1985 at 88, Richard in 1985 at 71, and Cecile in 1988 at 90. A few words

Mollie's father Louis Flaumenhaft, and her second mother,
Rachel Eisler Flaumenhaft, circa 1938. This photograph was
taken in the backyard of their own home at 130 Howard
Avenue, Brooklyn, N.Y.

should be said about Mollie's siblings. They, too, came up from Hester Street and also did well as teachers and businesspersons.

Max married June, and had two children, Hortense and Herbert. Max was in the retail clothing business. Of all her siblings, Max looked the most like Mollie—short, dark, and pleasant. Richard, Mollie's youngest brother, married Etta and had a daughter, Sandra. Richard had a job in Max's clothing store and later went on his own in merchandising. Richard was of medium height, thin, well spoken and pleasant, is said to have died of heart disease. Robert saw Max and Richard occasionally at family events mostly at Mollie's parents' home on Howard Avenue in Brooklyn.

Sadie, the oldest of Mollie's siblings, became a legal secretary in New York and married an attorney named Bodan, who predeceased her. They had no children. Robert remembers Sadie and Cecile helping him with school projects in elementary school. But Mollie had no contact with Sadie starting sometime before 1939 because of a falling out that Sadie did not understand and Mollie never discussed.

Al and Cecile became school teachers, like Mollie. Maybe that is why she kept in touch with them more over the years. Cecile visited us in our home in Lafayette when Sheff was eleven and Gemini five, and she brought them gifts from her trip to Russia. She was relatively tall, thin, well- spoken, and vivacious. Cecile spoke of her years as a principal of an elementary school and junior high school. Cecile married twice; neither husband was Jewish. Her first husband died unexpectedly shortly after their honeymoon. Later, the best man at their wedding, John Timmerman, became her second husband. He died in 1946. They had a daughter, Jean. Cecile died a widow, surviving her second husband by 42 years.

As a child Robert saw Mollie's brother, Al Flaumenhaft, on a number of occasions. Al married Lolly and had two children, Paul and Ruth. We visited with Al at an airport stop in New York in the 1980s. He was a high school English teacher in Brooklyn. Al was relatively tall and in his later years very thin. He followed the dietary recommendations of a physician in Florida, the details of which we never knew. He died of complications of phlebitis.

We also had Al's son, Paul Flaumenhaft, his wife and children to our home when Margaret, Sheff, and Gemini were children. Paul is a retired school principal. We visited Paul's family in their home in New York in the 1980s, where they hosted a dinner for us.

In reviewing Mollie's autobiography a few years ago, Robert lamented that he had not seen some of his maternal cousins since they were all children. They now all had children of their own. I encouraged Robert to visit his four surviving cousins (Herbert and Sandra were deceased). Our daughter Nancy had been asking to visit New York with him to see where he grew up. In September 2009 they made that visit. Beforehand, Robert contacted the cousins, which precipitated a reunion dinner that Jean Dattner (the daughter of Mollie's sister Cecile) and her husband organized and hosted. Nancy Nolan interviewed and recorded a video of the occasion, which we shared with all the children.

First cousins who attended the dinner:

Hortense Laub (and husband Bob), the daughter of Max Flaumenhaft

Paul Flaumenhaft (and wife Barbara), the son of Al Flaumenhaft

Ruth Nelson (and husband Ed), the daughter of Al Flaumenhaft

Jean Dattner (and husband Eric), the daughter of Cecile Flaumenhaft

Robert Nolan (and daughter Nancy), the son of Mollie Flaumenhaft

Robert had not seen Hortense or Ruth since childhood. Although these New York cousins all live relatively near each other, except for funerals they had not all met together in decades (except for Paul and Ruth, who are siblings). Robert had previously visited with his cousin, Jean, Cecile's daughter in New York.

Robert had observed over the years that Mollie kept in touch with the other teachers, Al and Cecile, who had common professional interests. However, Mollie did not seem to identify with the business activities of Max and Richard, with whom there was less contact. Mollie also had a forty-year alienation from Sadie, for reasons no one understands, but we suspect it may have involved something along perceived ethical lines. In Robert's view, the issue with Sadie could have been relatively minor by today's criteria. Robert's father often referred to Mollie as "Ethical Mary," which would always get a rise out of her.

We gave the video of the visit to our children, explaining that Hortense, Paul, Ruth, and Jean are their first cousins, once removed. The children of Hortense, Paul, Ruth, and Jean are our children's second cousins. The grandchildren of Hortense, Paul, Ruth, and Jean are third cousins to our grandchildren. Mollie would have been pleased with the family reunion. All spoke her praises as a brilliant woman.

AFTERWORD
Janiece's Notes on Mollie's Heritage

GENEALOGY DOCUMENTATION AND THOUGHTS FROM KIM FORMICA

In writing this book, we received help with genealogy documentation and thoughts from Kim Formica, a professional genealogist in Connecticut we met through *Ancestry.com*. She is researching another Flaumenhaft family, that of Naftali Flaumenhaft (born in 1840 in Galicia). He was a tavern keeper and owned an inn in Galicia where travelers would stop. Two of Naftali's children were born in Karsy (near Tarnow, Galicia). The oldest known Flaumenhaft was Naftali's father, Joel Flaumenhaft.

There is a Getze Pflaumenhaft (born 1875) about the same age as Naftali who was a farmer near Tarnow. Getze lived in Karsy, Poland during the Holocaust. He was murdered in 1945 at the age of 70 in the Shoah, along with his wife and daughter. Testimony about Getze from his great-granddaughter is at *YadVashem.org* (digital collections, Shoah names database), along with his picture.

Kim Formica told us about finding a Philadelphia branch of the Flaumenhafts as well as a branch that ended up in Rio de Janeiro, Brazil, after fleeing the Holocaust. There is a possibility that all four branches (Naftali, the Philadelphia branch, the Brazilian family as well as Zezil – Mollie's grandfather) are all related, but we do not know. All four branches came from Tarnow, or just outside the town.

We also learned from Kim Formica that the gravestones of Naftali's sons (Kalman and Irving Flaumenhaft) indicate they were Levites, descendants of Levi. Even today in Orthodox and Conservative Saturday morning services the first two of seven honors (aliya from the Torah) are given to the Kohains and then the Levites. Robert's cousin Hortense Laub affirmed that her grandfather Louis (Mollie's father) was a Levite.

THE NAMES FEIER AND FLAUMENHAFT

Our children have often asked about the family names. Mollie's mother's maiden name, Feier, is pronounced similar to *fire* in English. Mollie always thought that pronunciation was ironic since her mother had perished from a fire. However, *feier* actually means to celebrate in German.

Mollie's maiden name, Flaumenhaft is related to plums, since in German *pflaumen* means plums or prunes. The name Flaumenhaft seems to have been used in Galicia before 1800 when surnames came into common use. Kim Formica told us that Hugh Flomenhaft of the Philadelphia branch thinks that because *Pflaumenhaft* means having plums or full of plums, that there must have been an ancestor in the 1700's who had plum trees and lots of plums. That person could have become known as Joel (or whatever the first name) who was *Pflaumenhaft,* or "Joel having lots of plums". So the name Pflaumenhaft, and its variants became the family name or surname after 1800.

WHERE DID MOLLIE'S PARENTS ORIGINATE?

Mollie always said that her Orthodox Jewish parents (Louis and Breindel) were from Austria and Mollie's autobiography states that her father's family lived on a small farm in Austria. Her parents, however, were born in 1870 and 1871, respectively, long before 1918, when Austria became a separate country. In the U.S. census records of 1900 and 1910, Austria is listed as the birthplace of Mollie's father, Louis, and her second mother, Rachel. Interestingly, ten years earlier Louis and Breindel's Certificate of Marriage (1890) lists Galicia as the birthplace for both. Since the marriage certificate was issued only two years after Mollie's parents' entry into the United States, we believe it is more geographically accurate than what the family told the census takers ten years later. When Mollie's Aunt Dora returned to New York from a visit to her father in Europe, the ship's manifest shows Austria as Dora's native country, with Tarnow as her last residence in Austria. Tarnow is a town in Galicia.

When Mollie's parents were born and when they emigrated to the United States, Galicia was not a separate country but rather part of the Austro-Hungarian Empire. To say the family came from Austria rather than Galicia was not without merit.

Where is Galicia? Why the variation in place of origin? Most people have never heard of Galicia. This historical region in eastern Europe has belonged variously to Poland, the Hapsburg Empire, the Soviet Union, and, at present, the Ukraine. The area was first mentioned as *Galiciae* in Hungarian historic chronicles of 1206. It belonged at that time to Poland. When the first Partition of 1773 dismembered much of Poland, Galicia passed to the Hapsburg (or Austrian) Empire and was renamed the Kingdom of Galicia and Lodomeria. In 1867, the Hapsburg Empire became the dualist Austro-Hungarian Empire. In 1873 Galicia evolved into a semi-autonomous province within the empire, and Polish, rather than German, became the official language.

Galicia holds an important place in the history of the Diaspora. During the Crusades, pogroms had caused many Ashkenazi Jews in western Europe to flee eastward to Poland. By the thirteenth century, Poland had become a great center of Judaism and Galicia had acquired a substantial Jewish population. When Galicia passed to the Hapsburg Empire in 1773, it was poor, backward, and provincial compared to most other regions of the empire. Yet, for its Jewish population, the new Hapsburg rule proved relatively benign. Jews were allowed to engage in many professions and participate in political life.

Beginning in the 1880s, however, political repression and compulsory military service for young men produced a mass emigration of the Galician peasants and Jews to other parts of Austria-Hungary as well as to Germany, the United States, Brazil, and Canada. In 1888 Louis, Breindel, and Rachel seem to have come to the United States as part of this migration.

In her autobiography Mollie implies that the family's fear of compulsory military service may have led her father to leave his birthplace. Anti-Semitism may have been another reason. During the nineteenth century, anti-Jewish sentiment was rising in the Hapsburg Empire, with several anti-Semitic political parties taking root in the imperial capital of Vienna.

The outbreak of the First World War in 1914 put a temporary halt to the Jewish emigration from Galicia, which never again reached its earlier magnitude. In 1918 Galicia's status as a Hapsburg province ended. It became part of the newly formed Polish Republic. Later, under Nazi occupation in 1943, Galicia's Jewish population was wiped out. Any Flaumenhaft descendants left behind probably perished in the Holocaust.

We have concluded that Mollie's parents were Galician Jews. Her father's family lived on a farm in Galicia. They may have migrated to what is now Austria before coming to the United States. We do not know. There were farming areas near Vienna, but that was several hundred miles from Galicia and the other side of what later became Czechoslovakia. There may be another reason the family started indicating Austria rather than Galicia as its place of origin. Eastern European Jews did not wholly escape discrimination, even in the United States. German Jews, well established on the Lower East Side of New York City, often looked down on later arriving and less assimilated Eastern Orthodox Jews and ridiculed their traditional garments. Mollie described her father wearing his phylacteries. Perhaps it became economically advisable for Mollie's parents, struggling to make a living with their pushcarts and small grocery stores, to say that that they came from cultured Austria rather than from poor and backward Galicia. We will never know.

So was Mollie really of Austrian, Ukrainian, or Polish national origin? Our answer is none of the above. We think it wisest to think of Mollie as Jewish-American, born of parents who were Galician Jews who had lived in the Austro-Hungarian Empire. The close ties and often ghetto existence of Jewish people in Europe discouraged intermarriage of Jews with the people of their host countries. To say that Mollie or her parents were Austrian, Polish, or Ukrainian would be misleading. As Mollie liked to say, "I am an American."

WHAT MADE MOLLIE JEWISH?

Mollie's parents were Orthodox Jews. According to Jewish law, a Jew is a child born to a Jewish mother. (Reform and Reconstructionist movements have decided to accept both matrilineal and patrilineal descent, but that is not relevant in Mollie's case since both her parents were Jewish.) Prior to adulthood, Mollie clearly decided to depart from being an observant Jew. As a child she went to synagogue, attempted to learn Hebrew, and tried to study the religion. She became offended, however, by the inequity of the Orthodox practice of the men sitting downstairs with the women relegated to the balcony. The practice of giving the wealthy women front row seats in the balcony particularly offended her. Most of her high school teachers were Christian and very kind to her. Her Aunt Dora was an outspoken agnostic who also influenced Mollie to reject the practice of Judaism. The death of Mollie's mother resulting from a Jewish home ritual may have influenced Mollie, but she never mentioned that tragedy as a factor. To appease her parents, Mollie and John were later married by a rabbi, which is interesting because she states she would never have agreed to the converse (marriage by a priest for John's family, a request that never arose).

By the time Mollie was in high school she was following the principles of Ethical Culture, which shares many beliefs with Judaism. However, belief in god is not one of them. Mollie did not believe in a deity, so humanism or Ethical Culture resonated with her. Elizabeth Seelman, Mollie's English teacher at Girls' High School who became her lifelong friend, encouraged her to embrace Ethical Culture, as Elizabeth had done. Of course the Ethical Culture Society in Brooklyn was where Mollie met her future husband, which further confirmed her decision.

Mollie did not observe Jewish rituals (at least not consciously), but she did observe Jewish ethics. To be a Jew means to have a special role and purpose, a sacred mission. *Tikkun Olam* (literally, "repairing the world") refers to second-third century rabbinic legislation to remedy specific social ills or legal injustices. By the sixteenth century, kabalistic thought shifted the term from God's actions to human actions, giving the responsibility for perfecting the world to us. Mollie practiced *Tikkun Olam*. Throughout her life she struggled to right the wrongs in the world and to bring us toward transformation, healing, and perfection.

Mollie's overwhelming love of family, children, and grandchildren, and even her "Jewish mother" stereotype as manifested in the amusing "face in the window" story, shows how very Jewish she was culturally. Judaism focuses on behavior and the consequences of our behavior while we are alive. The concept of an afterlife is not important except for the eternal life of the soul that is undefined and unexplained. Immortality is achieved through living a good life, leaving behind a good reputation, and, most important, having children who will carry on the ethics their parents taught them. Mollie, or "Ethical Mary" as her husband teasingly called her, has certainly left us her legacy.

On a personal note, I am part of Mollie's legacy. I have decided to convert to Judaism. Although initially raised a Methodist, I have had a lifetime interest in becoming Jewish. Robert is Jewish because his mother was Jewish, and, in my opinion, he is ethically and culturally Jewish. Writing this biography about Mollie over the past two years as well as my study with a rabbi for the past year made me even more convinced that I should convert to Judaism. As part of the conversion ceremony, one is given a Jewish name. I decided upon Malka, Mollie's Jewish name, as my Jewish name, to honor this esteemed woman.

Grandchildren of Mollie F. Nolan: Patricia, Sheffield, Nancy (front) and Margaret, Douglas and Gemini (back), 2006.

CONCLUSION

We compiled this book so that our children and their children and others who read it will continue to remember and honor Mollie F. Nolan, her family, and the other brave souls who as first-generation Jewish-Americans came up from the depths of poverty on Hester Street to leave behind impressive legacies.

AUTHORS' BIOGRAPHIES

Robert L. Nolan is a pediatrician/attorney and advocate in Lafayette, California. Born in Brooklyn, his academic education includes: graduate of Townsend Harris High School; A.B. from NYU; M.D. from Yale University; J.D. and Master of Public Health from the University of California, Berkeley, and post-graduate pediatric training at Yale and Cornell medical schools. He is currently a clinical professor at UCSF and previously served on three other medical school faculties. He is the co-editor of *Appalachian and Rural Health* (Thomas, 1973) and the author or co-author of thirteen papers in public health. He is considered one of the founders of the National Health Service Corps. His career also included pediatric practice with both HIP and Kaiser Permanente and medical administrator of state and county public health programs in California. For his work he received formal resolutions of commendation from the California and West Virginia Legislatures as well as Contra Costa County (California). Dr. Nolan is also a combat veteran of WWII and a retired decorated naval officer (O-6).

A native Texan, **Janiece Simmons Nolan** has had a lifelong interest in writing, genealogy, and history, although her careers were in science and hospital administration. She is a Phi Beta Kappa with a B.A. (with high honors) and a M.A. in botany from the University of Texas, Austin. She earned a Ph.D. in biology at Tulane University, New Orleans, and a Master of Public Health from the University of California, Berkeley. Working as a research scientist at private institutes as well as during a postdoctoral at UC Berkeley, she published twenty-three articles in scientific journals. She is a retired decorated captain (O-6), U.S. Naval Reserve, Medical Service Corps, where she served as commanding officer of various hospital units. She was inducted into the Women's Hall of Fame by the Contra Costa County Commission for Women. Recently retired from a career in hospital administration, including eleven years as a CEO, she now has time to devote to writing. She contributed an essay entitled *Son of Southern Rebel* (about the grandfather she never knew) to the anthology *Roots and Tendrils, Prose and Poetry of a Berkeley Writers' Workshop* (2010). Her next book will be about this grandfather.

16239743R00072

Praise for Anne Perry's
CHARLOTTE AND THOMAS PITT novels

DEATH ON BLACKHEATH

"A truly unusual mystery distinguishes bestseller [Anne] Perry's twenty-
ninth Victorian puzzle featuring Charlotte and Thomas Pitt. . . .
Perry balances plot and character neatly before providing a resolution
that few will anticipate."

—*Publishers Weekly*

"Trickery, treachery and treason are combined in Anne Perry's latest
account of the dark side of nineteenth-century aristocratic London."
—*The Washington Times*

"Perry writes with great assurance about these Victorians stuck in
their notions of how to behave and how desperate they are to maintain their superiority—and how little all that will mean if England
falls."

—*New York Journal of Books*

MIDNIGHT AT MARBLE ARCH

"Without losing her grip on the refined language appropriate to the
day, Perry has written a sweeping and scandalous exposé of sexual
brutality amid the upper classes. . . . Perry has perfected a delicate
touch in approaching the untouchable."

—*The New York Times Book Review*

"Another splendid success. [Perry] is so familiar with life at this time that history, attitudes and culture are slipped in seamlessly so the reader sees the world as Victorians did. . . . This is a series to read from the beginning."

—*RT Book Reviews* (Top Pick)

"Absolutely crackles with suspense as it unfolds the dilemmas Perry is known for placing before her characters: moral, ethical, legal and personal. . . . Highly recommended."

—*The Historical Novels Society*

"Packed with intrigue."

—*The Huffington Post*

DORCHESTER TERRACE

"[A] magic kingdom of Victorian murder and intrigue."

—*The New York Times Book Review*

"The plot of *Dorchester Terrace* moves along in deliciously serpentine fashion and, given that we readers know what horrors really did follow from the assassination of an Austrian archduke, Pitt's dilemma has the pang of genuine urgency."

—National Public Radio

"[A] stately page-turner."

—*The Washington Post*

"Perry's Victorian England is well drawn, a broad-stroke portrait that gives readers the spirit of the time and place without getting mired down in too much detail, and Charlotte and Thomas remain two of the most vividly conceived protagonists in the historical-mystery genre. Another fine entry in an always entertaining series."

—*Booklist*

TREASON AT LISSON GROVE

"The action is nonstop and the characters ring true."

—HuntingtonNews.net

"Ms. Perry has always done her historical homework on the darker elements of the British ruling class, and she has outdone herself this time."

—The Washington Times

"A fast-paced Special Branch romp from beginning to end."

—Bookgasm

DEATH ON BLACKHEATH

ANNE PERRY

DEATH ON BLACKHEATH

A Charlotte and Thomas Pitt Novel

BALLANTINE BOOKS • NEW YORK

2015 Ballantine Books Trade Paperback Edition

Copyright © 2014 by Anne Perry
Excerpt from *The Angel Court Affair* by Anne Perry copyright © 2015 by Anne Perry

Published in the United States by Ballantine Books, an imprint of Random House, a division of Random House LLC, a Penguin Random House Company, New York.

BALLANTINE and the HOUSE colophon are registered trademarks of Random House LLC.

Originally published in hardcover in the United States by Ballantine Books, an imprint of Random House, a division of Random House LLC, in 2014.

This book contains an excerpt from the forthcoming book *The Angel Court Affair* by Anne Perry. This excerpt has been set for this edition only and may not reflect the final content of the forthcoming edition.

LIBRARY OF CONGRESS CATALOGING-IN-PUBLICATION DATA
Perry, Anne.
Death on Blackheath : a Charlotte and Thomas Pitt Novel / Anne Perry.
pages cm. — (A Charlotte and Thomas Pitt Novel)
ISBN 978-0-345-54842-9
eBook ISBN 978-0-345-54839-9 (eBook)
1. Pitt, Charlotte (Fictitious character)—Fiction. 2. Pitt, Thomas (Fictitious character)—
Fiction. 3. Murder—Investigation—Fiction. 4. Police—England—London—Fiction.
5. Women detectives—England—London—Fiction. 6. Police spouses—England—
London—Fiction. 7. London (England)—Fiction. 8. Great Britain—History—
Victoria, 1837–1901—Fiction. I. Title.
PR6066.E693D43 2014
823'.914—dc23

Printed in the United States of America on acid-free paper

www.ballantinebooks.com

2 4 6 8 9 7 5 3 1

Book design by Karin Batten

To Ileen Maisel

DEATH ON BLACKHEATH

1

Pɪᴛᴛ sᴛᴏᴏᴅ sʜɪᴠᴇʀɪɴɢ ᴏɴ the steps leading up from the areaway to the pavement and looked down at the clumps of blood and hair at his feet. Splinters and shards of glass lay on the steps below and above him. There was blood on those as well, and some of it had already congealed. The January wind whined across the open stretch towards the gravel pits in the distance.

"And a maid seems to be missing?" Pitt asked quietly.

"Yes, and sorry, sir," the police sergeant said unhappily. His young face was set hard in the gray early morning light. "Thought that seeing whose house it was, like, we should call you straightaway."

"You did the right thing," Pitt assured him.

They were in Shooters Hill, a very pleasant residential area on the outskirts of London. It was not far from Greenwich, where both the Naval College and the Royal Observatory from which the world took its time stood. The imposing house rising above them into the still, shadowed air was that of Dudley Kynaston, a senior government official deeply involved in matters of naval defense—a weapons expert of some kind. Violence so very close to his house was of concern to Special Branch, and thus to Pitt as its commander. It was a recent promotion for him and he was still uncomfortable with the extraordinary power it lent him. Perhaps he always would be. It was a responsibility that ultimately he could share with no one. His triumphs would be secret, his disasters appallingly public.

Looking down at the grim evidence at his feet, he would gladly have changed places with the sergeant beside him. He had been an ordinary young policeman himself when he had been this man's age, twenty years ago. He had dealt with regular crimes then: theft, arson, occasionally murder—although not many with any political implications, and certainly none to do with terrible threats of violence towards the country and the government.

Pitt straightened up. He dressed much more smartly these days, if a little untidily, but even his new woolen coat could not dull the knife-edge of the wind. He was cold to the bone. The chill was blowing up from the river a mile and a half away, not hard, but with the steady bitterness of the damp. From this height he could see the low-lying stretches to the east shrouded in mist, and hear the mournful wail of foghorns.

"Did you say it was reported by the first servant to get up?" he asked. "That must have been hours ago." He glanced at the wan daylight.

"Yes, sir," the sergeant replied. "Scullery maid, slip of a thing, but sharp as a tack. Scared the poor child half out of her wits, all the blood and hair, but she kept her presence of mind."

"She didn't run all the way to the police station in the dark?" Pitt asked incredulously. "It must be a mile and a half at least, from here."

"No, sir," the sergeant responded with some satisfaction in his voice. "Like I said, she's pretty coolheaded, and all of about thirteen, I would guess. She went in and woke up the housekeeper, a sensible sort of woman. She has the use of the telephone, so after she'd checked that the blood and hair were real, not just from some animals fighting or something similar, she called the police station. If she hadn't, likely we'd still be on the way here."

Pitt looked down at the blood, which could easily enough be human or animal. However, the strands of hair were long, auburn in the lantern light, and could only be human. The thought occurred to him that without the telephone to waken him at his home in Keppel Street on the other side of the river, he would have been having breakfast in his own warm kitchen now, unaware of any of this potential tragedy, and all the grief and complications that could arise from it.

He grunted agreement, but before he could add anything more he heard rapid footsteps along the pavement. The next moment, Stoker appeared at the top of the areaway. He was the one man in Special Branch that Pitt had learned to trust. After the betrayals that had led to Victor Narraway's dismissal, he trusted no one who had not earned it. Narraway had been innocent of any wrongdoing and, after desperate effort and cost, had been proved so. But the events in Ireland had still been the end of his career at Special Branch.

"Morning, sir," Stoker said with only the slightest curiosity in his voice. He glanced down at the lantern and the patch of stone steps illuminated by it, then at Pitt. He was a lean man with a strong, intelligent face, although it was a bit too bony to be good-looking, and too dour for charm.

"There was some sort of scuffle here, and a maid of the house appears to be missing," Pitt explained. He looked up at the sky then back at Stoker. "Make a note of exactly what you see. Draw it. Then pick up a few samples, in case we need them in evidence one day. Better hurry. If the rain comes it'll wash that whole lot away. I'm going in to speak to the household."

"Yes, sir. Why us, sir? A quarrel, a missing maid—what's wrong with the locals doing it?" He gave the sergeant a nod, but the question was directed at Pitt.

"Householder is Dudley Kynaston—naval defense . . ." Pitt replied.

Stoker swore under his breath.

Pitt smiled, glad not to have caught his exact words, although he probably agreed with them. He turned and knocked on the scullery door, then opened it, walking past the stored bins of vegetables and into the kitchen. Immediately the warmth wrapped around him, along with the rich aromas of food cooking. It was comfortable, everything in order. Polished copper pans hung from hooks, their sheen winking in the lights. Clean china was stacked on the dresser. Shelves were piled neatly with labeled spice jars. Strings of onions and dried herbs hung from the rafters.

"Good morning," he said clearly, and three women turned from their tasks to look at him.

"Mornin', sir," they replied almost in unison. The cook was a comfortably rounded woman, at the moment holding a large wooden spoon in her hand. A maid in a starched and lace-trimmed apron was setting out tea and toast ready to carry upstairs, and another maid was peeling potatoes. She had dark, unruly hair and wide eyes. As soon as he saw her, Pitt knew that she was the one who had gone outside and found the blood and glass. The sleeves of her gray dress were rolled well above her elbows, and her white apron was covered in smuts from relighting the stove.

The cook regarded Pitt apprehensively, unsure where to place him in the social scale. He wasn't a gentleman because he had come in through the back door, and he didn't have the natural arrogance of a man used to the attention of servants. On the other hand, he seemed very sure of himself in a different kind of way, and she could tell at a glance that his overcoat was of excellent quality. In the circumstances, he was probably a policeman of some sort, but he did not look like an ordinary sergeant.

Pitt gave her a brief smile. "May I speak to your scullery maid, please? I would appreciate it if you could give me a quiet room where we will be without interruption. If you wish the housekeeper to be with her while we speak, that will be acceptable." He phrased it as a request, but it was an order, and he held her eyes long enough to be certain that she knew that.

"Yes, sir," she said, her voice catching as though her mouth were dry. "Dora here can go with her." She gestured at the startled parlor maid. "I'll take that tray up to Mrs. Kynaston. Maisie, you go with the policeman an' tell 'im what 'e needs to know. And you be civil, mind!"

"Yes, Cook," Maisie said obediently and led Pitt as far as the door. Then she turned to him, looking him up and down with bright, critical eyes. "You look like you're froze to the bone. You want a cup o' tea . . . sir?"

Pitt smiled in spite of himself. "Thank you, that would be very nice. Perhaps Dora would bring us a pot?"

Dora was strongly disapproving. She was a parlor maid, not someone to fetch and carry cups of tea to the likes of policemen and scullery maids, but she could not find the right words to say this, so she nodded in assent.

Pitt's smile widened. "Thank you, very helpful of you." He turned and followed Maisie along the corridor to the housekeeper's sitting room. The housekeeper herself was no doubt about other duties necessitated by the alarming circumstances.

Pitt sat down in the armchair by the fire, which was newly lit and not yet warm. Maisie sat upright on the hard-backed chair opposite him.

"What time did you come down to the kitchen this morning?" Pitt started right away.

"'Alf past five," she replied without hesitation. "I raked out the ashes an' took 'em out ter the ash can in the yard. That was when I found the"—she gulped—"the blood . . . an' that."

"So you found the evidence at about quarter to six, would you say?"

"Yeah . . ."

"Was there anybody else nearby when you came out?"

She took a very deep breath, then let it out in a sigh. "Opposite's boot boy was there, but 'e wouldn't never 'ave done anything like that. 'Sides, 'e likes Kitty . . . I mean she were nice to 'im. 'E . . . 'e comes from the country an' 'e misses 'is family, like." Her dark eyes stared unwaveringly at Pitt.

"Who's Kitty?" he asked.

"Kitty Ryder," she said as if he should have known. "Mrs. Kynaston's lady's maid wot's missing."

"But how do you know for sure she's missing?" he asked curiously. It was possible that this Kitty had gotten up that early to leave on some specific errand, he thought.

"'Cos she in't 'ere," she replied reasonably, but he knew from the defiance in her face and her very slight sniff that she was perfectly aware of being evasive. He decided to leave it for the time being.

"So your first thought was that the hair on the steps looked like Kitty Ryder's?" he pressed.

"Yeah . . . some . . ."

"And you were afraid something had happened to Kitty?" he suggested.

"Yeah . . . I . . ." She stopped. She looked into his face and knew that somewhere there was a trap in the question, but she did not look away.

He heard Dora's footsteps in the passage. He hurried to his next question, before Dora could come in with the tea and remain as a chaperone, perhaps keeping Maisie from saying everything she'd like to say.

"So you immediately thought it likely Kitty could have been on the areaway steps sometime in the middle of the previous night, and possibly have had a quarrel that turned violent? Did she have a suitor?"

"A wot?"

"A young man?"

Dora came in through the door balancing a tray with a teapot, milk jug, sugar bowl, and two cups and saucers. She placed it on the table and stood back a little, her face stiff with disapproval.

Pitt nodded his thanks but kept his eyes on Maisie. "A young man," he repeated quickly. "I'm guessing Kitty had a young man and she went out at night to meet him. That was why when you saw the blood and hair you thought of her, and checked to see if she was home—and she wasn't. Is that right?"

Maisie stared at him with respect, and a new fear. She nodded silently.

"Thank you," Pitt acknowledged. "And did you find Kitty at all? Or any sort of note explaining where she had gone?" He asked that with a deep sense of impending sadness. Of course he already knew the answer.

Maisie shook her head. "She in't nowhere."

"Would you like a cup of tea?" he asked.

She nodded, still not taking her eyes from his face.

"Dora, would you pour two cups of tea, please?" Pitt requested. "I take mine with milk and no sugar. You'll know how Maisie likes hers. Then perhaps you would find either the housekeeper or the butler for me and have them come here."

Dora glared at him but did as she was told. She had been brought up to be very careful never to make trouble with the police, whatever sort they were.

An hour later Pitt had learned all that he could from the staff. He and Stoker made a complete record of the areaway with sketches and diagrams, then went together to the withdrawing room to speak first to Dudley Kynaston. If necessary they would also speak to his wife.

The room was spacious, as Pitt had expected. Surprisingly, it was also comfortable, as though it were arranged for the family's own pleasure, rather than for entertaining, or to impress. The carpets were mellow and well worn, the leather of the chairs creased into lines of comfort, cushions placed for ease. Kynaston was standing in the middle of the floor, but there was a pile of papers on the sofa where he had apparently been sitting. He must have heard their feet on the parquet of the hall, and risen to his feet. Pitt wondered if that was out of good manners or the instinctive desire not to be at a disadvantage.

Kynaston was a tall man, almost Pitt's own height. His face was handsome, regular featured, with thick fair hair graying at the temples. He looked unhappy, but not more anxious than any decent man should be at the thought of possible violence.

Pitt introduced himself and Stoker.

"How do you do?" Kynaston replied courteously, but only to Pitt, merely nodding towards Stoker. "I appreciate Special Branch's concern, but I don't know how I can help you. If my unfortunate maid is involved in this, I feel it is probably no more than an unusually vicious quarrel. Perhaps some young man had too much to drink and was reluctant to take 'no' for an answer. Unpleasant, but these things happen. I'm sure she will return." He was politely telling Pitt that he was wasting his time, and he did not have the air of a man making excuses.

"Is it usual for Miss Ryder to be about at this hour of the morning?" Pitt asked him.

Kynaston shook his head fractionally. "No, that is most unusual. I can't explain it. She is normally a very reliable girl."

Pitt felt more than heard Stoker fidget from one foot to the other behind him.

"You are sure she's not anywhere in the house?" Pitt asked.

"There's nowhere she can be." Kynaston looked confused. "She's never done this before. But, from what the butler tells me, the mess on the area steps indicates a rather nasty quarrel. It's all very unpleasant, and we shall have to let her go, but I hope she isn't seriously hurt. Beyond permitting you to search the house for yourself, and allowing you to question anyone you please, I can't think of any way in which I can be of help."

"Thank you, sir," Pitt responded. "Perhaps I could speak with Mrs. Kynaston? I'm sure she will know more about the domestic servants. As you say, it is probably no more than a quarrel that became violent, and once we have found Kitty Ryder and assured ourselves that she is all right, then we can close the issue."

Kynaston hesitated.

Pitt wondered if he was being protective of his wife, or afraid she might say something unintentionally indiscreet. It could be irrelevant to the hair and blood on the steps, possibly to do with some other matter entirely, one that he would like to keep private. So many times Pitt had investigated one thing, only to uncover secrets of a completely different nature. Privacy, once intruded upon, was never entirely the same again. He felt a moment's pity for Kynaston, and he regretted that he could not afford to indulge it.

"Mr. Kynaston?" he prompted.

"Yes . . . yes, of course," Kynaston said with a sigh. He reached over and rang the bell by the side of the fireplace. It was answered by the butler, a sober man, his pleasant face marred by an anxious frown. "Ah, Norton, would you please ask Mrs. Kynaston to come to the withdrawing room?" Clearly he had no intention of allowing Pitt and Stoker to speak with her alone.

Norton retreated and they all waited in silence until the door opened and a woman came into the room. She was of average height and at first of very unremarkable appearance. Her hair was thick but an ordinary shade of brown. Her features were regular, her eyes neither gray nor blue. When Pitt thought about it afterwards, he could not remember what she wore.

"I'm sorry to disturb you, my dear," Kynaston said quietly. "But it seems that the local police have called in Special Branch about the blood and hair on the steps. At least until we know what happened, and where Kitty has gone, we must allow them to pursue the issue."

"Good gracious!" she said with surprise. She looked straight at Pitt with sudden interest. "Is the safety of the nation so little threatened that you have time to investigate the misbehavior of a domestic servant?" Her voice was the one memorable feature about her. It was rich and soft. Pitt could not help thinking that if she sang she would do so beautifully, with the kind of timbre that made all the notes throaty and full of emotion.

Kynaston was clearly at a loss for words.

"I'm afraid we don't know for sure that it was Miss Ryder's hair, ma'am," Pitt replied for him. "Or her blood."

She was slightly taken aback. "I believe the hair found was of a reddish brown, which Kitty's is. But I imagine that would be true of many people. Are you saying, then, that this might have nothing to do with our house at all? The blood was found on the area steps, wasn't it? I suppose anyone might have been there."

Kynaston's face pinched momentarily. Then the instant he was aware of Pitt looking at him, he smoothed the expression away. "Of course," he agreed. "Although we do not get troubled by passing strangers. We have few neighbors." It was an unnecessary comment; Pitt knew they were mostly surrounded by open country, a few trees, and the large gravel pits that were common between Blackheath village and Greenwich Park.

"Really, Dudley," Rosalind Kynaston said patiently, "we might not be in the middle of a busy street, but we are not alone. And this time of the year, the shelter of the areaway must be a great deal pleasanter than the open in the wind."

Pitt allowed himself to smile. "No doubt," he conceded. "But could one of the people have been Kitty Ryder in this case, in your opinion?"

"I think so." She gave the slightest shrug, barely a movement of her rather graceful shoulders. "There's a young man she walks out with now and then. A carpenter or something of the sort."

Kynaston looked startled. "Does she? You never mentioned it!"

She regarded him with an expression that almost concealed her impatience. "Of course I didn't. Why on earth would I? I hoped it would pass, and I told her so. He is not particularly appealing."

Kynaston drew in his breath as if to say something, then let it out again, and waited for Pitt to speak.

"You don't care for the young man?" Pitt asked Mrs. Kynaston. "If she ended the acquaintance do you think he might have taken it badly?"

She considered for several moments before finally replying. "Actually, I do not think so. I believe he has a good deal of affection for her but that he has no real prospects. But also, to be frank, I think Kitty has more sense than to choose the area steps in the middle of a winter night to tell him so."

"She would have thought herself safe enough just outside her own scullery door!" Kynaston protested. His expression darkened. "Just how unsuitable was he?"

"He wasn't unsuitable, Dudley, he was just not as well as she might have done for herself," she explained. "Kitty is a very handsome girl. She could have been a parlor maid in the city, if she'd wished to."

"She didn't wish to?" Pitt was curious. He could tell Stoker, though silent, was also listening intently. What would keep a good-looking girl here in Shooters Hill if she could have been in one of the fashionable squares in London? "Has she family locally?" he asked.

"No," Rosalind assured him. "She comes from Gloucestershire. I don't know why she didn't take her chance in the city. I'm sure she had offers."

It might be irrelevant, but Pitt made a mental note to look further into the reason for Kitty's loyalty, if she did not very soon turn up alive and well.

"I suppose your advice that she could do better didn't go down very well with him," Kynaston observed, looking at his wife. He turned to Pitt. "We appear to have wasted your time. I feel if there is anything at all to deal with here, which there probably isn't, then it is a police matter. If Kitty doesn't turn up, or we have any reason to suppose she has been harmed, we'll report it." He smiled and inclined his head a little, as if it were a dismissal.

Pitt hesitated, unwilling to let go of the matter quite so easily. Someone had been hurt on the areaway steps, possibly badly. Had it been a daughter of the house rather than a maid, no one would be dismissing it.

"Could you describe Miss Ryder for me, sir?" he asked, without moving.

Kynaston blinked.

"How tall is she?" Pitt elaborated. "What build? What coloring?"

It was Rosalind Kynaston who replied. "Taller than I am, at least a couple of inches, and very handsomely built." She smiled with a dry, private amusement. "She had excellent features, in fact were she a society girl we'd say she was a beauty. She has fair skin and thick auburn hair with a wave in it."

"I think you're being overgenerous, my dear," Kynaston said with a slight edge to his voice. "She's a lady's maid who was being courted by a young man of very dubious background." He turned to Pitt again. "And as I'm sure you are aware, maids have a half day off at the weekends, but stepping out in this manner is not really acceptable—which, of course, is why she has done it on the sly. If you are still concerned, you might consider the possibility that she has eloped with him."

Rosalind was saved from making a reply by the entry into the room of another woman. She was taller, in fact only two or three inches short of Kynaston's own height, and her hair was silver blond. But it was her face that commanded attention, not by its beauty, which was questionable, but by the power of emotion in it, which was more arresting than mere regularity of feature. Her eyes were of a burning blue.

"Have you found the housemaid yet?" she asked, looking directly at Kynaston.

"Lady's maid," Rosalind corrected her. "No, we haven't."

"Good morning, Ailsa," Kynaston said, rather more gently than Pitt thought he would have, in the circumstances. "Unfortunately not. This is Commander Pitt of Special Branch."

Ailsa's delicate eyebrows rose. "Special Branch?" she said incredulously. "Dudley, you haven't called in Special Branch, have you? For heaven's sake, my dear, they have better things to do!" She turned to stare at Pitt with new curiosity. "Don't you?" she challenged him.

"My sister-in-law, Mrs. Bennett Kynaston," Kynaston explained. Pitt saw pain shadow Kynaston's face; it vanished almost immediately, but not without evident effort on Kynaston's part. Pitt recalled that Bennett Kynaston had died roughly nine years earlier. Interesting that his widow had kept such close touch with the family, and clearly had not married again. She was certainly handsome enough to have had many opportunities.

"How do you do, Mrs. Kynaston?" he replied to her. She was staring at him, her eyes wide, so he answered her question instead of waiting for her to reply. "A young woman is missing and there is blood, hair, and broken glass on the area steps—enough to indicate the possibility at least of a very nasty fight. The local police called us because they are aware of Mr. Kynaston's importance to both the navy and the government, and how serious any threat to him might be. If it turns out to be no more than a very unpleasant lovers' quarrel, then we shall leave it to them to take what action is necessary. At the moment Miss Ryder appears to be missing."

Ailsa shook her head. "You need to replace her, Rosalind. Whether she comes back or not, she is clearly no better than she should be, as they say."

A look of anger crossed Rosalind's face, but so quickly Pitt was not absolutely certain he had seen it at all. Had he imagined it? He knew how his own wife, Charlotte, would have felt about such high-handed instruction from anyone else—even her sister Emily, close as they were in affection.

Before Rosalind could frame a reply, Pitt intervened, speaking to Kynaston. "We shall keep the case open until Kitty Ryder is found, or you have some news of her, whatever it may be," he said. "In the meantime, she appears not to have taken any of her belongings with her. The housekeeper told me even her nightgowns and hairbrush are still in her room. In light of that, we have to assume she did not plan to leave. If you discover anything of value missing from the house, please inform the local police. I would suggest that you be more than usually diligent in making certain that the doors are locked at night. You might inform your butler of the possibility of robbery . . ."

"I will," Kynaston agreed. "This is all most unpleasant. She came to us with good references. But your advice is well placed, and I shall certainly take it. I am obliged to you."

"I don't believe Kitty would be involved in robbing us," Rosalind said with some heat, a slight flush on her pale cheeks.

"Of course you're reluctant to think so," Ailsa said gently, moving a step closer to her sister-in-law. "She was your personal maid, and you trusted her. One does! Usually one is right, but anyone can be misled, now and then. I understand she fell in with a very nasty type of young man, and we all know they can take people in—heaven knows, even in the best families, let alone a girl far from her home, working as a maid."

The truth of the remark was unarguable, but Pitt saw in Rosalind's face disbelief and frustration that she could not defend her feelings.

"Quite." Kynaston nodded at Ailsa and then turned to his wife. "Perhaps you could use Jane for a while. You like her, and she seems quite capable, until we get someone else to fill the place."

"What about Kitty?" Rosalind said sharply. "For heaven's sake, Dudley, she's only been gone a few hours! You're speaking as if she were dead and buried!"

"Even if she returns, my dear, she is obviously unreliable," he said more gently. "I think this is the best decision." He turned to Pitt. "Thank you again for your promptness, and your advice, Commander. We won't detain you any longer. Good day."

"Good day, sir," Pitt replied. "Ma'am," he acknowledged both women. Then he and Stoker left, going out through the front door into the deserted street. Rain was beginning to come across the open land of the heath.

"What do you make of that, sir?" Stoker asked curiously, turning up his coat collar as he walked. His voice was light, but when Pitt glanced at him he saw the doubt in his face. "There was a lot of blood on that step," Stoker went on. "More than a scratch, I reckon. If someone hit that girl it was pretty hard. She must be daft to go willingly with anyone who'd use her like that." Now the doubt had turned to anger.

"Perhaps she cut herself on the glass," Pitt said thoughtfully. He pulled the brim of his hat down and his scarf tighter as the rain increased. He looked up at the sky. "Good thing you made a sketch of it before this started. In twenty minutes there'll be nothing to see."

"There was blood on the glass," Stoker said. "And the hair. Torn out by the roots, from the look of it. Kynaston may be important to the navy, but I think he's covering something up . . . sir."

Pitt smiled. He knew Stoker's understated and quite delicate insolence. It was not directed at him personally, but more at their political masters, whom he knew Pitt occasionally disliked as much as he did himself. He was still nervous that Pitt might yield to them, and not absolutely certain whether Pitt's predecessor in command had done so or not. But Victor Narraway was a very different kind of man, at least on the surface. He was a gentleman, beginning as a junior lieutenant in the army, then through university in law, and as devious as an eel. Stoker had never been comfortable with him, but his respect for him was boundless.

Pitt, on the other hand, was the son of a country gamekeeper, and he had risen through the ranks of the regular Metropolitan Police. He had been promoted sideways into Special Branch, much against his will, when he had offended certain very powerful people and lost his job as superintendent in Bow Street. Pitt might think he was subtle, but to Stoker he was as clear as the rising sun.

Pitt was aware of all this as he replied, "I know that, Stoker. What I don't know is if it is something we should be concerned about."

"Well, if there's something messy going on in that house, and a maid gets the bad end of it, we should care," Stoker said with feeling. "Perfect setup for a spot of blackmail." He left the rest of his thought implied.

"You think Dudley Kynaston was having an affair with his wife's maid, and knocked her around on his own kitchen steps in the middle of a winter night?" Pitt asked with a smile.

Stoker flushed faintly and stared straight ahead, avoiding Pitt's eyes. "Put it like that, no, sir. If he's that crazy he wants putting in the madhouse, for everybody's sake, including his own."

Pitt was going to add that it was probably just what it looked like, but he wasn't sure what it looked like. The maids had found nothing missing to account for the glass. There was too much blood for a graze, and actually there was no way of telling if the blood was even human, let alone if it was that of the missing maid—who seemingly had gone without even taking her hairbrush. And was it even her hair, or did she just happen to have hair of a similar color?

"We'll have the local police keep an eye on it, and let us know if she comes back," he said to Stoker. "Or if she turns up anywhere else, for that matter."

Stoker grunted, not satisfied, but accepting that there was nothing more they could do. They trudged through the rain silently, heads down, feet sloshing on the wet pavement.

PITT ARRIVED HOME AT Keppel Street comparatively early, although at this time of the year it was already completely dark. The streetlamps gleamed like beacons through the rain, haloed in light for a brief space, darkness swirling between them.

Pitt went up the steps to his front door and was about to hunt through his always overstuffed pockets for his key when the door opened in front of him, bathing him in the glow of the inside lights and the warmth of the parlor fire where the passage door was open.

"Evenin' sir," Minnie Maude said with a smile. "D'yer like a cup o' tea before dinner's ready? My, yer in't 'alf soaked!" She looked him up and down with sympathy. "I reckon as it's rainin' stair rods out there."

"Indeed it is," he agreed, dripping steadily onto the hall floor as the front door closed behind him. He looked at her freckled face and her piled-up red-brown hair, and for a moment he imagined the missing maid from Kynaston's house and wondered again where she was. Minnie Maude was handsome, too, in her own way, tall and womanly, worldly wise, domestically capable, and naïvely full of trust. He felt a tightness in his chest at the thought of harm befalling her, of her winding up alone somewhere, perhaps hurt, cold to the bone, desperate for shelter. What if those were the circumstances Kitty Ryder faced now?

"Yer a'right, sir?" Minnie Maude's anxious voice intruded on his thoughts.

Pitt eased himself out of his wet coat and took off his sodden boots. He gave her his hat and scarf as well.

"Yes, thank you. And I will have a cup of tea. And I'll have something to eat. I can't remember what lunch was."

"Yes, sir. 'Ow about a couple o' crumpets?" she offered. "Wi' butter?"

He looked at her. She was about nineteen, four years older than his daughter, Jemima, who was far too rapidly growing into a woman.

Thank God Jemima wouldn't be a servant living in somebody else's house with only strangers to turn to.

"Thank you," he replied. "Yes . . . bring them to me in the parlor, please." He wanted to add something more, but there really wasn't anything to say that was appropriate.

After dinner, when Jemima and her younger brother, Daniel, had gone up to bed, he sat beside the fire in his usual chair, opposite Charlotte, who had abandoned her embroidery for the evening and sat with her boots off and her feet up, hidden by her skirts. The light from the gas brackets on the walls was a golden color, muted a little by the glass. It softened the lines of everything it touched: the familiar books on the shelves on either side, the few ornaments, each with its own attached set of memories. The long curtains across the French windows on to the garden were drawn against the cold. He could not imagine anywhere more comfortable.

"What is it?" Charlotte asked. "You are making your mind up whether to tell me, so it can't be a secret."

In the past, when he was still in the police, he had shared many of his cases with her. In fact, on some of them she had been something of a detective herself. She was acutely observant of human nature, and alarmingly fearless in pursuing what she felt was justice.

Of course, now so much more was secret and he could not share with her nearly as much as he used to, although he still would were he able. He was often tempted—only the cost restrained him. A betrayal of trust would damage him in his own eyes, and in hers. The loss of his position would destroy his career, and therefore also his ability to look after his family. He had faced that once when he was dismissed from the police, without the hope of ever being reinstated. He had powerful enemies, among them, unfortunately, the Prince of Wales, who would be only too delighted if Pitt's entire career were called into question.

Charlotte was waiting for an answer. No secrets of state were involved. So far it was nothing but a rather unfortunate domestic incident.

"Evidence of a fight on the areaway steps of a house on Shooters

Hill," he replied. "And a missing lady's maid. She was courting, so it's possible she eloped."

"I didn't think there were houses up on Shooters Hill," she responded, frowning a little. "If I mustn't know, then don't tell me, but what you've said so far doesn't make any sense."

"I know it doesn't make any sense," he agreed. "Blood and hair on the steps, and broken glass . . . and a missing maid at a time of day when she should have been there, and always has been in the past."

"Why you?" she said curiously. "If there's a crime involved at all, isn't it for the local police?" Then her face lit with understanding. "Oh . . . it's somebody important!"

"Yes. And you're quite right, if it's anything at all, it belongs to the local police. You said Jemima needs a new dress?"

She tucked her feet up a little higher. The coals settled in the fire with a shower of sparks.

"Yes, please . . . at least one."

"At least?" He raised his eyebrows.

"She's going to the party at the Grovers' as well as the other one," she explained. "It's quite formal."

"I thought she didn't want to go to the one at the Grovers'?" He was momentarily confused.

There was a slight shadow in Charlotte's face. "She doesn't," she agreed. "But Mary Grover was very kind to her, and Jemima promised she would be there to help."

Pitt remembered Jemima's argument on the subject, then he looked at Charlotte again. "Don't you think . . . ?" he began.

"The real reason she doesn't want to go is because the Hamiltons are also having a party that evening, and she wants to go there instead, because she likes Robert Hamilton."

"Then—"

"Thomas . . . she owes Mary Grover a debt of kindness. She will pay it. And don't tell me 'later.' 'Later' doesn't do."

"I know," he said quietly.

"I'm so glad." Suddenly she smiled, and it warmed her whole face with a melting gentleness. "I don't want to fight both of you—at least not at once."

"Good," he said, also relaxing, although he did not doubt for a second that she would have fought both of them—and won—had he forced her into it.

2

THREE WEEKS LATER, AT the end of January, Pitt was at breakfast in the warmth of the kitchen when the telephone rang. It was a marvelous instrument and had been of great service to him, but there were times when he resented its presence. Quarter past seven on a winter morning, before he had finished his toast, was one of them. Nevertheless he stood up and went out into the hall where the telephone sat on the small table, and picked it up. He knew no one would call him without good reason.

It was Stoker on the other end, his voice thick with emotion.

"They've found a body, sir." He took a breath, and Pitt could hear the sounds of footsteps and other voices around him. "I'm at the Blackheath police station," Stoker went on. "It's a woman . . . young woman, far as we can tell . . . handsome build . . ." He swallowed. "Reddish hair . . ."

Pitt felt his own throat tighten and a wave of sadness pass over him.

"Where?" he asked, although the fact that Stoker was calling from Blackheath told him that it was not far from Shooters Hill.

"Gravel pit, sir," Stoker replied. "Shooters Hill Road, just beyond Kynaston's house." He seemed about to add something, then changed his mind.

"I'll be there," Pitt replied. He had no need to tell Stoker that it would take him at least half an hour. Keppel Street was little more than a mile from Lisson Grove, where his office was, but it was a long way west and north of the river from Blackheath, let alone from Shooters Hill.

He put the phone back in its cradle and turned to see Charlotte standing at the bottom of the stairs, waiting for him to tell her what it was. She would know from his face, even from the angle of his body, that it was bad news.

"A body," he said quietly. "Young woman found in one of the gravel pits on Shooters Hill."

"I suppose you have to go . . ."

"Yes. Stoker's already there. That was him on the telephone. I suppose the local police called him."

"Why?" she asked.

He smiled bleakly. "Because the local police are very diligent—or because he's most likely kept checking on them in case they found Kitty Ryder's body. But I think they must also sense a bad case coming, and they'd very much like not to have to deal with it themselves."

"Can they pass it to you, just like that?" she asked dubiously.

"Since it's on Kynaston's doorstep, and might well be his maid who has been found, yes they can. If it turns out to be her, they'd have to give it to Special Branch anyway."

She nodded slowly, sadness pinching her face. "I'm sorry. Poor girl." She did not ask why anyone would kill her or if Kitty might have done something, such as attempting blackmail, in order to bring it on herself. She had learned over their sixteen years of marriage how complicated tragedies could be. She was just as blazingly angry at injustice as she had been when they first met, but now very much slower to judge—most of the time.

He walked back to the warm kitchen and its smells of coal, bread, and clean linen, to eat the last few mouthfuls of his toast, and drink his tea, if it wasn't cold. He hated cold tea. Then he would go out into the icy morning and find a hansom. By the time he got to the river it would be sunrise, and daylight when he got up the hill to the gravel pit.

Charlotte was ahead of him. She took his cup off the table and fetched a clean one from the Welsh dresser. "You've time for it," she stated firmly before he could get the words out to argue. She topped up the teapot from the kettle on the hob, waited a moment, then poured it.

Pitt thanked her and was drinking the hot—if a trifle weak—tea gratefully when Minnie Maude came in, carrying potatoes and a string of onions. Uffie, the small, shaggy orphan pup she had adopted a year ago was, as usual, practically treading on her skirts. At first they had tried to prevent him from coming into the kitchen, but it had not worked. If Charlotte had had any sense, she would never have imagined it would!

Pitt smiled, then thought of Kynaston's kitchen and how different it would be there this morning, if the body turned out to be Kitty's. "I don't know when I'll be back," he said quietly, and turned to leave.

HE REACHED THE GRAVEL pit just as the gray light spread over the waste where the earth had been dug and exploited. The wind from the east carried flecks of ice, stinging the exposed skin of his face and finding the vulnerable parts of his neck. In earlier days he would have worn a long woolen scarf, wound round and round to keep out the cold. Now he felt that would be a little scruffy and informal for his rank, and he had a silk one instead. It was difficult enough to impress people anyway. His predecessors had all been gentlemen from birth, and in many cases senior officers in either the army or the navy, like Narraway, assuming the obedience of others quite naturally.

"Morning, sir." Stoker walked towards him with an easy gait, his feet crunching on the frozen grass. He refused to huddle his body against the wind. "She's over there." He indicated a small group of men about fifty feet away, standing close together, coats whipping a little around their legs, hats jammed on their heads. The light of bull's-eye lanterns glowed with a false warmth, yellow in the gloom.

"Who found her?" Pitt asked curiously.

"The usual," Stoker replied with a shadow of a smile. "Man walking his dog."

"What time, for heaven's sake?" Pitt demanded. "Who the devil walks his dog up here at half past five on a winter morning?"

Stoker lifted his shoulders slightly. "Ferryman down on the Greenwich waterfront. Takes people who cross the river to be there before seven. Sounds like a decent enough man."

Pitt should have thought of that. He had come over the river by ferry himself but barely looked at the man at the oars. He had dealt with murders most of his police career, and yet they still disturbed him. He had never seen Kitty alive, but the accounts of her by the other staff at Kynaston's house had made her real, colored her as a girl quick to laugh and quick to make friends, with dreams for the future.

Stoker was watching him. He had to remind himself that the body might not be Kitty's. "So this man reported it to the local police station, and they remembered your interest and sent for you," Pitt said.

"Yes, sir. They telephoned my local station, who sent a constable around for me." Stoker looked uncomfortable, as if he were making some confession before it caught up with him anyway. "I came up here first, before calling you, sir, in case it wasn't anything to do with us. Didn't want to get you out here for nothing."

Pitt realized what he was doing—accounting for the fact that he was here first. He could have had his local police call Pitt, and he had chosen not to.

"I see," Pitt replied with a bleak smile, in this gray light, barely visible. "Where did you find a telephone up here?"

Stoker bit his lip, but he did not lower his eyes. "I went to the

Kynaston house, sir, just to make sure the maid had not returned after all and they had just forgotten to tell us."

Pitt nodded. "Very prudent," he said, almost without expression. Then he walked towards the group of men, who were openly shivering now as the wind increased. There were three of them: a constable, a sergeant, and the third whom Pitt took to be the police surgeon.

"Morning, sir," the sergeant said smartly. "Sorry to get you all the way up here so early, but I think this one might be yours."

"We'll see." Pitt refused to commit himself. He did not want the case any more than the sergeant did. Even if the body was Kitty Ryder's, her death probably had nothing whatever to do with Dudley Kynaston, but the danger of scandal was there, the pressure to solve the case quickly, the public interest the whole thing would attract. And the possibility of injustice, if it turned out there was something unsavory being covered up.

"Yes, sir," the sergeant agreed, the relief not disappearing a whit from his face. He indicated the oldest man, who was shorter than Pitt and slightly built, his brown hair liberally sprinkled with gray. "This is Dr. Whistler," he introduced him. He did not bother to explain who Pitt was. Presumably that had been done before he arrived.

Whistler inclined his head. "Morning, Commander. Nasty one, I'm afraid." There was a rough edge to his voice from perhaps more than the wretched morning, and an unmistakable pity in his face. He stepped back as he spoke, so Pitt could see behind him a rough cloth covering the body they had found.

Pitt took a deep breath of the air, cold and clean, then he bent to remove the cloth. In summer there would have been a smell, but the wind and the ice had kept it at bay. Still, Pitt was unprepared for what he found. The body had been severely mutilated. Most of the face was so damaged as to be unrecognizable: the nose split, the lips removed as if by a knife. The eyes themselves were gone as well. Only the arch of the brow was left to give an idea of their shape. The flesh was stripped from the cheeks, but the jawbone and teeth were intact. One could only imagine how her smile might have been.

Pitt looked away from her face, at the rest of her body. She was quite tall, almost Charlotte's height, and handsomely built, with a generous bosom, slender waist, long legs. Her clothes had protected her from the ravages of animals, and the normal decay had not yet reached the stage of disintegration. He forced himself to look at her hair. It was wet and matted from exposure to the elements, but it was still possible to see that when one took the pins out it would fall at least halfway down her back, and that once dry it would be thick and of a deep chestnut color.

Was it Kitty Ryder? Probably. They had said she was tall, handsomely built, and had beautiful hair the same shade of auburn as the hair found on the area steps.

He looked back at the surgeon. "Did you find anything to indicate how she died?" he asked.

Whistler shook his head. "Not for certain. I think there are some broken bones, but I'll have to get her back to the morgue to remove her clothes and look at her much more carefully. Nothing obvious. No bullets, no stab wounds that I can see. She wasn't strangled, and there's no visible damage to the skull."

"Anything to identify her?" Pitt asked a little sharply. He wanted it not to be Kitty Ryder. He would be very relieved if the body had no connection with the Kynaston house, except a reasonable proximity. More than that, he wanted it to be a woman he knew nothing about, even though they would still have to learn. Nobody should die alone and anonymously, as if they did not matter. He would just prefer it to be a regular police job.

"Possibly," Whistler said, meeting Pitt's eyes. "A very handsome gold fob watch. I looked at it carefully. Unusual and quite old, I think. Not hers, that's for sure. It's very definitely a man's."

"Stolen?" Pitt asked unhappily.

"I should think so. Most likely recently, or she wouldn't be carrying it around with her."

"Anything else?"

Whistler pursed his lips. "A handkerchief with flowers and initials embroidered on it, and a key. Looks like the sort of thing that would open a cupboard. Too small to be a door key. Might be a desk, or even a drawer, although not many drawers have separate keys." He looked across at the sergeant. "I gave it all to him. I'm afraid that's it, for the meantime."

Pitt looked back at the body again. "Did animals do that to her, or was it deliberate?"

"It was deliberate," Whistler replied. "A knife, not teeth or claws. I'll know more about it when I look at her more closely, and not by the light of a bull's-eye lantern when I'm freezing up here on the edge of a damn gravel pit at the crack of dawn. It looks like the bloody end of the world up here!"

Pitt nodded without answering. He turned to the sergeant, holding his hand out, palm up.

The sergeant gave him the small square of white embroidered cambric and a domestic key about an inch and three-quarters long, and the old and very lovely gold watch.

Pitt met his eyes, questioning.

"Don't know, sir. There's a few gentlemen as could have a watch like this. If someone picked his pocket he would have complained, depending where he was at the time, if you get my meaning?"

"I do," Pitt answered.

"Or he could have given it to her, as payment for services," the sergeant added.

Pitt gave him a bleak look. "It's worth a year's salary for a lady's maid," he said, looking again at the watch. "What about the handkerchief?"

The sergeant shook his head. "No ideas yet, sir. The initial on the handkerchief is an R. Seeing as how Mrs. Kynaston's name begins with an R, I thought I should leave that to you."

"There are only twenty-six letters in the alphabet, Sergeant," Pitt pointed out. "There must be scores of names beginning with R. If it had been Q, or X, that might have narrowed it down a bit. Even a Y, or Z."

"That was exactly what I was thinking, Commander," the sergeant replied. "And I'm sure Mr. Kynaston would have told me so, with some disfavor, if I had started out by asking if this was his wife's handkerchief." He seemed about to add something more and then changed his mind. Instead he turned to his own constable, standing a couple of yards away with his collar turned up and his back to the wind. "I expect the commander'll want you to stay until his own man gets here—more than Mr. Stoker, that is. So I'd better get back to the station." He gave Pitt a bleak smile. "That suit you, sir?"

"What happened to the man who found her?" Pitt asked, turning beside the sergeant and starting to walk back over the rutted ground towards the road.

"Got his statement, written and signed, then sent him on his way. Poor devil were a bit shaken up, but he's got his living to earn just the same," the sergeant replied.

"Do you know him?" Pitt said a trifle sharply.

"Yes, sir. Zeb Smith."

"But you *know* him?" Pitt repeated.

"Yes, sir." The sergeant increased his pace. "Zebediah Smith, Hyde Vale Cottages, about a mile or so over that way." He pointed north, towards Greenwich port and the river. "Had a bit too much to drink a couple of times—must be a few years ago now. Then he got married and settled down."

"Zebediah . . ." Pitt murmured, more to himself than to the sergeant.

"Yes, sir. Religious mother. We know where to find him, if we need him again. Frankly, sir, ferrymen are good witnesses. Don't want to get the reputation for giving them a hard time for no reason."

"Understood," Pitt acknowledged. "Did Mr. Smith tell you anything useful? Does he walk up here often? When was the last time? Did he see anyone else up here this morning? Any sign of someone? A figure in the distance, footprints? There's enough mud and ice to show them. What about his dog? How did it react?"

The sergeant smiled, a tight, satisfied expression. "He couldn't tell us a whole lot, sir. Except that he came up here yesterday morning as usual, and the body wasn't here then. Even if he hadn't seen it himself, his dog would. Good animal. Good ratter, apparently. Didn't see anyone else. I asked him that several times." He stepped over a ridge of tussock grass and Pitt followed. "Not a soul," he went on. "No footprints as make any sense. Looks like there's been an army up here, but not recently. Weather does that. No more to see a couple of hours ago than there is now." He looked down at the ground with a slight curl of his lip. "Useless," he added, regarding the cracked, rutted earth. As they came closer to the road, some of it was still frozen, more swimming in mud. "Anything could have passed that way."

Pitt was obliged to agree with him. "And the dog?" he asked again.

"Didn't see anyone else," the sergeant said. "Didn't bark. Didn't want to chase anything. Just found the body, an' howled!"

Pitt had a sudden vision of the dog throwing its head back and letting out a long wail of despair as it came across sudden death in the gray fog before dawn, shivering and alone amid the dripping weed heads and the few shadowy, skeletal trees.

"Thank you, Sergeant. I'll keep you informed as I may have to hand the case back to you."

"Ah . . . yes . . . sir," the sergeant said awkwardly.

Pitt smiled, although he felt very little humor. The last thing he wanted to do was disturb the Kynaston family again, but it had to be done sometime. Perhaps it was not only the most efficient thing to do it now but also the kindest. Then the news, which would inevitably reach them at some later point, would not be hanging over their heads like the sword of Damocles.

He came to the entrance to the pit, spoke briefly to the other sergeant there, then set out briskly to walk to the Kynaston house.

Because of the early hour of the morning, he went again to the back door. He did not want to be announced and have to ask permission to speak to the servants, with an explanation, and possibly an argument about the body in the gravel pit.

The areaway steps were scrubbed and clean, nothing worse on them now than a thin rime of ice, slick on top from the misty rain. He went down carefully and knocked on the scullery door.

After several moments it was opened by Maisie, the little scullery maid. For a moment she was confused. He was obviously not a delivery-man, and yet she was aware that she knew him.

"Good morning, Maisie," he said quietly. "Commander Pitt, Special Branch, you remember? May I come in?"

"Oh, yeah!" Her face lit with a smile. Then she recalled his original reason for coming, and suddenly she was terrified. "Yer found Kitty, 'ave yer?" She wanted to add more, but the rest of her thoughts were clearly too hideous to speak aloud.

"I don't know," he answered, still keeping his voice low so as not to attract the attention of the other servants in the kitchen a few yards away. "You will hear very soon, probably from the first delivery boy of the day, that we've found a woman's body up in the gravel pits, not far from here. It's difficult to tell who she is."

Maisie gulped, but she did not reply.

He pulled the handkerchief and the key out of his pocket. "Have you seen this handkerchief before, or one like it?"

She took it gingerly as if it were a live thing that might have bitten her. Very carefully she opened it out.

"It's pretty," she said with a shiver. "If she got one like this, mister, she's a lady. It's got summink stitched on it in the corner, 'ere . . ." She held it out.

"Yes, it's a letter R. I imagine it belonged to someone whose name begins with R."

"Kitty don't begin with an R," she said with certainty. "I can't read, but I know that much."

"The thing is," he said as casually as possible, "it may not be her own handkerchief. As you said, ladies have ones like this. It may have been given to her by someone . . ."

The understanding in Maisie's face was immediate. "You mean the woman wot you found could be Kitty, and someone give it 'er?"

"It's possible. If we could find out whose handkerchief it is, then it might help us to know if this is Kitty, or not."

"Did she drown in the pits?" Maisie asked. She was shaking now, as if they were standing outside in the wind and the ice.

"I don't know yet." He had no choice but to be honest. Evasion would only make it worse. He showed her the key. "Do you have any keys like this in the house?"

She frowned. "Everybody does. What's it for?"

"Probably a cupboard, or a desk drawer." He offered it to her.

She picked it up reluctantly, then walked over to one of the cupboards on the far side of the scullery. She tried it in the lock, and it would not fit. She tried a second, and a third with no success. On the fourth one it slipped in, and after a little difficulty, it turned.

"There y'are," she said, her face still white. "We all got cupboards a bit like that. Don't mean nothing. Mister, can't you do summink ter know if it's our Kitty?"

She had made the point well. It was a very ordinary key that might fit some lock or other in any of a hundred houses in the area, or for that matter, out of it. It probably served more as a handle than a device of security.

"She was only discovered this morning," he replied gently. "We'll do all we can to find out who she is. A few more questions and we may be able to say at least whether it is Kitty or not. If it isn't, then we need to know who she is. And you should go on believing that Kitty is somewhere alive and well, but perhaps too embarrassed to tell you why she ran off without saying good-bye to anyone."

Maisie took a deep breath and let it out shakily. "Yeah . . . yeah, I will. Can I get yer a cup o' tea? It's fair perishin' out there. Colder than a—" She stopped abruptly.

"Witch's tit," he finished for her. He was perfectly familiar with the expression.

She blushed hotly, but she did not deny that that was what had been in her mind. "I didn't say it," she murmured.

"Perhaps I shouldn't have," he apologized. "I beg your pardon."

"'S'all right!" Then she gave him a dazzling smile. "I'll get yer a cup o' tea, and tell Mr. Norton as yer 'ere." And before he could protest she whisked away around the corner into the kitchen.

Fifteen minutes later, and after a good hot cup of tea, Pitt was in the butler's pantry with a grim-faced Norton. It was quite a large room, painted cream and brown, and around the walls glass-fronted cupboards for the china and crystal in daily use. There were wooden horses for drying glass and tea cloths, a table for pressing cloths or ironing and folding newspapers. There were also all the usual keys, funnels, cork-screws, and—as was customary in most houses—a picture of the queen.

"Yes, sir, Mrs. Kynaston has handkerchiefs similar to this," Norton agreed. "But I cannot say that this one is hers. She does occasionally give such things away, if she has new ones, or if it is no longer . . . ser-viceable. Such as if it is frayed, or stained in some way. They do not last indefinitely." He looked at it again. "It is difficult to say, in this condi-tion, what state it would be if washed and ironed."

"Yes, it is," Pitt agreed. "But the monogram is clearly an R."

"Many ladies' names begin with an R," Norton pulled his lips tight. "As for the key, it is a very simple thing. I daresay half the houses in London have something it would open. I'm afraid we can be of no as-sistance to you."

"I have no wish that the poor woman in the gravel pit should be Miss Ryder," Pitt said with feeling. "But I am obliged to do all I can to find out who she was. She deserves a burial, and her family deserves to know what happened to her." He stood up from the stool where he had been sitting. "I preferred to come myself, since that was very much a possibility, rather than send a sergeant to disturb you at this hour."

Norton stood also. "I apologize, sir. I was ungenerous," he said a little awkwardly. "It was a kindness that you came yourself. I hope you find out who the poor creature is. Apart from the handkerchief, and the fact that the gravel pit is not far away, is there anything that made you think it was Kitty Ryder?"

"She was the height and build you described, and she had thick auburn hair," Pitt replied. "It is unusual coloring."

Norton was momentarily stunned. "Oh dear. Oh—I'm very sorry. I . . . this is absurd. Whoever she is she deserves our pity. Just for a moment the way you said that made it so much more . . . real." He cleared his throat. "I shall inform Mrs. Kynaston of your call, sir, and your consideration. May I show you out?"

It took Pitt some time to find Zebediah Smith at his home, and confirm with him what the sergeant had told him. He was not surprised to learn nothing new. His real purpose was to satisfy his own mind that Zebediah was as straightforward as he seemed. The man was still visibly shaken when he told Pitt how he had set out for his usual walk, and in the darkness the keen nose of his dog had scented something different and gone to find it. Then it sat and howled until Smith had come up to it himself and—in the light of his lantern—seen the pathetic corpse.

He shook his head. "Who'd do that to a woman?" he said miserably. "What kind of a . . . I suppose I gotta call 'im a man, although 'e ain't human. Can't call 'im an animal though. Even animals don't kill their own for nothing."

"There'll be a reason, Mr. Smith," Pitt replied. "It's my job to find it—when we discover who she is."

Zebediah looked up and met Pitt's eyes. "Ain't no reason to do that to anyone, sir, an' I don't care 'oo you are—government, police, nor nothin'—you find 'im, an' when you do, God 'elp yer what you do to 'im."

Pitt did not argue. He was satisfied that Zebediah was telling the exact truth, and also that since he walked the same paths every morning, the body could not have been there twenty-four hours earlier.

By mid-afternoon Pitt was in the morgue with Dr. Whistler. There was no place he disliked more. Outside, the wind had risen considerably. Gusting rain blew hard and cold one moment, then the next, in sheltered places, simply dripped with surprising power to soak through even the best coats. Now and then there were brief blue patches in the sky, bright, and then gone again.

Inside the morgue it seemed to be always winter. The windows were high, perhaps to conceal from the passing world what happened there. The cold was necessary to preserve the bodies as they were wheeled from one room to another for examination. Those stored for any length of time were kept in ice chambers, the chill of which permeated everything. The smell was mostly antiseptic, but it was impossible to forget what it was there to mask.

Whistler's office, where he saw Pitt, was warm and—had it been anywhere else—would have been quite pleasant. Whistler himself was dressed in a gray suit, and there was no outward sign of his grisly occupation, except a faint aroma of some chemical.

"I'm not going to be very helpful," he said as soon as Pitt had taken a seat in one of the well-padded but still uncomfortable chairs. They seemed to have been constructed to oblige one to sit unnaturally upright.

"Even the omission of something might be useful," Pitt said hopefully.

Whistler shrugged. "She's been dead at least two weeks. And it is as I said: that abomination was done to her face by a clean, very sharp knife."

Pitt said nothing.

"I can tell you she was moved after she was dead," Whistler went on. "But you must have concluded that, too. If she'd been lying there for a couple of weeks someone else would have found her before now. Apart from other people who walk their dogs on the paths across the old gravel pits, there's Mr. Smith himself."

"As you said," Pitt observed drily. "Not much help so far. I've spoken to Mr. Smith. I agree, she wasn't there yesterday. If she's been dead a couple of weeks, where was she all that time? Do you know that? Or can you at least make an educated guess?"

"Somewhere cold, or the deterioration would be worse than it is," Whistler answered.

"Brilliant." Pitt was now openly sarcastic. "At this time of the year, that narrows it down to anywhere in England except the home of somebody who has decent fires in all the main rooms. Even then it could be someone's outhouse."

"Not quite." Whistler pursed his lips. "She was very clean, apart from a smear or two of mud and bits of gravel and sand caught up in her clothes, likely from the pit itself. Wherever she was kept for the time in between death and being put in the gravel pit, it was clean. I suppose that could be useful?" He shrugged. "It more or less rules out anywhere outside."

"More than that." Pitt sat forward a little. "If you're quite sure about that: no rats? Absolutely no rats?"

Whistler took his point. There were rats almost everywhere, in cities and the country, in the sewers, in the streets and gutters, in people's houses, even cellars, potting sheds, and outhouses of every kind. One did not see them so often, but any food left lying, certainly any dead and rotting body, they would have found.

"Yes." Whistler nodded, his eyes meeting Pitt's squarely for the first time. "You may safely conclude that wherever she was, it was cold and clean, and sufficiently well sealed that neither flies nor rats could get in, or the damage to her body would've been much worse. Of course there are no flies at this time of year, but there are always beetles of some sort. Narrows it down quite a lot."

"Any idea how she got there?" Pitt pursued.

"Impossible to tell. I can't find any marks of ropes, or tell whether she lay on slats, or boards, or anything else. You've got a nasty one . . ."

Pitt looked at him coolly. "That also I had worked out for myself."

"I'll let you know if I find out anything more," Whistler said with a faint smile.

"Please do." Pitt rose to his feet. "For example, how old she was, any distinguishing marks that might help identify her, what state of health she was in, any healed injuries, old scars, birthmarks? Particularly, I would like to know what killed her."

Whistler nodded. "Believe me, Commander, I very much want you to find out who did this and then exact everything from him the law allows, in some attempt at payment for it."

Pitt looked at him more closely, and for an instant saw, behind the defenses, a quiet belligerence, the sense of helplessness and pity for the agony of a stranger now beyond his aid. Whistler was embarrassed by his own grief and hid it behind a bitter professional detachment. Pitt wondered how often he had to do this sort of thing, and why he had chosen it instead of a practice with the living.

"Thank you," Pitt said gravely. "If I learn anything that might be useful to you I'll see that you are informed."

Outside again he walked quickly. The air was cold and had the sting of sleet in it, its odor was the sourness of soot and smoke, the smell of horse dung and swift-running gutters, impersonal, ordinary, but he breathed it in with relief.

Questions were teeming in his mind. Was the body Kitty Ryder? He hoped profoundly that it wasn't, but he couldn't help but feel it probably was. After all, what were the odds of it being another woman who happened quite by chance to resemble her, at least superficially?

How had she died? And where? Had she been kept where she was killed, or had she been moved first and then last night taken to the gravel pit? Why? What had necessitated that?

If he knew where she had been, would that also tell him for certain who she was? And therefore quite possibly who had killed her, how, and why?

As he came to the first major street corner he saw the newspapers for sale. The black headlines would soon be up—"Mutilated Corpse Found on Shooters Hill! Who is she? Police Are Keeping Silent!"

The press was like hounds on the scent of blood. Inevitable, even necessary—he pictured Zeb Smith's dog, tracking the body long before any human would've been able to—but he flinched at the thought all the same.

CHAPTER

3

Iᴛ ᴡᴀs ᴡᴇʟʟ ᴀꜰᴛᴇʀ five by the time Pitt was again in the Kynaston house, this time standing in the morning room opposite Kynaston himself. It was dark outside by this hour, but the fire had probably been lit all day and the room was warm. In other circumstances he might have appreciated the elegance of the furniture, the books on the many shelves, even the paintings. They were a curious choice, most of them snow scenes, clearly not anywhere in Britain by the scale and magnificence of the mountains. There was a soaring beauty to them, and yet a sense of intimacy in the detail that indicated the artist was familiar with them. He wondered why Kynaston had chosen them, but today he was too preoccupied to give them more than a glance.

Kynaston was waiting for him to speak. He stood in the middle of a thick Turkish carpet, his face tense and puzzled.

"I expect you have heard already," Pitt began. "There has been a body found early today, before dawn, at the gravel pit to the east of here.

It's that of a young woman, but it is so damaged that it is not possible to make an immediate identification. I am very sorry, but we cannot say if it is Kitty Ryder or not—at least not yet."

Kynaston was very pale, but he kept his composure, even if it was with difficulty. "I take it from the way you phrase it that it could be. Do you believe that it is?"

"I think it is probable, yes," Pitt admitted, then instantly wondered if perhaps he should have been more cautious.

Kynaston took a deep breath. "If she is unrecognizable, poor creature, why do you believe it is Kitty?"

Pitt had seen people fight the inevitable before. It was the natural instinct to deny tragedy as long as possible. He had done it himself but had always had to give in, in the end.

"She is the same general height and build as Kitty," he replied quietly. "Her hair is auburn." He saw Kynaston's body tense even more and the muscles along his jaw tighten. "And she had in her pocket a lace-edged handkerchief with the letter R embroidered on it," he continued. "Your butler says Mrs. Kynaston has some like it and that she occasionally gives away old ones."

There was a long moment's silence, then Kynaston straightened his shoulders a little. "I see. Yes. It does seem . . . probable. Nevertheless we shall not leap to conclusions. I would be obliged if you did not tell the rest of the household that it is Kitty . . . until there is no doubt left. Then we shall have to deal with it. My butler and housekeeper are both excellent people. They will help the more emotionally affected of the staff."

Pitt took the gold watch out of his pocket and saw Kynaston's eyes widen and the color drain from his face. "This was found on the body also," he said very quietly. "I see you recognize it." It was not a question.

"It . . . it's mine." Kynaston's voice was a croak, as if his mouth and lips were dry. "It was taken out of my pocket a couple of weeks ago. Somewhere on the street—damn pickpockets! The fob and chain were taken, too. Kitty didn't take it—if that's what you're thinking!"

Pitt nodded. "I see. I'm afraid it happens. Now, I would like to speak to both your wife and your sister-in-law, if that is possible. I appreciate that they, too, will be distressed, but either of them may have knowledge that would help us."

"I doubt it." Kynaston's mouth pulled down in a gesture of distaste. "I think you would learn more from the other maids . . . if anything is known at all. Girls talk to each other, not to their mistresses."

"I was not thinking of confidences so much as their observations of Kitty," Pitt answered. "My own wife is a very good judge of character. I imagine Mrs. Kynaston is also. Women see things in other women, whatever their social station. And no woman who runs a house well is ignorant of the character of her maids."

Kynaston sighed. "Yes, of course you are right. I wished to spare her this distress, but perhaps it is not possible."

Pitt smiled a trifle bleakly, knowing in his mind exactly how Charlotte would have reacted had he tried to conceal such a thing from her. "If you would be good enough to ask her to give me half an hour or so of her time . . ."

"What about the other maids?" Kynaston did not move. "Or the housekeeper? Female staff are her concern."

"I will have Sergeant Stoker speak to them, when he is finished with the local police."

"I see," Kynaston said thoughtfully. "I see." Still he hesitated.

This time Pitt did not help him. He had long learned that silence can betray people as much as words, sometimes in the subtlest of ways.

"I . . ." Kynaston cleared his throat. "I would like to be present when you speak to her. My wife is . . . is easily distressed. If indeed it is Kitty, she will take it extremely hard."

Pitt did not want Kynaston there, but he had no excuse to deny him at this point. Had it been Charlotte, and Gracie Phipps or Minnie Maude who had gone missing, she would have been completely distraught at the idea of them having been hurt at all, let alone killed in a violent scuffle. For that matter, so would Pitt himself.

"Of course," he agreed. "I shall be as circumspect as possible." He was probably being more gentle than was wise. If the body was that of Kitty Ryder, then Rosalind Kynaston feeling a great deal of pain was inevitable, no matter how tactful he was.

Kynaston excused himself and returned twenty minutes later with not only Rosalind Kynaston, but his sister-in-law, Ailsa, as well. Both of them were immaculately dressed as if ready for an evening outing.

Rosalind wore a beautifully tailored costume of dark blue. It was a cold color for winter, but with pale lace at the throat it became her well enough. There was a dignity in her manner, though she was gaunt and pale. When she met Pitt's eyes her hand instinctively reached out to clasp on to something. Kynaston offered his arm, and she ignored it.

Beside her, Ailsa, taller and so very much fairer, looked magnificent in soft grays. Pitt could not have said exactly how, but he recognized the latest cut in her sweeping skirt, short enough not to touch the ground and get wet. The whole costume needed only a fur hat to be perfect, and no doubt she had such a thing. She took Rosalind's arm, without asking her permission, and guided her to the large, soft sofa, easing them both into it, side by side. She stared at Pitt with sharp blame in her blue eyes.

Kynaston remained standing, as though he felt that to sit down would somehow relax his guard.

"We do not yet know what happened to Kitty, Mr. Pitt," Ailsa said a little brusquely. "My sister-in-law told you that we would inform you if we did."

"Yes, Mrs. Kynaston, I know that," Pitt replied. The woman irritated him and he had to remind himself that although she certainly did not look it, she was probably afraid, more for her sister-in-law than for her own sake. The thought flickered through his mind that she might be more aware of the domestic realities than the younger and apparently more delicate Rosalind. He had a sudden cold vision of Kynaston's possible affair with a handsome maid: quarrels, embarrassment, even an attempt at blackmail, a flare of temper out of control.

Was that what he saw in Ailsa's vivid eyes, and the fear of everything that exposure would bring? To whom? Scandal to Kynaston? Or disillusion to Rosalind? But he was days ahead of himself, and quite probably mistaken.

Ailsa was waiting, somewhat impatiently.

"I am sorry to inform you that we have discovered the body of a young woman up at the gravel pit to the east of here," Pitt told her. "We do not know who she is, but we would like to assure ourselves, and you, that it is not Kitty Ryder." Out of the corner of his vision he saw Kynaston relax a little. It was no more than a slight change in his stance, as if he breathed more easily.

Ailsa gave the ghost of a smile. Rosalind did not stop staring straight at Pitt.

"Why don't you find out who she is first? Then you would have no need to disturb my sister-in-law at all," Ailsa said with an edge of criticism in her voice. She did not like Pitt, and she was not trying to conceal the fact. It might not have anything to do with the case, but he wondered why. Rosalind did not seem to have any such feelings. But perhaps she was too numb to feel anything. Did she usually need Ailsa to protect her?

If the body were that of Kitty Ryder, Pitt suspected that there was going to be a difficult mass of emotions to untangle in the Kynaston household, relevant and irrelevant alike. Everyone had secrets, old wounds that still bled, people they loved or hated, sometimes both.

"You would have heard of it within a day or two at the outside anyway," Pitt assured her. "And if we have not eliminated the possibility that it is anyone from your house, hearing of it that way would've been far more distressing."

"For goodness' sake, why don't you know if it was her?" Ailsa demanded. "She was a perfectly recognizable young woman. Get the butler, or someone, to go and look at her. Isn't that your job?"

Rosalind put her hand on her sister-in-law's sleeve. "Ailsa, give him a chance to tell us. I daresay he has his reasons."

Pitt avoided the answer, aware of Kynaston's eyes on him and a sharp, almost electric tension in the air.

He looked at Rosalind. "Mrs. Kynaston, I imagine that, like most ladies, you have a number of handkerchiefs, some of them embroidered with your initials?"

"Yes, several," she replied with a frown.

"Why on earth does that matter?" Ailsa snapped.

Kynaston opened his mouth to reprove her, and changed his mind. He looked even tenser than before.

Pitt took the recovered handkerchief out of his pocket and passed it across to Rosalind.

She took it, damp, in her fingers and dropped it instantly, her face white.

Ailsa picked it up and examined it. Then she looked up at Pitt. "It's a fairly ordinary lace-edged handkerchief, made of cambric. I have half a dozen like it myself."

"That one has an R embroidered on it," Pitt pointed out. "Does yours not have an A?"

"Naturally. There are thousands like these. If she was not the kind of person to own one herself, she could have stolen it from someone."

"Did Kitty Ryder steal it from you, Mrs. Kynaston?" Pitt asked Rosalind.

Rosalind gave the slightest shrug: a delicate gesture but unmistakable. She had no idea. Picking it up again between her fingertip and thumb, she passed it back to Pitt.

"Is that all?" Kynaston asked.

Pitt replaced the handkerchief in his pocket. "No. She also had a small key, the sort that might open a cupboard or a drawer."

No one responded. They sat stiff and waiting, not glancing at each other.

"It fits one of the cupboards in your laundry room," Pitt added.

Ailsa raised her delicate eyebrows slightly. "Only one? Or did you not try the rest? In my house such a key would have fitted all of them."

Rosalind drew in her breath as if to speak and then changed her mind.

Was it anger in Ailsa, or fear? Or simply defense of someone she saw as more vulnerable than herself? Pitt replied to her levelly, politely. "I am aware that there are only a limited number of types of keys, especially of that very simple sort. I have cupboards in my own house, and I have found that all the doors in one piece of furniture can be opened by the same key. This one opened one set of doors, but nothing in your kitchen or pantry, for example."

Ailsa did not flinch. "Are you concluding from this . . . evidence . . . that the unfortunate woman in the gravel pit is Kitty Ryder?"

"No, Mrs. Kynaston. I am hoping there is some way of proving that she is not." It was perfectly honest: he would very much rather she were someone about whom he knew nothing, whose friends or relatives he would meet only when there was no hope left of her being alive. It was easier, he admitted to himself. You went prepared.

Kynaston cleared his throat, but when he spoke his voice was still hoarse. "Do you wish me to look at this poor woman and see if I recognize her?"

"No, sir," Pitt said gently. "If you will permit me to take your butler, Norton, he will know her better and be in a position to tell us, if it is possible, whether this is Kitty Ryder or not."

"Yes . . . yes, of course," Kynaston agreed, breathing out slowly. "I'll tell him immediately." He seemed about to add something, but glancing first at Ailsa, then at Rosalind, instead he said good-bye to Pitt with a brief nod and turned to go and seek Norton.

"That is all we can do for you, Mr. Pitt." Ailsa did not rise to her feet, but her dismissal was clear.

"Thank you for your consideration," Rosalind added quietly.

PITT AND NORTON TRAVELED to the morgue by hansom cab. Norton sat bolt upright, his hands clenched in his lap, knuckles white. Neither of them spoke. There was no sound except the clatter of the horse's hooves and the hiss of the wheels on the wet road, then the occasional splash as they passed through a deeper puddle.

Pitt let the silence remain. Norton could have felt anything for the girl he was perhaps going to identify: indifference, irritation, dislike, respect, even affection. Or the clearly intense emotion he suffered now could be quite impersonal, simply a dread of death. Anybody's death was a reminder that it was the one unavoidable reality in all life.

Perhaps he had lost someone else young: a mother, a sister, even a daughter. It happened to many people. Pitt was lucky it had not happened to him—at least not yet. Please God—never!

Or it might be that Norton feared that if it was Kitty, then her murder had some connection with the Kynaston house and someone who lived in it, either family or staff.

And there was the other possibility also, as there was in every household, that a close and intrusive police investigation would expose all kinds of other secrets, weaknesses, the petty deceits that keep lives whole, and private. Everyone needed some illusions; they were the clothes that kept humans from emotional nakedness. It was sometimes more than a kindness to purposefully avoid seeing; it was an act of decency, a safeguard for oneself and others.

It was Pitt's duty to watch this man as he looked at the body, read all his emotions, however private or, for that matter, however irrelevant. He could not find justice or protection for the innocent without the truth. But he still felt intrusive.

It was also his duty to interrogate him now, while he was emotionally raw and at his most vulnerable.

"Did Kitty often go out with the young carpenter?" he began. "That was very lenient of Mrs. Kynaston to allow her to. Or did she do it without asking?"

Norton stiffened. "Certainly not. She was allowed her half day off, and she went out with him sometimes, just for the afternoon. A walk in the park, or out to tea. She was always home by six. At least . . . nearly always," he amended.

"Did you approve of him?" Pitt asked, now watching his face for the feeling behind the words.

Norton's shoulders tightened—he stared straight ahead. "He was pleasant enough."

"Had he a temper?"

"Not that I observed."

"Would you have employed him, if he had a domestic ability you could use?"

Norton thought for a moment. "Yes," he said at last. "I think I would." A faint smile crossed his face and vanished. Pitt could not read it.

They reached the morgue and alighted. Pitt paid the driver then led the way inside. He stayed close to Norton because he was afraid the man might faint. He looked white, and a little awkward, as though he were not certain of his balance.

As always, the place smelled of carbolic and death. Pitt was not certain which was worse. Antiseptic always made him think of corpses anyway, and then of loss, and pain. He hurried without meaning to and then had to wait for Norton to catch up when he reached the end of the passage and the door to the cold room that they wanted.

The attendant seemed to disappear into the gray walls, the sheet that had fully concealed the corpse in his hands. Now it was covered only as much as decency required. She looked even more broken and alone than she had lying sprawled out in the gravel pit on the freezing grass.

Norton gasped and choked on his own breath. Pitt took his arm to support him if he should faint.

There was no sound but an irregular dripping somewhere. Norton took a step closer and looked down at the body, the blotched flesh coming away from the bone, the hollow eye sockets, the ravaged face. The auburn hair was thick and tangled now, but it was still possible to see where clumps of it had been torn out.

Norton backed away at last, staggering a little, uncertain of his footing although the floor was even. Pitt still kept hold of him.

"I don't know," Norton said hoarsely. "I can't say for certain. God help her, whoever she is." He began to shake as though suddenly the cold had reached him.

"I didn't expect you would," Pitt assured him. "But you might have been able to say that it was *not* her. Perhaps the hair was slightly wrong, or the height . . ."

"No," Norton gulped. "No . . . the hair looks right. She . . . she had beautiful hair. Perhaps it was a little darker than that . . . and hers was never . . ." He motioned to the tangles. "She was always very careful of her hair." He stopped abruptly, unable to control his voice.

Pitt allowed him to walk away and go out of the room into the cold, tiled passage, then along to the door to the outside and the steady drenching rain that held nothing worse than physical discomfort. They still did not know if the woman from the gravel pit was Kitty Ryder, or some other poor creature whose name and life they might never learn.

The next morning Stoker finished all the inquiries he could make locally, and on leaving the police station in Blackheath he walked up the rise towards Shooters Hill. He was careful to keep his footing on the ice. Pitt had said little yet as to how they would approach the staff in the Kynaston house regarding Kitty Ryder. Stoker was surprised how much he still wanted to find her alive.

Without realizing it he had increased his pace, and he had to steady himself. The footpath was treacherous. Perhaps someone could tell him a detail, a fact that would prove that the woman they had found in the gravel pit was not her, could not be, from some quirk or other: a birthmark, the shape of her hands, a particular pattern in the way her hair grew—anything. Maybe there was something the butler, Norton, had been too emotionally overwrought to notice.

It was all ridiculous. He knew that. One woman's life was as important, as unique as another. He knew nothing about Mrs. Kynaston's maid, except what Pitt had told him. If he had met her he might have found her just as ordinary, as trivial, as most other people he knew. To allow his imagination to become involved was bad detection. He knew that, too. Facts. Deal with the facts only. Allow them to take you wherever they lead.

He reached the areaway steps where he had first found the blood and broken glass. He noticed that they had been swept clean, apart from a few iced-over puddles where endless feet coming and going had worn a dip in the stone.

He knocked on the door, and after a few moments it was opened by Maisie. She looked at him blankly for a moment, then lit up with a smile when she recognized him.

"Yer come ter tell us yer found Kitty, an' the body in't 'er at all?" she said immediately. Then she screwed up her eyes and looked at him more closely. Her voice caught in her throat. "It in't 'er—is it?"

She was only a child and suddenly Stoker, in his mid-thirties, felt very old.

"I don't think so." He meant it to sound gentler, but he was not used to softening the truth.

Her face crumpled. "Wot d'yer mean, yer don't think so! Is it 'er or not?"

He resisted the temptation to lie outright, but only with difficulty. "We don't think it's her," he replied carefully. "We just need to be sure. I have to ask all of you some more questions about her."

She did not move aside. "Din't Mr. Norton go ter look at 'er?"

"She's in a bad way. It didn't help a lot," he replied. "Can I come in? It's cold out here, and you're letting it all in with the door open."

"S'pose so," she said grudgingly, stepping back at last and allowing him to go past her into the scullery.

"Thank you." He closed the door firmly behind him. The sudden warmth made him sneeze and he blew his nose to clear it. Then he smelled the onions and herbs hanging on the racks.

Maisie bit her lip to stop it trembling. "I s'pose yer want a cup o' tea, an' all?" Without waiting for his answer, she led him into the kitchen where the cook was busy preparing dinner, rolling pastry ready to put on top of the fruit pie on the counter.

"You got those carrots prepared then, Maisie?" she said sharply before she noticed Stoker following. "You back?" She looked at him with disfavor. "We only just got rid o' yer gaffer. 'E bin 'ere 'alf o' yesterday upsetting everyone. Wot is it now?"

Stoker knew how irritated people were when interrupted in their work, not at all inclined to tell you what you needed to know. He wanted them to be at ease, not merely answering what he asked, but filling in the details, the color he could not deliberately seek.

"I don't want to interrupt you," he said, filling his tone with respect. "I'd just like you to tell me a little more about Kitty."

Cook looked up from her pastry, the wooden rolling pin still in both hands. "Why? She ran off with that miserable young man of 'ers, didn't she?" Her face crumpled up with anger. "Stupid girl. She could 'a done a lot better for 'erself. Come ter that, she couldn't 'ardly 'a done worse!" She sniffed hard and resumed her smoothing and easing the shape of the piecrust.

Stoker heard the emotion in her voice, and saw it in the angry tightness of her shoulders and the way she hid her face from him. She had cared about Kitty and she was frightened for her. Anger was easier, and less painful. He knew from relatives in service, old friends he seldom saw, that few household servants had family they were still in touch with. If they stayed for any length of time the other servants became family to them, full of the same loyalties, squabbles, rivalries, and intimate knowledge. Kitty might have been the closest this woman, bent over her pastry, would have to a daughter of her own.

Stoker wanted to be gentle, and it was almost impossible.

"Probably she did," he agreed. "But we didn't find her, so we've got no proof of it. We've got to know who this woman is in the gravel pit. I'd like to know for sure it's not her."

She looked up at him, her eyes filled with tears. "Yer saying as that 'orrible . . . fool . . . did this to 'er?"

"No, ma'am, I'm saying I'd like to prove it's got nothing to do with this house at all, and keep the police from having to trouble you."

She sniffed and searched for a handkerchief in her apron pocket. When she had found it and had blown her nose, she gave him her full attention. "Well, what do you want to know about Kitty? She might 'a been a fool about men, goin' an' picking the stupidest great lummox she could find." She glared at him, daring him to argue.

"How did she meet him?" Stoker asked.

"Came an' did a carpentry job 'ere," she answered. "Kept coming back even after it were finished, just to see 'er."

"Was she frightened of him?" He tried to keep the sudden anger out of his own voice, and his face.

"Not 'er! Ask me, she were sorry for 'im," she responded. "More fool 'er! 'E played on it. 'Oo wouldn't?"

"She was gentle?" he said with some surprise. The idea he had in his mind was of a strong woman, handsome and sure of herself. But the cook might know of a vulnerable side to her that her mistress didn't.

The cook laughed and shook her head. "Yer just like all men, aren't yer! Think because a woman's 'andsome, an' got a mind of 'er own, that she can't be 'urt, can't cry 'erself ter sleep when no one sees 'er, like anyone else. She were worth ten of 'im, any day, an' 'e knew it." She was obliged to blow her nose again, hiding the tears on her face.

"Did that make him angry with her?" Stoker asked.

"Didn't think so." She glared at him. "You tellin' me I'm wrong?"

He did not answer. He needed to know more: for example, if it was indeed Kitty lying in the morgue, how had she come by the gold watch that had been stolen from Dudley Kynaston?

"Who else did she know?" he asked. "Anyone who gave her expensive presents?"

"No!" the cook snapped back at him. "If she were a fool like that, you think she'd 'a bin a lady's maid?" There was contempt in her voice, and she was too hurt to try to govern it. He was only a policeman of sorts and she had done nothing wrong to fear him. "If you mean to stay in a quality house like this, you don't never let your greed get the better o' you," she said witheringly. "You're thinking just because she got soft over a young man wot wasn't worth it, that she were stupid all the time? Well, she weren't. If she'd 'a been born in the right family, and learned 'ow ter be'ave 'erself like a lady, she could 'a married the best an' never 'ad ter work a day in 'er life. Yer take wot life gives yer, an' get on with it. You, too, an' all!"

Stoker smiled, something he did not often do on duty. Most of his work was grim—and, more often than not, he did it alone. Perhaps he was too sober? He felt he would have liked Kitty Ryder, if he had known her.

"You are quite right," he conceded. "So apart from her choice in admirer, she was wise in her friends."

"I'm not sayin' as she didn't 'ave some daft ideas," the cook said more amiably. "An' some dreams as wouldn't never 'appen. Course she did. Wot girl don't? An' she could fight 'er corner if she'd a mind to. But not like some, she could own up if she were wrong . . . sometimes, any'ow."

"Thank you, you've been very helpful. I'd like to speak to the rest of the staff, if you please." He did not expect them to add much, but it was possible some of those nearer Kitty's age might know other things, details he could use. He had spoken to them before, but this was different. Now there was the matter of the gold watch. The handkerchief could've belong to anyone, but the watch was unquestionably Kynaston's, and stolen from him, but seemingly by a pickpocket in the street. So then it was essential that they prove beyond any reasonable doubt that the woman in the gravel pit was someone else. That was his job, in order to protect Dudley Kynaston. Then the presence of the watch would be a coincidence—probably!

Late that same afternoon Pitt received a message that he should report to the Home Office at his very earliest convenience. Perhaps seven o'clock that evening would be a good idea.

He read the note at quarter past six, but knew that he had no choice but to make the suggested time convenient. So after changing his wet jacket and his muddy boots, he took a hansom. At ten past seven, he entered a pleasant room with portraits of home secretaries of the past, some of their faces from every child's history books, pompous and un-smiling.

Pitt glanced at the newspapers on the table near the fireplace. The headlines caught his eye. "Mutilated Corpse in Gravel Pit Still Unidentified." And underneath it: "Police Say Nothing!" Pitt deliberately looked away.

He waited for a further twenty minutes before being greeted by a well-groomed young gentleman who came in and closed the door behind him.

"So sorry to keep you waiting, Commander Pitt," he said with a slight smile, as though he was doing Pitt a service by being well mannered, given his own importance.

Pitt thought of several terse replies, and then how he could not afford to make them.

"I was the one who was late, Mr. Rogers," he said equally politely. "I could not come here covered in mud."

Rogers's fair eyebrows rose. "Mud?"

"It is raining outside," Pitt said, as if perhaps Rogers had not noticed.

Rogers glanced down at Pitt's immaculate polished boots and then up at his face.

"We found a body in a gravel pit at Shooters Hill before dawn yesterday," Pitt explained. "I had occasion to go back there."

"Yes . . . yes. About that . . ." Rogers cleared his throat. "Extremely distasteful, of course. Have you identified her yet?"

"No. There is a possibility that it is the missing maid from Dudley Kynaston's house, but the butler was unable to confirm or deny the body is her."

"Really?" The young man's eyes widened. "I find that hard to believe. Is the man lying, do you suppose? I assume he did look? He didn't . . . evade it, turn away? Faint?"

"She has been dead for some time, and is badly mutilated," Pitt told him. "Apart from her very serious facial injuries, the flesh is beginning to decay. I can go into detail, if you wish, but I imagine you would prefer that I didn't. Her eyes are missing, but her hair is unusual."

"Yes, I see," the man said hastily. "That makes it difficult . . . I appreciate the . . ." He stopped. "However, the important thing is that you cannot say for certain that it is Kynaston's maid, correct?"

"Correct," Pitt agreed.

The young man relaxed the stiff line of his shoulders. His voice, when he spoke, was suddenly softer. "Excellent. Then it will not be difficult for you to leave the matter to the local police. She is probably some prostitute who was unfortunate in her choice of customer. Sad and extremely ugly, but not a Special Branch matter, and certainly nothing to do with Kynaston. The home secretary asked me to convey to you his appreciation of your discretion in stepping in so quickly, just in case the local police were clumsy and caused any degree of embarrassment to the Kynaston family, and therefore to the government. We have enemies who would seek to profit from even the slightest appearance of an . . . unfortunate association." He inclined his head slightly. It was a dismissal.

Pitt wanted to argue, to point out that the issue was not finished yet and it was too soon to assume it settled. But he had been dealing with crimes and investigation all his adult life. He understood both gossip and authority. He had learned how to use them, not always successfully. Reason agreed with the young man, instinct spoke against him. It had not been phrased so, but he knew this was an order. It was part of his new position that he should not require anything blunter.

"Of course," he said quietly. "Good evening."

The young man smiled. "Good evening, sir."

PITT WAS HOME LATER than he had wished to be, and he found that the rest of the family had already eaten dinner. Charlotte, however, had waited for him. She offered him the choice of the kitchen or the dining-room table, and he chose the kitchen. It was warmer, both literally and in the sense that it was the room at the heart of his family's life. Their closest friends had sat around this table in anxiety, working on desperate challenges, in grief, when they seemed beaten, and in celebration, when victory was grasped.

Now he was there, eating hot beef stew with vegetables, lots of onions, and dumplings.

The discovery of the woman's body in the gravel pit was in no way secret, reported, as it had been, in the newspapers. Of course the usual speculations had accompanied the few known facts.

"Is it the missing maid?" Charlotte asked, leaving her own portion of stew untouched.

"I wish I knew," he replied when he had swallowed his mouthful.

"Are they going to admit it, if it is?" She looked at him directly, demanding his attention.

He smiled in spite of himself. He should have known she would say that, or something like it. She had learned to curb her tongue over the years, but never her thoughts, and never with him.

"Not if they can help it," he replied.

"Will you go along with that?" she persisted. "I suppose you'll have to. Is Kynaston really so important? Thomas, for heaven's sake, do be careful."

He heard the sudden gravity in her voice and realized she was genuinely afraid for him. She had been proud when he was promoted, and never for an instant doubted he was able to fill Narraway's position. Furthermore, until now she had concealed almost completely her understanding of the danger of the job. Or was it that he had never told her the worst? There were whole areas he could not speak of, not as he had in the past when he was merely a policeman.

"My dear, it is simply a missing maid," he said gently. "It could be she ran off with a young man who had been courting her. If it is her body in the gravel pit, it is a tragedy. But regardless of who it is, it is a young woman dead. The fact that she used to be Mrs. Kynaston's maid—if it is her—draws attention to him it would be better to avoid, no more."

She waited for a moment, then relaxed and smiled. "I saw Emily today." Emily was her younger sister, now married to Jack Radley, for some time a member of Parliament. "She knows Rosalind Kynaston slightly. She says she's very quiet and frankly rather boring."

Pitt took another mouthful before he replied. "Emily is easily bored. How is she?" He had not seen Emily since Christmas. Once she and

Charlotte had helped in some of his more colorful cases, particularly those involving the wealthy and socially prominent, where they had access, while he, as a policeman, was sent round to the servants' entrance. It felt like a long time ago now. Emily's first husband had had both wealth and title, and had died tragically. For a short and desperate time in her life, Emily had been suspected of his murder. That, too, was well in the past.

Charlotte shrugged very slightly. "You know how it is in winter."

He waited, expecting her to add something. Instead, she stood up, went to the stove, lifted a treacle pudding out of its steaming pan and turned it out, upside down onto a large plate, watching with satisfaction as the rich, melted golden syrup ran down its sides. She knew it was one of his favorites. There was nothing more enjoyable at the end of a long, cold, wet day. He found himself smiling in anticipation, even though he was quite aware that she had deliberately evaded his question about Emily, which had to mean that there was something wrong.

4

I T WAS TWO MORE days before Pitt heard from the police at Shooters Hill—or to be more precise, from the police surgeon, Dr. Whistler. He received a short note, sealed in an envelope and delivered by a messenger who did not wait for an answer.

Pitt read it a second time.

> Dear Commander Pitt,
>
> I have further examined the body of the woman found in the gravel pit on Shooters Hill. I have learned a number of facts, which change the situation quite fundamentally. It is my duty to report these to Special Branch so you may act as you believe appropriate in the interests both of the state, and of justice.
>
> I shall be in my office in the morgue for the rest of the day, and at your service.
>
> Yours sincerely,
>
> George Whistler, MD

Pitt obeyed the summons immediately. His first thought was that Whistler had found some way of confirming that the body was indeed Kitty Ryder, and that she had in fact been murdered in a way that would connect her death with the Kynaston house.

There was nothing to keep him at Lisson Grove. The matters in hand were all routine and very capably handled by others. He informed the appropriate people where he was going. Fifteen minutes later he was in a hansom on the long, traffic-clogged journey first to the river, across Westminster Bridge, then eastwards to Greenwich and the morgue. He was cold and uncomfortable in the hansom. He had several miles to cover, and the ice on the roads made the journey even slower than usual.

Finally he stood in Whistler's office. His coat was on the stand by the door and the warmth was slowly seeping back into him, thawing out his hands and allowing his tense shoulders to ease a little.

Whistler had lost the slightly aggressive air he had had earlier. In fact he looked distinctly unhappy, as if he did not know how to begin.

"Well?" Pitt prompted him.

Whistler was also standing, but closer to the fire. He pushed his hands hard into his trouser pockets. "Rather a lot of things to tell you, I'm afraid," he replied. "On more detailed examination of the body, it became apparent that she had died considerably earlier than I had thought . . ."

Pitt was confused. "Don't you tell the time a person has been dead from the degree of decay?"

"Will you let me finish?" Whistler snapped, his temper fraying at the first touch.

Pitt realized with a jolt that the man was more than merely annoyed with himself for having to alter his diagnosis. Something was disturbing him more deeply, even brushing him with a kind of dread.

Whistler cleared his throat. "Bitterly cold temperatures, below freezing, can delay the decaying process greatly, even put it off altogether, if they persist without break. This is why people keep ice houses for meat storage." He hesitated, but Pitt did not interrupt again.

"This body was kept at or below freezing for some time, and the decay was slight. But, as we discussed before, she was not kept at the place where we found her; she was not in the open at all, or scavenging animals would have got to her—at the very least, insects would have. Therefore she was in a very cold and completely enclosed place. Do you follow me so far?"

"Yes. She was kept in a place that was clean and cold. We knew that already. Perhaps somebody's ice house?" Pitt mused.

"Precisely. The gravel pit is so close to a public footpath—granted, one used very infrequently, particularly at this time of year, but all the same, still used, and by people with dogs. So I had assumed she must've been placed there during that night—but, based on my initial assessment of her injuries, that she was killed perhaps two weeks before we found her." Whistler was watching Pitt closely. "It seemed to make sense that possibly someone killed her, in an unplanned attack, and then had to consider how to dispose of her body. It took him time to find a way of getting her up to the gravel pit unseen, and considering the circumstances, without anyone else's assistance."

"A reasonable assumption," Pitt agreed. "No longer tenable?"

Whistler grunted and let his breath out between his teeth. "It is. But, I examined the body very closely for the cause of death. While doing so I realized that the decay was much further advanced than I had supposed from the exterior. She had been kept somewhere extremely cold and"—he took a deep breath before continuing—"she had been cleaned up quite a lot after the injuries that caused her death . . ."

"What?"

Whistler glared at him. "You heard me correctly, Commander. Someone made an attempt to clean her up, then kept her body somewhere very cold, but thoroughly sealed. And don't waste your time asking me for an explanation. I can only tell you the facts. Understanding them is your business, thank God!"

"And the cause of death?" Pitt felt cold again, in spite of the bright fire.

"Extreme violence," Whistler replied. "Blows hard enough to break her bones, specifically her shoulder blade, four ribs, the humerus in her left arm, and her pelvis in three places. But all of that happened some time before the mutilations to her face. That is my point!" He stared at Pitt, his outrage at the brutality of it all apparent. "Her death happened around three weeks before the mutilation, at the absolute minimum."

Pitt was appalled. It was one of the most savage beatings he could imagine. And then to mutilate her face after she had died, to store her body and clean up her wounds before disposing of her in the pit! Whoever did it must have been completely insane. No wonder Whistler looked so wretched. If she were a prostitute it was no ordinary quarrel she had fallen victim to, it was an attack by a raving madman. And if he could do that once, how long would it be before he did it again?

Suddenly the room seemed not warm and comfortably protected from the elements. It was more like a suffocating, airless imprisonment from the clean, driving sleet outside, and he longed to escape into it.

"What with?" he asked, his voice wavering a little. "What did he use?"

"Honestly?" Whistler shook his head. "This side of a lunatic asylum, I would say he ran her down with a coach and four. Some of the injuries could have been caused by horses' hooves or carriage wheels. Considerable impact, from several directions, and it could have happened all at once, like horses panicking."

A momentary fury welled up inside Pitt. The man could have told him that in the first place. Hideous accidents happened. The damage and the pain were the same, but the horror was nothing like that of imagining a homicidal human being doing such a thing deliberately. He longed to actually hit Whistler, which was childish, and he was ashamed of himself. Nevertheless it was true. He clenched his fists and kept his voice level, even if it was tight and grated between his teeth.

"Are you saying that this woman's death could have been a traffic accident, and not a crime at all, Dr. Whistler?"

"It could have been any number of things!" Whistler's answer rose to all but a shout. "But if it was a traffic accident, why in God's name was it not reported to the police?" He waved his arms wide, only just missing the bookcase. "Where the devil was the body for the weeks before he disposed of her? And why put her out in one of the Shooters Hill gravel pits for that poor soul walking his dog to find?" He drew in a deep breath. "And why the terrible mutilations so long after her death?"

This time it was Pitt who was silent.

Whistler gave a shuddering sigh and fought to regain control of himself. He looked slightly embarrassed by his emotion and avoided meeting Pitt's eyes. Perhaps he thought himself unprofessional, but Pitt liked him the more for it.

"Anything further about who she was?" Pitt asked at last. "Something not obliterated by this . . . lunatic?"

"Probably in good health, as far as I could tell at this stage," Whistler answered. "No apparent disease. Organs all fine, apart from beginning to decay. If you find whoever did this to her, I hope you hang him! If you don't, don't come back to me for any help!" His glare swiveled to Pitt, then away again. There was a faint flush in his cheeks. "She was probably a domestic servant. There are signs, little things, you know? Good teeth. Well nourished. Clean nails, good hands, but several small scars from burning, the sort you see on a woman who does a lot of ironing. Difficult things not to burn yourself with now and again, flatirons. Especially if you're ironing something fiddly, like lace, or gathered sleeves, delicate collars, that kind of thing."

"A lady's maid . . ." Pitt said the inevitable.

"Yes . . . or a laundry maid of a more general sort. Children's clothes are fiddly, too."

"So you still have no idea whether it is Kitty Ryder or not?"

"No, I haven't. Sorry. But I can tell you this victim wasn't a lady. Ladies don't do their own ironing. And she wasn't a prostitute—much too clean and healthy for that. She must have been in her mid- to late twenties. On the streets, by that age she'd have looked a lot worse. A servant. Or maybe a young married woman, taking in laundry, though that's less likely. Everyone around here has their own servants for that sort of thing. And she'd had no children. With the injuries and the rot I don't know if she was still a virgin."

"Thank you," Pitt said grimly, as a matter of courtesy; it was the last thing he actually meant. He did not want the case, and he knew that Whistler would rather not have found the evidence, or have had to tell him about it. It was all inevitable now: the slow, sad unraveling of whoever's tragedy it was. "Have you told the local police?" he added, almost as an afterthought.

A bitter amusement flashed in Whistler's eyes. "Yes." He did not add their reaction, but Pitt could guess it. They would be delighted if they could claim this was a problem they would have to give up to Special Branch, just in case it should end up involving Dudley Kynaston.

Pitt took his damp overcoat and hat off the coatrack and put them on. He said good-bye to Whistler and went out into the passage, and then the cold street again. He could have got a hansom here and ridden all the way back to Lisson Grove, but he preferred to walk down to the river and sit in a ferry on the choppy gray water, alone with the wind and the rain, and think what he was going to do next, and how he was going to do it. He could get a cab on the far side.

There were too many questions unanswered. If this were the body of Kitty Ryder, had it also been her blood and hair on the steps of the Kynaston house? Had she been taken by force, struggled against whoever attacked her? If so, the only suspect so far seemed to be her suitor, but why would he have done such a thing? If he had killed her there, it had been an extraordinarily violent quarrel to conduct so close to an inhabited house. Why had no one heard anything? In fact, why had she not screamed, and brought the whole household out?

And if he had killed her why had he not left her there and escaped as fast as he could? She was a big woman for someone to have carried anywhere. If he had run off into the night, leaving her dead in the alleyway, he had an excellent chance of never being found. London was a large city to lose yourself in, and there was the whole of the countryside beyond that! Or, if you were desperate enough, ships sailed every day from the Pool of London for every part of the world.

Pitt looked across the rough water at them now: masts jostling against the sky in the distance; steamers heavier, and more solid; barges and lighters threading between them. A man could lose himself here in a day, never mind three weeks. None of this made sense. What was he missing?

The silent ferryman at the oars and the rhythmic slap of the water on the sides of the boat helped him to concentrate.

If it was Kitty, where had she been from the time she left Kynaston's house until she was placed in the gravel pit? Was she killed straight away, or later? Why put her in the gravel pit anyway? Why not bury her? That made no sense. It was almost as if someone had intended her to be found.

The longer he considered it, the uglier and more senseless it appeared. He still hoped it was not Kitty at all, but he knew he must proceed as if it were.

WITHIN TEN MINUTES OF his return to Lisson Grove, Stoker materialized in Pitt's office. Pitt felt a touch of amusement at his prompt appearance. Stoker would have heard that Pitt had been summoned by Whistler, and must have been watching for Pitt to return. He entered the office and closed the door behind him and stood expectantly, waiting to be told.

Pitt did so, briefly.

Stoker listened in silence. His strong, bony face was unreadable, except for the increased pallor. He looked down at the floor, his shoulders hunched a little, hands in his pockets.

"No choice, have we?" he stated. "This doesn't make any sense. There's a major part of it we don't know anything about." He looked up, his blue-gray eyes brilliant. "Maybe it has nothing to do with the young man she was courting, sir. It could all be in the Kynaston household. According to what I learned about her from the other servants, she was smart and didn't miss much. A lady's maid gets to know a lot of things, that's why they stay in places a long time. You can't afford to let them go, 'specially not to a position with anyone in your own circle."

"What are you suggesting?" Pitt faced the inevitable. "That she was blackmailing someone in the house, and they refused to pay? Or that they killed her simply because she knew?"

Stoker winced. "Either one, sir. Maybe she knew what they'd do and she tried to run away, an' that's where they caught her?"

"And she didn't cry out?"

"Couldn't you kill a woman without letting her scream, sir? I could."

Pitt imagined it: Kitty terrified because she knew what she had seen, or heard, running out of the house, even in the dark in the winter. She would have gone through the dimly lit kitchen and scullery to the back door, struggling with the bolts on the doors, flinging them open and going outside into the bitter air, scrambling up the steps. Had she known her killer was only yards behind her? Or had he come silently, his footsteps masked in her ears by her own pounding heart? There had been a brief, terrible fight on the steps, a blow—fatal sooner than the killer had realized. He had gone on pounding, beating, until the hysteria had died down inside him and he saw what he had done.

Then what?

He had moved the body quickly. Where to? A cellar? Somewhere bitterly cold, until he could move it again. And some mischance had delayed that.

Pitt looked at Stoker's face and saw a trace of the same thought in his eyes.

"If it was someone in the house, it was most likely Kynaston," Stoker said aloud. "We'd better find out."

There was no argument to be made, only careful plans, and perhaps something of Dudley Kynaston himself to be learned before they began. "Yes . . ." Pitt agreed. "I'll start with Kynaston tomorrow. You start with Kitty Ryder."

STOKER DID NOT WAIT until the morning.

He knew he had already learned all he could about Kitty Ryder from where she had lived and worked.

He and Pitt had naturally checked with police all over the area to see if there had been similar attacks, and found nothing.

Stoker himself had spoken to the institutions that kept the criminally insane. No one had escaped. There was no record of such mutilations anywhere else.

No matter where else they looked, they were turned back to Kitty herself, and her connections with the Kynaston house.

Stoker lived alone in rented rooms. He had no family in this part of London. In fact only he and his sister Gwen were left anyway, and she lived in King's Langley, a short train journey away. Their two brothers had died in childhood, and his other sister in giving birth. His work filled his life. He realized how much, with an awareness of suddenly being anonymous as he walked along the wet pavement from the island of light beneath one streetlamp through the mist and shadows to the island beneath the next.

Other people seemed to be moving more rapidly, heads bent, as if hurrying towards some purpose. Were they eager for what was ahead of them? Or only weary of what was behind?

Stoker had begun in the navy as a boy, and the hard life on a ship had taught him the worth of discipline. One might argue with men, trick or deceive them, even bribe them, but no one argued with the sea. The bones of those who had tried littered the ocean's floor. He had learned both obedience and command, at least to a moderate level, and had expected his life to follow that path.

Then an incident while in port had involved investigation by Special Branch, and he had been recruited by Victor Narraway, at that time its commander. It was a different life; more interesting; in its own way more demanding, certainly of his imagination and intelligence. He found to his surprise that he had a considerable skill for it.

Then Narraway had been forced out. It was only Pitt who had been loyal to Narraway and eventually saved his reputation, perhaps his life, but not his position. Pitt had inherited that himself, much to his embarrassment and dismay. He did not wish to profit from Narraway's loss. Nor did he, frankly, think that he had the necessary skills or experience to succeed.

Of course he had not said so to Stoker, possibly not to anyone at all. But Stoker was a good judge of men, and he saw it in a dozen tiny details. Less so now, perhaps, after a year, but still there, to one who had recognized them before.

Stoker liked Pitt. There was an innate decency in him it was impossible to disregard. However, occasionally he worried that some quality in Pitt would stay his hand when he should strike. The position he now held demanded ruthlessness, and therefore an ability to live with mistakes, to forgive himself and move on, not allowing the memory of them to debilitate him.

And yet even with that realization, he did not want Pitt to change. It saddened him that perhaps such change was inevitable. He might even be driven to take a lead in that himself one day.

Kitty Ryder troubled him also, though he had never even met the woman or seen a likeness of her. He pictured her in his mind: something like his sister Gwen, who had thick, soft hair and a quick smile, nice teeth, one a little crooked.

Even though he did not see her more than perhaps once a month, the closeness between them was always in his mind. Gwen would have been a good lady's maid, if she had not married young and started a family. She was lucky; her husband was a decent man, even if he was away at sea too much of the time.

He came to the pub where he ate frequently and went inside to the noise and the warmth. He ordered a steak and kidney pie, but even while he ate, his mind was on Kitty. What had she been like? What made her laugh, or cry? Why had she apparently loved a man that everyone else thought was unworthy of her? Why did any woman love such a man?

He had to laugh at himself—here he was, sitting alone in the pub, angry over the fate of a woman he had never met and who was probably nothing like Gwen at all!

He paid for his ale and walked out into the cold, wet night. She was the victim, at the very least, of a hideous mutilation and abandonment. He was a detective, so he should find out about her. He took a hansom back up to the Shooters Hill area and went into the café near the Pig and Whistle on Silver Street. He was not naturally convivial but it was part of his job to mix with people, start casual conversations and ask questions without seeming to.

It was growing late, and he was all but ready to give up when the waiter, refilling his tankard, responded to his casual mention of Kitty.

"'Aven't seen 'er lately," he said with a shrug. "Pity. We'd music sometimes. She used ter sing real sweet. Don't like them 'igh, tinkly sort o' voices, but 'ers were low and gentle. No edge to it, if yer know what I mean? Not as she couldn't carry a jolly good tune, an' make us laugh, an' all."

"She came in here often?" Stoker tried to keep the eagerness out of his face, avoiding looking at the man's eyes.

"Yer know 'er, then?" the waiter asked curiously.

"No." Stoker forced himself to drink some of the fresh cider before he went on. "Friend o' mine liked her quite a lot. He hasn't seen her in a month or so either. Maybe she got a new place . . ." He let the suggestion hang in the air.

"More fool 'er," the waiter said drily. "Got a good position, it don't do to change it. She never spoke like she meant ter. But then she kept 'er own counsel, that one. Never talked loose, like." He shook his head. "'Er and 'er ships . . . real dreamer, she was. 'Ope she landed on 'er feet." He turned to the room. "Drink up, gents. I ain't stayin' open all night."

"Ships?" Stoker said quietly. "What kind of ships?"

The waiter grinned. "Paper ones, mate. Pictures of all kinds o' ships: big ones, little ones, foreign ones what sail out east, like up an' down the Nile. She kept 'em an' stuck 'em in a book. Learned all about 'em, she did. Could tell yer where they went an' 'oo sailed 'em. Will yer be wantin' another pint, then?"

"No, thank you," Stoker declined, but he pulled a sixpence out of his pocket and put it on the table. "But here's for the last one, and have one yourself."

The waiter snatched it up instantly and smiled. "Thank you, sir. You're a gent."

Stoker went outside into the rising wind, walking down towards the river to catch a ferry across. He would have a better chance of finding a cab on the other side for the long ride home.

By the time he reached the north bank and climbed the steep stairs up to the road, the night was clear. The moon lit the water so he could see the real ships riding on the tide, dark hulls on the silver-black spars against a paler sky.

Pitt was at the Kynaston house on Shooters Hill by half past eight the next morning. Any later and he might have missed Kynaston himself, and Rosalind would almost certainly refuse to see him without her husband present.

This time, at Pitt's request they met in Kynaston's study. Pitt had no time alone in the room, which he would have preferred. However, even as they spoke he looked more closely at what he was able to see without obviously staring.

Kynaston sat behind his desk. It was a large, comfortable piece of furniture with a patina of age, and suitably untidy. The sand tray, sealing wax, pens, and inkwells were easily to hand, not set straight since last used. The books on the shelf behind were there for reference, not ornament. The sizes were odd, the subjects aligned rather than the appearance. There were several paintings on the walls, some of ships or seascapes, one of a striking snowscape with trees, and mountains of some height in the distance, like the ones pictured in the morning room.

Certainly it was not a depiction of any part of Britain.

Kynaston saw Pitt looking at it.

"Beautiful," Pitt said quickly, scanning his memory to find some suitable comment to make about the piece from his earlier days in the police when he had dealt with theft, frequently of works of art. "The clarity of the light is extraordinary."

Kynaston looked at him with a spark of sudden interest. "It is, isn't it!" he agreed. "You get it in the far north, almost luminous like that."

Pitt frowned. "But it's not Scotland, surely? The scale is more than artistic license . . ."

Kynaston smiled. "Oh, no, it's pretty accurate. It's Sweden. I've been there, very briefly. My brother, Bennett, bought that one. He . . ." A shadow of pain crossed his face as if the sharpness of loss suddenly revisited him. He took a breath and started again. "He spent some time there and grew to love the landscape, especially the light. As you observed, it is quite extraordinary." A pleasure came back into his voice, the timbre completely different. "He always used to say that great art is distinguished by a universality, some passion in it that speaks to all kinds of people; combined with something unique to the artist that makes it totally personal, the sensitivity of one man, an individual eye." He stopped as if a memory had transported him and the present time and place were forgotten.

Pitt waited, not because he expected to deduce anything of value either from what Kynaston had said, or the way in which he had said it, but because to have interrupted with some trivial comment would have broken the possibility of any understanding between them.

Instead he let his eye wander a little towards the other pictures in the room. The pride of place above the mantelpiece was taken by a head-and-shoulders portrait of a man of about thirty, bearing so strong a resemblance to Kynaston that for a moment Pitt thought that it was he, and the artist had taken too much of a liberty, perhaps for dramatic effect. Kynaston was striking-looking, but this man was handsome, an idealized version with thicker hair and bolder eyes, a face of almost visionary intensity, and dark-eyed, where Kynaston's eyes were blue.

Kynaston followed his gaze.

"That's Bennett," he said quietly. "He died years ago. But I expect you know that."

"Yes," Pitt answered quietly. "I'm sorry." He knew nothing of the circumstances, except that they were sudden and tragic, a man of great promise dying on what seemed like the eve of achievement. It had been an illness of some sort. There was no suggestion of scandal.

Kynaston's face suddenly looked bruised, as if the grief were still raw. He made an effort to dismiss it and regain his composure. He raised his eyes and looked squarely at Pitt. "But I presume you are here over this wretched body in the gravel pit—again. There is absolutely nothing I can tell you, except that we are missing no more servants." He sighed.

Pitt decided bluntness was the only course open to him. Tact would allow Kynaston to dismiss him.

"We know a little more about her now," he replied with a slight smile, as if they were discussing something trivial and not particularly unpleasant. "She had no signs of disease, or of life on the streets in any manner. In fact, she was well fed and well cared for, very clean apart from the surface dirt of having lain in the gravel pit. She did have slight burns on her hands, as many maids do who have occasion to do a lot of ironing. Such burns are distinct from those of a cook or a scullery maid."

Kynaston paled. "So it is Kitty? But how? This body was just found, and Kitty has been missing for weeks . . . surely you'd be able to tell . . ."

"Though the body was just found, the police surgeon says that this woman actually died at least three weeks earlier and was kept in a cold place, sufficiently sealed that no animals or insects could get to her. This is all information I imagine you would prefer Mrs. Kynaston did not have to know . . ."

"Good God, man! What on earth are you suggesting?" Kynaston was now ashen. He searched for words and was unable to find any.

"That it is possible that the body is Kitty Ryder's, and that her disappearance, most probably her murder, is a very ugly issue. Your work for the government is sensitive. There are those who disapprove of it. This is not going to be dealt with quietly and discreetly," Pitt replied, "unless we can prove almost immediately that her death had nothing whatever to do with her employment or residence in this house. I know of no way of doing that, beyond damaging speculation, except to find out exactly what really did happen—and possibly, that the woman in the gravel pit is not Kitty at all. To do that, I need to know all that I can about her: not in polite whispers, but openly and provably, the less attractive as well as the good."

Kynaston looked as if he had been struck and was still absorbing the pain, unable to respond.

"Why . . ." he stammered. "Why in God's name would anyone kill the poor girl and then leave her body in the gravel pit . . . weeks after she was—" He stopped.

"I don't know," Pitt responded. "Obviously there are many things we do not know, and we need to learn them as soon and as completely as possible. Stoker will do all he can to learn about Kitty and to follow up on the young man she was courting, in the possibility that she is alive and well, or if not, that it was he who killed her, or someone she met after she left here . . ."

"And you?" Kynaston asked hoarsely.

"I shall do what I can here, on the much worse assumption that the body is hers and that she was killed because of her associations here." He met Kynaston's eyes and saw the fear in them. "I'm sorry," he added. "But the scrutiny is bound to be close—and unpleasant. The only defense is to be prepared."

Kynaston leaned back in his chair slowly and let out his breath. "All right. What is it you wish to know? I hope you will have the decency to keep my wife out of this as much as possible." That was a statement, almost an order.

"As much as possible, of course," Pitt agreed, thinking how different Rosalind Kynaston seemed from Charlotte. Charlotte would resent being kept out of it, protected from reality, as she would see it. And she would unquestionably think the murder of a servant in her house to be her business.

"Murders have motive," Pitt said. "And usually some event that caused them to happen at the time and place in which they did. I would like to see your diary, and that of Mrs. Kynaston, for the two or three weeks before Kitty disappeared, please, sir."

"Neither my wife nor her engagements can have any effect on—" Kynaston began.

Pitt raised his eyebrows very slightly. "You think Miss Ryder's death may have more to do with your life than with your wife's?" he said with some surprise.

"I don't think it has anything to do with this house at all!" Kynaston snapped. "It is you who are supposing it."

"No, sir, I am supposing that the police and the newspapers will take a close, and possibly prurient, interest in all events in this house, and we need to be able to answer every question, preferably with corroboration, even with proof, before they are allowed to do that in print."

Kynaston flushed. He picked up a leather-bound book from the desk near his elbow and passed it across to Pitt.

"Thank you." Pitt took it and rose to his feet. "If you can give me a place where I can read it, and take any notes that are necessary, I'll return it to you before I leave. Perhaps you would be kind enough to lend me Mrs. Kynaston's diary as well; then I can accomplish this exercise all at the same time?"

Kynaston's face tightened, but he handed over her diary. "I can't see how it can help anything, but I suppose you know what you're doing." He did not sound as if he believed it. "My appointments are quite public."

Pitt thanked him without adding anything.

Norton offered him a small, rather chilly room, which appeared from its furnishings to be a sitting room for summer use, facing onto the garden, and without a fireplace. Pitt thanked him as if he had not noticed the cold.

He read through both the diaries, making notes. He was looking not for Kynaston's social engagements so much as where they were the same as Rosalind's and where they were not, and for any discrepancies. He found a few, but they were easily explained as carelessness, even misreading of Kynaston's own handwriting, the mistaking of a 5 for an 8, a date or an address wrongly copied down.

He smiled as he read Rosalind's more casual accounts of invitations, and side notes as to what to wear, and why. She was apparently aware that Kynaston was making excuses about certain functions he chose to avoid.

There were notes in the back of his diary as to purchases, gifts, and invitations. Kynaston had a weakness for good brandy and cigars, membership of clubs Pitt knew were extremely expensive, first-night tickets for the best theaters and operas, several appointments with a very good tailor indeed. He was a man who cared about his appearance, and was not loath to indulge his tastes.

There were a few errors and one or two omissions, but it seemed natural for the unedited diaries of a man with very human foibles. Had all details been exact, it would have raised Pitt's suspicions.

Thoroughly chilled, but determined not to show it, he returned the diaries to Norton and took his leave.

Outside he walked briskly to get warm again, and while irritated that he had found nothing of value, he could not help a certain liking for Dudley Kynaston, and a feeling that perhaps Rosalind was a more interesting woman than her rather colorless appearance suggested.

CHAPTER

5

Two MORNINGS LATER, AND well into February, Pitt was at his desk reading reports regarding a case in Edinburgh when Stoker knocked. Almost before Pitt had replied, he came in and closed the door behind him. His face was grim and flushed from the sting of the wind in the street.

"Have you seen the billboards this morning, sir?" he asked without preamble.

Pitt felt the warmth of the room fade. "No, I came by hansom. I wanted to be early and deal with this business in Edinburgh. Why?" He named his worst fear. "They haven't identified the body as Kitty Ryder, have they?"

"No, sir." Stoker never exaggerated the suspense, which was a quality about him that Pitt valued. "But apparently one of the members of Parliament raised rather a lot of questions about the body we've got, and asked what we are doing to ascertain if it is her or not."

Pitt was stunned. "In Parliament?" he said incredulously. "Have they nothing better to do?" A flicker of expression crossed Stoker's face and disappeared too rapidly to be readable.

"'Can the prime minister assure us that everything possible is being done to protect not only the safety but the reputation of Mr. Dudley Kynaston, a naval inventor of great importance to the safety and welfare of this country?'" he quoted. "That sort of thing, then others asking about his family's safety, and so on." His eyes met Pitt's squarely; there was no hostility in them, only questions.

Pitt put away the papers to do with the case in Edinburgh. He swore fiercely, and without apology.

"Exactly my opinion, sir," Stoker agreed. There might or might not have been amusement in his eyes.

"Who was it who was asking these . . . questions?" Pitt inquired. "Doesn't the idiot realize that by asking them in Parliament, where they will be reported by the press, he is making Kynaston's vulnerability all the greater? Sometimes I wonder who the devil elects these people! Don't they ever look at them first?"

"That's rather the trouble, sir," Stoker said grimly.

"Elections?"

Again the smile touched Stoker's lips then vanished. "No, sir, that's a separate problem altogether. The MP in the case was Somerset Carlisle, who is really rather good."

Pitt drew in his breath to respond, and let it out again in a sigh. He would not have described Somerset Carlisle as "rather good." He was brilliant, eccentric, and personally loyal, even when at great cost to himself. He was also unpredictable, unreasonable, and beyond anyone's control, as far as Pitt knew. Even Lady Vespasia Cumming-Gould herself, whose friend Carlisle had been for years, seemed to exercise very little influence over him. Pitt thought back to the long-ago episode in his career involving Somerset Carlisle and corpses that would not remain buried. He remembered the nature of the detection and scandal it had caused. He had to remind himself that this was a different case altogether. The whole issue of the supposed resurrectionists was well covered over, and Pitt would very much rather it remained that way.

Stoker was still waiting, but his face reflected his awareness that he seemed to be awakening ghosts.

"Perhaps I had better go and see Lady Vespasia." Pitt stood up and moved towards the coat stand in the corner of the room. "It's a bit late to get ahead of this, but I'd like to be as close behind as possible."

"Are you sure you want to be out of the office when they send for you, sir?" Stoker's face was unreadable.

"I'm damn sure I'd like to be miles away," Pitt said fervently. "But I'll be within reach—if Lady Vespasia is at home. If I'm sent for, leave me a message there and I'll go straight to Whitehall."

Stoker looked dubious.

"I want to know what's going on!" Pitt told him, taking his coat off the stand and putting it on as he went out of the door.

VESPASIA WAS STILL AT breakfast but her maid was used to Pitt turning up without announcement, and frequently at inconvenient times. She simply tightened her lips a little and went to bring fresh tea.

In her youth Vespasia Cumming-Gould had been accepted by many to be the most beautiful woman of her generation. As far as Pitt was concerned, she still was, because for him beauty was a quality of the mind and the heart as much as of physical perfection. Her hair was silver and her face now reflected decades of passion, grief, and laughter, and a courage that had seen her through triumph and loss of many different kinds.

"Good morning, Thomas," she said with some surprise. "You look tired and exasperated. Sit down and have some tea, and tell me what has happened. Would you like something to eat as well? Toast, perhaps? I have a new and most excellent marmalade. It is so pungent I can feel it right through my head."

"It sounds like exactly what I need," he accepted, pulling out the chair at the opposite side of the table from her and sitting down. He had always liked this yellow breakfast room where she often took all her meals when dining alone, or with only one guest. It felt as if the sun always shone here, regardless of the weather beyond.

The maid returned with the second cup and saucer, and Vespasia requested more toast.

"Now tell me what has occurred," Vespasia said as soon as they were alone again.

He had never hesitated to tell her the truth, even when perhaps it was indiscreet, and never had she betrayed his trust. She knew many people's secrets, and the fact that she had not relayed them to him only increased his certainty of her judgment. Briefly, between mouthfuls of toast, and the marmalade that was as good as she had claimed, he told her about the missing maid and the body in the gravel pit on Shooters Hill.

"I see," she said at last. "It is a dilemma, but I do not yet understand why you think I can be of help. You are far better able to pursue it than I."

"I am expecting a telephone call here, any moment, and I apologize for requesting it be forwarded to me without asking your permission . . ."

"Thomas! Please reach the point of this visit before that happens!"

"It will be from someone in the prime minister's office asking me what I know, and what I am doing about it," he explained.

Her silver eyebrows arched even higher. "You told the prime minister about it? For heaven's sake, Thomas, why?"

He swallowed the last of his toast. "No, I didn't! That is exactly the point. He knows because there were questions in the House, yesterday evening."

"Oh dear . . ." In her mouth the words were extraordinarily expressive, even catastrophic.

"Asked by Somerset Carlisle," he finished.

"Oh dear," she said again, a little more slowly. "Now I see why you have come to me. I'm afraid I have no idea how he came to know of the affair, or why he should raise it in the House." She looked worried. "I assume you are involved because the body may be that of the Kynastons's poor maid? Tragic as it is, it would not concern Special Branch otherwise, would it?"

"No, it wouldn't. And I still have considerable hope that it is not Kitty Ryder—"

"But you fear that it is?" she interrupted him. "And that either her death involves the Kynaston household, or it will be made to look as if it does? Why? To ruin Kynaston personally, or to embarrass the government?" She refilled his cup from the pewter teapot.

"I don't know," he replied. "But if it is to embarrass the government it seems rather a poor effort. It's tragic and sordid, if the poor girl was killed because of some romantic involvement . . . perhaps with one of the male servants, or with . . ."

"Don't be so delicate, Thomas," Vespasia said briskly. "If it has anything at all to do with the household, it will be with Kynaston himself. Or at the very least there will be the suggestion of his being entangled with the poor girl in some way. Frankly it sounds most unlikely to me, and I do not believe that Somerset Carlisle is naïve enough to become involved in such a thing. Certainly not in order to embarrass the government!"

"That was my conclusion." He sipped the tea. It was hot and fragrant. "Therefore it is something else, but why is he asking questions in the House, instead of coming to me? If it is of any legitimate concern to him anyway."

"I have no idea," she replied, passing him more toast. "But I shall certainly do what I can to find out."

"Thank you," he said. He was just about to eat it when there was a knock on the door. The maid came in quietly.

"Excuse me, my lady, but there is a message on the telephone for Commander Pitt."

"What is it?" Vespasia asked.

The maid turned to Pitt. "The prime minister requires that you go to Downing Street immediately, sir, where a government official is waiting to speak to you."

Vespasia sighed. "You had better take my carriage, Thomas. Send it back when you reach there. There is no convenient place for it to wait for you, and I believe I have some errands to run myself. Good-bye, my dear, and good luck."

"Thank you," Pitt said grimly, putting the cup down again and rising to his feet. He finished the toast as he went out into the hall.

HE HAD ONLY FIFTEEN minutes to wait in one of the outer rooms in the prime minister's offices before he was escorted into a larger and much warmer room to face one of the prime minister's assistants, a well-upholstered man whose look of ease belied his nature. It must have been well cultivated.

"Morning, Pitt. Edom Talbot," he introduced himself. He was a burly man with a very ordinary face, except for remarkably penetrating eyes; it was impossible to tell if they were gray or brown. He was a man it might be easy to underestimate, but probably most unwise to do so. He did not invite Pitt to be seated, although there were two comfortable leather chairs near the fire, which was already burning up well.

"Good morning, Mr. Talbot," Pitt replied, trying not to sound wary.

Talbot wasted no time with niceties. "We've got a few nasty questions we don't know how to answer. Can't afford to be caught on the wrong foot again." He looked critically at Pitt. "I suppose we could say the fellow who asked them did us a kind of backhanded favor, though. Brought it to our attention, and we won't be caught out this time." He stared at Pitt almost unblinkingly. "We expect the answers from you, sir. Or if not, then a damned good explanation that'll do in the meantime."

"Yes, sir," Pitt returned his steady gaze. "What were the questions?"

Talbot looked bland. "Good," he said with almost no tone in his voice. "Look at the press with that blankness. Know nothing." Then suddenly all the muscles in his neck and shoulders tightened and his mouth went into a thin, flat line. "But don't damned well try it on me, sir!"

Pitt felt his temper flame, but he controlled himself as if nothing had changed. He did not ask again for the questions but waited for Talbot to continue.

"You've got your nerve, I'll say that for you," Talbot observed. "Or else you're too damned stupid to understand the issue. I suppose, God help me, I'll find out which soon enough. Who is the woman whose body was found in the gravel pit on Shooters Hill? What happened to her, and how did she get there? What the hell has all this got to do with Dudley Kynaston? Or anyone else in his house? And when are you going to get this damned great mess sorted out? And most importantly, how are you going to keep the lid on it until you do? And if you can't do the job, then tell me, and we'll get Narraway back, damn his hide!"

With an effort, because he knew he must be careful, Pitt began at the beginning. "We do not know whose body it is." He measured his words and kept his voice unnaturally calm. "It is too far decomposed to be easily recognizable, beyond the fact that she was probably a lady's maid, or a laundress of sorts."

"How do you know that?" Talbot interrupted, his eyebrows raised.

"Burn marks on her hands, such as you get in the use of a flatiron," Pitt said with satisfaction.

"I see. Go on! How do you propose to find out who she is, then?"

"First by eliminating the possibility that it is Kitty Ryder, Mrs. Kynaston's maid," Pitt replied. "I presume that's all you really want?"

Talbot grunted, but it was vaguely a sound of appreciation.

"What happened to her is harder to ascertain," Pitt continued. "How she got there is not known, and may never be. Certainly she did not walk to the place where she was found. She seems to have been dead for some time before she was put there. Probably she was kept somewhere extremely cold. I dislike the thought of it, but it might be the time to examine Mr. Kynaston's cold rooms, icehouse and so on, rather more thoroughly." He was satisfied with the look of extreme distaste in Talbot's face.

"As to what it has to do with Dudley Kynaston," Pitt said. "I am hoping that we can prove that it had nothing to do with him. And if the body is not that of Kitty Ryder, then there is no connection with him at all."

"If it's as badly decomposed as you say, how the devil do you presume to prove that it is not her?" Talbot asked, his eyebrows raised so high his forehead was ridged like a plowed field.

"By finding her somewhere else, alive and well," Pitt told him.

Talbot considered the reply for several moments.

Pitt waited. He had learned the value of silence, requiring the other person to speak first.

"That would be the best possible outcome," Talbot said finally. "And the sooner the better. In your opinion, how likely is it that such will be the case?"

Pitt did not need to weigh that before answering. "Unlikely," he said grimly. "We may have to settle for merely identifying the body as someone else, for which we need luck as well as skill."

Talbot nodded. He had expected as much. "Then what we need from you is that you find out, beyond reasonable doubt, preferably beyond any doubt at all, who this unfortunate woman is and how she met her death. If it has to do with Kynaston, then prove it, but do nothing further. Report back to me before you act. Is that understood?"

"I can't order the police—" Pitt began.

"That is precisely why Special Branch will deal with the case!" Talbot snapped. "Tell them whatever you want! Spies, secret documents, whatever serves the purpose, but keep them out of it."

"We'll be a lot longer finding Kitty Ryder alive without police help," Pitt pointed out, with a sharpness to his voice.

Talbot gave him a long, cold stare. "Be realistic, man! The woman is dead. Identify her, or prove the body is someone else's. And either prove Kynaston's guilt or his lack of connection with the whole affair. Report to me. If this woman is his maid, then find out if this connection with him is bad luck or someone taking advantage of a miserable coincidence. Or worse than that, a deliberate ploy to implicate him. And if it is that, then we need to know by whom."

"And why?" Pitt added with a touch of sarcasm.

"I can work that out for myself," Talbot said tartly. "Report to me any significant progress that you make, and do so discreetly. I need all details. Do not stop until you have them."

"Exactly what is Kynaston doing that is so important?" Pitt asked.

"You do not need to know that," Talbot answered immediately, his eyes hard and angry.

"I'm head of Special Branch!" Pitt snapped, his temper rising at the absurdity of Talbot's first ordering him to search for answers, and then keeping him half blind. "If you want me to do my job, then tell me what I need to know."

"You need to know what your instructions are," Talbot retorted. "If this is a piece of dramatic stupidity, we will deal with it accordingly. Thank you for coming so soon. Good day."

Pitt did not move. He opened his eyes very wide. "Stupidity?" he repeated the word as if it were meaningless. "Someone beat a young woman to death, concealed her body for three weeks, mutilated her face until it was unrecognizable, then dumped her in a gravel pit. If that is regarded by Her Majesty's Government as mere dramatic stupidity, what does it regard as a vicious crime?"

Talbot paled, but he did not flinch. "You have your instructions, Commander Pitt. Find the truth, sooner rather than later, and report it to me. Dispensing justice is not your job."

"I wish that were true," Pitt said bitterly. "Too often it is exactly my job. Or perhaps that is something you were not aware of?"

Talbot's face was white, mouth pinched at the corners. "Kynaston is of great importance to the government, and his work is both secret and sensitive. It may even be the key to our survival in any future war. That is sufficient information for you. It is also highly confidential. Now stop arguing the issue and making excuses. Do your job. Again, Commander Pitt, good day to you."

"Good day, Mr. Talbot," Pitt replied with some satisfaction, even if it lasted no longer than it took him to reach the street. Regardless of what Talbot said, he needed all the information he could gather regarding Dudley Kynaston's value to the government, not only to find out what Kitty Ryder might have learned that made her dangerous, but who else might profit from Kynaston's downfall, for any reason. And if he was actually innocent, then who had engineered his appearance of guilt?

There was only one man to ask, and that was Victor Narraway. And he would prefer to consult him without others, particularly Talbot, knowing he had done so.

Narraway, like himself, was one of the few people who owned a telephone in his own home. Since his forced retirement from the leadership of Special Branch, he had been elevated to the House of Lords, but that was more of a sop to his reputation than a real opportunity to be of use. Previously he would not have been at home at this hour, but now there was a reasonable chance he would not have gone to the House of Lords, or to one of his clubs for luncheon. Such things grew stale quite quickly to a man of Narraway's intelligence. Also, since he had no part in political affairs, he felt sidelined, no more of interest to those who used to hold him in awe. He had never said as much, but Pitt had heard it in his silences.

As IT TURNED OUT, Pitt had to wait about half an hour for Narraway to return from a brief walk. Considering the weather, Pitt imagined he had gone at all only as a matter of discipline. Narraway had begun his career in the Indian Army, and the virtues of abstinence and hard, strict self-mastery had never entirely left him.

Narraway's manservant offered Pitt a late luncheon, which he accepted gratefully, realizing that he was actually quite hungry. He was just finishing an excellent slice of hot apple pie, served with cream, when he heard the sound of the front door closing, then Narraway's voice in the hall.

Narraway came into the sitting room, having removed his overcoat. His thick hair was flattened a little where his hat had been, and his lean, dark face colored by the cold.

He glanced at the plate where the apple pie had been, and which now held only Pitt's folded spoon and fork.

"You came for more than luncheon, I presume?" he said with a slight lift of curiosity. He walked towards the fire, which was burning strongly where the manservant had added fresh coals. He stood in front of it from habit, holding his hands out to catch the heat.

"Luncheon seemed like a good idea," Pitt replied with a tight smile. "Since I spent my own luncheon time being hauled over the coals in Downing Street by a rather officious man by the name of Talbot."

Narraway straightened up, forgetting the fire. He stared at Pitt with interest. "I imagine you are at liberty to tell me what about, or you would not have come here? And it is both urgent and discreet, or you would have suggested luncheon at some restaurant. Please don't disappoint me . . ." He said it lightly, but Pitt caught the flash of emotion, the sincerity there, before Narraway concealed it again.

"It seems a shame not to have you deduce what it's about," Pitt said drily, in part to cover the fact that he had caught Narraway's moment of vulnerability.

Narraway sat down in the chair opposite and crossed his legs elegantly, hitching the knee of his trousers so as not to spoil the line. "Have you got time to wait for that?" he asked, his eyes bright with amusement.

Pitt smiled back. "No, I haven't. Did you read about the young woman's body found in the gravel pit on Shooters Hill?"

"Of course. Why? Ah! I see." He sat forward again. "Is that what Somerset Carlisle was referring to in his questions to the House yesterday? I saw that headline on the sandwich boards as I passed. I admit I didn't make the connection. Why the hell would Carlisle think a dead woman on Shooters Hill was anything to do with Kynaston, or might endanger him and his family? What danger? Who was the woman?"

"Probably doesn't have anything to do with Kynaston," Pitt replied. "But his wife's maid is missing, and she answers the description."

"Bit thin, isn't it? Wouldn't half the young women in Greenwich or

Blackheath answer it?" Narraway was looking at him steadily, waiting for the missing facts that made sense of it.

"Taller than average, handsomely built and with thick auburn hair?" Pitt asked. "Gone missing in the last three weeks? No, they wouldn't. And there was evidence of a scuffle outside Kynaston's house, not to mention the gravel pit is only a short walk from there."

Narraway nodded. It was so slight a movement it was barely visible. "I see. Are we supposing Kynaston was having an affair with this maid? Or that she learned something about either Mr. or Mrs. Kynaston so potentially damaging that Kynaston killed her? Seems a little drastic, and honestly pretty unlikely. But I suppose those are the crimes that catch us out."

"My question is, why does Carlisle care?" Pitt countered. "We have far more vulnerable members of the government than Kynaston! I could name half a dozen whose private lives would be open to question—if that were his purpose."

Narraway's mouth twisted in a wry smile, his black eyes bright. "Only half a dozen. For God's sake, Pitt, where are your eyes?"

"All right, a couple of dozen," Pitt conceded. "Why Kynaston?"

"Opportunity," Narraway answered. "The corpse turned up near his house, correct?" He pulled his mouth into a thin line. "I'm slipping. That isn't a reason to raise the subject publicly. The real question is what for? What does Carlisle want?" He thought in silence for a few moments before looking up at Pitt again. "Kynaston works for the War Office. But that's extremely vague. I think we need more precise information than that. At least you do," he corrected himself. "And you need to know a lot more about Kynaston professionally, too."

"Don't you know? I asked Talbot and was told fairly tersely to mind my own business."

"Good," Narraway responded. "Then there's something there. You'll get the door shut in your face. I've got a few favors I can call in . . ."

"Or threats you can hold over people," Pitt said a little bitterly. "I'm beginning to learn the power of this job."

"That's the favor," Narraway answered. "I won't carry out the threat.

Lesson, Pitt—never carry out a threat unless you absolutely have to. Once it's done, you've no more power with it."

"If I never do it, why would anyone believe that I would?" Pitt asked reasonably.

"Oh, you'll have to, once or twice," Narraway assured him, a shadow passing over his eyes as if memory darkened them for a moment. "Just put it off as long as you can. I hated doing it—you'll hate it even more."

Pitt remembered a large party, a house full of laughter and music, and a scene where a man lay on a tiled floor, blood pooling out from the shot with which Pitt had killed him.

"I know," he said almost under his breath.

Narraway looked at him with a moment's intense compassion, then that, too, vanished.

"I'll see what I can find out about Dudley Kynaston," he promised. "Might take a couple of days. Keep on trying to identify your corpse. You might be lucky and find out it's not your missing maid, but don't count on it."

Pitt stood up. "I'm not," he said quietly. "I'm preparing for the next round."

It came exactly as Pitt had expected. Nothing further had been learned about the identity of the woman in the gravel pit, nor had Stoker been more fortunate in finding any trace of Kitty Ryder. A few days later Narraway telephoned Pitt and invited him to call by just after dark. He would have invited him to dinner, but he knew of Pitt's desire to be at home with his family. If he envied him that, he disguised it so well Pitt had seen no more than perhaps a glimpse of it.

He offered Pitt a brandy, something that Pitt very seldom accepted, though he did on this occasion. He was tired and cold. He needed the fire inside as well as burning in the hearth.

Narraway got to the point immediately.

"Kynaston is cleverer than he looks, and—at least professionally—a lot more imaginative. He works on the design of submarines for the navy, and now particularly on submarine weapons, which is a field of its own: obviously different from weapons fired above the water."

"Submarines?" Pitt realized the yawning gap in his knowledge. He frowned, not wanting to make a fool of himself. "You mean like in Jules Verne's, *Twenty Thousand Leagues Under the Sea*?"

Narraway shrugged. "Not quite that clever yet, but definitely the naval warfare of the future, and not so far in the future either. The French were the first to launch a submarine not relying on human power for propulsion—*Plongeur*, back in '63, then improved on in '67. Fellow called Narcís Monturiol built a boat forty-six feet long, could dive down nearly a hundred feet and stay down for two hours."

Pitt was fascinated.

"The Peruvians, of all people, built a really good submarine during their war with Chile in '79. Then the Poles had one about the same time."

"Didn't we do anything?" Pitt interrupted with chagrin.

"I'm getting to it. Our clergyman and inventor George Garrett got together with a Swedish industrialist Thorsten Nordenfelt and made a whole series, one of which they sold to the Greeks. In '87 they improved it and added torpedo tubes for firing underwater explosive missiles. That one, sold to the Ottoman Navy, was the first to fire a torpedo while submerged." He closed his eyes and for a moment his jaw tightened. "One can only begin to imagine the possibilities of that on an island like ours, whose survival depends on our navy guarding not only our trade routes but our shores themselves: in fact, our existence."

Pitt's imagination was already there, racing and yet cold with fear.

"The Spanish are working on it, too," Narraway went on. "And the French have an all-electrical-powered one. It will be only two or three years before they're common."

"I see," Pitt said quietly. Indeed he did, all too terribly clearly. Britain was an island. Without their sea-lanes the British could be starved to death in weeks. The importance of submarine weapons could hardly be exaggerated—which is why they had to value people like Dudley Kynaston, and be prepared to go to great lengths to protect him.

"I can't see why Talbot wouldn't tell me that," Pitt said, both puzzled and angry.

"Neither can I," Narraway agreed. "I can only suppose that he thought you had been told already." Then he hesitated. "Also, I imagine he feared that if he did mention it, you would have gone on to ask a lot more questions, and the answers to those might be rather more . . . delicate." Narraway was tense, sitting back in his chair as if casually, but Pitt saw the strain in the fabric of his jacket as his shoulders hunched very slightly.

Pitt could not leave it unasked. "Technically delicate, or personally?"

"Personally, of course," Narraway said with a wry twist to his lips. "Technically is probably irrelevant, and would require a great deal more study than you have time for in order to understand. Are you aware that Dudley had a brother, Bennett, a couple or so years younger than he?"

"Yes. There's a picture of him in Kynaston's study, above the mantel." Pitt could see it as clearly as if it were before him now, even the eyes, the contours of the face. "He placed it in the best wall space, and the best light," he added. "And he will see it every time he comes into the room. Strong resemblance to Dudley, but even better looking. But he's been dead for several years. What could he have to do with all this?"

"Probably nothing," Narraway agreed. "But there were whispers of scandal concerning him some years ago. I haven't been able to uncover it, which means they took very great care indeed to hide everything, or disguise it as something else. I haven't even been able to learn if Dudley is aware of it himself. Apparently at least some elements of it happened abroad. Again, I don't know where. The only thing I gathered from both sources I tried is that Bennett was not to blame for it. Of course that may or may not be true."

"At the time of his death?" Pitt asked.

"No, some years before."

"Which would mean it was at least a decade ago, or longer," Pitt concluded. "Kitty Ryder would have been a child."

"It's relevant only in that it reveals Dudley Kynaston's sensitivities," Narraway pointed out. "And therefore his immediate reaction to conceal things that perhaps other people would not, even if he were completely innocent. He and Bennett were very close, as you have deduced from the portrait in the study."

Pitt thought about it for a few moments. It would account for Dudley Kynaston's behavior, the unease Pitt had sensed, even the tiny errors of omission in his diaries.

"Yes," he said with a degree of relief. Perhaps Kitty Ryder was likable, but unwise, and she had eloped with the young man the household staff so disapproved of, and the woman in the gravel pit could turn out to be unrelated to the Kynaston house.

Narraway saw the sudden ease in his face. "Protect Kynaston as long as you can," he said quietly. "We need as strong a navy as possible. There's a hell of a lot of unrest in the world. Africa is stirring against us, especially in the south. The old order is changing. The century is almost worn out, and the queen with it. She's tired and lonely and growing weaker. In Europe they're looking for change, reform. We may think we are isolated, but it's a delusion we can't afford. The English Channel is not very wide. A strong swimmer can make it, let alone a fleet of ships. We need to have the best navy in the world."

Pitt stared at him. None of what Narraway had said was unknown to him, but put together like this, it was a darker picture than he had allowed himself to see.

He did not answer. Narraway knew he understood.

6

CHARLOTTE HAD NOT SEEN her sister Emily for several weeks, and had not spent much time alone with her when they could talk to each other in more than formalities since before Christmas. She decided to write a letter to Emily asking if she would like to take luncheon and, if the weather permitted, to walk in Kew Gardens. Even if it was cold, the massive glasshouses filled with tropical plants would be warm, and a pleasant change from sitting inside.

Emily wrote back immediately, agreeing that it would be an excellent idea. She had married extremely well, just before Charlotte had married Pitt, and had gained a title and a very large fortune, if not a commensurate happiness. Tragically, George had been killed in circumstances to which they never referred. Emily found herself a very wealthy widow with a son, in whose name both the title and the inheritance were vested.

Later she had fallen in love, wildly and quite irresponsibly (so she told herself) with the handsome and charming Jack Radley. He had no profession and no inheritance at all. Everyone else had agreed with her that it would be a disaster, and in their first few years together Jack had done little but enjoy himself, and be excellent company. Then the ambition had seized him to do something of value, and he had fought very hard to win a seat in Parliament. Emily had been enormously proud of him, as indeed had Charlotte. He had more than justified their belief in him.

Young Edward's inheritance allowed Emily to live quite nicely, without using up what would rightfully be his when he reached majority. This was a little while in the future because he was roughly the same age as Jemima, who was now fifteen. Emily kept a carriage for her personal use, and it was in that that she came to pick up Charlotte for their luncheon.

She came into the house in Keppel Street, barely glancing at its hallway, so much smaller than her own. Nor did she look at the stairs, which went straight up to the first-floor landing, not in the sweeping arc of those at Ashworth House, never mind those at their country seat, which could accommodate twenty guests without inconvenience.

Charlotte was still in the kitchen, giving Minnie Maude last-minute instructions for dinner, and warning her not to let Uffie steal the sausages, which he was presently creeping towards, imagining no one would notice him.

"See that Daniel and Jemima have no more than hot soup when they come in from school," Charlotte added, picking up the little dog and putting him back in his basket. "And that they go straight upstairs to do whatever homework is assigned them."

"Yes, ma'am," Minnie Maude agreed, giving Uffie a stern look. He thumped his tail happily in reply.

Emily was looking extraordinarily dashing, wearing the very latest fashion in capes. It was double-breasted, with two rows of large fancy buttons down the front. It was very becoming, and from the way she walked it was apparent that she knew it. The whole outfit was a mixture of blues and greens, an up-to-the-minute, daring combination, frowned upon only a year ago. Her hat was positively rakish. She was younger than Charlotte, only just approaching forty, and had always been slender. Her fair hair had a deep wave to it, the finer tendrils curling delicately. With her porcelain skin and wide blue eyes she had a refinement approaching beauty, and she never failed to make the best of it.

Charlotte felt a little drab beside her, even though her skirt had the latest cut, with five pieces making the fullness fall very gracefully to the back. But it was an ordinary terra-cotta in color. She would have added a cape, but she had little spare income to spend on memorable clothes she could not afford to be seen in next year, and the year after, and probably after that, too.

She hugged Emily quickly and stood back to admire her. "That's wonderful," she said sincerely. "You manage to make winter look as if it is fun."

Emily smiled suddenly, lighting her face, and only then did Charlotte realize that Emily had looked tired the moment before. She made no remark on it. The last thing any woman wanted to hear was that she did not look fresh. It was almost as bad as being told one looked ill, and approaching the worst of all—old.

Charlotte reached for her hat, a rich brown ordinary felt one. It was nothing like as beautiful as Emily's, but it did suit her richer coloring, and she knew it.

They had an excellent luncheon. As always, it was Emily's gift. They had become so used to that over the years that they ceased to argue about it, even though since Pitt's promotion Charlotte's means were considerably improved. Still, they were not in the same sphere as Emily.

They spoke of family matters, how their children were faring. Besides Emily's son, Edward, she had a younger daughter, Evangeline. Children changed so rapidly there was always something to report.

They also spoke of their mother, Caroline Fielding, who had scandalized everyone by remarrying after their father's death—and to an actor, of all things! Not only that, but he was very considerably younger than she was. Life had changed radically for her. She had a whole new set of occupations and issues to engage her mind and her emotions, and to worry about. And she was happier than she had imagined possible.

"And Grandmama?" Charlotte said finally, over dessert. It was a subject she would have preferred to ignore, but it hovered between them unsaid, and with such weight that eventually she surrendered.

Emily smiled in spite of herself. "Nearly as appalling, as always," she said cheerfully. "Complaining about everything, although I think it is merely habit, and her heart is no longer in it. I caught her actually being nice to the scullery maid last week. I swear she'll live to be a hundred."

"Isn't she there already?" Charlotte asked waspishly.

Emily's eyebrows shot up. "For goodness' sake, do you think I asked her? But if you did, then please tell me the answer. I have to have some hope to cling on to!"

"What if she's only ninety?"

"Then say nothing," Emily responded instantly. "I couldn't bear it—not another ten years."

Charlotte looked down at the folded napkin and the empty plate. "It could be twenty . . ."

Emily said a word she would later deny ever having used, and they both laughed.

They rose from the table and had the carriage sent for, and agreed that a walk in Kew Gardens would be just what they would most enjoy.

The air was cold and bright, but with no wind at all it was very pleasant. Many others seemed to have had the same idea, as the gardens were scattered with people.

"I suppose you don't get the opportunity to help Thomas with cases anymore," Emily remarked, as they passed several very handsome trees. Neither of them bothered to read the plaques in front saying what they were, and which were their countries of origin. "All too secret," she added, referring back to Pitt's cases.

"Not much," Charlotte agreed. She heard the wistfulness in Emily's voice. She even felt a little of it herself. Looking back, some of their adventures, which had been dangerous or even tragic at the time, now were softened by memory, and only the better parts remained.

"But you have to know something about them," Emily insisted. "Don't you?"

Charlotte glanced sideways at her, just for a moment, and saw a hunger in her, almost a need. Then it vanished, and as they passed a couple of well-dressed women she smiled at them charmingly, full of confidence. The old Emily was there again, beautiful, funny, intensely alive, brave enough for anything.

"This particular case he is working on is very . . . shapeless," Charlotte relented and answered the question. "Thomas was called in because they found the body of a woman in a gravel pit up on Shooters Hill. For a little while they were afraid it might be Dudley Kynaston's missing maid . . ."

Emily stopped abruptly. "Dudley Kynaston? Really?"

Charlotte had a sharp stab of misgiving. Perhaps she was breaking a confidence to have told Emily so much?

"It's confidential!" she said urgently. "It could cause an awful scandal, quite unjustifiably, if people started to speculate. You mustn't repeat it! Emily . . . I'm serious . . ."

"Of course!" Emily agreed smoothly, beginning to walk again. "But I know something already. Jack said Somerset Carlisle was asking questions in the House about Kynaston's safety."

"Somerset Carlisle?" Now Charlotte was intrigued, and touched with a cold finger of fear. She had not forgotten about Carlisle and the resurrectionists either. "What else did Jack say?" she asked, attempting to keep the urgency out of her voice.

Emily's mouth tightened and she gave an elegant shrug of her slender shoulders, but it was a tiny movement, as if her muscles were tight. "Not very much. I asked him because I know Rosalind Kynaston a little, and I suppose it would really be her maid, not his. But Jack didn't answer me."

"Oh." It was a meaningless response, except to acknowledge that she had heard. Had she also understood? Was this one answer that closed Emily out perhaps because Jack did not know anything more, or what he did know was in confidence? Or had he just not been listening closely enough to realize that Emily wanted an answer?

They walked for a few moments without speaking again. They passed exotic trees, palms whose structure was utterly unlike the oaks and elms they were used to, or the soaring, smooth-limbed beeches. On the ground there were ferns, almost like green feathers a Cavalier might wear on his hat, but far larger. Emily buried her hands in her muff, and Charlotte wished that she had one.

"What is Rosalind Kynaston like?" Charlotte said to break the silence before it grew too deep to disregard.

Emily gave a tiny smile. "Ordinary enough, I suppose. We spoke little about anything in particular. She's older than I am. Her children are all away, married, or at school. I don't believe she sees them very often."

"There are hundreds of other things to talk about!" Charlotte protested.

"Gossip," Emily said tartly. "Have you any idea how boring that is? Half of it is complete rubbish. People make it up in order to have something to say. Who on earth cares anyway?"

It was mid-afternoon and the days were lengthening again. The sky was clear and the lowering light shone brightly and a little harshly on their faces. For the first time Charlotte noticed the very fine lines in Emily's once-perfect skin. Actually they were the marks of laughter, emotion, thought. They were not unkind. They even gave her face more character, but they were lines nonetheless. She did not for a second doubt that Emily had also seen them. Of course they were there in Charlotte's face, too—more of them, a little deeper—but she did not mind. Did she?

Pitt was a little older than she, and time had touched him with a brush of gray at the temples. She liked it. She was beginning to find youth less interesting, even callow at times. Experience lent depth, compassion, a sharper value to the good things. Time tested one's courage, softened the heart.

But did Emily see it that way? Jack Radley was remarkably hand-some, and her own age. Men matured nicely. To some people, women simply got older.

As if reading her thoughts and taking them further, Emily spoke again.

"Do you suppose that Kynaston was having an affair with the maid, and got her with child, or something? Then he had to get rid of her?" she asked.

"That's a bit extreme, isn't it?" Charlotte said with surprise. "She far more likely ran off with her young man."

"To a gravel pit, in the middle of winter?" Emily said with an edge of sarcasm. "Have you lost your imagination? Or do you think I have? Or is this your way of telling me you can't discuss it with me?"

Charlotte heard the hurt in her voice beneath the surface irrita-tion. She wanted to turn and study Emily's face more closely, but she knew that in doing that she would make an issue of something that was too delicate to force.

"We don't know that it was her body in the gravel pit," she said instead. "If it wasn't, and we accuse a government scientist of what amounts to murder, we are hardly guarding the safety of the state. In fact," she added, "we are doing the enemy's work for them."

Emily stopped, her eyes wide. "Now that is a really interesting thought."

Charlotte's heart sank. Unquestionably she had said too much now. How could she get out of it? She had never been able to fool Emily; they knew each other far too well. Emily, the youngest of the three sisters, had always been the prettiest, possibly a little spoiled, and forever trying to catch up. Socially and financially, it was many years since she had overtaken Charlotte. The memory of their elder sister, Sarah, murdered in the terrible affair of the Hangman of Cater Street, was one that Charlotte seldom touched. There was a pain of grief still left, and also regret over the stupid quarrels, and a nameless guilt that she was dead while Emily and Charlotte were alive, and happy. There was too much darkness in it, the kind of thick, heavy shadow that eats the light.

"That's all it is!" Charlotte said, more sharply than she had intended. "A thought."

Emily smiled, a sparkle in her eyes.

"Anyway, the person who's drawing attention to it is Somerset Carlisle, and he's hardly an enemy of the country. Nor is he stupid enough not to understand what he's doing."

"Maybe we could find out?" Emily suggested.

Charlotte had no quick answer. She was trying to extricate herself from the difficulty she had created by raising the subject at all. She shivered very visibly. "Could we do it walking again? I'm freezing standing here."

"You don't want to," Emily started to move, actually quite quickly, making conversation difficult. "Stop tiptoeing around me, Charlotte. You're as bad as Jack."

Charlotte stopped again, colder than she had been even the moment before. What was this about? Was Emily bored and losing interest in gossip and pointless parties? Or was it really about Jack? Certainly it had little if anything to do with Dudley Kynaston or the body in the gravel pit.

Emily was still walking away, though she had slowed down. Charlotte hurried to catch up with her. There was no point in being subtle now; in fact it might only make things worse.

"Do you really know Rosalind Kynaston?" she asked a little breathlessly. Charlotte wanted desperately to help her sister, and yet the slightest clumsiness would close off the opportunity, perhaps for a long time. She knew even as she was doing it that it might be dangerous, and Pitt would not approve, but she knew also that what she had thought was temper on Emily's part was really pain.

They had known each other all the life they could clearly remember. Sharing was woven through all childhood. It was nothing to do with toys, lessons, dresses, books; as little children they had run hand in hand. As girls they had shared secrets and laughter, quick squabbles. As young women there had been adventures, hope, falling in love, and heartbreak—all experienced together. Now, probably more than halfway through life, there was also disillusion, coming to terms with certain kinds of pain, inequalities that would always be there.

Emily shook her head. "Not very well, but that could be mended. In fact, it will have to be, if Jack takes a position with Dudley Kynaston. He's likely to be offered it. It must be a promotion." And yet there was no lift in her voice, no excitement.

Charlotte hesitated, then decided honesty was the only safe choice. "But you don't like it? Or is it just this messy maid business that worries you?"

Emily kept her eyes forward. "I don't know why you say that . . ."

"Shall I explain it?" Charlotte asked. "Or would you rather talk about something else?"

Emily pulled her mouth into a grimace. "I'm not as sure as he is that it would really be upward. I think it's rather more sideways. Honestly . . ." She gave a little sigh and looked away again. "Promotion carries some burdens as well. He could be away more . . . a lot more."

"Oh . . ." Charlotte immediately wondered whether Emily was going to miss him, or if she was more worried about what he might do far from home, and perhaps if he would miss her as much. As far as Charlotte knew, Jack had not been unfaithful to Emily, even in thought, but before marriage he had certainly been widely experienced, and had not hidden the fact. The novel thought of being completely faithful to one woman was part of the new adventure of marrying. So also, of course, was the equally novel experience of being financially far more than comfortable, with at least two very fine homes of his own, instead of living most of the year as a guest in someone else's house, there because he was charming, entertaining, and always agreeable—but never secure.

He was a member of Parliament commanding considerable respect from his peers, and being offered advancement entirely on his own merit. Emily had begun as the privileged one; now Jack made his own way. Charlotte realized with surprise that that was a bit like herself and Pitt, except that all she had possessed at the beginning was an excellent upbringing and the entrée to certain circles in society, no money at all.

The change that Pitt's promotions had brought delighted her, especially the respect he was now accorded by those who had previously condescended to him. The only disappointment was the inability to take part in his cases, no excitement, no detection. With a second jolt of surprise she realized that she, too, had become a trifle bored. She was definitely affected with a feeling that she was repeating the same tasks over and over, and perhaps they were not really either as useful or as interesting as she had once imagined.

Emily had waited as long as she was going to. "Is that all you have to say?" she demanded.

"I know what you mean about promotion," Charlotte answered. "It brings more money, and more responsibility, but not necessarily more satisfaction. And certainly not more fun." Then, afraid she had given away too much about herself, she hastened on. "What does Jack say?"

Emily gave a slight shrug. "Not a great deal. In fact, not enough. He says he wants the promotion, but it isn't the exact truth." She glanced at Charlotte, then away again, and kept on walking. Their surroundings were like some otherworldly forest, hard winter sunlight reflecting back off the glass-domed ceiling while groups of strangers walked under extraordinarily shaped trees and trailing vines, pretending they had not seen each other so they did not break the spell of being in another world.

"The trouble is," Emily went on, "I don't know which part of it is the lie, or what it's for. Is it self-protection, so if he doesn't get the promotion he can tell me he really doesn't mind? Or is he after the position for some reason he doesn't want me to know?"

Or possibly he just did not consult Emily anymore, not as he used to, but that was not a thought that Charlotte wanted to speak aloud. On the other hand, maybe he wanted the job very much, and he was afraid Emily's advice would be negative.

"Do you know much about it?" Charlotte asked.

"The position? Not a lot. After the last disaster, none of which was Jack's fault, I don't know whether to encourage him or not, and he isn't telling me enough for me to make an intelligent comment anyway. I . . .

I don't know whether he doesn't trust me, or if he doesn't care what I think . . ." Now the misery was so heavy in her voice she seemed on the brink of tears.

Charlotte said the only thing she could.

"Then we must find out. It is better to find out the worst and deal with it than to spoil something that wasn't actually the worst at all, by fearing and being filled with an unjust suspicion." She looked at Emily's face. "I know that's very easy to say, and you think I've never experienced it."

"You haven't!" Emily said sharply. "Thomas would no more look at another woman than grow wings and fly in the air! If you dare patronize me, so help me, I'll push you and your best dress into that pile of wet soil over there—and you'll never get the smell out as long as you live!"

"An excellent solution to all problems," Charlotte said disgustedly. "Push it into the manure. It'll make us all feel so much better—for about five minutes . . ."

"Ten!" Emily snapped. Then in spite of herself she began to laugh, even though the tears running down her face were not really those of amusement.

Charlotte put her arms around her and hugged her briefly, then stepped back. "We had better get started," she said in a businesslike way. "We must get to know Dudley and Rosalind Kynaston, and the possibility of Jack being offered a position with Kynaston is the perfect excuse."

Emily put her shoulders back and lifted her chin a little. "I shall begin immediately. I'm freezing standing here. I thought tropical jungles were supposed to be warm! Let's go home and have some tea by the fire, and hot crumpets soaked with butter."

"An excellent idea," Charlotte agreed. "Then I shall have to have a whole wardrobe of new dresses, a size larger."

"You could give me that one," Emily said, regarding it with pleasure. "I could have it taken in to fit me!"

Charlotte pretended to slap her, and she tripped over a piece of fallen branch, only just righting herself before she overbalanced. This time Emily really laughed, a swift, bubbling sound full of delight.

"How kind!" Charlotte said under her breath, then couldn't help laughing as well.

THE ARRANGEMENT WAS FULFILLED three days later when Charlotte and Pitt met Emily and Jack at the theater. There had been no further progress either in finding Kitty Ryder alive, or in identifying the body on Shooters Hill. Other news had overtaken the issues raised in Parliament by Somerset Carlisle's questions. However, it was only a matter of time before they would need to be addressed more urgently. Pitt had not deluded himself that the case was over, and Charlotte was quite aware of the tension in him above that of the usual concerns of his position.

It was the opening night of a new play, and therefore something of an occasion. Emily had been both fortunate and clever to obtain four tickets. Formal dress was required, which Pitt hated. On the other hand, he enjoyed seeing Charlotte wear a really beautiful gown of warm coral and russet tones with even a touch of hot scarlet in the brocade. It was brand new; the skirt was perfectly flat at the front and around the hips, not a line possible for everyone. It widened like a bell at the bottom, so cleverly was it cut. It was unadorned; the beauty of the fabric said everything.

Glancing at herself in the looking glass for a final time, Charlotte had to admit that even without expensive jewelry she looked striking. She could not afford such things and did not wish Pitt to be extravagant in giving them to her. She wore no necklace at all. This was rather a daring decision, but it only drew attention to her still smooth jawline, her slender throat, and the warmth of her natural coloring. Her thick dark chestnut hair was coiled upon her head, and there was a slight flush in her cheeks. Her pearl and coral earrings were perfect.

Pitt did not say anything, but the admiration in his eyes was more than sufficient. Even Jemima was impressed, although she was reluctant to say so.

"That's a nice gown, Mama," she muttered as Charlotte reached the top of the stairs. "Better than the green one."

"Thank you," Charlotte accepted the compliment. "I prefer it myself."

Pitt bit his lip to hide a smile.

"You look very handsome, Papa," Jemima added, this time more wholeheartedly.

Pitt did not imagine for a moment that he was handsome—distinguished at best—but in his daughter's eyes he was, and that was of far more importance. He gave her a quick hug and then followed Charlotte down to the waiting carriage, which had been hired for the occasion.

It was a gusty evening with an edge to the wind, but at least it was dry.

They arrived in good time, but the theater foyer was already quite crowded. From the moment they came up the steps into the arc of the glittering lights, Pitt saw people he knew, albeit professionally rather than socially. He was absorbed into nods of acknowledgment, brief words of greeting, a smile here or there. They were his acquaintances, not Charlotte's, which was a radical change from the early years of their marriage when she had known everyone and he had been there only because of her. She found herself smiling, walking with her head a little higher. She was proud of him . . . actually, very proud.

Charlotte was the first of them to see Jack. She was struck again by how handsome he was. The few extra years had given him maturity, a sense of something more than simple good looks. The sharp light was unkind in showing more than one might see in the gaslight or candlelight of a withdrawing room, but the few lines around his mouth and at the corners of his eyes gave him character.

Emily was a step or two away, speaking to someone else. Her fair hair gleamed, almost like an ornament in itself, making her diamond earrings unnecessary. She was wearing a gown of lilac pink threaded with silver and stitched with tiny pearls. It was gorgeous in itself, and of course had the perfect new skirt, but it did not flatter her as a cooler shade would have done. Also, it was going to clash with Charlotte's gown about as much as it was possible for two colors to detract from each other. Perhaps they should have consulted together first? But Charlotte had little choice, and Emily had a room full of gowns. The fashion rage at the moment was turquoise, and it would have been perfect for her!

Too late now. The only option was to carry it off with bravado. She walked over towards Emily, smiling as if delighted to see her.

Emily turned from her conversation to see Charlotte almost beside her, and a moment later they kissed cheeks lightly.

Jack turned also, and the appreciation in his eyes as he saw Charlotte was unmistakable. The evening was already off to a shaky start.

General polite greetings and trivial conversation continued for another few minutes until Jack seemed effortlessly to have guided them towards a couple who were striking-looking—at least the man was. He was tall with a mane of thick, fair hair and strong features. The woman was more ordinary, but beautifully dressed. Her face was gentle, but there was no fire in it, no passion. Her gown, on the other hand, was stitched—one might say encrusted—with turquoises and tiny beads of crystal, and of course was made with the new, five-piece cut of skirt as well; the full, bell-like bottom had yet more beads dancing just above the hem.

The man's eyes mirrored Jack's appreciation of Charlotte, then as he turned to Pitt, the light faded from them and he paled visibly.

"May I present my brother and sister-in-law, Mr. and Mrs. Thomas Pitt," Jack said courteously. "Mr. and Mrs. Dudley Kynaston . . ."

Kynaston swallowed. "Commander Pitt I have met. How do you do, Mrs. Pitt?" He bowed very slightly to Charlotte.

"How do you do, Mr. Kynaston?" she responded, trying to keep the sudden flame of interest out of her expression. "Mrs. Kynaston." She was fascinated. Neither of them was what she had expected. Her mind raced for something harmless to say. She must engage them in conversation of some sort. "I believe the play is quite controversial," she began. "I hope that is true, and not just a fiction to spark our interest."

Rosalind looked surprised. "You like controversy?"

"I like to be asked a question to which I don't have the answer," Charlotte replied. "One that makes me think, look at things I think I am familiar with, and see them from another view."

"I think you will find some of these views might make you quite angry, and confused," Kynaston said gently, glancing at his wife before turning to Charlotte.

"Angry, I can well believe," Pitt said with a discerning smile. "Confused, I think less likely."

Kynaston was startled, but he did his best to hide it.

Jack stepped in to bridge a rather embarrassed silence. He looked at Kynaston. "Have you seen reviews of the play, sir?" he asked with interest.

"Hotly varying opinions," Kynaston answered. "Which I suppose is why they are sold out this evening. Everyone wishes to make up their own minds."

"Or accept such an excellent excuse for a glamorous evening," Emily suggested. "I can see all sorts of interesting people here."

"Indeed," Rosalind smiled back at her. For a moment her face had a surprising vitality, as if a different person had looked out through her rather ordinary eyes. "I think that is the main reason for most of them coming."

Emily laughed and looked across an open space at a woman in a gown of outrageous green. "And an excuse to wear something one could not possibly wear except in a theater! It will probably still glow when the lights go down."

Rosalind stifled a laugh, but already she was looking at Emily as an ally.

A few moments later they were joined by a grim-faced man and a tall woman with flaxen hair that gleamed like polished silk, a porcelain fair skin, and amazing blue eyes. She led the way and joined the group as if she were quite naturally a part of it. The man stopped a yard or so away, and Charlotte felt Pitt stiffen beside her.

The woman smiled. She had perfect teeth.

"Commander Pitt. What a pleasant surprise to see you here." Her eyes slid to Charlotte, obliging Pitt to introduce her.

"Mrs. Ailsa Kynaston," Pitt said a little awkwardly.

For an instant Charlotte wondered if Pitt had made a mistake, using her Christian name; then she remembered that Bennett Kynaston was dead. She was Dudley's widowed sister-in-law. She acknowledged her with interest, and turned to the man now moving forward. He also seemed to know Pitt, but inclined his head to Charlotte politely. "Edom Talbot, ma'am," he said, introducing himself.

"How do you do, Mr. Talbot?" she replied, meeting his hard, steady eyes. She wondered how Pitt knew him, and whether it was as an ally or an antagonist. Something in his manner suggested the latter.

The conversation continued, mostly consisting of meaningless polite observations, the sort of thing one says to new acquaintances. Charlotte took part as much as was necessary, but mostly she studied Rosalind and Ailsa Kynaston. Ailsa must have been a widow for some time. She was striking to look at and clearly self-composed and intelligent. She could easily have married again, had she wished to. Had she loved Bennett Kynaston too much ever to consider such a thing?

But then, if anything happened to Pitt . . . Even the thought of it chilled her and caught the breath in her throat. Charlotte could not imagine marrying anyone else. She felt a sort of sympathy for the woman standing only a couple of yards from her. Looking at her now as the rest of them discussed what was rumored of the play, she could see a tension in the other woman's body, in the ruler-straight way she held her back and the proud tilt of her head.

"Mrs. Pitt?"

Suddenly she realized that Talbot had been speaking to her, and she had no idea what he had said. If she replied foolishly it would reflect on Pitt. Honesty was the only course open to her.

"I beg your pardon," she smiled at him as charmingly as she could, although she did not feel it in the least. "I was daydreaming and I did not hear you. I'm so sorry." She made herself meet his eyes warmly, as if she liked him.

He was flattered; she could see it in the sudden ease in his face. "The theater is the place for dreams," he replied. "I was asking if you agree with your sister's opinion of the leading actress's last performance."

"As Lady Macbeth," Emily put in helpfully.

Charlotte remembered reading a critic's response to it and hesitated, wondering if she could get away with quoting him. She would look such a fool, so much too eager to impress, if she were caught. "I read it was rather too melodramatic," she replied. "But I didn't see it."

"Because of what the critic said?" Talbot asked curiously.

"Actually that would have made me more inclined to look for myself," she replied without hesitation. Then she remembered what Emily had said of the performance. "But Emily did tell me a few other performances were . . ." She shrugged slightly, not willing to repeat the negative opinion.

"And of course you believed her?" Talbot said with a laugh.

"I had a sister, too," Ailsa said quietly, her voice tight with a strain she could not disguise. "Though she was younger than I, not older. But I would still have taken her word for anything . . ."

Charlotte saw Emily's face and the shock of realization in it—that Ailsa had just assumed *Charlotte* was the younger of the two. Jack was startled, then embarrassed. Clearly he had no idea what to say.

It was Pitt who broke the silence. "Unfortunately my wife lost her elder sister many years ago. It is a memory we don't go back to, because it was in very painful circumstances."

"My sister also," Ailsa said, looking at him with interest, almost challenge. "Forgive me for having raised the subject. It was clumsy of me. Perhaps we should go into the theater and find our seats."

THE FOLLOWING DAY CHARLOTTE put off a dressmaker's appointment and went instead to visit her great-aunt Vespasia or, to be more accurate, Emily's late husband's great-aunt. Outside of her direct family, she could think of no one in the world she liked better, or trusted more. February was still winter, in spite of the slightly lengthening afternoons, and they sat in front of the fire while rain beat against the windows out onto the garden. Charlotte put her feet as close to the fender as she could, in the hope of drying out her boots and the hem of her skirt.

Vespasia poured the tea and offered the plate of wafer-thin egg-and-cress sandwiches. "So you did not enjoy your visit to the theater," she observed, after Charlotte had mentioned it.

Charlotte had long since abandoned prevarication with Vespasia. In fact, she was more honest with her than with anyone else. She felt none of the emotional restrictions that she had with her mother, or with Emily. Even with Pitt she was sometimes a little more careful.

"No," she said, accepting the tea and trying to judge how soon she could sip it and let its warmth slide down inside her. Certainly she would burn herself with it now. "The conversation lurched from the edge of one precipice to the edge of another, and finally, for Emily, toppled over into the abyss."

"It sounds disastrous," Vespasia responded. "Perhaps you had better tell me the nature of this abyss?"

"That she isn't funny or wise or beautiful anymore. And, more specifically, that Jack is no longer in love with her. I suppose it is the sort of thing we all have nightmares about some time or other."

Vespasia looked very serious. She did not even pick up her cup. "Possibly," she replied. "Has something happened to Emily in particular, to make her feel this way?"

"I don't think so. But she is restless—bored, I think. We used to be involved in so much. Not always as exciting or pleasant as it seemed; looking back on it now, I know that, and I think Emily does, too. But being a good society wife, and an attentive mother to children who need you less and less, hardly exercises the imagination. And it is certainly not exciting . . ." She saw the understanding in Vespasia's expression and stopped. "I think at the heart of it she is very aware that she will soon be forty, and a part of life is slipping out of her grasp," she added.

"And Jack?" Vespasia inquired.

"Jack is as handsome as ever, in fact I think more so. A few added years suit him. He is not so . . . shallow."

"Ooh!" Vespasia gave a tiny wince, so small as to be almost invisible.

Charlotte blushed. "I'm sorry . . ."

"Don't be." Vespasia picked up her cup at last and took a sip, then offered Charlotte the sandwiches again before taking one herself. "Which particular precipice did Emily fall over yesterday evening?"

"Someone assumed that she was my older sister."

"Oh dear." Vespasia sipped her tea again. "Sibling rivalry is a snake you can never quite kill. I'm afraid Emily has been used to being a step ahead for rather too long. She is finding it hard to adjust to being a step behind."

"She isn't behind!" Charlotte said instantly.

Vespasia merely smiled.

"Well . . . she needs something to do, I mean something that matters," Charlotte tried again. "The way we used to when we could help with Thomas's cases, before they were secret."

"Be careful," Vespasia warned.

Charlotte thought of denying that the affair of Kynaston and the missing maid was in her mind, but she had never deliberately lied to Vespasia, and their friendship was too precious to begin doing it now, even to defend Emily.

"I will be," she said instead. It was halfway to the truth.

"I mean it, my dear," Vespasia's voice was very grave again. "I know Thomas is inclined to believe that Dudley Kynaston is not involved with this missing maid, and possibly even that the body in the gravel pit was not her. He may be right. That does not mean that Kynaston has nothing to hide. Be very careful what you do . . . and perhaps even more careful what you arrange for Emily to do. Her mind is filled with her own misgivings: her fear of boredom, and thus of becoming boring herself. Her beauty, to which she has been accustomed, beginning to lose its bloom. She will have to learn to rely on character and charm, style, even wit. It is not an easy adjustment to make." She smiled with deep affection. "Especially when your older sister has never relied on her looks and has already learned wit and charm, and now at the age when other women are fading, she is coming into bloom. Be gentle with her, by all means, but do not be indulgent. None of us can afford the errors that come with carelessness, or desperation."

Charlotte said nothing, but she thought about it very deeply as she took the last sip of her tea. Regardless of Vespasia's advice, and the wisdom she knew it held, she was going to involve Emily. She had to.

Stoker stood in front of Pitt's desk, his face bleak, and oddly bruised-looking.

"How did you find it?" Pitt asked, looking at the sodden wet tangle of felt and ribbon on his desk. It was barely recognizable as a hat. It was impossible to tell what color it had been, except from the tiny flash of red on what was left of a feather.

"Anonymous tip-off, sir," Stoker said quietly. "Tried to trace who it came from, but no luck so far. Just a note in with the post."

"What did it say, exactly?" Pitt asked. He was pursuing it as a matter of course. He did not seriously think it would prove of any value.

"Just that the sender had been out walking in the early morning and sat down on a frozen log, then saw this odd-looking mass of what appeared to be fabric. He poked it with a stick and then realized that it was a hat. He knew there'd been a body found up near there, and wondered if it might have any connection."

"Those words?" Pitt said curiously.

"No, I'm elaborating a bit." Stoker grimaced. "Word for word, it was more like 'Was sitting on a log up the gravel pit where that woman got found. Thought this might have something to do with it, like maybe it was hers.'"

"What kind of paper?" Pitt asked. "Pen or pencil? What was the writing like?"

Stoker's mouth pulled tight. "Ordinary, cheap paper, written in pencil, but no real attempt to disguise the hand. Bit of a scrawl, but perfectly legible."

"And the spelling?" Pitt asked.

"Right spelling," Stoker replied. "But there was nothing difficult in it. Simple words."

Pitt looked at what was left of the hat, and then up at Stoker. He did not need to ask the question, but he did anyway.

"Why do you think it's Kitty Ryder's?"

Stoker answered as if his throat were tight and he had to force the words out. "The red feather, sir. I got to know one of the barmaids at the Pig and Whistle who was a friend of Kitty's . . . Apparently they had tea together on their days off. Kitty really wanted a hat like that and she saved up to buy it. It was the red feather that mattered, because it was unexpected. In a way it didn't fit in with the rest of it, and it made people look, and smile. At least that's what Violet said—Violet Blane, the barmaid."

"I see. Thank you."

Stoker did not move. "We'll have to go back to Kynaston, sir."

"I know that," Pitt agreed. "Before I do that I want to go over all the statements he's made and everything we know about him. So far all we have is that Kitty worked for him, and that the woman in the gravel pit had his watch, which he says a pickpocket took, which his wife confirms. Which means nothing. We've searched the house and found nothing. None of the servants know anything of use. We've been over the cellars and the icehouse and found no trace of Kitty, or anything at all out of order. And the servants were in and out of there all the time anyway."

"Yes, sir," Stoker said flatly. "I've got notes as to what Violet said, and if you compare it with Mrs. Kynaston's diaries, and then his, I think you'll find a few places where it doesn't match."

Pitt did not answer, but opened one of the drawers beside the desk and took out his notes from the Kynaston diaries, then held out his hand for Stoker's notebook.

"Why didn't we find the hat when we looked before?" he asked.

"Probably too intent on the body," Stoker replied. "It was thirty feet away. If you didn't see the red feather you wouldn't have seen the rest. It looks like leaves on mud."

That was true. It had been found now only by chance.

"Thank you. I'll look at all the notes again, then I'll go and see Kynaston this evening. He won't be there at this time of day."

Even so, Pitt was a little early. He disliked having to harass the man again. He personally liked him, therefore he determined to finish this business tonight and get it over with. He did not want to give Kynaston the chance to come home, change, and then go out to dinner somewhere.

After meeting Kynaston and his wife and sister-in-law at the theater, this was even more unpleasant. He stood uneasily in Kynaston's morning room, staring at one bookshelf after another, unable to concentrate on the titles. Occasionally he paced. He had actually been invited by Mrs. Kynaston to wait in the withdrawing room, but he felt guilty about accepting it when his purpose was far from social.

He had been there less than half an hour when he heard Kynaston come in through the front door, and within minutes he was in the morning room, smiling.

Pitt's heart sank, and he felt his throat tighten. He walked forward from the fireplace.

"Good evening, Mr. Kynaston. I'm sorry to intrude on your time, but I have further questions I need to ask you."

Kynaston indicated the chair near the fire, and, when Pitt sat down, he took the other one himself. He looked slightly puzzled, but not yet alarmed.

"Has there been some further development?" he inquired.

"I'm afraid there has. We discovered a hat at the gravel pit, near where the body was found." He watched Kynaston's face as he spoke. "It's in a state that makes it impossible to identify, but it is an unusual shape, as much as we can make out, and quite clearly it still has a small red feather tucked in the ribbon where the crown meets the brim. It is distinctive, and one of Kitty's friends we have spoken to says that she had wanted exactly such a hat with a red feather—that she had spoken to her about it on several occasions."

Kynaston blanched, but he did not avoid Pitt's eyes. "Then it was Kitty . . ." he said very quietly. "Perhaps it was foolish, but I was still hoping that it wasn't. I'm so sorry." He took a deep, rather shaky breath. "Will you be looking for the young man she was walking out with? I believe he was a somewhat itinerant carpenter. He went where the work was a lot of the time." There was an edge to his voice, but it was not anger, and—as far as Pitt could judge—it was not fear either. Was he really so sure of himself, and his own safety?

"Of course," Pitt agreed. "We haven't searched diligently enough for him yet. Admittedly, I think we are guilty of also hoping that the body was not hers."

"But now . . . ?" Kynaston's mouth pinched at the ugliness of the thought, and with something that appeared to be pity.

"His name is Harry Dobson," Pitt replied. "And yes, we will ask the police farther afield to cooperate with us in finding him. So far we've looked only locally."

"If he's any sense he'll have gone away as far as possible," Kynaston observed with a grimace. "Liverpool, or Glasgow, somewhere with a lot of people where he can get lost. Although I suppose it's not hard to lose yourself in London, if you're desperate enough. Even ship out . . . go to sea. He's able-bodied."

"That's possible, too," Pitt admitted.

"Thank you for telling me." Kynaston gave a bleak half-smile. "I will inform my wife, and the staff. They'll be upset, but I imagine they will be half expecting it." He leaned forward as if to rise to his feet.

"I'm sorry, sir," Pitt said quickly. "But that is not all."

Kynaston looked taken aback, but he relaxed into the chair again, waiting for Pitt to explain.

Pitt drew in his breath and held Kynaston's gaze. "It is not just a matter of finding this wretched young man and charging him, which is a police matter. I'm Special Branch, and my concern is the safety of the state . . ."

Kynaston was now very pale, and his hands were clenched on the arms of his chair, knuckles white.

"And therefore exonerating you," Pitt continued. "And anyone else in this house. Unfortunately questions have been asked in the House of Commons as to your part in this, and also about your personal safety, under the circumstances. I have to be able to assure the prime minister that he has no cause for concern."

Kynaston blinked, and there was a long silence as the seconds ticked by on the clock on the mantel. "I see," he said at last.

"I've checked over all the questions I asked you previously," Pitt replied. He knew already that he was going to turn up something private and painful. It was there in Kynaston's face and in the stiff angles of his shoulders. He would like to have stopped his questioning now. Possibly what would be revealed had nothing to do with Kitty Ryder's death, but then it might have everything to do with it. He could not afford to believe anyone without proof.

"I have nothing to add," Kynaston told him.

"You have a few errors to correct, Mr. Kynaston," Pitt answered. "And a few omissions to fill in rather more fully. And before you do, sir, I would prefer to tell you in advance than embarrass you afterwards, I shall be checking with other people, because this matter is too serious to allow even unintentional misstatements of fact."

Kynaston did not answer. It had gone beyond the point of pretense that he was not deeply uncomfortable.

Pitt could have asked him the questions one by one, and tripped him in the lies—or if they were, the errors—but he loathed doing so. This had to be lethal, but it could be quick.

"Your diary states that you went to dinner with Mr. Blanchard on the evening of December fourteenth . . ." Pitt began.

Kynaston moved very slightly in his chair. "If I had the date wrong, is it really important?" he said reasonably.

"Yes, sir, because you left the house dressed for dinner, and according to our inquiries, you did not see Mr. Blanchard. Where did you go?"

"Certainly not anywhere with my wife's maid!" Kynaston said sharply. "Perhaps the dinner was canceled. I don't remember. Has Special Branch really got nothing better to do than this?"

Pitt did not answer his question. "And just over a week later, on December twenty-second, again you have Mr. Blanchard's name in your diary, and again you did not see him," he went on.

Kynaston sat absolutely motionless in the chair, unnaturally so. "I have no idea where I went," he replied. "But it was probably an engagement to do with a society I belong to, and couldn't possibly have anything less to do with my wife's maid." He swallowed, his throat jerking. "For God's sake, do you do this to everybody? Read their diaries and cross-question them as to whom they dined with? Is this what we pay you for?" There was a faint flush of color in his cheeks.

"If it has nothing to do with Kitty Ryder's death, then it will go no further," Pitt said, perhaps rashly. He felt grubby pursuing something that was clearly private, and embarrassing. Were it not, Kynaston would not be still trying to avoid offering an answer.

"Of course it has nothing to do with it!" Kynaston snapped, leaning forward suddenly. "If anyone killed her, then it was this wretched young man she walked out with. Isn't that obvious, even to a fool?" He looked away. "I apologize, but really, all this probing into my life is unnecessary and completely irrelevant."

"I hope so," Pitt said sincerely. He had to pursue this to the bitter end. "There are a few errors in your diaries, which is to be expected. We all get hours or dates wrong from time to time, or forget to note something at all, even do so illegibly. It is only the occasions when you left home, dressed for dinner, and consistently did not go where you stated that I am asking you about. There are at least a dozen of them in the last two months."

Kynaston's face now had colored.

"And I will not tell you, sir!" His voice wobbled a bit. "Except that it had nothing whatever to do with Kitty Ryder. For God's sake, man! Do you think I am dining out in full evening dress with a lady's maid?" He managed to sound incredulous, even though his voice cracked a little.

"I think you are going somewhere that you feel the need to lie about," Pitt answered. "The obvious conclusion is that it is with a woman, but that is not the only possibility. I would prefer to think that, rather than finding out something else you feel the need to keep secret from your family, and from the police, and Special Branch."

Kynaston blushed an even darker shade of scarlet. He caught Pitt's implication immediately. Pitt regretted it, but the man had left him no choice. He waited.

"I dined with a lady," Kynaston said in little more than a whisper. "I shall not tell you who it was, except that it was certainly not Kitty Ryder . . . or anyone else's . . . servant."

Pitt recognized that that was the truth, and also that Kynaston did not intend to reveal who it was. The question in Pitt's mind was whether Kitty Ryder might have known of it, and asked for some kind of favor not to tell her mistress. There was no purpose in asking Kynaston, though. He had already implicitly denied the affair had anything to do with Kitty. If he was lying, Pitt would have to catch him out later.

Pitt stood up. "Thank you, sir. I'm sorry I had to pursue such a thing, but when a woman is violently murdered, and her body dumped in a gravel pit, we don't have much choice."

Kynaston winced.

"That is more important than anyone's sensibilities as to privacy for their indiscretions," Pitt concluded.

Kynaston stood up also, but he said nothing more except to wish Pitt a good evening, icily and as a matter of form.

Outside in the cold, damp night, the wind was blowing clouds across the stars and streetlamps dotted occasionally here and there. Pitt was glad to walk briskly for some considerable distance. He was likely to find a hansom easily to take him all the way back across the river to Keppel Street.

What should he tell Talbot? That Kynaston was having an affair, but with some woman he could dine with in full formal clothes? Certainly not a servant of any kind. Someone else's wife? That was the obvious conclusion, although perhaps not the only one.

Had Rosalind Kynaston any idea?

Possibly she had. It was then conceivable that she did not mind, as long as he was meticulously discreet. Pitt knew of marriages where such agreements were made.

It did not answer the question as to whether the bright and observant Kitty Ryder had been aware of it. If so, then it had to have been deduction. There was no way in which she could be in an appropriate place to have observed such a thing.

Deduced from what? What could she have seen or heard . . . or overheard? A conversation on the telephone, perhaps? A letter left open? A coachman's gossip?

Was she really so quick, so very acute a judge? Was Kynaston so desperate and so callous as to beat a maid to death for her knowledge of his affair? He was embarrassed that Pitt had deduced it, but Pitt had seen no rage in him, not the slightest suggestion of violence of any sort, physical or political. He had not threatened Pitt's job or his position.

Was it necessary to report this to Edom Talbot?

He had reached the main road and found a hansom. He was sitting in it bowling along at a good speed by the time he reached the conclusion that it was, but he was still undecided exactly what he would say.

HE WAS STILL COLLECTING his evidence next day when a message came to his office requiring him to report immediately to Downing Street. It had to be Talbot, but how could he know what Pitt had learned the previous evening already? Surely that was impossible? Unless Kynaston had gone there ahead of Pitt, in order to—what? Complain? Deny the charge? Confess privately to Talbot who his mistress was, instead of to a mere policeman? Did he have far more influence in government than Pitt had imagined?

Pitt had no choice but to obey. He put his papers in a small case so that, if Talbot demanded it, he could show him the statements. Then he went out into the street to catch a hansom.

He sat all the way through the traffic, turning over in his mind how much he would tell. He would be finished if he were caught in a lie, but he might get away with an omission.

Why was he even thinking of concealing the truth from Talbot?

Because he did not believe that Kynaston had murdered Kitty Ryder to keep the secret of an affair. It was too extreme for a man who appeared to be neither violent nor particularly arrogant. Nothing Pitt had learned of him suggested either. And he had learned a considerable amount. Kynaston was proud of his family heritage. He had mourned the loss of his brother, Bennett, deeply; in fact the grief was still there in him, masked beneath the surface. To all outward appearances he had been a good father and a dutiful husband, if not a passionate one.

Certainly he liked a few luxuries in his dress and in his dining, but even with his favorite wines—of which there were several—no one had seen him seriously inebriated, and never in any circumstances aggressive.

His passion and imagination seem to have gone into his work. Pitt knew that only from the high esteem in which he was held by the senior naval officers who were involved with his inventions, though he had not heard this from them himself. It had been passed on to him by the appropriate authorities. Could that be an omission he needed to rectify? Underwater ships firing explosive missiles, invisible from the surface, might well be the warfare of the future. Britain was behind in the race, and—as an island—peculiarly vulnerable. She had no land borders with any other country across which to import food, raw materials, munitions, or any kind of help.

He arrived at Downing Street unusually nervous. His palms were sweating even in the cold, and he took his gloves off. Better to be dry, if numb.

He walked to the step and was let in almost immediately. There was always a policeman on duty and he was recognized without having to state his name.

Inside, he was shown immediately to the room in which he had met Talbot before. Talbot was waiting for him, pacing the floor. He swung around angrily as soon as Pitt came in and started to speak before the footman had closed the door, leaving them alone.

"What the devil are you playing at?" Talbot demanded. "I would prefer to think you're incompetent rather than deliberately attempting to deceive Her Majesty's Government. Did you not understand my distinct command that you report to me—here—any further development in the Kynaston case? What is it in that which is unclear to you?" His cheeks were red, his nose pinched at the nostrils, and his jaw tight. He glared at Pitt as if his fury were slipping out of his control.

"I was checking some of the evidence before I reported it to you," Pitt replied. Damn! That sounded so feeble, so obviously an excuse, and yet it was the truth. "I wished to—" he began again.

"You wished to evade the issue!" Talbot said furiously. "What about this bloody hat you found in the gravel pit?"

"It's not bloody," Pitt corrected him.

"God damn it, man! Don't you dare tell me when to swear and when not to! Who the hell do you think you are, you jumped-up—"

"There was no blood on the hat . . . sir," Pitt said between his teeth.

Talbot stared at him. "What the hell are you talking about?"

"There was no blood on the hat," Pitt repeated.

"That is totally irrelevant. Was it the maid's hat or not?" Talbot said slowly between his teeth, as if Pitt were simple.

"I don't know," Pitt replied. "But that is also irrelevant to Kynaston, unless we can prove that he had some illicit relationship with her, or that she knew of something else he was doing and threatened him."

"And you have basically proven that! The man is having an affair! But you did not think it necessary to report that fact to me, as I commanded you to," Talbot said grimly. "I wonder if you would care to explain that? I rather think we are back to the beginning again." His voice grated, full of ragged edges. "Are you so arrogant that you think you can take decisions on this matter without reference to your superiors, or have you some reason of your own for protecting Kynaston from the truth? Just how well do you know him? You force me to ask."

Pitt felt the heat rise up his face. Any answer he could give was going to sound like an excuse. And yet if he had come to Talbot earlier, before he was certain of Kynaston's affair, he would have been equally to blame for maligning an important man in the government's plans for naval defense, not to mention the moral and civil wrong of false accusation. It would have brought Special Branch into disrepute and made its future work harder. It might even have earned Pitt's own removal from leadership.

A sudden horrible thought flashed into his mind that this was the purpose of Talbot's rage. This was an excellent platform on which to build the means of getting rid of Pitt altogether. He drew in his breath to frame some kind of a reply just as the door opened and Somerset Carlisle came in, closing it quietly behind him. He was older than when they had first met, but the remarkable arched brows and the quirky humor were both still there on his face. It was only the deepening of the lines that changed him, made one aware that it was over a decade since that first meeting.

"Ah! Pitt," he said cheerfully. "Delighted to find you here."

"You are interrupting a private conversation—" Talbot snarled at him.

"Yes, of course I am," Carlisle cut across the rest of his remark. "Just wanted to tell Pitt that I found the piece of information he was looking for." He smiled at Pitt, gazing straight into his eyes. "You were quite right, of course. The hat was no more Kitty Ryder's than it was mine! Some damn fool was wanting to distract attention from his own rather stupid mistakes . . . drinks locally now and then, so he knew about the poor woman's disappearance, and the body you found in the gravel pit, of course."

Talbot tried to interrupt, but Carlisle carried on without taking the slightest notice of him.

"Knew she'd had a hat like that, poor girl, and bought one the same. Put a red feather in it." He smiled even more widely and reached his hand into his pocket. He pulled out a rather crumpled piece of paper. "Got the receipt. You'll see it's dated for the day before your informant found the hat."

"And the timing of all this is pure coincidence, I suppose?" Talbot said sarcastically.

"Hardly," Carlisle replied with exaggerated patience. "He was the one who found it!"

Talbot was standing motionless, his face filled with bafflement and even further mounting anger.

Carlisle was still smiling, as if the atmosphere in the room were one of cooperation, not open enmity.

"Policeman's job to be skeptical," he went on, now looking at Pitt. "Good thing you were. Made a highly embarrassing mistake if you'd reported to Downing Street that the body was Kitty's on evidence discovered by the man who put it there. Looked a bit of a fool. Not good for the reputation of Special Branch." He shook his head. "No doubt some journalist would have got hold of it and put it all over the front pages. Somehow or other they find these things." He shrugged. "And then, of course, they put all kinds of other bits of fact—and imagined fact—together and come up with accusations. Too late to apologize when you've ruined a man."

Pitt had recovered from his amazement, although he had no idea how Carlisle had known he was here, or become involved in the matter at all.

"Exactly," he agreed aloud.

Talbot was still fighting the issue, his body stiff, his face pale.

"What unbelievable good fortune that you happened to be aware of all this . . . eccentric behavior, Mr. Carlisle," he said, the sarcasm still in his voice. "I suppose we should be grateful some extraordinary chance took you to . . . what?" His voice became even more grating. "How was it you learned that this particularly irresponsible man knew of Ryder's passion for a hat with a red feather, and also exactly where her body was found, and that he should purchase such a hat, plus feather, of course, and place it there? Such a piece of good fortune seems . . . beyond belief." He pronounced the words slowly, giving every syllable emphasis.

Carlisle merely smiled a little more widely.

Pitt's heart was racing, but he dared not intervene. He had no explanation either.

"And of course that you should also, purely by chance, know exactly where Commander Pitt was," Talbot went on. "And race here just in time to rescue him from having to give me some explanation as to why I had to hear of the whole apparent farce from someone else, and demand he explain to me why he had not reported to me, as I had instructed him. I suppose you have answers for all that also?"

Carlisle spread his hands in an elegant gesture, rather like another shrug of his shoulders.

"The man who bought the hat is a constituent of mine," he said calmly. "He's been in trouble a few times for trying to draw attention to himself."

"Kitty Ryder's desire for a hat with a red feather was not in the newspapers," Talbot said icily. "And your constituency is miles from Shooters Hill."

Carlisle laughed. "For heaven's sake, man! People move around. He's a hound for scandal. He went and drank at the Pig and Whistle. He asked questions, listened to gossip. And as to finding Pitt here—I called his office and was told he's been sent for to come here. Not exactly the work of a genius." His eyes were bright, his arched eyebrows even higher. "Anyway, I'm delighted if I've saved you embarrassment—not to mention poor Kynaston." He turned to Pitt. "If your business here is finished, I'll walk to Whitehall with you."

"Yes . . . thank you," Pitt agreed quickly, then turned to Talbot. "I shall keep you informed of anything I learn that is relevant to Mr. Kynaston, especially should we find out the identity of the woman in the gravel pit. Good morning, sir." And without waiting for Talbot to answer or give him leave to go, he turned and followed Carlisle out of the door, through the hallway, and into the street.

They walked several paces along the quiet pavement, past the usual police presence, since Downing Street was the home not only of the prime minister but also of the chancellor of the exchequer.

"Was any of that true?" Pitt asked quietly as they turned into Whitehall.

Carlisle's expression barely changed. "Close enough," he replied.

"Close enough for what?" Pitt demanded, still uneasy.

"To pass muster, should Talbot choose to have it investigated," Carlisle replied. "Don't ask anything further, because you don't want to know, and I certainly don't want to tell you."

"Does the hat have anything to do with Kitty Ryder?"

"Nothing at all, except that she did want one."

Pitt let his breath out slowly. "I'm extremely grateful."

"You should be," Carlisle agreed pleasantly. "Don't cross Talbot; he's a nasty bastard. Doesn't mean Kynaston's innocent, of course. Just can't hang a man on a manufactured piece of evidence. And . . . and I wouldn't like to see you replaced by someone a lot worse. Good luck! Watch your back!" And with that he turned and walked in the opposite direction, leaving Pitt to go east, and down to the river.

It was only as he was nearing the riverbank and could hear the slurping of the incoming tide that Pitt allowed the wave of relief to run through him, and with it, a sudden warmth. He realized how close he had come to giving Talbot a reason to dismiss him. Of course he knew that many people did not find him a suitable person to follow Victor Narraway, who was undoubtedly a gentleman.

Pitt himself was the son of a disgraced gamekeeper, transported to Australia for theft when Pitt was a boy. He could scarcely remember him, only the shock and the indignation, his protest of innocence that was disregarded, then his mother's grief. She and Pitt had been allowed to remain in the large country estate; indeed, Pitt had been educated with the son of the house, to encourage the boy. It would not do for a servant's son to outdo the heir, and it was felt this might prevent such a thing. Although looking back on it now, Pitt thought that that had been an excuse to mask a kindness that was always intended.

Still, it was hardly a background to equal Narraway's, or one that a man such as Talbot—and to be honest, many others—would be happy with. He must remember that, and not let anger or complacency lead him into error again. Carlisle had rescued him this time, and Pitt was beginning to appreciate now just how much. He had been gracious enough to make light of it, as if it were in his own interest, rather than in Pitt's, but that was a courteous fiction.

That there was also an antipathy between Carlisle and Talbot was clear, and Pitt would be wise to remember that and avoid being caught in the middle. Nevertheless, his step was light as he made his way to the ferry.

STOKER SAT AT THE kitchen table at his sister's house. He quite often came here on his days off. King's Langley was an ancient and very pleasant village in Hertfordshire beyond the outskirts of London, about an hour's journey on the train. Gwen was the only family he had left, and quite apart from that, he really liked her. All his best memories were somehow attached to her. She was two years older than he and had looked after him in the earliest times he could recall. It was she, more than the schoolteacher, who had taught him to read. She was the one who encouraged him to join the navy, and to whom he had recounted his adventures, enlarging the good and mostly skipping over the bad. Perhaps that was why he remembered the good so clearly, trying to share it with her, seeing her eyes widen, her holding her breath as she waited for the next turn in his stories.

It was also Gwen who had traveled miles by train, spending the little money she had, to come and visit him in hospital when he was injured. And of course it was Gwen who told him off when she thought he was wrong. She who had brought him the news of their mother's death, and she who nagged him about putting flowers on the grave, saving for the future, and even occasionally about getting married.

Now she was cooking dinner for her husband and children when they came home. He watched her with pleasure because the kitchen was warm and smelled of baking pastry and the clean sheets drying on the airing rail above them. There were strings of onions hanging in the corner and a small dresser with plates on it, and two copper pans, the pride of her possessions. The shine and the color of them were too good to spoil with overuse.

He must get her something else pretty some time. It was too long since he had last done so. Her husband was a hard worker, most of the year at sea, as Stoker himself had been. But money had a long way to go to support a wife, and four children who grew out of their clothes and were always hungry.

Stoker was full of thoughts of Kitty Ryder, and relief that the hat with the red feather was not hers. He had not realized until Pitt told him about Talbot, and Carlisle's rescue of the situation, that he had been sad at her death. It was ridiculous! He had never even seen the woman!

Gwen was looking at him.

"What's the matter, Davey?" she asked. "You've got a face on you like a burst boot! You said the hat wasn't hers. She could still be alive."

He looked up. "I know. But if she is, why doesn't she come forward and say so? Everybody in London knows we're trying to identify the body in the gravel pit and that there's speculation it's her. And don't tell me she can't read! I know she can."

"Are you staying to dinner? You're welcome, you know. You're always welcome," she assured him.

He smiled at her, quite unaware how it lit his face. "I know. And no, I'm not. I've got to be on duty tomorrow." That was not strictly the truth; he chose to be. But he had also made a good assessment of the meat in the stew and how if he accepted a portion, someone else would go without—almost certainly Gwen herself.

"They work you too hard," she criticized.

"We've been over that," he reminded her. "I like the work, Gwen. It matters. I don't tell you much about it because it's secret. But Special Branch keeps us all safe, if we do it right."

"What about this new guv'nor, Pitt?" she asked. "Does he work as hard as you do? Or does he go back to a nice big house somewhere with servants to look after him and parties to go to?"

Stoker laughed. "Pitt? He's not a gentleman, Gwen. He's an ordinary man, like anyone. Worked his way up. He's got a decent home, on Keppel Street, but no mansion. You'd like his wife. I don't know her well, but she's not all that different from you." He looked around the room quickly. "Kitchen's bigger than this one, but like it; smells of clean laundry and bread as well."

She looked at him and smiled back. "So why the face? And you might be Special Branch, an' all that, but you never could fool me, and you can't now, so don't waste both our time trying it."

"Where is she?" he said simply.

"In love with the man she ran off with?" she suggested, reaching out to pour him another cup of tea.

He raised his eyebrows. "It's been over four weeks since she disappeared. No one's that much in love."

She shook her head. "You know, Davey, sometimes I worry about you. Have you ever been really in love? You haven't, have you? When you are, you can't see anything else, believe me. You walk into a hole in the road, because your head's in the air and your eyes full of dreams. Would you like some cake?"

"I will gladly take the cake. But as a rule I try to avoid falling into holes in the road," he answered.

She stood up, still looking at him. "You've got your head screwed on all right, so tight it's a wonder you can fasten your shirt collar." She opened the pantry cupboard and took out the cake, cutting a really large wedge for him and putting it on a plate.

"Thank you." He accepted the cake, taking a bite of it immediately. "That isn't the answer, though, Gwen," he said with his mouth full.

"She knew something, and that's why she ran away. And the only thing that'd be safe for her is if she came out from wherever she's hiding and told people. Then there'd be no point in hurting her, it would only prove she was right."

"For heaven's sake, use your common sense!" she said exasperatedly. "Who's going to believe a lady's maid over a lord, or his wife?"

"He's not a lord, he's an inventor of some sort, working on experiments with new undersea weapons."

"Under the sea?" she said incredulously. "To kill what? The fish?"

"Ships," he said succinctly. "Hole them under the waterline, where they'll sink."

"Oh." She paled. "And you're saying he isn't a gentleman either?"

"No! He's a gentleman, and he's got money and influence. And I suppose you're right, she'd have to have proof, and maybe she doesn't. I've got to find her, Gwen. I've got to prove what happened to her, I just don't know where else to try!"

She looked at him as if he were five again, and she were seven. "What do you know about her?" she said patiently.

He described what he knew of her appearance. "And she came from the country," he added. "Somewhere in the west. The local police looked to see if she'd gone home, and she hasn't."

"Well, she wouldn't, if she were hiding, would she!" Gwen said, shaking her head. "But she might go somewhere like it."

"We thought of that. We can't find a trace of her at all." He heard the note of panic in his voice and deliberately lowered it. "She was very handsome to look at, easy to notice. And she was quick, and sometimes funny, so the other staff said, and her friends at the local pub. They were all surprised she took up with Harry Dobson. Said he wasn't anywhere good enough for her."

"Nobody ever is," she said with a sudden wide smile. "But we love you anyway!"

She was teasing him and he relaxed a little, taking several more bites of the cake. She was a good cook, and the taste of it carried him back in memory to being home on leave from the sea, and sitting in another kitchen, before she moved out here to King's Langley. Everything had been different there—sparser, poorer, much smaller, back door opening into a small, grubby yard—all except the cake. She never stinted with cake.

"She liked the sea," he went on. "Used to carve little boats, real little tiny ones, out of soft wood. What kind of a man would kill her just because she couldn't help seeing that he was having an affair? And he was. Pitt caught him in lies and he had to admit it. But Pitt doesn't think Kynaston killed her. I think he's off on another world sometimes."

Gwen frowned. "It doesn't make sense," she agreed. "Who's she going to tell?"

"His wife," he replied.

"Oh, for goodness' sake!" she said impatiently. "Do you think she doesn't know? What's she going to do about it? Nothing—except pretend she didn't see. It's not a crime, just a betrayal. And nobody else will want to know, I can promise you that. It could upset all sorts of apple-carts to be admitting to that kind of thing . . . unless . . ." She stopped.

"Unless what?" He put the last of the cake into his mouth.

"Unless it's with someone that really matters?" she answered thoughtfully. "Someone whose husband would throw her out. That could happen, and then she'd be ruined. That's . . . possible . . . I suppose."

"How do you know about things like that?" he said curiously.

"For goodness' sake!" she repeated. "I was a laundress before I got married! I didn't live all my life inside a box with the lid on, Davey!" She stood up again. "You'd better go and catch your train, before it gets late and you're out half the night. And don't leave it so long next time." She came around the table and hugged him. He felt the warmth of her body, the softness of her hair, and how strong her arms were when she clung to him. For a moment he hugged her hard in return, then put on his coat and went out the door, into the yard, and up the steps without looking back at the lights, or to see her standing there watching him.

While Stoker was in the train rattling through the darkening countryside back to London, Pitt was in the chair beside the fire in

Vespasia's sitting room with its warm, pale colors. He was so comfortable it was an effort to keep awake. The fire was burning low, its embers glowing, the light reflecting in the facets of the small crystal vase in which were a few delicate snowdrops. He was startled at how richly their perfume filled the room. There were faint sounds of footsteps in the hall, and now and then the patter of rain on the window. It was only the urgency of the matter weighing on his mind that prevented him from relaxing.

"Suspiciously, at the very last moment," he finished, describing the events of his rescue by Somerset Carlisle.

"And the very best moment," she added drily. "That sounds exactly like Somerset, although unusually fortunate, even for him. I see that troubles you . . ."

"I've been thinking about it," Pitt admitted. "Carlisle was the one who had asked the question in the House, making the whole issue far more public than it had been before. And yet he not only rescued me from Talbot, he rescued Kynaston, for the time being, from a situation that at the very best would have been embarrassing. At worst it would have brought him into suspicion of having killed and mutilated Kitty and put her body in the gravel pit. Why?"

"Somerset is a good man," Vespasia said quietly, her mouth curving in a sweet smile, "if, as you say, a trifle eccentric now and then."

"That is a magnificent understatement," he observed.

She smiled very slightly. "I only overstate things when I am so angry I have lost my vocabulary," she answered.

He raised his eyebrows. "I don't believe you ever lose your vocabulary. I have seen a fluency from you that would stop a horse in full gallop, or freeze a duchess at twenty paces."

"You flatter me," she protested, but through laughter. "I would like to think that his principal purpose was to make a fool of Edom Talbot, a man he loathes, but I appreciate that that could be no more than an agreeable side effect." The amusement in her face died completely. "But you say that Dudley Kynaston is unquestionably having an affair, and that you think it is possible that Kitty, being bright, observant, and no doubt bored, may have been aware of this? You are certain, I presume?"

"The evidence is there, and he did not deny it," Pitt said unhappily. "I just don't believe he would kill his wife's maid because she had deduced that he was lying about where he had been. Either that is not the case at all, and is merely incidental, or there is something far more important that I'm missing. And where did she learn it? Why won't she come forward now, or at least send some kind of a message that she's alive? Maisie said she could read and write!"

"Who is Maisie?"

"The scullery maid." Pitt remembered Maisie's eager face. "Kitty was her . . . example. She not only liked her, she admired her. Maisie means to learn to read."

"Just how ambitious was Kitty?" Vespasia asked doubtfully. "Sufficient to improve herself, but not so rash as to exert a little unwelcome pressure? Are you sure, Thomas?"

"What could it gain her to attempt blackmail on Kynaston? Not a lot more than dismissal, and possibly a police charge. And she can't have been stupid enough to imagine anything else. The magistrates would not be very kind to her. They can't be seen to allow servants to gather information about their masters and then use it that way." He smiled ruefully and almost without bitterness.

"Of course not," she agreed, her face reflecting an unaccustomed sadness. "It would be the end of the world, as most of us know it. And yet it will certainly happen, inch by inch. Nothing is more inevitable than change, for better and for worse. Perhaps it is the approaching close of the century, but I feel it is a very mixed prospect. Events seem to be moving faster and faster."

He looked at her face. It was still beautiful, still full of passion and vitality, but he also knew there was a fragility in it, a power to be hurt that he had not appreciated before. Her century was ending, and she could not know what lay ahead.

Could Pitt say anything that would comfort Vespasia? Or would it be clumsy, and in reality make her more fragile?

He changed the subject completely. "Do you trust Somerset Carlisle?"

She gave an abrupt little laugh, light and full of generous amusement.

"My dear! What a question. That depends very much upon what we are talking about. To be honest, yes, I do. To be generous and risk anything at all for what he believes? Unquestionably. To have values the same as mine, and to behave responsibly? Not in the slightest."

"I owed him a lot today," Pitt answered. "I think Edom Talbot would be delighted to see the back of me from Special Branch. I am not the sort of man he judges suitable for the position, neither intellectually nor socially, especially the latter."

"I have no doubt of it," she agreed. "For all that he is not quite a gentleman himself, he intends to become one. And yes, you owe Somerset a considerable debt. Now if you do not mind, my dear, I have plans for this evening, and I need to get ready."

"Of course." He rose to his feet immediately. "Thank you for your advice, as always." He leaned forward and kissed her very lightly on the cheek, then felt instantly embarrassed for the familiarity of it. He could not remember having had the courage to do it before.

WHEN PITT LEFT, VESPASIA turned to the telephone and found herself curiously nervous. Beneath the muslin ruffles of her cuff, her hand was trembling a little. She steadied it and picked up the phone. When the operator asked whom she wanted, she gave her Victor Narraway's number.

It rang three times, and she was about to change her mind when he answered, giving simply his name.

She cleared her throat.

"Good evening, Victor. I hope I am not troubling you?"

"I am not certain how to answer that and be both courteous and truthful," he said with a degree of amusement that she could discern, even in a voice distorted by the machine.

"It is serious enough, I think, that you may dispense with courtesy," she replied. "And not all of the truth may be necessary . . ."

He laughed. "You always trouble me, but I should be bored without it," he said. "What is it that is so serious? I presume I may help? Or at least that there is that possibility?"

She was relieved, but also nervous, which was extremely unusual for her. She was accustomed to being in control of any social situation.

"Will you dine with me, and I can explain to you the situation I believe I am observing?"

"I should be delighted," he said immediately. "May I suggest a place where we may eat well, but not fashionably, and therefore be able to discuss without interruption whatever it is that troubles you?"

"I think that would do very nicely," she accepted. "I shall dress accordingly."

"You will still cause a stir." The idea seemed to please him. "You cannot help it, and I should regret it bitterly if you tried."

For once she could think of no suitable answer, except to say that she would see him in just over an hour.

In spite of what she had said about dressing quite ordinarily for dinner, she did not do so. Indeed, she took great care, choosing a gown of a dark blue-gray so soft that in the shadow it looked almost indigo. The line of the neck and the sweep of the skirt were both very flattering, and cut in the fashion of the moment. Deliberately she wore no jewelry, except very small diamond drop earrings. Her shining silver hair was ornament enough.

In the carriage as it made its way through the windy darkness of the streets, she was deep in thought, turning over and over in her mind the things that Pitt had told her.

There was a major part missing, in the sense of it. Now in the flickering light and shadow of the carriage interior, she could no longer deny that. She was almost certain who it was that had made it appear that Dudley Kynaston was deeply involved in the disappearance, probably even the murder of Kitty Ryder. The thought was painful.

She did not regard Kynaston as a close friend. She had met him perhaps half a dozen times, but she did know of his importance to the navy, even if not any of the details of his particular skills. Remembering his face, his voice, his pleasant but slightly detached manner, she found it hard to imagine any circumstances in which he would feel a sufficiently violent and totally uncontrolled emotion that he would sink to such an act. And why, for heaven's sake? What could possibly be gained by it?

If his marriage were precious to him, would he have carried on a dalliance with a maid, however handsome she was? Even if his wife were too ill to offer him the usual comfort, or was of a chill disposition and refused him, most men had more sense than to take their pleasure within their own households—it being discovered would be disastrous. However, such a thing would usually be regarded as shabby, not ruinous. One could dismiss a maid easily enough. All it required was an accusation of petty theft, or even unseemly conduct. Many maids had found themselves on the street for less, and without a "character" with which to gain another position.

The carriage slowed as traffic became more congested. It happened frequently, but now it annoyed her because she was anxious to speak with Narraway.

It seemed far more likely that Kitty Ryder had been too clever and too observant for her own good. Even so, had she been reckless enough to try blackmail? What Pitt had said suggested that she was intelligent. A wise girl would have affected to know nothing, and expected in due course to be rewarded for her loyalty and discretion—as she no doubt would have been.

According to Pitt, Kynaston had admitted having an affair, but with a woman of at least his own social class. But his wife's lady's maid was not in a position to know who the woman was, surely?

Would it ruin the woman if it became public? Depending upon whose wife it was, that was indeed possible, if unlikely. Vespasia could think of a few candidates.

And of course there was the far more serious alternative: that the woman in question was the wife of someone who could ruin Kynaston's career and thwart any ambitions he might have for higher office. No reason would ever be given. Some might guess, but that would not save Kynaston.

It was still a stretch of coincidence and imagination to connect it with the disappearance and probable death of Rosalind Kynaston's maid.

The traffic cleared, and once again they were rattling through the early evening darkness. Vespasia was certain that there was some other crucial part of the picture that she had not seen, something that would change it entirely. It must be something that would explain why Somerset Carlisle, her friend for so many years, had asked questions in the House of Commons as to Dudley Kynaston's safety, with regard to the apparent dramatic and brutal murder of one of his servants.

And now it appeared that Somerset had also most fortunately rescued Pitt from a profound embarrassment, and even fatal damage to his career, when facing Edom Talbot in Downing Street. His appearance, so perfectly timed, was explainable. If he had called Pitt's office, as he had claimed, Pitt's staff would know where he was, because he would not have left without telling them. As for the other information, Somerset was a member of Parliament, therefore anything known to the House of Commons might well be known to him, even if it were not said openly where the public might hear.

But there were other matters, like his apparently close following of the case of Kitty's disappearance. Then there was the coincidence that a member of his constituency, which was many miles from Shooters Hill, should follow the case even more closely, and drink at the Pig and Whistle, an hour's journey from his home, in order to learn that Kitty had wanted a hat with a red feather in it. Then, according to Somerset, he had gone to a third area and bought just such a hat. He had also known where to place it, once again in Shooters Hill, in the right spot to have been missed by the police in their search around where the body was found, and yet still close enough that it was easy to believe it was hers.

And then there was the coincidence that someone found it, when only the red feather was noticeable in the surrounding mud and tussocks of dead grass.

No simple event in itself was unbelievable, just all of it together, particularly when coupled with the long history she knew of Somerset Carlisle. He had been willing to help Pitt, at her request, using his considerable influence in Parliament, even at times when it was embarrassing or inconvenient to himself. That had been true ever since Pitt had investigated the bizarre affair of the decently buried corpses that kept reappearing around Resurrection Row.

What could Dudley Kynaston have done to warrant this seeming setup? Whatever Rosalind's character, betrayal of a wife was hardly unique, if ugly. Certainly it was not motive to stir Somerset to such action.

Or was Vespasia wrong in suspecting Somerset's involvement at all? She would very much like to think so.

She arrived at the restaurant. It was one of Narraway's favorites, small and elegant with windows that overlooked the river.

Narraway was already waiting for her, as she had expected. He was always fifteen minutes early, just to avoid any possibility of her having to wait for him. He rose to his feet and came towards her, his face lit with pleasure. He was still as lean and straight as when she had first met him, although his thick black hair had more gray in it than even a year ago. He was a little taller than she, but she was tall for a woman, and carried every inch of her height as if she balanced a crown on her head.

He took both her hands, lightly, and kissed her on the cheek. Then he stepped back and regarded her with his usual intensity, as if he could read not her thoughts but her emotions.

"Is it this miserable business of Pitt's?" he asked quietly as they were escorted to their table.

"You know me too well," she replied. "Or have I been reduced to the periphery of social life where I can have no other anxieties?" she said with a smile. She intended to keep the conversation light. Oddly, she still found herself nervous, not willing to trespass onto emotional ground.

"I know you well enough to be perfectly aware that there are issues in society that might interest you, or annoy you," he answered. "But your heart is engaged only where you care. Which suggests your family . . . even if slightly extended." There was a flicker of something in his face that she could not identify, except as a kind of sadness, there and then gone again. Narraway had never married, and he had no family left. She had never thought it appropriate, or even kind, to inquire further. That there had been lovers come and then gone again, she knew perfectly well. It was not something one discussed.

They had been seated and ordered their meal before she answered his question.

"Thomas is in something of a cleft stick," she said, sipping her wine, which had been brought just before the hors d'oeuvres. "The evidence seems to indicate that Dudley Kynaston is involved in this poor servant's death, and yet they have no definite proof that the body is hers, even though they cannot find her alive. Kynaston admits to having an affair, but with someone of his own social rank, and Pitt does not believe he would kill anyone to conceal that."

"And you?" Narraway asked, watching her reaction.

"It seems a little . . . excessive," she replied. "And I agree, I had not thought Kynaston a man of such . . ."

"Stupidity?"

"I was going to say 'passion.'"

"Sometimes people have far more passion than they appear to," he said quietly, his eyes on her face, tracing the outlines of it as if to make it indelible in his mind. "Everyone else thinks them cerebral and a trifle cold because they keep their feelings hidden."

She looked back at him. She wanted to press for his precise meaning and was afraid to. It would leave her exposed as caring too much for the answer.

"Do you think Kynaston is one of them?" she asked instead, taking another sip of the wine. "I find I know less about him than I thought. I remember his brother, Bennett. He died young . . . well under forty. He had great promise, so it was particularly upsetting. Dudley took it very hard."

"I remember," Narraway said thoughtfully. "But that was several years ago—eight or nine, I think. They were very close, I believe."

They were interrupted by the arrival of the main course of a delicate whitefish, dense-fleshed and tender. It was dessert before that particular conversation resumed. In the meantime they spoke of the kind of art, theater, music they both enjoyed, and laughed at current political jokes.

"You did not ask to see me as an excuse to dine," Narraway said at last, the gravity back in his face. "I might have done, but *you* have never needed to prevaricate." He was smiling very slightly as he said it, but his concern was real, and it would be a rebuff to pretend she did not hear it.

"I can though," she admitted. "But I won't. I think there are strong currents beneath the surface of this. I feel them, but I don't know what they are. In fact, the more details I discover, the less can I make sense of it. It seems an absurd mixture of trivia and tragedy."

He watched her without interrupting. His eyes looked almost black in the light from the chandeliers.

"A maid running off with a suitor is very inconvenient, but it happens quite often," she continued. "I think I have lost at least three that way, perhaps four, if you count a scullery maid. But a woman beaten to death and her body left in a public but deserted place, to be scavenged by animals, is both grotesque and tragic."

He nodded. "And they appear to be connected. Pitt was only called in because the missing maid worked for a man of great importance to the navy, and thus to the safety of the country. What else?"

"Kynaston, by his own admission, is having an affair, which is grubby but far from unique . . ."

"By his own admission?" Narraway interrupted.

"Yes. When Thomas taxed him with it, he did not try to evade it."

"Which does not mean it is necessarily true," he pointed out.

She was startled, and about to argue when she suddenly realized what he meant. "Oh! You think it is something worse? That an affair would be preferable to the truth?"

He gave a small, slight smile. "I don't know, only that we should not assume anything for which we have no proof."

"Of course not. You are quite right," she agreed. "So that is another strange contrast, an admitted affair, which may conceal something worse, or at least something he has a greater desire to keep secret. Victor, what do you know of this man Talbot? Why does he so desire to be rid of Thomas? Is it something as simple as prejudice because Thomas has no family background or military experience? That, too, is grubby, but sadly it is not uncommon.

"He has the government's confidence," Narraway said thoughtfully. "But the government has no real experience of criminal deviousness as opposed to moral or political." He sighed. "You may be right, Talbot dines at the right clubs and Pitt doesn't. He will never be one of them; you have to be born to it, and of course go to the right schools."

"Pitt is better as he is, right schools and clubs or not," she said sharply. Then she felt the color hot in her cheeks as she saw the laughter in his face.

He leaned forward across the table. "I know that, my dear. I am as aware of Pitt's worth as you are, professionally even more so. And in my own way, I am also fond of him."

She looked down, avoiding his eyes. "I apologize. Of course you are. I did not mean to doubt you. This conflict has me . . . wrong-footed."

He touched her hand where it lay on the table, gently, and only for a moment.

"How charmingly you understate it. You make confusion about violence and murder sound like a missed step in a dance. I fear we shall run out of music before we reach that point. May I say what I think is really troubling you?"

"Could I prevent you?" she asked. Her voice was soft, but the words were a trifle defensive.

"Certainly," he replied. "Just tell me that you are not yet ready to trust me with it—or perhaps that you do not wish to."

"Victor, I'm sorry. I am behaving with a discourtesy you do not deserve. I am evading the issue because I am afraid of it."

"I know," he said so quietly she barely heard him above the murmur of conversation around them. "It is Somerset Carlisle, isn't it?" he continued.

"Yes . . ."

"Would Pitt have let it go had Carlisle not asked the question about Kynaston in the House?"

"I think so. That made it impossible," she agreed.

"And what are you afraid of—exactly?" he pressed.

She must now either answer him honestly, or deliberately refuse to.

He moved very slightly back again, no more than an inch, but she saw the shadow in his eyes. It was a moment of decision about far more than the admission as to what she feared regarding Carlisle: it was the moment where she and Narraway could move closer, or move apart.

The minute seemed to stretch endlessly, isolated as if it were unreal, an island in time. She was afraid because where it led to might be painful. The chance to prevaricate was slipping out of her hands.

He shifted back an inch farther.

"I am afraid that Somerset might have engineered the whole thing," she said huskily. "I don't mean that he killed anyone," she amended. "I can't believe that any cause, however intense, would make him do that . . ." She took a deep breath. "But I think he may have used the police finding that tragic corpse; the continued disappearance of Kitty Ryder; the whole absurd episode of the hat with the red feather, which could have been hers and wasn't; and the man who supposedly put it there, and found it, and so opened up the whole case again."

"Only to blow it apart and rescue Pitt?" he asked curiously, but the shadow had gone from his face and his eyes were grave, and gentle. "For heaven's sake, why?"

"That is what troubles me," she confessed. "It is the mountain that is filling the sky, too big to see its boundaries, and yet too far away to touch. He is maneuvering Pitt, Victor. That is what I am afraid of. And I have no idea why, so I can't help."

"Have you warned him?" he asked.

"Thomas? Of what? He can remember Resurrection Row, and the

bodies all over the place, not to mention various other . . . irregularities since."

His eyebrows shot up. "Irregularities! What a wonderful term for them! Yes, my dear, Somerset Carlisle has an art for irregularities that amounts to genius. What injustices does he care about enough to do this?"

"I don't know: murder, betrayal, corruption at the highest level, treason?" The moment she said that last word she wished she had not. "Or perhaps some personal debt of honor. He wouldn't tell me, and place me in the position of having to betray his trust in order to stop him."

"But he would use Pitt, who showed him such unwise compassion before?"

"Maybe that's why Somerset rescued him from Talbot?" she suggested.

"You are being too idealistic," Narraway replied sadly. "He is perfectly prepared to use Pitt because he needs him, but I wish we knew for what purpose." He looked at her steadily, and this time she did not look away. It was an admission of something, a difference in the relationship between them, and she was not as afraid of it as she had expected to be. In fact she felt a relaxing of tension inside herself, almost a warmth.

"We are going to do something about it, aren't we?" he asked.

"Oh, yes," she answered. "I think we have to."

Again his fingers touched hers across the table, just tip to tip. "Then you must begin," he told her, "with Carlisle. I shall find out a great deal more about Mr. Talbot."

She smiled. "Indeed."

THE FOLLOWING MORNING OVER breakfast Vespasia returned her mind to the question of Kynaston and his involvement in Pitt's case. She was concerned primarily for Pitt, because she was troubled by a fear that there was some element in it far more dangerous than a simple illicit affair. However, she had no idea yet what it was, except that it was ugly enough to provoke a particularly grotesque murder.

Which was why it also troubled her that Jack Radley had apparently been offered a position working more closely with Kynaston. She had grown fond of Jack for himself, but she would care about him regardless because he was married to Emily. Emily's first marriage had been to Lord George Ashworth, who had been her nephew. The close affection had remained after George's death. Indeed, she now felt the same kind of bond with Charlotte also, perhaps even closer. They were in some ways more alike in nature.

If Kynaston were guilty in any way of Kitty Ryder's death, then the stain of it would extend to those close to him professionally. And because of this suspicion, she could not rid herself of the fear that this ugly affair was more than a personal matter. Somerset Carlisle might deplore the betrayal of an affair, but she believed he would not appoint himself to any kind of judgment regarding it. He was too wise to imagine that such things were one-sided.

Was to suspect Carlisle in this the inevitable result of common sense, or was it an unfair prejudice, a leap to conclusions based on the past?

She was not hungry. The crisp toast sat uneaten in the rack, all except for one piece taken with her boiled egg. Only the hot, fragrant tea appealed to her. This morning she must see Somerset Carlisle and ask him exactly how he was involved, and oblige him either to tell her the truth or to lie to her. If for some reason, even a good one, he lied, then that would open a chasm between them, perhaps narrow, but a division nevertheless, one that could never again be completely closed. It would break a thread of trust that had been there for years, delicate and strong, like silk, throughout all kinds of fortune, good and bad.

She had not appreciated before quite how precious that was to her. She had scores of acquaintances, but they had not known the people Vespasia had wept for. They had not lain awake at night, cold with dread because they knew what had actually transpired, and the terror that had not come to pass. For them it was not life, it was the pages of history.

Not that Carlisle was her age—he wasn't—but he had a fire, an idealism, for which he was willing to risk his own comfort, even his life. She admired him for that, and she was obliged to admit she liked him deeply. She did not yet wish to know exactly how he was involved in Dudley Kynaston's life, or what he knew about Kitty Ryder.

If she faced it with any degree of honesty, she was not yet prepared to deal with that knowledge. So long as she did not ask, she had left herself room to believe as she wished. Once she knew, she would be obliged to speak to Pitt and tell him all she was aware of and for which there was proof.

And yet, of course, if she did not, she was responsible for what might occur out of his innocence.

Was Pitt naïve? No, that was not the word, he was simply not as subtle and devious of mind as she was—or as Carlisle was.

Even the tea ceased to appeal to her. She rose from the table and walked out of the yellow dining room and across the hall to the stairs. It was too early yet to see Carlisle. First she would address the problem of Emily's unhappiness.

Emily was delighted she had come, and welcomed her into the magnificent hallway with its marble floor and sweeping double staircases. Emily was so pleased, Vespasia immediately felt guilty that she had come for such a specific purpose. If Emily had any suspicion of that, she gave no sign of it at all.

"It's lovely to see you," she said warmly. She looked well, if a little pale. "I get so tired of snatching a word or two at some function, and having to be polite to everyone else."

She led the way into a garden room, which was light and airy, even in the wintry February morning where brief bars of sunlight shone between bands of cloud. The fire was burning and the air was warm. If one closed one's eyes it was possible to believe in the illusion of summer. Vespasia was flattered that the shades so closely resembled those she had chosen for her own sitting room, which also faced onto the garden. They were subtle and yet there was depth to them, so nothing in the room seemed chill or bleached of life.

"Indeed, so do I," she agreed, sitting in one of the chairs by the fire. When she was settled and comfortable, Emily took the other. She was facing the light and Vespasia noted a tightness in her skin. It was perhaps due to nothing more than the usual effects of winter when one went outside less often, and riding in the park was hardly a pleasure. There was no gray in Emily's fair hair, but there were tiny lines in her delicate skin and a shadow in her eyes.

"Did you come for any special reason?" Emily asked. She was a little more direct than her usual manner. After her encounters with Charlotte, was she afraid that there might be?

"No, but if there is something you wish to speak of, then I am always happy to hear." Vespasia practiced the sort of evasion she had perfected over the years, both in society and within family. There were so many things one approached circuitously.

Emily smiled and relaxed a little. "Loads of gossip," she answered lightly. "Did you hear that wonderful story from America in the newspaper?"

Vespasia hesitated for a moment, uncertain if there was something behind Emily's remark. "I hope you are about to tell me," she answered.

"You haven't?" Emily said happily. "That's marvelous. It's absolutely gruesome. Her name was Elva Zona Heaster. Her death was ruled natural, but her mother claimed that her ghost came back and said her husband had broken her neck." Emily smiled and her eyes were dancing. "And to demonstrate, the ghost turned its head right around as she was describing her death, and walked away forwards, but with her head on backwards, still talking to her mother!"

Vespasia stared at her, incredulous.

"In a little town in West Virginia," Emily continued. "Honestly!

That's more interesting than that Margery Arbuthnott is about to marry Reginald Whately, which is probably totally predictable." Suddenly there was a flat note in her voice as the laughter vanished.

Vespasia affected not to have noticed. "Such news does seem to be very repetitive," she agreed. "And unless you know them well, it is not interesting. I used to find it easier to pretend I cared than I do now. It seems to me there are so many things more important."

"What is important, Aunt Vespasia?" Emily said with a slight shrug. It was an elegant gesture, very feminine, and yet there was a thread of hurt through it, something deeper than the words.

"Anything that concerns those you love, my dear," Vespasia answered. "But that is not for social conversation. We often do not tell people what matters to us. It is not always easy to say it even to those we know well, because we care what they think of us."

Emily's eyes widened with momentary disbelief.

"Do you think I am too old to feel pain?" Vespasia asked, knowing there was no other way to reach whatever it was that coiled so tightly inside Emily, crushing the woman she used to be, than by exposing her own vulnerabilities.

Emily blushed scarlet. "No, of course I don't!"

"Yes, you do," Vespasia said gently. "Or else you would not be so embarrassed that I have observed your own pain. I assure you, pain does not lessen just because you have known it before. It is new each time, and cuts just as sharply."

"What would hurt or frighten you?" Emily's voice was husky now. "You are beautiful, wealthy, admired by everyone, even those who envy you. You are safe. No one can take from you all the wonderful things you have done. See some people's faces when you walk into a room. Everyone looks. No one ever thinks of ignoring you." She took a deep breath and let it out slowly. "You cannot lose who you are . . ."

"Is that what frightens you, losing who you are?" Vespasia looked at her carefully, searching her eyes. "What frightens me is no one else knowing who I am—not what I look like, or what I said that might have interested or amused them, but what I feel like inside." She gave a rueful little sigh. It was not the time for mock modesty. "It has always been pleasant to be beautiful; it is certainly not a gift one should be ungrateful for." She moved perhaps an inch. "But love concerns the beauty that is within—and the pain, the mistakes, the dreams, the things that make you laugh, and cry. Love is about how you deal with failure and own your mistakes. It is about tenderness and the courage to admit your own need, to be grateful for passion and generosity of soul. That has nothing to do with whether your nose is straight or your complexion without blemish."

Emily stared at her, tears welling up in her eyes.

"I don't know whether Jack still loves me or not," she whispered. "He doesn't talk to me anymore, not about things that matter. He used to ask my opinion. It's . . . it's as if I've already said everything he wants to hear, and I'm not interesting now. I look in the mirror and I see a woman who's tired . . . and boring." She stopped abruptly, her silence begging for a reply.

Vespasia could not answer her immediately and in the way she wanted. This was too deep an unhappiness to allow a quick remedy.

"Are you bored, Emily?" she asked. "There comes a time when society is not enough, no matter how much you cannot afford to offend it. I remember very vividly when I arrived at that point the first time." That was absolutely true. She had been younger than Emily, and bored stiff with being ornamental but completely unnecessary. It was a time she preferred not to think of. She had children she loved, but their daily needs were cared for largely by servants. Her husband was not unkind—he had never been that. He was simply without the fire in his soul or the flight of imagination she hungered for. But none of that did she intend to tell Emily, or anyone else.

Emily's eyes were wide, the tears forgotten. "I can't imagine you bored. You are always so . . . so engaged in things. You are not just being . . . kind to me . . . are you?"

"I think you mean 'patronizing,' don't you?" Vespasia asked frankly.

"Yes, I suppose so, but I didn't mean to say it," Emily admitted, then gave a small, very reluctant smile.

"I'm sure you didn't." Vespasia smiled back. "And no, I am not being either kind or, I hope, patronizing. Do you imagine you are the only woman who finds mere comfort insufficient? Of course it is different when you don't have it in the first place. But one can become accustomed to it very quickly. Perhaps a little downfall is helpful in that way. Not of the physical kind, but of the emotional sort? One can very quickly learn the value of something when you fear losing it. We take the light for granted, until it goes out. You are used to turning on the tap and getting water. You have forgotten what it is like to have to go to the well with a bucket."

Emily's eyebrows rose. "Do you think going to the well would make me feel better?"

"Not at all. But if you did so a few times, turning on the tap certainly would. But I mentioned it only as an example. Tell me, is Jack going to work for Dudley Kynaston, do you know?"

"No, I don't know! That is one of the many things he has not discussed with me." There was a moment's conflict in Emily's face; then she made a decision. "I would like to tell you to ask Charlotte. She seems to know everything. But that would only cut off my nose to spite my face, as they say. Somerset Carlisle was asking questions about Kynaston in the House. What do you make of that? Do you think there is really something wrong?" Now her concern was sharp and very visible.

Vespasia knew exactly what she was afraid of. It was not so long ago that Jack had received a promotion from a remarkable man, in high office and who had favored him. That man had proved to be a traitor, and Jack was fortunate to have escaped with his own reputation intact. Was history going to repeat itself? It was not an unreasonable fear.

"I dare say Jack is as concerned as you are," Vespasia said. "He will feel that he has let you down if he makes another error of judgment. And yet Kynaston may be totally guiltless in the disappearance of this unfortunate maid. She may simply have gone off with a young man and be living happily somewhere well outside London." She sighed. "Or, of course, she may have made a most unfortunate choice of lover, and it was indeed her body in the gravel pit, and she would have been perfectly safe had she stayed at the Kynaston house. Maybe Jack is trying to postpone his decision until Thomas has proved the matter one way or the other."

"That would be pretty difficult," Emily pointed out. "It's going to be obvious what he's doing, and why. He would be letting the whole world know that he thinks Kynaston might be guilty."

"Quite so," Vespasia agreed. "And that is enough to embarrass him, and make him wish he could be more decisive. I would lie awake at night were I to be faced with such a decision."

"Then why doesn't he ask me?" Emily demanded.

"Possibly because he is stubborn, and proud. And also perhaps because he does not wish to burden you with the choice, because if it should turn out badly he will take the blame himself."

"Do you think so?" There was a lift of hope in Emily's voice.

"Expect the best," Vespasia advised. "Then you will not be filled with guilt if you receive it. In the meantime, for heaven's sake find yourself something in which to be interested. You fear being boring because you are bored with yourself. And I do not mean that you should play at being detective! That would be dangerous, and highly undignified."

"What do you want me to do? Go and visit the poor?" Emily's face was filled with horror.

"I don't think the poor deserve that," Vespasia said drily.

"Some of the poor are very nice!" Emily protested. "Just because . . . oh! Yes. I see."

"Exactly my point, my dear," Vespasia replied. "They do not deserve to be patronized either. Do something useful."

"Yes, Great-aunt Vespasia," Emily said meekly.

Vespasia looked at her with alarm. "You intend to find out about Kynaston! Don't you?"

"Yes, Great-aunt Vespasia. But I shall be very careful, I promise you."

"Well, if you must meddle, find out about his wife. And if you say 'yes, Great-aunt Vespasia' again I shall . . . think of something suitable to control your impudence."

Emily leaned forward and kissed her gently. "Bed without any supper," she said with a smile. "Cold rice pudding in the nursery? I hate it cold."

"I daresay you are well acquainted with it!" Vespasia observed, but she could not keep either the affection or the amusement out of her voice.

CHAPTER

9

Emily's resolve remained strong for at least two days. It crumbled only when she faced Jack across the breakfast table on the third morning. He sat studying a folded copy of *The Times*. At least he did not hold it open so that he was entirely hidden behind it, as she had seen her father do on more than one occasion.

"Has something now occurred?" she asked, trying not to sound either plaintive or sarcastic, which was not easy as she felt a little of each.

"The world situation is worrying," he replied, without lowering the newspaper.

"Is it not always?" she asked.

"I pulled the court circular for you." He indicated a couple of sheets he had folded and placed on her side of the table. "*The Times* doesn't do fashion."

She felt her temper flare up like fire in dry wood.

"Thank you, but I already know exactly what is fashionable, and probably possess it, and frankly I couldn't be less interested in the appointments for the day of numerous royal grandchildren and their families. I have no intention of attending any of them." She sounded waspish, and she knew it. It embarrassed her because it displayed her vulnerability, and yet she did not seem to be able to help it. "I am much more interested in politics," she added.

There was a minute or two's silence, then he folded the paper and put it down. "Perhaps I should get you a copy of Hansard," he suggested, referring to the written report of what had transpired in Parliament.

"If you can't remember what happened, then I suppose I shall be reduced to that," she responded, this time not even attempting to be polite.

Jack remained impassive, if a little pale. "I can remember exactly what happened," he said levelly. "I just don't remember anything of the remotest interest. But I was not there all day. Is there something about which you have a particular concern?"

She felt the tears prickle her eyes, which was ridiculous. Grown women, approaching forty, did not weep at the breakfast table, no matter how alone or unnecessary they felt. The only way to stop it was to replace hurt with anger—carefully controlled.

"You didn't think that I might from time to time wonder about Dudley Kynaston and the disappearing maid, not to mention the mutilated corpse found within a quarter of a mile of his home on Shooters Hill? Of course, if you have declined the offer of a position with him then it is no longer my husband's future at stake, not to mention my own, it is simply a matter of speculation, much as any other particularly grotesque murder might be."

Jack was very pale now, and a tiny muscle was ticking on the right side of his face.

Emily swallowed the lump in her throat. Perhaps she had gone too far?

"I am quite aware of the public speculation on the subject," he said gravely. "I am also aware that neither the police nor Special Branch has identified the corpse as being that of Kitty Ryder. Somerset Carlisle, who is as irresponsible as a man can be, has used his Parliamentary privilege to suggest that the body is Kitty Ryder, and that her death is connected with her service in Kynaston's house, but there is no proof of it, or even any evidence."

"People won't care about that!" she said hotly.

"I care!" His voice was hard, angry in a way she had never seen before, and it chilled her deeply. This was not the man who had wooed her, adored her, held her in his arms as if he would never let her go. This was someone she barely knew.

Loneliness drowned her, sweeping her off her balance like a riptide.

"I've learned better," he said grimly, measuring each word. "I'm surprised you haven't. When George was killed . . . murdered . . . many people thought it was you who had done it. Do you remember that? Do you remember how afraid you were? How you felt everyone was against you, and you couldn't find any way to prove your innocence?"

Her mouth was dry. She tried to swallow and couldn't. "Yes," she whispered. Now, suddenly, she could remember it hideously well.

He looked at her very steadily across the table. "And what would you think of me if I assumed Dudley Kynaston was guilty of having murdered his wife's maid, brutally, breaking the bones in her body and mutilating her face, when we don't even know that she's dead? Would you admire me for that? Even if I did it so that I wouldn't be stained by association should it turn out to be true?"

She took a very deep breath and let it out in a sigh.

"I would not admire you," she said quite honestly. Then continuing in the same vein: "But I would have appreciated your talking it over with me, so I understood what you were doing, and why. I don't know how to interpret silence."

He looked startled, as if it required a moment or two of thought before he understood. "Don't you?" he said at length. "I thought you understood that . . . I told you . . ."

"No, you didn't!" She shook her head. "I don't know what you're thinking, and I don't know what you're going to do."

"I don't know myself," he said reasonably. "I really can't believe Dudley would have an affair with a maid . . ." He stopped, looking at the lopsided, rueful smile on her face. "Not that he's so righteous, Emily! I know perfectly well that plenty of men do! I just don't think Dudley Kynaston's taste runs to maids! Even handsome ones!" He was very slightly flushed. She saw it in his face, and the way his eyes almost avoided hers, and then didn't.

"You know who it is, don't you?" she said with conviction.

"Who what is?"

"Jack! Don't play games with me! You know he's having an affair. You know with whom! Which is why you don't think it is with the maid . . ."

He was on his feet, and she stood up, too. "Why on earth don't you tell Thomas? You could save Kynaston . . . practically from ruin! Thomas isn't going to make it public. He'll keep it just as secret as you do, if it . . . oh!" She stared at him, looking into his beautiful, long-lashed eyes, still feeling the beat of her heart shaking her. "It's worse than the maid! Could it really be? Like whom? Someone he can't ever be seen with . . ." Her imagination raced.

"Emily, stop it!" he said firmly. "I said I didn't think maids were his taste, that's all. I don't know the man that well, and I certainly don't have his confidence in romantic affairs! Or even merely lustful ones. I very much want to work with him, but I don't know if it will be possible. I'd rather err on the side of thinking too well of him than of assuming his guilt before there's even proof of a crime he might be involved in. Wouldn't you? Isn't that what you want?"

She did not answer. She wanted him safe, and she wanted him to talk to her. Above all she wanted him to love her the way he had before he became a member of Parliament. But to say so would be appallingly childish, embarrassingly so. She blushed hot at the idea he might even guess that that was what she meant.

"I imagine I might," she agreed. "But there's something in your voice that makes me think you don't trust him, for all your generous words. I daresay you are right, and he wouldn't have an affair with a maid, or even take advantage of her in something less emotional than an affair. But there is something wrong, you just don't know yet whether it is something you should take notice of or not."

He looked disconcerted for a long moment, then he smiled, with the same warm, easy charm she had known right from the beginning. She should stop telling herself she was not still in love with him. She knew better than to believe such a lie anyway.

"You have a gift for putting things horribly plainly," he said with a degree of approval. "You would never be a success in Parliament. I don't know how you do it in society. I wouldn't dare!"

"You have to smile when you say things people don't want to hear," she replied. "Then they think you don't really mean it. Or at worst, they aren't sure that you do. And it's quite different for me anyway; nobody needs to care very much what I think. They can always discount it, if they want to. Except, of course, if I tell them they look marvelous and are up-to-the-minute in fashion. Then, naturally, I am talking perfect sense, and my opinion is infallible."

He looked at her for a moment, not sure himself how much to believe. Then he shook his head, kissed her briefly but softly on the cheek, and left the room.

It was better than it might have been, not yet a disaster, but it was still very much too close to the brink.

She must *do* something! And not with Charlotte this time. Regardless of who did what, Charlotte always got the credit.

Emily was ideally placed to spend an afternoon with Rosalind Kynaston. She looked through the newspaper that Jack had discarded and found a suitable event, and another for tomorrow, and the day after. Then she used her telephone to call Rosalind and invite her to an exhibition of French Impressionist paintings, and then perhaps afternoon tea. Very deliberately she did not invite Ailsa. She did not like her, and felt Rosalind was not herself around her sister-in-law.

She was happily surprised when Rosalind replied that she had no engagements that afternoon that could not be put off, even though it meant that Emily was not nearly as well prepared as she would like to be as to exactly how she would conduct herself to gain the best advantage she could. She knew perfectly well that she wanted to acquire some information that would assist Pitt, and therefore Jack, in determining what had happened to Kitty Ryder, and who had caused it. She would very much like the perpetrator not to be anyone in the Kynaston house.

She took great care dressing. The pink had been a disaster. Simply because of the memory of that awful night, apart from anything else, she would not wear it again. In fact, she might well avoid all warm, light colors! She had sufficient means to choose anything she wished. With her fair hair and pale skin, especially after the winter, something delicate and cool was the obvious choice. How had she been so foolish as to do otherwise? Desperation is never a good judge!

She chose a very pale teal, halfway between blue and green, with a white silk fichu at the neck. She regarded herself critically in the glass, and was satisfied. She must now forget the whole dress issue and concentrate on what she would say.

THEY MET ON THE steps of the gallery, Rosalind arriving only moments after Emily. They greeted each other warmly and went inside. It was a very pleasant day, but the wind still had a February bite to it.

"I apologize for such inconsiderate haste," Emily said as they reached the entrance hall. "I just had a sudden urge to go somewhere simply for the sake of it, not just to be correct, and seen, and have to make conversation with everyone."

"I was delighted," Rosalind said with feeling. She glanced at Emily very directly. "We shall play truant from obligation for a whole afternoon." She did not add anything about her sister-in-law, but somehow her presence—or lack thereof—hung in the air between them. The very absence of her name was notable in itself.

Emily knew she must not be too direct too soon. She smiled as they walked towards the first gallery.

"I have always liked Impressionist paintings. They seem to have a freedom of the mind. Even if you don't like the work itself, it offers you a dozen different ways to see it and interpret it. Something that is strictly representational forces on you its reality straightaway."

"I never thought of that," Rosalind said with very evident pleasure. "Perhaps we could stay here all afternoon?" She did not add how much the idea appealed to her; it was clear in her face.

The first room was taken up almost entirely with paintings of trees, light on leaves, shadows on grass, and impressions of movement in the wind. Emily was happy to gaze at them for their own beauty for quite some time, and allow Rosalind to do the same, although she did glance several times at her face and study the expression in it. Rosalind was clearly troubled. Emily had been right in her observation that the subtle nature of the art allowed a great deal of one's own emotion to come to the surface, the dark as well as the light. It had been a dangerous place to come for that reason—so much feeling could be laid bare. But one mistake of too much candor too soon could destroy it all, like smashing a mirror, so that you would never know what the reflection had been.

She moved up to join Rosalind in front of a pencil drawing of wind-blown trees.

"Doesn't it make you wonder what was going on in the mind of the artist?" she said quietly. "There is so much strain in those branches. Some of them look close to breaking."

"I suppose everyone has their own wind, and their own darkness," Rosalind said quietly. "Perhaps that is what real art is. Any good journeyman can capture the individual and reproduce what the eye sees. A genius can capture the universal in what everyone feels . . . or perhaps not everyone, but people of a thousand different sorts."

There would never be a clearer opportunity. It was almost as if Rosalind were seeking an opening to speak.

"You are right," Emily agreed quietly so that anyone else entering the room would not chance to overhear her. "This drawing looks as if the branches are all hugging each other in the darkness, afraid of the violence outside."

"I see the violence inside, and the darkness beyond," Rosalind said with a tiny, tense little smile. "And I see them huddling, but not together except by chance."

Emily affected not to have noticed anything raw or painful in her words, but her heart was hammering in her chest. "What about the picture over there?" She indicated one also of branches, but utterly different in mood. It made one smile simply to look at it. "To me it is the complete opposite, and yet the subject is the same."

"The light," Rosalind said without hesitation. "In that one the wind is warm, and the branches are dancing in it. All the leaves flutter, like frills, or skirts."

"Dancers," Emily said thoughtfully. "That's right—absolutely. You know what intrigues me about dancing? It is very difficult for someone else to tell how your partner is holding you, lightly, supportively, or so tightly you are bruised and you know you cannot escape. I wonder if someone has painted real dancers the way this artist has painted the branches. It would be something to attempt, wouldn't it? If you were a painter?"

"Perhaps that is what group portraiture is about," Rosalind suggested.

Emily laughed. "Not if you want another commission!"

Rosalind spread her hands in a tiny little gesture of submission. "Of course," she agreed. "You must paint people the way they wish to be seen. But would any great artist do that, except to earn enough to live on?"

"Can anyone afford not to make accommodations?" Emily asked in return.

By then they had moved to the next room where most of the paintings were seascapes, or views of lakes and rivers.

"I like the sea pictures better," Rosalind observed. "The open horizon." She hesitated a moment. "That one is beautiful and terrible—the loneliness in it, even despair. It looks like a gravel pit, deserted and filled in with water."

Emily said nothing, waiting.

"I'm sure you must have heard that my lady's maid is missing," Rosalind went on, looking at the painting, not at Emily. "And that there was a body found in the gravel pits near us. We don't know yet whether it is Kitty, or not."

"Yes," Emily agreed. "It must be dreadful for you . . . I can't imagine." She could imagine very well, but it was not the time to be speaking about herself, or the tragedies of her own past.

"The worst part is the suspicion," Rosalind went on. "I can't help hoping she is alive and well somewhere, for everyone's sake. But she wasn't an irresponsible person at all. Everyone is suggesting that she ran off with the young man she was courting, but I don't believe it. I can't. She liked him, but she wasn't in love. Ailsa says she was, but I know better. Either she's dead, or she ran away for some other, real reason." For a moment Rosalind's face looked as utterly bleak as the painted gravel pit on the wall.

Emily felt she must say something, not only because she could not let the opportunity slip out of her grasp, but out of ordinary kindness.

"Are you sure you are not letting your fondness for her make you overlook her faults?" she asked gently. "Wouldn't you rather think she was flighty and on rare occasions selfish, rather than dead? After all, who could she be so afraid of that she would run off into the night without a word?" Dare she take it any further? If she did, it must be now! She hesitated only a moment. "Wouldn't you have sensed it? A look in her face, a clumsiness perhaps, an inattention to detail? It is very hard to conceal fear great enough to make you run off alone into a winter night! It was January then, wasn't it? I don't really like to go out in January even wrapped up and in a carriage, and knowing I will come back to my own bed."

Rosalind turned a little and stared at her, hollow-eyed. "Neither do

I," she said in a little above a whisper. "But I have been safe, physically safe, all my life. I'm not a servant, and I don't know anything that could be dangerous."

"What could she know?" Emily seized the chance offered her. "It would have to have been something she couldn't tell you . . ."

"That is what frightens me," Rosalind replied, her voice now so strained it was barely recognizable. "There is nothing about me that is even interesting, let alone threatening to anyone. It must be about my husband, or my sister-in-law." She took in a deep breath and let it out. "Or Bennett. He's been dead nearly nine years, and yet it is as if he still lived in the house somewhere just out of sight. No one ever forgets him."

Emily thought for only a moment. "You mean Ailsa still loves him too much to consider marrying again?"

Rosalind did not answer immediately. She appeared to give the matter thought. "I'm not sure," she said at length. "She does accept various social invitations from other men, but they seem to cool after a while. So yes, perhaps you are right. That is what she tells Dudley, anyway. But Dudley loved Bennett profoundly. Even for brothers, they were very close." She smiled, and there was a deep warmth to it. "That is one of the nicest qualities about Dudley: he is totally loyal, and if he judges at all, then he judges kindly. He was always protective of the young, and of course Bennett was younger than he. I remember Dudley with our sons. He was patient, no matter how exasperating they were at times . . . and they were. In fact, he was gentler than I . . . I am ashamed to admit."

"And your daughters?" Emily said with interest.

Rosalind shrugged. "Oh, he was always patient with the girls, and with me. And with Ailsa, for that matter. Women don't tempt him to be otherwise. I'm not certain if that is because he doesn't expect so much of us . . ."

"Some men just *are* patient," Emily agreed. She thought momentarily of Jack with Evangeline. She could twist him around her little finger, and he did not even bother to deny it.

She looked at Rosalind, deciding what line to pursue, intensely aware of the distress in her. "Ailsa seems to be strong-willed enough not to need a great deal of protection," she observed. "Am I jumping to too quick a judgment?"

"No, not at all," Rosalind said instantly. "I . . ." She shook her head. "No, I am at fault. I should not judge either. To me Ailsa seems immensely strong, but she was torn apart by Bennett's death. It was just that with her it seemed on the outside to be anger, even rage that fate had taken from her the one man she loved. I . . ." She shook her head again. "I never loved in that kind of way. Perhaps because I have children? I don't know. If Dudley died I would miss him terribly. I expect every day I would be aware of the emptiness, all the things he said, did, cared about . . . everything. I would weep inside, as he still does for Bennett, I know. But I don't believe I would rage at fate."

Emily thought how she would feel if Jack were to die. Alone . . . as if she would be alone for the rest of her life. If she knew beyond doubt that he really had left her, either openly, physically, or just by being emotionally absent, then she would rage! Her anger might be beyond control, at times, but it would be a defense against tears. She knew that almost as if it had actually happened. It would be as if the sweet wine of life had turned to vinegar. The thought was cold and real inside her.

"What was he like . . . Bennett?" she asked.

Rosalind gave a little laugh. "Like this picture, with the sunlight in the trees," she answered. "Do you think we should move on? Are we stopping other people from studying this one?" She glanced around to see if anyone was waiting, but no one else was in the room except a couple of men staring at a different picture over on the opposite wall.

"Probably," Emily agreed. "We'll see what's in the next room."

It turned out to be landscapes in various moods, all of them profoundly beautiful in their own way. With so much passion around them it was easier to be honest than it might have been in a more conventional place.

"What was Bennett like?" Rosalind repeated Emily's question. "When I think back on it, I didn't see him nearly as often as one would suppose, from the impression he made on me. He was very like Dudley in some ways: his interests, his mannerisms, his sense of humor. But he was quicker, more certain of himself. He had boundless dreams, and he had few doubts that one day he would achieve at least most of them. In a way that's why it was so difficult to realize he was dead. It all happened very quickly. One day he was ill, and in a week he was gone. We couldn't grasp it—especially not Dudley. After all that had—" She stopped.

Emily waited. They were standing near a broad, sweeping landscape with huge skies: the left side was filled with blue distance, the right a driving storm coming in rapidly, darkening everything, heavy with threat.

"We thought the worst was past," Rosalind said simply, as if everyone would know what she meant.

Perhaps it was indelicate, but Emily could not now leave it.

"He had been ill before?" she asked.

"Bennett was in Sweden," Rosalind said after a moment or two. "Many years ago now. Before he ever met Ailsa. I don't know what happened. Dudley was frantic. I've never seen him so desperate. He received a message and dropped everything. He went to Sweden the very next day, and I didn't hear from him for weeks. When he returned he brought Bennett with him, and they never told me what happened. Bennett looked ashen, and thin. He stayed with us. Dudley wouldn't let him out of his sight."

The two gentlemen walked past them talking earnestly.

"He used to have nightmares," Rosalind continued when they were out of earshot. "I heard him crying out in the night. Dudley never told me why, and gradually it passed. Bennett regained his strength and went back to his work. A year or two after that he met Ailsa and shortly after they were married."

"Then the illness returned?" Emily said, her heart heavy with a sense of tragedy. "But this time it was too swift, and there was nothing they could do to help him?"

"I suppose so," Rosalind answered, looking suddenly away from the painting and at Emily. "But that was all long before Kitty came to us, and there was definitely nothing about it that was anything except tragic. I . . . I wish I could do something to help in this mess! Dudley has had more than enough pain."

Emily looked at the racing clouds in the painting and the heavy shadow they cast on the land. She shivered involuntarily.

"That sounds self-pitying, doesn't it!" Rosalind said, annoyed with herself. "We have a beautiful home. Dudley's work is terribly important, and he is extremely good at it. We have money and position, and healthy sons and daughters, and here am I with the arrogance to speak of pain."

"Not knowing the truth is always painful," Emily said with sincerity. "No matter how much you love, if you are afraid of losing it all, then the icy edge of that storm is upon you already."

Rosalind smiled, and there were tears in her eyes. She put her hand on Emily's arm in a quick gesture, then withdrew it again.

"Would you care for afternoon tea? I know it is a little early, but I should like to take you to a small place I know will be open and is quite delightful."

"An excellent idea," Emily agreed.

ALL THE WAY HOME in her carriage afterwards Emily thought over everything that Rosalind had said, and even more what she had left unsaid. Over tea they had spoken of many things, mostly totally trivial, often even funny. Rosalind was well informed about a number of subjects. She spoke with enthusiasm about music, and had some knowledge of various pianists. She was interested in the history of glass, going back to ancient Egypt and forward to present-day Venice and the glass features in Murano. Emily began to hope with some energy that Jack would find himself working for Dudley Kynaston. She would enjoy a further friendship with his wife.

A friendship with his sister-in-law did not even occur to her until she realized how seldom Rosalind had mentioned Ailsa. In fact, it had been only once more, to say that they had gone together to some event that had been Ailsa's idea. Apart from that, they had had an interesting and entertaining afternoon without thought of her at all.

And yet Ailsa had appeared on other occasions to be so large a part of the Kynastons' life. Was it actually only a kindness, including her because she appeared to have no other family?

Thinking back on the few times she had been in the company of both women, Emily remembered Ailsa always seeming to be in charge, like the elder sister, although she was probably several years younger. But there had been little actual warmth between her and Rosalind.

Was that of any importance at all? Possibly not. Nevertheless Emily wanted to find out a bit more about Ailsa Kynaston. Preferably when not in Rosalind's company, though. Among many other things she had learned about Rosalind was that she was far wiser and more observant than she affected to be.

Creating the opportunity to observe Ailsa was now the challenge. If Ailsa were indeed at the heart of the problem—somehow connected with the disappearance of Kitty Ryder—then it might be dangerous to openly inquire about her. The thought did not deter Emily, but she knew she must plan with care. She would find out Ailsa's interests, what plays she liked, what exhibitions, who in her circle of friends Emily herself might also know.

As it turned out, fate played directly into Emily's hands. She accompanied Jack to a formal party with several other people in government; previously she had said she would not go, afraid that she would appear clinging and a trifle possessive. Now her purpose regarding Ailsa changed everything. She was also determined to support Jack not just tacitly but positively, and oblige him to be aware of her and happy that she was present.

She dressed carefully in her favorite shade: pale green, more delicate than the earliest leaves, known as "waters of the Nile," or in the far more sophisticated French "eau de Nil." It was the softest silk, floating when she moved, and the sheen of it caught the light. Naturally it was the latest cut: soft at the shoulder and neck, smooth and slender at the hip. Pearls might have been more appropriate considering the name of the color, but she wore diamonds. She wanted the fire and the sparkle.

She was satisfied as she swept down the stairs towards Jack, who was waiting for her at the bottom, that she had achieved the result she wished. He said nothing, but his eyes widened and he gave a little sigh of satisfaction. So far, she was succeeding.

The effect of her entrance at the party was also gratifying. However, it took only a few minutes to realize that she certainly had no monopoly on beauty or attention. Moments later Ailsa Kynaston arrived, sufficiently late to ensure everyone was aware of her, but not enough to be discourteous.

She was dressed in cream and gold. It was a daring combination for a woman of such pale coloring, but she carried it superbly, with a confidence that challenged anyone to find fault with her.

However, what took Emily's attention was the fact that she was on the arm of Edom Talbot, whom she knew to be one of the men closest to the prime minister, even though he held no specific government position. But Emily knew from Charlotte that Talbot had taken a dislike to Pitt, and made his investigation of the Kynaston affair more difficult than it needed to be. Or perhaps it was not Talbot's intention, rather his necessity, because of the sensitivity of Kynaston's position with the navy.

Looking at him very carefully now, Emily saw a man striking in appearance because of his height and casual strength. He carried himself as if he had tested and proved his physical superiority many times. There was a kind of unspoken arrogance in his posture, something slightly intimidating.

Did Ailsa find that pleasing? To Emily that arrogance seemed slightly ill bred. A gentleman did not ever intentionally make others feel uncomfortable, unless given pressing cause to.

Some women found dangerous men attractive. Emily considered their taste, conversely, to be a sign of some kind of inner weakness. And weakness was dangerous. It was those aware of their own disadvantage that often attacked others.

Someone spoke to her, and she made a light and meaningless reply, smiling with the charm she had always known how to use.

Jack said something to her that she did not hear. She was busy watching Edom Talbot and Ailsa Kynaston, studying the way they moved together, who spoke and who listened, how often they met each other's eyes, or smiled. Who was leading?

At first it seemed to be Talbot. He knew more people, and introduced them to her. She was gracious, but not eager. Nothing in their conversation seemed so very interesting. He clearly admired her striking appearance, but then so did at least half the men in the room, and the women both envied and resented it.

Emily had not been paying attention to her own duties. She gave Jack a dazzling smile and joined in the conversation.

It was over half an hour before she could watch Ailsa and Talbot again. Now Ailsa was leaning toward him, smiling. Then she spoke to someone else, and a moment later turned back to Talbot. He did not take his eyes from her, almost as if he could not. She was flirting with him, but so subtly only Emily, an expert at such things herself, was aware of it. Others walked by, made some passing observation, smiled, laughed, and moved on.

Talbot put his hand on Ailsa's arm, high, near the shoulder, as if to pull her a little closer to him. It was an oddly proprietorial gesture, almost intimate. Her face was turned away from him as she had been speaking momentarily to someone else. But Emily saw the flash of something in her expression—more than distaste, it was almost hatred. Then deliberately Ailsa allowed herself to be drawn toward him before finding an excuse to move in a different direction.

Was she holding back because of the memory of Bennett, the lost husband she could never forget? Or something else entirely? Perhaps something she knew of Dudley Kynaston and the adopted family whose loyalty to her she was repaying with a kind of protection now?

But protection from what? Could it be the same knowledge that Kitty Ryder had run away from? Or was killed for?

Perhaps Emily had been completely wrong in her estimation of Ailsa. That was something she had to find out. She must force herself to know her better, in spite of her instinctive dislike of her. Emily knew scores of people, perhaps hundreds. At least two or three of them must know Ailsa. She would begin looking for the best way forward tomorrow.

10

"You bring 'er back 'ere by 'alf past five, you 'ear me, young man? I don't care 'oo you are, special police or not," the cook said fiercely, staring at Stoker as if he were an errant bootboy.

Stoker smiled, but Maisie got the answer in before he could speak.

"Yes, Cook. Mr. Stoker's a Special Branch policeman. 'E wouldn't never do nothing wrong." She lifted her chin up even higher and met Cook's eyes directly, something she would not normally dare to do. But today she was in her best dress, the only one that she never used for work. The footman had polished her boots for her until the cat could see its face reflected in them. Mrs. Kynaston's new lady's maid had put her hair up so that it was tidy, even at the back where she couldn't see it herself. She was going out to tea with Mr. Stoker, to be asked some important questions, so important they couldn't be asked where other people might overhear them.

Stoker became serious again. "We shall have tea, and then I shall bring her back," he promised.

Cook gave Maisie a stern warning. "You be'ave, Maisie. Don't you go gettin' ideas above yourself or givin' no cheek, you understand? And if you go repeatin' gossip what's none o' your business, you'll find yourself out on the street with no place. You watch your tongue, and that imagination o' yours."

"Yes, Cook. I won't say nothin' at all but the truth." Then, without waiting for the cook to add anything more, she turned and walked away, her chin high, her back as straight as if she had been carrying books on her head.

Suddenly Stoker wished he had had a daughter. An old love of his had wanted to marry and settle down. She had been pretty, with dark eyes like this odd little scullery maid's. Stoker had been frightened by the idea of such responsibility. He had hesitated too long. By the time he had come back from the voyage, Mary had found someone else. It had hurt for a long time.

He caught up with Maisie and they walked together, he being careful not to outpace her. They went down Shooters Hill Road towards Blackheath until they came to the tea shop, where he had already reserved a table for them.

"This your table, then?" she asked as he pulled out the chair and she sat down, more than a little self-consciously arranging her skirts.

"For now it is," he told her. "Would you like tea? And some cakes?"

She was too impressed to speak as the waitress stood ready to take their order. She had never been waited on before, or called "Miss."

"Tea for two, and your best cakes, please," Stoker requested. He was loath to admit it, but he was enjoying himself. However, time was short, and he had a lot to ask her. He could not afford to wait until they began tea.

"We found a hat up at the gravel pit we thought was Kitty's," he began. "But then we learned that it wasn't. Some stupid man put it there on purpose, just to get himself noticed."

Maisie frowned. "That's wicked. 'E just wanted ter make us all scared and sad, so's 'e'd be talked about? Is 'e daft, or summink?"

"I'd say so. But we found the receipt for the hat, and for the red feather, so we know it wasn't hers."

Her eyes were bright. "So mebbe she in't dead, then?"

"I'm going to believe she isn't," he said firmly.

"But some poor cow is." She bit her lip. "An' yer still gotter find out 'oo she is, an' 'oo done that to 'er?"

"If it isn't Kitty, and isn't anything to do with the Kynaston household, then it's the police's job to find out," he replied.

" 'Cos you're special, right? And Mr. Kynaston's special?"

He drew in breath to explain it a little less self-importantly but, seeing her bright face, changed his mind.

"Something like that," he agreed awkwardly. "But I still want to find Kitty, and prove she's alive."

She put her head a little to one side. "Ter save Mr. Kynaston?"

He found himself slightly uncomfortable. Her eyes were bright, almost black, and both quick and innocent at the same time. He hesitated as to how he should answer her. He needed information from her, and yet if she caught him in any deception at all he would lose her trust, and therefore her honesty. He would also find that painful. He was getting soft.

"Mostly," he agreed. "But I'd like to find Kitty just to know she's all right as well."

The tea came, with a whole plate full of little cakes and pastries. Maisie looked at them, then up at Stoker, then back at the plate.

"Which one would you like?" he asked.

"The chocolate one," she said instantly, then blushed. "Course, if you like it, the one with the pink sugar on it'd be all right."

He made a note not to take the one with the pink icing, which he rather liked the look of, too.

"I'll take the apple tart," he assured her. "You begin with the chocolate." He considered asking her if she would pour the tea, then changed his mind. He did ask her how she liked hers, and then poured for each of them.

She ate the chocolate cake slowly, savoring each mouthful.

"To find Kitty, I need to know more about her," he began. "I know a few things. She could sing really nicely. She liked the sea, and ships, and used to collect pictures of ships from all over the world—with different kinds of sails."

Maisie nodded with her mouth full. As soon as she had swallowed she answered. "Real clever with 'er 'ands, she was. Course, bein' a lady's maid an' all, she could sew real well, even mend lace when it got tore." Her eyes filled with tears. "Please find 'er, mister. Tell us she's all right . . . I mean . . . alive, an' well . . ."

"I will," he promised, and knew even as he was saying it how rash he was being.

Maisie sniffed. "D'yer think she just went off wi' that great dollop, 'Arry?" She looked at the last piece of chocolate cake on the plate. "But why couldn't she 'ave told us? Why don't she even write a letter, nor nothin'?"

"Are you sure she can write?" he asked.

"Yeah! She used ter write lists an' things. She were teachin' me." She looked again at the chocolate cake.

"Why don't you finish that, and then take the pink one?" he suggested. "I'm going to have that one with the raisins."

She looked at him to make sure he meant it, then did as he said, taking a delicate sip of her tea in between.

He hid his smile. Perhaps he was going about this the wrong way. Maybe he should be looking not for where Kitty would go, but for where Harry Dobson would choose.

"What was he like, this . . . dollop?" he asked.

Maisie giggled at his use of her word. "'E were all right. Crazy about Kitty, 'e were. Thought as the sun shone out of 'er eyes. An' I s'pose that's worth summink, in't it? She just smiled at 'im, an' 'e were made."

"But he wouldn't suit you?" he concluded. "Why not?"

She looked down at the pink-iced cake, a little embarrassed. "I in't never goin' ter be pretty like 'er, but I want ter better meself, all the same. I'd want someone wi' a bit o' fire, like; someone as wouldn't let me run rings around 'im." She stopped, ashamed of her words. It was too self-revealing to say what she meant to somebody who didn't know her—or any man at all, for that matter.

"You might have to work hard to find someone you couldn't run rings around, Maisie," Stoker warned. "But I heard that Kitty was ambitious, too. Was that wrong?"

Maisie sighed. "I s'pose when yer fall in love yer kind o' lose yer wits. Least that's wot they say." She bit into the pink cake, then looked at it. "This 'as got cream in it, all squashy and sweet."

"Don't you like it?" he said quickly. "You don't have to eat it. Choose another . . ."

She looked up at him. "Oh, I like it. It's a bit like bein' in love, though, in't it? I s'pose yer don't know it's goin' ter 'appen until yer already bit into it, eh?"

"Maisie, you are so clever sometimes you worry me. All these cakes are for us, so take as many as you like. Tell me more about Harry Dobson, and if you really think she liked him enough to have gone off with him . . . without telling anyone. She must have had a reason for that. What might it be?" He drank some of his tea and added a little more, to keep it hot. Then he took another cake, because he was sure she would not take another until after he had. He had seen her count them, and she was going to be scrupulously fair.

"Do you think he would have made her go secretly?" he asked.

She shook her head. "No! 'E wouldn't 'a made Kitty do nothin' as she didn't want. I reckon she must 'a bin . . ." She hunched her shoulder a little and gave a tiny shiver, then she looked up at Stoker. "Mebbe she were scared? I used ter think as she knew one or two things as she'd sooner not a' knowed about the mister an' missus, like. Then I thought as it were just talk. But mebbe it weren't? D'yer think?"

"I think that's very possible," he agreed, trying not to make too much of it and twist what she was going to say. "Any idea what she knew?"

She shook her head. "There are things as I don't want ter know. Me ma always said that, told me not to see things or 'ear things as I shouldn't. An' if I did, ter forget it like it never 'appened."

"Very wise indeed," Stoker said gravely. "I am telling you exactly the same thing, and I mean it just as much as she did. Now tell me more about Harry Dobson. We've asked the regular police, but nobody seems able to find him. Did he do any special kind of carpentry work? Windows, doors, floors? Any particular builder he worked with?" He reached for the teapot. "And have some more tea. If you'd like more cakes, we'll ask for them."

She took a deep breath, scooped up all her courage, and asked for another chocolate cake.

"Kitty said as 'e were goin' ter get a place ter work on 'is own, like," she answered. "'E were good at doors. Wanted ter make fancy ones, carved, an' all that. But 'e could 'a gone anywhere for that."

"Where did he come from?" Stoker persisted. This looked more hopeful.

"Dunno," Maisie admitted. "North o' the river, I think."

"Thank you. That'll narrow the search quite a bit."

She frowned. "Should I 'a said that before? Nobody asked. It were only wot 'e wanted. I dunno as 'e ever did it."

He smiled at her. "Maybe he didn't, but it's worth a try."

She sighed with relief and ate the cake.

STOKER HAD NATURALLY BEEN assigned to other cases since the failure to identify the body in the gravel pit and then the assumption that it was indeed that of Kitty Ryder. Those cases could not be ignored; they genuinely affected the security of the country. Therefore it was wiser that he continue to look for Harry Dobson in his own time. He did not relish trudging around the streets, in and out of public houses, music halls, taverns, but it was very possibly a task that he would gain little from doing at midday. He had learned a lot from Maisie that would narrow the search. He must forget the local area and go north of the river and at least try to find someone who specialized in good doors, ones with carving.

It took him four evenings walking in the late February rain, his sodden trouser legs flapping around his ankles, his boots letting in the water from puddles and overflowing gutters. He spoke to local builders from Stepney, Poplar, then headed east to Canning Town, then north to Woolwich before he finally found Harry Dobson.

Stoker stood in the sawdust of the carpenter's workroom and faced a fair-haired young man with heavily muscled arms and mild eyes.

"You Harry Dobson?" Stoker asked. Could this be the young man Kitty Ryder had run off with, abandoning her position, and her warm, safe home on Shooters Hill? Stoker had expected to dislike him, to see in his face some evidence of the nature that would abuse a young woman who trusted him. He saw instead only a young man who was slow, careful. At the moment, he seemed a little sad, as if he had lost something and had no idea where to look to find it again.

"Yeah," the carpenter said quietly. "You the feller with the warped doors?"

"No, actually I'm not." Stoker felt like apologizing. He stood blocking the doorway, but there was another entrance behind Dobson, leading into a timber yard. "Sorry. I'm looking for the Harry Dobson who courted Kitty Ryder, who worked up on Shooters Hill."

The color leached out of Dobson's skin, leaving him almost white, his eyes dark hollows in his head.

Stoker tensed, expected him to turn and bolt out of the other door.

For seconds the two stood staring at each other.

Finally Dobson spoke. "You . . . you police?"

"Yes . . ." Stoker was rigid, all his muscles tight, expecting to have to chase this man, try to bring him down before he escaped. He was sick with misery at the thought, and also physically very aware of the other man's strength. He was solidly built, muscular, and with powerful arms. Stoker was as tall, and wiry, but he had nothing like the sheer strength of Dobson. He would have to rely on speed, and years of experience in hard and dirty fighting.

Dobson took a deep breath. "You come to tell me they got 'er after all?"

Stoker was stunned. "Got who?"

"Kitty!" Dobson said desperately. "'Ave you come to tell me they killed 'er? I begged 'er not to go, but she wouldn't listen to me." He gasped as if someone were preventing him from breathing. "I promised I'd look after 'er, but she wouldn't listen." He shook his head. There were tears in his eyes, and he did not even seem to be aware of them.

"No!" Stoker said quickly. "No . . . I haven't come to say that at all! I don't know where she is. I'm looking for her."

The color and the light came back into Dobson's face. "You mean she could be all right?" He took a step forward eagerly. "She's still alive?"

Stoker held up a hand. "I don't know! The last I heard about her for sure was the night she ran away from Shooters Hill, way back in January."

"She was with me then," Dobson responded. "I promised to look after 'er, an' I did. Then all of a sudden, about a week ago, she said she gotter go again, and there weren't nothing I could do to stop 'er. I begged 'er, told 'er I didn't want nothing except to keep 'er safe." He shook his head. "But she wouldn't listen . . ." A look of helplessness washed over him again, and Stoker was suddenly moved to an intense pity for him.

"She's probably all right," he said gently. A wave of relief went through him, that the body they had found was not Kitty's after all. "And she maybe was right to go. If I could find you, so could others. I don't suppose you have any idea where she went?"

"No . . ."

"Perhaps that's wise, too," Stoker conceded, difficult as it was. "I'm a policeman, and I haven't heard of anyone finding her in the last week, dead or alive, so she's probably fine for now. You did the right thing."

"What about 'er?" Dobson pressed. "What if they find 'er, then?"

"We'll do all we can to see that we catch them before they do." Stoker made a wild promise. He knew perfectly well that he was being unprofessional about this. Pitt's influence was rubbing off on him!

Dobson nodded slowly. He believed him. "Thank you, sir," he said solemnly.

"But you have to help me," Stoker resumed a more serious manner. "I can't catch them without your help . . ." He remained vague, wanting to find out exactly what Dobson knew without betraying that he knew very little himself.

"Anything!" Dobson agreed eagerly.

"Why was she afraid of them? I need you to tell me what she believed."

"She saw things and heard them," Dobson answered straightaway. "She knew as there were something really bad going on in that house. I mean worse than just people pinching the odd thing 'ere and there, or messing around with other people's wives, an' such."

"Not an affair?" Stoker was surprised, immediately wondering if Kitty had told Dobson the truth. "What, then?"

Dobson shook his head. "She didn't say. I asked her, told her to go to the police, but she said the police wouldn't be no good. For a start, she didn't think they'd believe 'er, considering who Mr. Kynaston is, but also she said the police could be in on it anyway. And there in't no use getting angry with me! Don't you think I'd tell you, if I knew?"

"Yes," Stoker said frankly. "I think you would. Thank you, Mr. Dobson. If we find Kitty we'll keep her safe . . ."

"You can't," Dobson said instantly. "You don't know who's after 'er. I don't even know for sure who it was." That was a challenge, not a question.

"No," Stoker admitted. There was a chill inside him as if a gust of cold rain had drenched his clothes, touching his skin with an icy hand. He drew breath to promise that he would find out, then he realized he had made enough extravagant promises for today. This one he would make silently, and to himself.

————

THAT SAME EVENING, PITT was sitting by the fire in his home on Keppel Street. The long curtains across the French windows were closed, but he could hear the wind and rain beating against the glass. The children were in bed. He and Charlotte were sitting quietly by the fire.

It was Charlotte who raised the subject of the unidentified woman in the gravel pit again.

"Do you think it's over?" she asked, putting her embroidery aside.

Pitt liked watching her sew. The light flashed on the needle as it moved in her hands, weaving in and out, and the faint click of it against the thimble on her finger was rhythmic and comforting.

"What's over?" He had not been paying attention. To be honest, he was nearly asleep in the warmth of his home, with Charlotte so close he could have leaned forward and touched her.

"The Dudley Kynaston case," she answered. "I keep waiting every day for Somerset Carlisle to raise it again in the House. You know the hat wasn't Kitty's, but you don't know that the body wasn't—do you?"

He sighed, forcing his attention back to the issue. "No, and there's no further evidence, so there's nothing to pursue. We have to let it go."

"But you do know there's something wrong!" she protested. "Didn't Kynaston admit to you that he had a mistress?"

"Yes, but it wasn't Kitty Ryder."

"You believe him?" Her brow was puckered.

"Yes, I do." He sat up a little straighter. "From everything the other servants say, Kitty was a handsome girl, with an ambition to better herself, not to have an affair that could cost her her job. Or worse than that, get her with child and then out on the street with no money, no position, and no future. I believe Kynaston. I really don't think a quick fumble with his wife's maid would be worth killing her to keep secret. I don't know why Kitty went, but I can't see her succeeding in blackmailing him or—from what the other servants say of her—even trying it. It looks as if she ran off with Dobson and then perhaps was too ashamed to come home again."

"Maybe she was with child already, and she married him?" Charlotte suggested. "I suppose you looked at all the marriage registers?"

Pitt smiled. "Yes, my darling, we did."

"Oh." She was silent for several minutes. There was no sound but the flickering of the fire, and the rain against the windows.

"Then what is Somerset Carlisle doing?" she said at last. "Why did he raise the question in the House? He must have had a reason. For that matter, how did he even know so much about it?"

"I don't know," Pitt confessed. "The information is not so difficult to get; he may have friends in the police, or in the newspapers."

She frowned. "What could he know that we don't? It has to be about Kynaston, doesn't it?"

"Or his mistress," he said thoughtfully. "He may have ways of finding out, on a personal level, that we don't."

"Would it matter?" She was puzzled, her embroidery still ignored. "I mean would it matter to Somerset? If Kynaston was having an affair with someone he knew, or cared about, surely it would be the last thing he would want exposed publicly, wouldn't it?"

Pitt considered the possibility of the woman being someone Carlisle disliked, but as soon as the thought formed in his mind he discarded it. Carlisle was unpredictable in many ways—eccentric at times, to say the least—but he would not have descended to using his privilege of parliamentary questions for the purpose of conducting a private vendetta.

Charlotte was watching him. "What is it?" she asked.

"I don't know. Talbot's involvement troubles me, but I can't put my finger on why. Carlisle dislikes him profoundly. It's there in his manners and his voice, polite and perfectly controlled so there's nothing to get hold of. I don't like Talbot either, and I'm perfectly sure he doesn't like me. But as far as I know, it's just because I'm not the sort of gentleman he thinks should hold this position." He felt suddenly self-conscious saying this. Charlotte was the daughter of a family of both very comfortable means and long-accepted social position—not high society like Vespasia, but far beyond the servant status of his own family. A generation earlier he would have been Charlotte's footman, not her husband. He was more conscious of it than she. Talbot's attitude had brought it back again to the forefront of his mind.

"Then he's a fool," Charlotte said angrily. "It is too important a position to just hand to people merely because they had titled fathers. We can't afford anything but the best. To try to undermine that is disloyal to the country. Of which I shall remind him, should he be rash enough to make such a remark in my presence."

He laughed, but it was a little lopsided. He knew that she was perfectly capable of doing exactly that.

"Are you going back to Carlisle?" she asked.

"Not until I have something specific to ask him," he answered. "We know each other too well for me to fool him for an instant. I wish I were as good a judge of him!"

"I'm glad you're not much like him," she said gently.

Pitt was in his office in the morning, reading through reports from various officers around the country, when, after a brisk knock on the door, Stoker came in. Today there was nothing stoic about him. His usually bleak, rather bony face was alight with satisfaction. His eyes shone.

Pitt was in no mood for preamble. "What is it?" he demanded.

"I found Harry Dobson," Stoker said immediately. "He's set up in his own workshop now; that's why we couldn't find him. Ordinary sort of bloke, but decent. I checked on him. No record with the police. Pays all his debts. Nothing bad known about him—"

"Get to the point, Stoker. Where is Kitty Ryder?" Pitt interrupted.

"That's it. She ran off from Shooters Hill with Dobson because she knew something that scared her so badly she thought she'd be killed if she stayed. Wouldn't tell Dobson what it was, but it was bad enough that when she heard the hat with the red feather in it was found, she thought someone was after her again and she moved off. Wouldn't tell him where she was going. Maybe she hadn't decided." His face tightened. "Or she meant to keep on moving, too scared to stay in one place."

"That's what Dobson told you?" Pitt asked.

"I believe him," Stoker insisted. There was absolute certainty in his voice, in his face, and in the way he stood square in front of Pitt's desk. "I think he cares about her, and to be honest, I don't think he's got the wits to lie anyway. It fits in with everything else we know."

"Still leaves a lot unanswered, even though I'm relieved she is alive," Pitt said unhappily. What was she frightened of? Who did she think was pursuing her? Like Stoker, he wanted to believe that she was alive, that Kynaston had not harmed her, that the body in the gravel pit was definitely not hers—and, of course, if he was honest with himself, something that the local police could deal with. But Dobson's word was not concrete proof.

"Sir?" Stoker said a little sharply.

Pitt brought his attention back to the moment. "I suppose you checked with the locals that at least some of them had seen her with Dobson after the night she disappeared?"

"Yes, sir. Only got one, but I didn't find Dobson till yesterday late afternoon. I was lucky he was still working."

"Late?" Pitt said curiously.

"Yes, sir. About seven o'clock." There was a very faint color in Stoker's lean cheeks.

"Your own time," Pitt remarked.

Now the color was deeper. "I thought it mattered, sir," he said a little defensively.

Pitt leaned back in his chair and regarded Stoker with interest and a growing sense of sympathy. This pressing need to follow up a missing person, to the point where he did it in his own time, was a side of Stoker he had not seen before. It was interesting that Stoker was embarrassed about it, too. Far from feeling irritation or contempt for him, Pitt liked him the better for it. It showed a gentleness, a vulnerability he had not thought Stoker possessed.

"It probably does," he agreed. "So now if we say we can safely believe she is alive, that the body was not hers, then the question is, what did she learn that was so terrible, or she thought was so terrible, that she fled without taking anything with her, or giving notice to anyone? And why has she not got in touch with the Kynaston house, or the police, to say that she's alive and well?"

"I've been thinking about that," Stoker said, regaining a little of his composure. "It's pretty plain from what she said to Dobson that she thought someone had come after her, and she wouldn't tell Dobson who. But nobody does that about an affair, whoever it's with."

"No," Pitt conceded. "In fact I wonder now if Kynaston confessed to one at all only in order to satisfy our curiosity and get us to stop looking for anything further."

Stoker bit his lip. "Can't get away from that one, sir."

"For heaven's sake, sit down!" Pitt told him. "We've got to go back to the beginning on this. Did Dobson say if the blood and hair on the areaway steps were hers? If they were, how did they get there? I assume he didn't fight with her? Were they put there to mislead? Did someone try to stop her? Who? It's hard to believe it was any kind of coincidence."

Stoker colored again. "I didn't ask him. I'll go back and do that. Most likely seems to me that it was some kind of accident. Maybe she tripped."

"One accident I can believe in," Pitt answered. "Two I can't. Whose body was it in the gravel pit? The local police can't find anyone missing, and they've checked for several miles around. Whoever it is, poor woman, she died violently, then was kept somewhere for weeks between the time of her death and the time she was found in the gravel pit. And she was appallingly mutilated. There's no accident whatever in that."

"No, sir. Someone's playing a very funny game with us. The stakes must be high."

"Very high," Pitt said gravely. "And I'm not sure we even know who the players are."

"Is Mr. Carlisle a player, or a pawn?" Stoker asked.

"That's another thing I don't know," Pitt replied. "I've known him a long time. I think it will be wise to assume he's a player."

"On whose side?"

"Ours—I hope."

"And Mr. Kynaston?"

"I think that is where we begin. Delegate everything else for the time being."

"Yes, sir."

Pitt had sat up very late the previous evening, rereading all the papers he had on the Kynaston case. He thought of it in those terms because the root of it lay in Kynaston's house. He had finally gone to bed at about half past one, when the pages were swimming before his eyes and he was only wasting time looking at them.

He was jerked out of sleep by Charlotte's hand on his shoulder, gentle but quite firm, shaking him. He opened his eyes and saw pale gray daylight in the room. It was the first of March. The sun was rising earlier every day. The equinox was less than three weeks away.

"Sorry. I slept in," he mumbled, sitting up reluctantly. His head felt thick, and there was a dull ache at the back of his neck.

"It isn't all that late," she said quietly. Her voice was soft, but he had known her too long and too well to miss the strain in it.

Suddenly he was truly awake. "What's happened?" His mind raced over thoughts first of his children, then of Vespasia, or even Charlotte's mother. Now he was cold, clenched up.

"They've found another body in one of the gravel pits up on Shooters Hill," she answered. Her face was anxious, her brow furrowed.

All he felt was a wave of relief, as if the warm blood had started to flow in his body again. He threw off the covers and stood up.

"I'd better get dressed and go. Who called you? I didn't hear the telephone."

"Stoker's here waiting for you, with a hansom. I'll make him a cup of tea and a slice of toast while you're dressing, and there'll be some for you when you come down."

He drew in his breath to argue, but she was already at the door.

"And don't tell me you haven't time!" she called. "The tea will be ready to drink, and you can carry the toast with you."

Fifteen minutes later he was washed, dressed, hastily shaved, and sitting beside Stoker in the cab. They were going as fast as possible through the broadening daylight, rattling over the cobbles heading south.

"Local police called me," Stoker told him. "Haven't been there yet, came straight for you. They said this one's worse. A lot worse."

"Another woman?" Pitt asked.

"Yes. But with fair hair." Stoker did not look at Pitt as he said it. Perhaps he was ashamed of it, but there was relief in his voice.

"Does anyone know who she is? Any of the local police recognize her?" Pitt asked.

Stoker shook his head. "Not at the time they called. Maybe they've got further now."

Neither of them spoke for the rest of the journey as the hansom slowed a little going up the incline through Blackheath and then onto Shooters Hill. Here the countryside was bare, the wind raking the grass between the few clumps of trees, which were none of them yet in leaf. Some of the gravel pits were filled with water after the winter rains.

Pitt prepared himself for the blast of the wind, which would be heavy and damp when he got out. He tried to imagine the sight that was waiting for them, as if foreknowledge could blunt the edge of the impact.

"I ain't waitin' for yer," the cabby said gravely, his face windburned, half hidden by the muffler around his neck and chin. "I'nt fair ter me 'orse."

"Wouldn't think of asking you." Pitt climbed out a little stiffly and paid the man generously.

The driver found a sudden change of manner. "Thank you," he said with surprise. "Good o' yer . . . sir." Then, before Pitt could have the chance to change his mind, he urged his horse on, turned in a circle, and headed back down towards Greenwich to find another fare.

Pitt and Stoker walked into the wind towards the group of men they could see huddled about a hundred yards away. The tussock grass was rough and the ground between littered with small stones and weeds. In moments their boots were covered with pale, sandy mud.

Some movement must have caught the eye of one of the men because he turned and then started to walk toward them, the loose ends of his scarf flapping. Before he reached them he stopped, nodding to Stoker, then speaking to Pitt.

"Sorry, sir. Looks too much like the last one not to let you know. Over this way." He started to walk back, head bent, feet making no sound on the spongy earth.

Pitt and Stoker followed, each consumed in their own thoughts.

The sergeant in charge was the same man as before. He looked tired and cold. "Mind those tracks there," he directed, pointing at what there was of a pathway. "Looks like a pony and trap, or something of the sort. Might have nothing to do with the body, but more than likely it was what the swine brought her here in."

"So she didn't die here?" Pitt asked.

The man bit his lip. "No, sir. Looks just like the other one back a few weeks ago. Even got the same kind of hair, same sort of build. From what you can tell, she must a' bin real 'andsome when she were alive.

We'll need the doc to tell us for sure, but I reckon that wasn't all that lately. Week or two, at any rate."

"Hidden from view?" Pitt asked.

"That's just it," the sergeant replied, "she wasn't. She was right out there for anyone passing to see. Couldn't hardly miss her, poor creature."

"So she was put there very recently?"

"Last night. That's why the wheel tracks are worth something, or might be."

"Who found her?" Pitt asked.

"Young couple." The sergeant pulled a grim face. "Bin out all night. Walking the girl home so she could pretend as she'd been in 'er own bed, like. Not fooling anyone now!" He gave a bark of laughter.

"At least they reported it," Pitt observed, keeping pace with him. "They could have just kept going. Then it might have been a lot longer before we found her. Could have been more wind and rain, and we wouldn't have found the cart tracks. How far do they go?"

"Far as the main track over there," he pointed. "Then they get lost in all the gravel ruts. But then it's reasonable that's the way he came. Isn't really any other way."

"Which means she was deliberately brought here," Pitt pointed out just as they reached the group. They were all standing close together, giving the illusion of sheltering each other, although the wind managed to pick them out, whip everyone's scarves and coattails, and bend the grasses around their feet.

They parted slightly to allow Pitt to walk through and look down at the corpse that lay in the shallow dip in the ground. Her clothes were spread out around her, dark and lacking any distinguishing shape or color in the wet early light. Her hair was immediately noticeable because it was thick and fair, a little longer than average. Pitt thought that in life it would have been beautiful.

Her face was harder to appreciate because it was already distorted by death, and, as with the earlier corpse, it had been obscenely lacerated by a razor-sharp blade. The eyes, nose, and lips were missing. It was worse, because decomposition had begun, and small night animals had already reached her. As the sergeant had told him, she had been dead some time before she was placed here.

"What killed her?" Pitt straightened up, trying to tamp down the horror and pity that welled up inside him. His whole body was shaking, and he could not control it. He looked from one to another of the men. "I can't see anything obvious."

The sergeant spoke quietly, his voice hoarse. "We'll need the police surgeon to tell us for sure, but 'er inside is broken up pretty bad, and both her legs are broke, high up, across the . . ." He drew his own hand across his upper thighs. "God knows what did that to 'er."

"But no blood," Pitt said with surprise. He looked at the ground near her and saw nothing to mark the proximity except the claw marks of small animals. "And she wasn't here yesterday evening?" he went on.

"She'd 'ave bin seen, this close to the main paths," the sergeant answered. "And 'er clothes are damp but not soaked. There's the cart tracks as well. No, she was put here after dark yesterday. God alone knows what for! But if we catch the swine what did it, you won't need the hangman . . ."

One of the young men cleared his throat. "Commander Pitt, sir?"

Pitt looked at him.

"Sir, she's lying kind of odd, like her spine's bent, or something. But I were 'ere when we found the first one, sir, an' she were lying exactly the same way—I mean absolute exactly. Like it's the same thing all over again."

Pitt had a flash in his mind's eye of the woman they had thought was Kitty. It was exactly the same, as if she had the same internal pain twisting her back.

The wind was rising, whining a little in the branches above them and rattling as it knocked the dead weed heads together.

"You're right. Well observed," Pitt said. "I presume the police surgeon is on his way?"

"Yes, sir."

"Good. Anything else about her? I suppose no one has any idea who she is?"

"No idea at all, sir. Except the quality of her dress an' jacket suggest she could be another maid. Looked at 'er 'ands, an' she's got little burns an' scars on them, too, like she did a lot of ironing or cooking, or that kind of thing. An' . . . there's a handkerchief in her coat pocket, an embroidered one with lace an' an R stitched on it. Far as I can recall it's a pretty exact match for the one we found on the other body. An' worse than that, sir, we found this on 'er."

He took an envelope out of his own pocket and opened it. Inside was a gold chain with a very beautiful fob on it, also gold, about an inch in diameter, but of an irregular shape. It was slightly indented around the circumference, like a five-petaled rose. On the reverse were the initials BK in an ornamental script. Bennett Kynaston? It had to be the missing chain and fob from Dudley Kynaston's watch that he claimed was taken from his pocket.

"I can just imagine what the papers will make of this," Pitt said grimly. "Let me see the handkerchief, too, please?"

The man bent and picked it out of the dead woman's pocket. He passed it to Pitt. It was a small square of white cambric, lace-edged and embroidered with an R in one corner, with tiny flowers. It was an exact match for the earlier one.

"I'll go and speak with Kynaston," Pitt said to the sergeant, then he turned to Stoker. "Stay here. Speak to the couple who found her. Learn all you can. I'll catch up with you at the police station, or the morgue. Make damn sure this gets priority."

"Yes, sir," Stoker and the sergeant replied as one.

Pitt was cold and hungry when he knocked on the front door of Kynaston's house on Shooters Hill. This time he had no interest in the area steps, or the servants except as they might corroborate anyone else's story.

The door was opened by Norton, the butler, who regarded Pitt with unhappy misgiving. No one with any manners called at this hour. It could only mean bad news.

"Good morning, sir. May I help you?" he said very coolly.

"Thank you." Pitt stepped inside, forcing Norton either to let him in or deliberately to bar the way. "I apologize for my boots. They are unfortunately filthy. I have been to the gravel pit . . . again." He knew his voice was shaking. His body was tense, muscles locked tight across the shoulders and in his belly, as if he were as cold as the mutilated body up on the wind-combed grass a thousand yards away. He had tried, really tried, to get it out of his imagination, to concentrate on his job, to watch and listen to the present, but he could not.

Norton was pale. He swallowed hard. "I'm sure the bootboy would be able to do something for you, sir. Perhaps you would care for a pair of slippers in the meantime? And a cup of tea?"

Pitt was bitterly cold, and he realized his throat was dry. He was also on duty regarding a particularly vile crime. To accept cleaner footwear was a necessary courtesy to the housemaids who would have to try to clean the carpets after him. Tea and toast was a luxury, and therefore an indulgence.

"That is very kind of you," he replied. "Slippers would be a practical courtesy; the tea is unnecessary. I require to speak to Mr. Kynaston before he leaves the house. You will doubtless hear about it very soon, so I'll just tell you—I'm afraid there has been another body found in the gravel pits." He saw Norton's look of horror. "It is not Kitty Ryder," he added quickly. "In fact, it is quite possible that Kitty is still alive and well." Instantly he knew he should not have said so much. Certainly Norton would tell his master. Pitt had given away his opportunity to catch Kynaston unaware. "I'm sorry, but it cannot wait," he added.

"Yes, sir." Norton bowed his head very slightly in acknowledgment. "I shall inform him immediately. If you would like to wait in the morning room, it is agreeably warm. See if these slippers will fit you."

Pitt obeyed, taking off his prized boots, then following Norton to the morning room, slippers in his hand.

Kynaston came only moments later, his face grave and anxious. He closed the door behind him and remained standing.

"Norton tells me you have found another woman's body in the gravel pits," he said without preamble.

"Yes, sir, I'm afraid so. This one also has been mutilated, and appears to have been dead some time, but placed there only last night."

The last dregs of color drained out of Kynaston's face. He swallowed hard, as if something constricted his throat.

"For God's sake, man, why are you telling me this?" he demanded huskily. "Do you imagine that it is Kitty at last?"

So Norton had not told him! Interesting. Had he not had the opportunity, or was his loyalty more divided than one might suspect?

"No, sir, I think that is not possible," he replied. "This woman has fair hair, very little like the description of Kitty Ryder. Also we have found Harry Dobson, and he says Kitty ran away with him, but has since left him. We checked, and neighbors and local shopkeepers have seen her, alive and well, since she left here."

"And you couldn't have told us this before?" Kynaston said in a sudden explosion of fury. His eyes were blazing, the color dark in his cheeks. "What the devil is the matter with you, man? Whatever you think of me, what about my wife's feelings? Or those of the other servants? She was part of our household! We cared about her!"

Pitt felt the lash of his words, but curiously it pleased him. The man was showing some sign of ordinary decency.

"We have only just found out, sir," he answered levelly. "Sergeant Stoker worked in his own time. This morning I was woken with the news of this second body, which also has a handkerchief identical to the one we found on the first body, and to several your wife possesses." He took the gold watch fob out of his pocket and laid it on the table between them. "And she also had this . . ."

Now Kynaston did sit down, hard, as if he were uncertain his legs would support him much longer. His face was ash pale. "That is my watch fob. It used to be my brother's. That's why I was so upset when it was stolen."

"And where did you say the theft happened, sir?" Pitt remembered perfectly where Kynaston said it had been taken, but he wanted to see if he could catch Kynaston out with an inconsistency by asking again.

"Oxford Street. It was crowded. I only realized when I went to check the time later. Someone is trying to make it appear that I am involved in this," he said desperately. "God knows why! I have no idea who this woman is, what happened to her, or how she got there. Any more than I had for the first one, poor creature." He looked up. "If she is not Kitty, for which I am profoundly grateful, who is she? She's still someone, violently dead and her body discarded. Why aren't you doing everything you can to find out who she is, and who did this to her?"

Pitt controlled his own feelings with some difficulty. He had seen this body, and the first one.

"That's a regular police job, Mr. Kynaston. I'm Special Branch, and my job is the security of the country. And in this case, to safeguard you and your reputation so you can continue with the work you do for the navy."

Kynaston buried his head in his hands. "Yes . . . I know that. I'm sorry. Tell me when this latest body was put there, if you know, and I'll account for wherever I was."

"Some time last night," Pitt told him, "before light this morning, probably at least an hour before. I can't tell you closer than that at the moment. I might be able to after I've seen the police surgeon, and he has had time to look at her more closely. She's been dead quite awhile."

"How . . . how did she die?"

"I don't know that either. But perhaps we can exclude you before we've learned that. Where were you from sundown yesterday until, let's say, a quarter to six this morning?"

Kynaston looked vaguely surprised. "I was in bed most of the night, like anybody else!"

"From sundown yesterday evening, sir?"

"I dined out . . . at my club. I'd been working late in the City. I didn't want to come all the way home to eat. I was tired, and hungry."

There was a sharp edge to his voice, but Pitt could not tell if it was from irritation or fear.

"Did you dine alone?" Pitt asked. "Would one of the stewards remember you?"

"I had things to consider for a meeting. I was in no mood for idle conversation, however agreeable. But certainly the steward will remember me. Ask him."

"Yes, sir, I will. If you will give me the name of the club, and the address. And if you recall which steward it was who served you, I'll speak to him personally. What time did you leave?"

"I didn't look at the clock. Half past nine, roughly."

"And you got home at what time?"

"The traffic was bad. Some stupid accident; man not in control of his horses. I was late. Ask Norton, he'll tell you. I think it was about eleven."

"Did you speak to Mrs. Kynaston?" Pitt and Charlotte shared a bed, but he knew that many people with large houses did not necessarily do so, especially when they had been married for some time. Kynaston's sons were at boarding school or university and both his daughters were married.

"It was unnecessary to disturb her at that time of night," Kynaston replied. His mouth twisted in a bitter smile. "But if you think I crept out of the house unseen, found some wretched woman's body and somehow or other carried it up to the gravel pits and left it there, then returned home to my bed again, you might ponder how I managed to do it without disturbing anyone and getting my clothes sodden. Or how I even carried her! It wasn't in my carriage. The groom would know if I'd disturbed the horses, and I certainly didn't do it in a hansom cab!"

Pitt smiled back at him. "Frankly, sir, I don't think you did it at all. But someone did. All I have to do is be satisfied that it could not have been you, or anyone in this house . . ."

"Norton? Have you lost your wits?" Kynaston said incredulously. "The coachman? The bootboy?"

"No, sir. I never considered Norton a possibility. But your observation about the horses, and the idea of anyone doing such a thing in a hansom, very nicely rules him out as well. Actually, we think it was probably a pony and trap."

"I don't have one."

"Yes, sir, I know that."

Kynaston sighed. "I suppose it's your job. I'm damned glad it isn't mine! I imagine someone has to do it."

Pitt was stung. "Yes, sir. And sometimes it is extremely unpleasant, full of darkness and tragedy." He took a breath. "But if it were your wife or daughter lying out there you would wish me to do everything in my power to learn the truth, whoever it inconvenienced."

He expected Kynaston to lose his temper, but instead he began to tremble and went so ashen that had he not been sitting already he might well have fallen.

"I'm sorry," he said very quietly. "I spoke without thinking. This whole business is deeply distressing."

Pitt wished he had not been so harsh. And yet he had meant what he said, even if he knew instantly that he should not have said it. Perhaps it would be wiser now to leave the matter of the supposed affair until Kynaston was more composed. "I'll keep you informed, sir, should we actually find Kitty Ryder. But it was certainly not her body in the gravel pit, either the first time or now."

"Thank you. Norton will see you out."

Pitt went into the hall where Norton handed him his clean and polished boots and retrieved the slippers. Pitt thanked him.

Pitt spent the rest of the morning checking what Kynaston had said. He did not disbelieve him, but he wanted to have the proof so he could rebut any accusations made by journalists. More importantly he needed be able to answer any questions firmly, even tartly, that Somerset Carlisle might again raise in the House, under the privilege afforded him as a member of Parliament.

By two o'clock in the afternoon he was tired and miserable. His stomach was gnawing at him with hunger, so much so that he felt light-headed as he sat at one of the tables in a pub. Eating a big steak and kidney pudding with a glass of cider helped little.

Kynaston had been at his club, but he had left at least an hour earlier than he had said, and arrived home an hour later than he had told Pitt. Neither had there been any recorded incidents of traffic accidents or other delays. He had had Stoker speak to a number of hansom drivers, as they were the most reliable source of information as to the traffic conditions on the streets. It was part of their livelihood to know. Word of delays, accidents, and mischance of any sort spread like fire among them. There was hardly a street in London they did not frequent, let alone the way from Kynaston's club in central London to his home on Shooters Hill.

The barmaid passed by, checking that he was satisfied with his meal. He smiled his thanks and took another mouthful.

Why had Kynaston lied? Clearly he was afraid, but of whom? Of what? Where had he been for nearly two hours that he had not accounted for?

Perhaps the matter came back to his mistress again? The issue of Kitty Ryder's disappearance had all but died from the public's mind. The newspapers' attention had been taken by other things. The police wished to identify the first body but had already pursued it as far as they could. Kynaston might reasonably have believed that life was back to normal. Only the discovery of this new body in the gravel pit brought the whole thing flooding back to mind.

Pitt kept on eating, warmer at last.

No doubt the newspapers would have banner headlines on this second wretched discovery. They would sell thousands of extra copies on the sheer horror of it. They would go after Kynaston again because he was a public figure. It was a temptation they would not even try to resist.

Why in heaven's name had he lied? He must surely have foreseen that?

Pitt knew he must weigh how he would answer Edom Talbot, when Talbot sent for him, as he assuredly would.

Then another thought occurred to him. Was it conceivable that Kynaston knew who had killed those women? Was he protecting him willingly? Or was he afraid of him? Was someone he loved in jeopardy of far deeper involvement than Kynaston could protect them from?

Pitt finished his meal without the enjoyment such cooking deserved, emptied his glass of cider. He went out to find a hansom to take him to Downing Street to report this latest event to Talbot—although no doubt Talbot would have heard of it already, at least the facts.

Pitt was correct in that assumption. He was ushered in immediately, and Talbot saw him within ten minutes. Only an interview with the prime minister himself could take precedence over this.

Talbot came into the room stiff with fury. His hands fumbled with the doorknob and he ended up slamming it in spite of himself. This was the residence and the office of the prime minister of Great Britain, and he could not afford such a loss of self-control. He clearly blamed Pitt for it.

"What in heaven's name are you doing, Pitt?" he demanded in a low, angry voice. "I thought you had this thing under control!"

Pitt knew that he could not afford to lose his own self-mastery. Narraway would not have, whatever he felt. He had a temper—Pitt knew that very well—but Narraway just had too much dignity to allow someone else to manipulate him. That thought was helpful. He clung to it.

"We did, sir," he replied stiffly, "until this new body was found. We have no idea yet who she is. I'm waiting for the police surgeon to tell me what he has found, or can deduce. My first priority was to see if Mr. Kynaston could provide proof that it has nothing to do with him, or anyone in his house."

"And did you?" Talbot could not conceal his fear. His face was strained, the muscles of his neck so tight he could barely turn his head without a wince of pain. His high, stiff collar had to be biting into him.

"To my own satisfaction," Pitt answered. "But it won't satisfy the police, or the newspapers, if they get hold of it. It certainly wouldn't satisfy a jury."

Talbot seemed not to be breathing, yet a nerve jumped in his temple.

"Be precise, man," he snapped. "What are you talking about? The prime minister can't deal in *what's* and *if's* and *maybe's*. Is Kynaston implicated or not? If that damn fool Carlisle asks questions in the House again, the prime minister has to have a decent and absolute answer! And I have to be able to assure him that it is accurate. And in spite of appearance to the contrary, that Special Branch knows what the devil it's doing!"

Pitt kept his voice level with a considerable effort.

"This woman had a gold watch chain with a very unusual fob. The first one had the actual watch, you will remember . . ."

"Half the well-to-do men in London have gold watches," Talbot snapped. "Probably most of them have a chain and fob of some sort."

"The watch was Kynaston's," Pitt said levelly. "He admitted it. The fob he owned to as well. It has the initials BK on it. He said it had belonged to his brother, Bennett, and was of sentimental value to him. He said it had been stolen from him by a pickpocket, in Oxford Street, or near it."

Talbot was silent for a moment.

Pitt waited.

"And do you believe him?" Talbot said at last.

"I don't know. There was a handkerchief like the first one as well."

"It means nothing!" Talbot said sharply.

"And the watch and fob, on two different women, both dead and mutilated, and left in the gravel pits?" Pitt asked. "Does that also mean nothing? On the other hand, we have evidence that the Kynastons' maid was seen alive and well sometime after the first body was found, and the second one does not resemble her."

Something almost palpable eased inside Talbot. "Seen alive after the first body was found? Then for God's sake leave Kynaston alone! You can't prove anything! Maybe this pickpocket is your homicidal lunatic!"

"Perhaps. But when I asked Mr. Kynaston to account for his whereabouts at the time the body was left in the gravel pit, he lied about it."

"So he's got some business, or pastime, he doesn't want to discuss with the public!" Talbot raised his eyebrows very high. "Haven't we all? He was gambling, drinking, or whoring, for all I know, or care. He wasn't murdering some wretched woman and dumping her body in the gravel pits right outside his own damn doorway!"

"I was hoping for something definitive for the newspapers," Pitt explained. "They might consider any of the pastimes you mentioned worthy of public attention, and I'm sure we would rather they didn't." He kept the smile from his face with difficulty. It might well have been more of a sneer.

Talbot started to make a remark, then thought better of it. "Keep me apprised," he ordered instead. "Do try to get this thing solved and out of the newspapers."

"Yes, sir."

THE EVENING DARKNESS HAD closed in and it was dripping sporadic rain when Pitt reached the police surgeon at the morgue. He knew the woman from the gravel pit would have been given priority. Surely Whistler would have all the information he needed by now?

He found Whistler in his office looking tired and a little gaunt. His clothes were rumpled and his tie had come undone. A kettle was steaming gently on the top of a wood-burning stove in the corner, and altogether the room was very pleasant, apart from its proximity to the morgue itself. All real ease was torn away by the knowledge that within thirty feet of them there were cold rooms with corpses in them, and tables on which those same corpses would duly be cut open and examined.

When Pitt went in, Whistler was in the act of taking his work jacket off and replacing it with a more casual one. His hands were pink, the skin a little raw, as if he had just scrubbed himself as hard as he could with an abrasive brush.

"I was expecting you," he said wearily. "In fact I thought you'd be here waiting, like a dog for its dinner." He sat down behind his desk, which was covered with papers in no apparent order.

"Would it have been worth the wait?" Pitt asked, closing the door. He was grateful that he did not have Whistler's job. Even if his clients were beyond pain, and Pitt's were not, they were also beyond help.

Whistler sighed. "Tea?" he offered. "It's colder than a witch's heart in that damn morgue." Without waiting for Pitt's reply he moved the kettle into the middle of the stove and watched while it boiled. He talked as he made the tea in a battered pewter pot, which must once have been quite handsome.

"Cause of death is fairly obviously a very bad fall," he said. "From the look of the poor creature, might have been out of a window. Two stories up, at least, maybe higher. Lot of broken bones, some of them downright splintered. Only good thing about it is that she probably didn't know much about it."

Pitt winced. "How long ago?"

"Ah!" Whistler poured the boiling water into the teapot and inhaled the fragrant steam. "That's the more difficult part. At least two weeks ago, but I'd bet my money on more like three. But just like the other one from the gravel pit, she'd been kept in a cold place. Couldn't have made a better job of it if I'd had her here. And I assure you, I didn't! No apparent marks of depredation, except a little bit from insects. Hadn't been out there more than a night. But I expect you know that. Do you take milk?"

"Yes, please." Pitt was losing his taste for eating or drinking anything, even as chilled as he was.

"Sugar?"

"No . . . thank you."

"Got no cake. Need to stop eating so much. Cut up too many fat people and seen what's inside 'em to want to become one." He passed Pitt one of the mugs. "Here."

"Thank you. So she was kept for a couple of weeks at least? You're certain?" he asked.

Whistler looked at him sharply. "Of course I'm certain! You've got a bloody lunatic here! The sooner you, or someone else, gets hold of him and locks him up, the better."

Pitt asked the question he had been dreading. "Are you certain she was murdered?"

Whistler's eyebrows shot up almost to his hairline. "What? Man, half the bones in her body were smashed. She didn't walk herself up to the gravel pit in the middle of the night!"

"I'm not suggesting she put herself there," Pitt said patiently. "But could she have died from an accidental fall, and someone else put her there?"

"Two or three weeks after she died? And for God's sake—the mutilations! That's not done by animals or nature—it's grotesque, man: moral obscenity!" Whistler took a deep breath, then let it out slowly. "But I suppose it's not impossible her death itself was accidental—if you can look at it in isolation," he conceded. "But why? Why would any sane man keep the victim of an appalling accident for weeks, mutilate her, and then dump her up at the gravel pit—and right where she'd be sure to be found? If he wanted to get rid of the body, why not bury her? Or even drop her, with a few stones around her waist, in one of the shallow lakes around there? By the time the summer dried them out, she'd be unrecognizable. There wouldn't be a cat in hell's chance of finding out who she was, or who put her there. If she was ever found at all."

Pitt thought about it. "Well, he doesn't appear to have been interrupted, so he had time to do whatever he wanted. He must have wanted her to be found."

Whistler stared at him. "So we've got a lunatic on our hands."

"Perhaps . . ."

"If this one isn't, I pray to the Good Lord we never get one that fits your idea of what is!" he said disgustedly.

"Anything else you can tell me?" Absentmindedly Pitt drank the tea. For all the makeshift preparation of it, it was actually very good. After the subject of the conversation, and the fear that was forming in his mind, he was glad of the tea's warmth.

"I'll write up a full report for you," Whistler promised. "But I doubt it'll help you much. As far as I can tell, she was a well-nourished woman in her late twenties. From the state of her it's hard to tell a lot. A few odd scars on her hands, just like the other one. Could have been a maid or laundress, or a young woman with her own house, but no one else to do the chores. But if she was poor, she still ate well. Her hair must have been beautiful, and she was tall and nicely curved in all the right places. Does that help?" He put his cup down and added more hot water to it.

"Not that I can see," Pitt admitted. "We'll get the local police this side of the river to find out if anyone's missing that it could be. Thank you, anyway."

"Sorry I can't tell you when she died, closer than by a week or so. Can't very well rule anyone out over that."

"Can't even tell who put her there," Pitt replied. "For whatever that might be worth!"

Pitt thanked him and left, glad to get outside into the wind, away from the heaviness and the closed air of Whistler's office.

He walked for a little distance, deep in thought. He was not ready yet to decide his next actions, although it was too late to do much else this evening. When he got home he would have dinner, then help Jemima with her homework, or at least make suggestions. He would have a quick game of dominoes with Daniel, who was getting pretty good at it. Another year or two and he would have lost the chance. Daniel and Jemima would be bound up in their own futures. Jemima would probably be in love.

Charlotte would understand if Pitt continued working, but that was not an excuse to do so. Regardless of her wishes that he solve the case, he wanted to spend time with her for himself, time that had nothing to do with Kynaston, or dead women, or possible treason and threats to the state.

Walking home alone in the dark, the wind blustery around him, he would think.

Was someone trying to make Kynaston appear guilty of killing these women? It was an outlandish idea! Worse than eccentric, it was absurd. Since Kitty was alive, at least until a few days ago, the first body could not have been hers. Yet the suggestion that it was had been deliberately created by leaving the distinctive gold watch there. By whom? But more than that, why? Had there been a pickpocket at all? It was totally believable, and impossible to disprove.

He crossed a main thoroughfare and had to wait for a couple of carriages to pass.

Was Somerset Carlisle behind it? This was bizarre and macabre enough for him! It took Pitt back all those years to the case in Resurrection Row, and the corpses then. He remembered with a shiver and a strange, twisted amusement the resolution of that case. Perhaps he should have had Carlisle prosecuted then? But he had not. It was one of the very few occasions when he had bent the rules. His own sense of justice forced him to. Had Carlisle always known that? Yes, he probably had.

And now that Pitt knew Vespasia so much better, cared for her as much as he cared for anyone in his own immediate family, it was still impossible to prosecute him! Carlisle had been her friend—and his—in times of disappointment, or need. He had never found any request for help too dangerous or too troublesome to fulfill.

He increased his pace a little, walking along the pavement.

And he also owed Carlisle for the rescue from his embarrassment, possibly even a major disgrace, in front of Talbot. Not that Carlisle would ever attempt to collect the debt! And that made it heavier to carry.

Damn the man, and his charm, his courage, and his outrageous behavior!

In the morning Pitt resolved to have Stoker, and whatever other men he needed, dig more deeply into every aspect of Kynaston's life, his relationships past and present, personal and professional. Had he rivals for office? What exactly was his financial position? What were his debts, or expectations? And, of course, who was the mistress he guarded so carefully? And lied about? Had he rivals there, other than the woman's husband, of course? He could not now afford to ignore any of these things, distasteful as they were to pursue. The watch and the fob made them impossible to overlook.

12

Victor Narraway awoke early the following morning and was not in the least surprised to find Pitt at the door as he was about to begin breakfast. Last evening's newspapers had been full of the discovery of another mutilated body in the Shooters Hill gravel pits. Narraway had already lain awake for some of the night, thinking it over and over. He had fallen asleep at almost three in the morning, exhausted and without any further useful thoughts.

He welcomed Pitt in and asked his manservant to bring him breakfast. Pitt declined it and Narraway ignored him.

"You're going to sit here and talk to me. You might as well eat," he pointed out. "I don't think well on an empty stomach, and neither do you. Has this new body got anything to do with Kynaston?"

The manservant appeared with an additional cup and saucer. Narraway thanked him and poured tea for Pitt without asking him.

"Appears to have," Pitt replied, taking the tea and thanking him for it. After the first sip, he appreciated that he was hungry as well. "She had a gold watch chain and a highly unusual gold fob, which Kynaston admitted was his, from the watch he claims was stolen from his pocket in Oxford Street. He made no insurance claim because its sentimental value was irreplaceable. It used to belong to his late brother, Bennett."

Narraway stopped eating for a moment. "Do you believe Kynaston about the robbery?" he asked, not taking his eyes from Pitt's.

"I have no idea," Pitt admitted. "It seems extremely fortuitous, and yet he does not seem to me to be lying. Somebody could have stolen it, and left it on the body—like the watch left on the first body. The question is why. Is this personal or professional?"

"Any reason why it should be personal?" Narraway asked the question without hope that Pitt would have found any such reason. They were both working towards the answer they did not want, and he seemed to know it.

It was Pitt's job to find this truth, whatever it turned out to be. It was not Narraway's; the government had dismissed him. He owed no more loyalty towards them than the average citizen did. No—that was not true, not completely. Old loyalties could not be disregarded.

"Carlisle." Pitt had remained silent, so Narraway finally said what they were both thinking.

Pitt nodded. "It is he who is drawing attention to Kynaston in Parliament. What is the disappearance of Kynaston's wife's maid to Carlisle unless he has some deeper motive for raising the subject? Why would he do that?"

"Have you spoken to him?"

The manservant came in silently with Pitt's breakfast: eggs, bacon, fried bread, and fresh toast.

Pitt thanked him and began to eat with relish.

"No," he answered after a few minutes. "I've been putting it off . . ."

"You don't want to know," Narraway said drily. "Neither do I, but I think you have to." He smiled very slightly. "I don't."

Pitt looked at him steadily. The amusement died out of Narraway's eyes and he colored very faintly, just a flush across the bones of his cheeks.

It told Pitt all he was seeking to know. Narraway loved Vespasia enough to blind himself deliberately so he could protect Carlisle, because he was her friend. Pitt felt a sudden wave of emotion, a happiness that surprised him. But he would say nothing of that now, even though he was aware of a strange aloneness where he had counted on an ally. And yet it also pleased him. It was something he had not thought Narraway to be capable of, and from the awareness of it now, neither had Narraway himself.

"But I will have to do it soon," Pitt continued aloud. "I will be happy if he has some believable story to explain it."

"Very subtle," Narraway said sarcastically. "Really, Pitt, you could do better than that!"

Pitt raised his eyebrows. "Do I need to?"

"No—no, you don't. And I daresay I would have criticized you if you had. Have some toast."

Pitt accepted the toast.

"I do think Kynaston is the key, given what we know about Kitty running off," Pitt said after he swallowed the first bite. "Plus he seems to be prepared to lie, even if it brings him into suspicion of having dumped this second body in the gravel pit."

"You had better be careful about it," Narraway warned. "Have all your reasons ready to explain why you're digging into the very private life of a man whose skills at invention are extremely important to the country."

"If it's really just an affair, why won't he tell me and clear himself from suspicion of murder?" Pitt argued. "I don't approve of him being in bed with another man's wife, but it isn't my concern, unless he's endangering the security of the country. I'm not going to expose it. Good heavens, I've spent all my adult life in the police! Does he imagine I haven't seen every kind of affair you can think of, and a few you wouldn't have?"

Narraway smiled. "I know. You can't leave the job half done. I'm just warning you to be careful. Talbot already dislikes you . . ."

"I hardly know him!" Pitt protested.

Narraway shook his head very slightly. "You are naïve sometimes, Pitt. Talbot doesn't need to know you to resent your rise to a position usually occupied by someone of considerable social standing, and frequently a military or naval background as well. The fact that you're the best man for the job is irrelevant to him."

"Why on earth—" Pitt began.

"Because he's from the same sort of background, you fool!" Narraway said with exasperation. "And he knows society's closed to him. You don't care, and that gives you a kind of grace, God help me, that allows you to be accepted. Added to which—and believe me I understand it—you know too many people's secrets for anyone to risk offending you."

"And you?" Pitt asked.

"Or me either," Narraway admitted. "And neither do I care." He stopped suddenly.

"And I have never minded that I married above me," Pitt added wryly. "Or hardly ever . . ."

Narraway drew in his breath, then let it out again soundlessly.

"It's not an insult," Pitt said gently. "I don't think there are any royal princes left for Vespasia to marry upwards, nor would she want to."

"I hope not," Narraway said with emotion. Then he changed the subject abruptly, a slight pinkness coloring his cheeks. "Be careful of Talbot. Carlisle will not be there the next time to risk his neck rescuing you. You owe him a debt on that—which I suppose you are acutely aware of?"

"Yes . . . but . . ." He had been going to say that it would have no effect upon his actions in confronting Carlisle over the bodies in the gravel pits; but he wondered if that were true. "I suppose I shouldn't have—" he began.

"Don't be a fool, Pitt," Narraway snapped. "You can't go through life without owing anybody. The real debts are hardly ever a matter of money: they are about friendship, trust, help when you desperately need it, a hand out in the darkness to take yours, when you're alone. You give it when you can, and don't look for thanks, never mind payment. You grasp it when you're drowning, and you never forget whose hand it was."

Pitt said nothing.

"Carlisle won't call you on it," Narraway said with conviction. "You've turned a blind eye to his misdemeanors a few times."

"And he's helped me more than once," Pitt answered. "Of course he won't call me on it! But I'll be aware of it myself."

"It's more than that." Narraway reached for the teapot and refilled both of their cups. "It will be impossible to hide the fact that you're digging into Kynaston's private life. Are you certain you are prepared to deal with whatever you find? Ignorance is sometimes a kind of safety. And with the reactions of other people whose personal habits wouldn't bear being made public, you could lose some valuable allies. You'll find out enough you don't want to know in this job; it's a balancing act: know, but pretend that you don't. You need to be a better actor than you are, Pitt, and less of a moralist, at least on the surface. Your job is to know, not to judge."

"You make me sound like a provincial clergyman with more self-righteousness than compassion," Pitt said with disgust.

"No," Narraway said, shaking his head. "I'm just remembering how I used to be—at your age."

Pitt laughed outright. "When you were my age, you were twenty years older than I am!"

"In some things," Narraway agreed. "I'm twenty years behind you in others. Ask the questions you need to. Meanwhile, I will find out what I can and tell you just what is relevant, and no more."

Pitt did not argue. "Thank you," he said quietly.

THE FOLLOWING DAY PITT received a rather stiff request to meet his brother-in-law, Jack Radley. Since it was apparently about the Kynaston case, Pitt could hardly refuse. He saw Jack alone, if hardly privately, on the Embankment not far from the House of Commons. It was a fresh, windy day with the usual chill of early March. The air was cold off the river, salt-smelling, and too brisk for one to enjoy lingering, so they walked along quite quickly together.

Jack came straight to the point.

"What business is it of Special Branch if Dudley Kynaston has a mistress, let alone who she might be?"

Pitt could hear the sharp edge of criticism in Jack's voice, something he was unused to. They had many differences of view, but they had usually been amicable. The tone of this took Pitt by surprise.

"If it wasn't my business I wouldn't ask," he replied. "Although I hadn't realized I was so obvious."

"Oh, really!" Jack was impatient. "You're asking about where he was, who he was with, attendance at different theaters or dinners—then cross-checking. Everybody can work out what you're looking for." He hunched his shoulders against the chill and pulled his white silk scarf a little higher. "You don't suspect him of theft, or embezzling naval petty cash, or cheating at cards, do you? Or even being a little drunk and talking too much. Anyone can tell you Dudley Kynaston is a decent man from a good family who behaves like a gentleman and is intensely loyal to his country and all it means." He turned to look at Pitt. "If he has a mistress, what of it? Maybe his wife is a crashing bore, or one of those chilly women who would break something if they laughed, or loved!"

Pitt caught him by the arm and swung him round so he was obliged to stop. They stood face-to-face in the wind.

"You say that with a lot of feeling, Jack." Pitt allowed it to sound like an accusation. He had not entirely forgotten Jack's reputation before his marriage.

Jack colored; his eyes under his amazing eyelashes were dark with temper. "You're a self-righteous idiot sometimes, Thomas. You may have been promoted to be the guardian of the nation's secrets, but no one appointed you arbiter of our morals. Leave the poor man alone, before you ruin him with your suspicions."

"I wouldn't give a damn about his affair," Pitt said between his teeth. "Except that I'm trying to prove he didn't have anything to do with the murder of two women!! But I can't do that if he keeps on lying to me about where he was at the relevant times."

"I thought you didn't know when the second woman was killed," Jack retaliated instantly.

"I don't!" Pitt was raising his voice now, too. "But I know within a few hours when she was dumped at the gravel pit, and I'm pretty certain how she was carried there. If Kynaston would tell me where he was, and I could confirm it, I'd be certain it was not he who did it."

"Why the hell would you even suspect him?"

"You know better than to ask that," Pitt replied. "You know perfectly well I can't tell you."

The anger drained out of Jack's voice. "It must be intensely private . . ."

"I need to know about this for myself!" Pitt said exasperatedly. "I'm not going to tell the world. If he isn't guilty he's wasting my time, but I'll let go of it and allow the regular police to do their job. If this case is no threat to Kynaston, it's nothing to do with Special Branch."

Jack looked at him with disbelief. "You really think Kynaston's desperation to hide who his mistress is could be a threat to the security of the state? Come on, Thomas. That looks a hell of a lot like an upstart officer wielding his new powers to embarrass his social superiors, because he can. You're better than that."

Pitt was stunned. He stood in the bright light, and the cold wind off the water chilled him right through his coat as if it were made of cotton.

"Kynaston's maid ran away the night before the first body was found, Jack," he replied, his voice shaking not only with anger but with a degree of hurt. "Because she saw or heard something that made her fear for her life. And that's not a supposition! She's been seen and spoken to since. Not by us—we can't find her—but by others with no interest in this affair. Now there's a second woman dead and mutilated and dumped in the same gravel pit. Physical evidence, which he doesn't deny, links him to both dead women. Kynaston isn't telling the truth about where he was, and won't tell us anything except that he's having an affair. But he must prove it, or allow his mistress, even discreetly to Special Branch, to say where they were. She could just confirm that he was actually with her. There are questions here that need to be answered. He works on highly sensitive state secrets for the navy. Wouldn't you want something better than an evasion, for that reason alone?"

Jack looked as if the wind drove through his coat, too. The last of the anger drained out of him, and his face was pale and tight. "Do you think he killed anyone?" he asked very quietly.

"I don't want to," Pitt replied. "But he's hiding something a lot more than the name of a woman he's having an affair with."

Jack said nothing.

"Would you sooner be publicly accused of murder than privately accused of infidelity?" Pitt demanded.

"It doesn't make sense," Jack agreed unhappily, his face filled with concern, his shoulders hunched. "Is he protecting someone, do you think? He counts family loyalty terribly highly."

"Of course he does," Pitt agreed sarcastically. "That's why he has a mistress!"

Jack winced as if Pitt had slapped him. "Perhaps that is more loyal than leaving a wife and publicly humiliating her," he said so softly that the whine of the wind almost took his words away.

Pitt stared at him. It was a possibility that had not occurred to him. Then a worse thought followed hard on its heels. Was Jack speaking of Kynaston, or of himself? Charlotte had told him of Emily's unhappiness, but he had also seen it. She was without color, all the fine lines on her face drawn downwards. It was not absurd that Ailsa Kynaston had taken her for Charlotte's elder sister. Was that, at the heart of it, why Jack so resented Pitt's pursuit of Kynaston's affair? Sometimes Pitt wished he did not have to know so much. This kind of knowledge could isolate you from all human closeness. He could not tell Charlotte. Her love of Emily, and her own candor, would betray it instantly.

"I know you've been offered a position close to Kynaston," he said aloud. "Be careful, Jack. Think hard before you accept it. You have a lot to lose."

"You said there is physical evidence linking Kynaston to the murdered women?" Jack asked. "Are you certain?"

"Absolutely. Don't ask me about it because I can't tell you. It doesn't prove guilt, but it's highly suggestive. If you have any influence with him, Jack, tell him to explain himself. I can't let it go!"

Jack stared at him long and steadily, then gave a very slight nod and turned and walked away, back towards the Houses of Parliament.

Pitt could not tell Charlotte about his conversation with Jack. She knew him far too well: even if she did not ask, she would deduce from his discomfort that there was something he would not discuss. Her imagination would make the worst of it, probably that the rift between Jack and Emily was deeper than she had thought. She and Emily might quarrel at times over all sorts of little things, but underneath it she was intensely loyal. Entwined through all her life's memories were the images of Emily as the younger sister, the one two years behind whom it was Charlotte's job to protect. It had nothing to do with duty, or with need, for that matter. Emily had been supremely able to look after herself—until now.

THAT EVENING PITT SAT in his big chair by the fire watching Daniel and Jemima working on a large jigsaw puzzle. After some time he became aware of a pattern, not only in the picture beginning to take form on the card table but in their behavior also. There were three years between their ages. Jemima was always those few steps ahead. It would be like that through life, until age began to be a disadvantage. Now it was all in Jemima's favor. But as he watched, he saw her mind leap to a recognition, her hand reach for the piece then fall back again. She smiled as Daniel suddenly made the same recognition and put the piece in the right space.

Pitt felt a sudden rush of emotion, almost overpowering. He could see something of himself in Jemima, but so very much more of her mother. That kind of discreet gentleness, the quiet selflessness, was exactly what he had observed in Charlotte, time and again. Jemima was not yet sixteen, and there it was, the instinct to nurture, to protect.

How could he protect Jack, or Emily, in this wretched business, without crossing the boundaries of his own morality?

Jack had made a bad error of judgment with his loyalties once before. There would be those very happy to remind his superior of it, and throw his wisdom into doubt. The safety of the state was Pitt's duty, above and beyond that to those he loved. No one in the public trust could favor his own family. It would be, perhaps, the ultimate betrayal of the oath he had taken, and the faith in him he had accepted.

And yet he learned secrets he did not want to know, vulnerabilities he could not protect. He had his own network of debts and loyalties; it was what made life precious: the honor, and the caring. Without such things it was empty, a long march to nowhere.

Carlisle had done favors for all of them, in one case or another, especially for Vespasia. If Carlisle was involved—and Pitt was becoming increasingly afraid that he was—could Pitt ever trust Vespasia in this?

Perhaps Victor Narraway was the only one he could trust without placing an intolerable burden on him.

But thinking back on their last meeting, perhaps he, too, was now compromised? He cared for Vespasia far more deeply than mere friendship. After all the fancies and hungers of his youth, and adventures since then, even his care for Charlotte, was this to be the love of his life, the one that touched him too deeply to heal over, or pass by?

What were Vespasia's feelings for him? Were they more than friendship, interest, affection? No man, especially one so sensitive under the shell as Victor Narraway, could settle happily for that! If you are in love, you want it all.

Pitt was alone in whatever action he took, or refrained from. He was more truly alone than he could ever recall. Whatever he did about Somerset Carlisle, it was solely his judgment to make. Was he really the right man for this job? He had the intelligence and the experience to detect. He had pursued and found the truth on many occasions where others had failed. On that his promotion was deserved. But had he the wisdom? Did he understand people with money and power, ancient privilege of history and title, pride and loyalty stretching intricate webs into all the great families in the land, and in some cases beyond and into Europe?

Was he himself free from all debt and loyalty, all emotional pity that could corrupt? He looked at his family around him in the twilight. And it reached much further than that: to Vespasia, Narraway, Jack and Emily; further still to Charlotte's mother and her husband. To Somerset Carlisle, even. To all the people who had shared the moments of his life, to whom he owed if not compassion, then at least honesty.

He did not want to know if Carlisle had placed those dead women in the gravel pit, but he knew he could no longer evade the issue.

If Carlisle had placed the bodies, then where had he obtained them? Pitt refused even to imagine that he had killed them himself, or for that matter paid someone else to. That meant they were already dead. Where would he find corpses that he could take? Not a hospital. He could hardly claim to be a relative, because that would be unbelievable. Nor, for that matter, could he prove he was an employer or other benefactor.

Therefore he had done it secretly, but certainly with some help. Possibly he had a manservant of some sort that he trusted, or even more likely, someone much closer to the edge of the law whom he had helped in the past, and who was now willing to return the favor.

There were always unclaimed bodies in a morgue, people who had no close relative willing to bury them. It would not be difficult to claim some past association and then offer to provide a decent burial, out of pity. Then what? Bury a coffin full of bags of sand, or anything else of the appropriate weight.

That would answer the question of where the bodies had been kept so chilled and clean. It would also explain the timing of discovery of them—only when Carlisle could find one that was suitable. They needed to be young women of the servant class, unclaimed by anyone else, and who had died violently. He must have combed all London for them!

If, of course, he had done it at all!

There was no evidence, only Pitt's previous knowledge of Carlisle and his belief about his character.

What proof could he find? He could have his men look through all the records of recent deaths of women in the London area, those that were violent and resulted in the kind of injuries the gravel pit corpses had sustained. Then see which were unclaimed by family, and if some benefactor had offered to pay for a funeral.

Then what? Exhume them to see if the corpses were there, or bags of sand instead? Perhaps, but only as a last resort, and he would need far more to justify it than a desperate imagination.

He would have the inquiries made, discreetly. No exhumations until he had evidence.

But why? What was Carlisle's connection with Kynaston? He would have to look into the man's private interests apart from politics and social reform, the numerous battles against injustice. Who were his friends, other than Vespasia? Was there anyone in particular he might have turned to for help in this extraordinary undertaking? Were there any other connections that were worth exploring?

He must do it with great care, and disguise his reasons for asking. If he spoke to more than a very few, Carlisle would undoubtedly hear of it and know exactly what he was doing.

One friend of Carlisle whom Pitt spoke to was a highly respected architect by the name of Rawlins. Pitt took him to luncheon at a discreet and expensive restaurant. He gave the pretext of making a check on Carlisle in order to trust him with Special Branch information and engage his help in Parliament.

"He is erratic," Rawlins said. "I wanted to build towers and spires that reached to the sky. Somerset wanted to climb them!" He gave a wry smile. "I liked him enormously; still do, although I don't see him so often. But I never understood him. Never knew what he was thinking." He sipped the very good red wine they were having with their roast beef.

Pitt waited. He knew from the look of concentration on Rawlins' face that he was searching memory, struggling to understand something that had long eluded him.

"Then he went off to Italy without finishing his degree," Rawlins spoke slowly. "Couldn't understand why at the time. He was in line for a first; he could have been an academic."

"A woman?" Pitt suggested. So far there had been no mention of any love affair, only dalliances, nothing to capture the heart.

"I thought so at the time," Rawlins conceded. He gave a slight shrug and sipped at the wine again. "I learned long after that it was to fight with some partisans who were struggling for Italian unification. He never spoke of it himself. I only heard it from a woman I met in Rome, years later. She spoke of him as if his exploits were woven through the best and most fulfilling part of his life. I think she might have been in love with him."

He smiled ruefully. "I remember I was jealous. In her words, he sounded funny, impossibly brave, absolutely harebrained—but not un-recognizable as the man I had known."

He sighed and took another mouthful of the excellent meal. "He ended up in an Italian prison somewhere in the north, with both his shoulders dislocated. Must have hurt like hell. He never spoke of it. I haven't any idea what happened, or who did it. I could give half a dozen guesses as to why, though."

Pitt avoided Rawlins's eyes, looking instead down at his own plate. "Did you ever know him to commit violence against anyone?" he asked. "Perhaps in the conviction that the end justified the means?" He did not want the answer, and he almost denied the question in the next breath. He could feel his muscles tense, as though he were waiting for a blow.

"I can't tell you," Rawlins said quietly. "Not in a way that would be of any value. I never knew him to choose violence, in fact, as a student I saw him go to some lengths to avoid it. He was argumentative, but never quarrelsome. But I do know that he was a man of intense passions. I don't believe anything would stop him doing something he believed to be necessary in a cause he cared about. He had too much imagination, and not enough sense of fear. He was an all-or-nothing sort of man. Judging by his speeches in Parliament, and the little I know of him now, he still is. Actually, I don't think that kind of thing changes. I'm sorry I can't be of more help."

"Any friends I should worry about?" Pitt asked casually.

"Worry?"

"Fringes of the communal underworld, that sort of thing?"

Rawlins smiled. "Carlisle? Quite possibly. He's a man of eclectic tastes and peculiar loyalties. But if he makes a promise, he won't break it."

"That's rather what I thought," Pitt agreed.

They finished the meal speaking of other things. Rawlins was a pleasant man, intelligent and courteous. Pitt found him not only easy to like but easier to believe than he would have wished.

Nothing he had heard in the course of the conversation had painted a picture of Somerset Carlisle that was in any way different from the man he already knew, the man who had played such a grotesque and dangerous game with the corpses in Resurrection Row.

If anything, Pitt was worse off, because it drew a picture of a man he not only liked, and was compelled to admire, but one very capable of doing precisely what Pitt had feared.

13

PITT ARRIVED LATE AT his office on the following morning, having been held up by a traffic accident on Euston Road. The whole thing had turned into chaos as everyone tried to find a way around it, and ended by getting jammed in a total impasse where no one had room to turn and extricate themselves.

Stoker was waiting for him, looking grave. "Don't bother taking your coat off," he said as soon as Pitt was in through the door.

Pitt stopped. "Not another body!"

"No, sir, still the same one. Whistler wants to see you. And if you don't mind, sir, I'd like to come along, too."

Pitt had no objection to Stoker coming, but he was curious, and desperate for a little hope. "Why?" he asked.

Stoker stared back at him, his dark gray eyes clear. "I want to know more about what kind of a man does this to a woman. I want to know who it is that Kitty Ryder thinks she's running away from."

"No more progress with finding her?" Pitt asked.

"Not much." Stoker stopped, took a deep breath, and went on. "But I'm not giving up." There was a faint color in his bony face, just a smudge of pink across his cheeks. He looked at Pitt defiantly, offering no explanations.

"Well, if you succeed, you can ask her all the questions." Pitt jammed his hat on again. "But we can't wait for that. We'd better go and see Whistler. Just what I feel like first thing on a cold wet morning: get stuck in a traffic jam, then a visit to the morgue. Come on!" He led the way back out into the rain.

Pitt and Stoker had to wait several minutes to find a hansom. It was always like this on wet days. No one was willing to walk.

Finally they found a cab and splashed through the puddles to scramble inside, their sodden trouser legs flapping, coats flying open in the wind.

It was a long way from Lisson Grove to Blackheath, which was on the other side of the river and considerably farther east.

"If someone's trying to make Kynaston look guilty of this, even if he isn't, then it's someone with a pretty good knowledge of his household," Stoker said after a few minutes. "And he knows Kynaston himself, too. Either he knows why Kynaston keeps on lying, or he's got some kind of a hold over him so he doesn't tell us the truth." He sat huddled in his damp coat, looking sideways at Pitt in the gray daylight.

"I'm afraid that's unarguable," Pitt agreed. "What I need to know is, why? To what end? I wish I could think it was personal vengeance of some sort, but we haven't found any kind of reason for it."

They turned from Seymour Place right into Edgware Road then left and right again into Park Lane.

"Well, I daresay Rosalind Kynaston would be pretty angry if she knew about the mistress," Stoker pointed out. "And she could have taken the watch and fob easily enough."

"She might hate him," Pitt replied reasonably, "but she wouldn't ruin him. If she did, she'd be ruining herself at the same time. His disgrace would be hers as well. And if he lost his income, that's also hers! You told me she comes from a respectable background, but she has no independent wealth. Unless you think she's got a lover, too! One who would marry her, in spite of whatever this does to her reputation? I suppose it's possible, but I can't see it as likely, can you?"

Stoker thought for a moment. "I don't know women that well, sir. Not as you must, with a wife and a daughter . . ."

"I'm not sure any man really knows women," Pitt said drily. "Let us agree that perhaps my ignorance is not as total as yours. What about it?"

"Mrs. Kynaston doesn't look to me like a woman who's got a secret lover, sir." Stoker assiduously avoided his eyes. "I remember when my sister Gwen was first in love with her husband, didn't know that much about him, but, by heck, I knew she had something going on. Little things, like the way she did her hair, the way she took care with what she wore, not just some of the time, but all of it. That little secret smile, like the cat that got the cream. And even the way she walked with a little swish of her skirts, as if she knew she was going somewhere special."

Pitt couldn't help laughing, in spite of the cold and the discomfort inside the rattling hansom squashing them together. He had seen exactly what Stoker was describing in Charlotte, years ago when he had been courting her. He hadn't understood it then: the happiness one moment, despair the next, but always the vitality. She had seemed to glow with life.

He had seen it in Emily, too, when she was beginning to think seriously about Jack Radley. But that was another subject, and at the moment one of more pain than pleasure.

And, of course, now it was also beginning in Jemima. How quickly she was growing up. Pitt knew which young men she liked and which held no interest for her. She was so pretty, brave, and vulnerable, like her mother, imagining she was sophisticated, but as easy to read as an open book. Or was that only so to him, because he loved her and would have protected her from every pain, if that were possible?

Charlotte's father, on the other hand, would have protected her from the social, not to mention financial, disasters of marrying a policeman! The only fate worse would have been not to marry at all, and that judgment call was a fine thing. Thank heaven her mother had more emotional sense.

Would he have sense, when it came to Jemima marrying someone?

Not necessary to think of now. It was years away. Years and years!

They were moving steadily south towards the river. No doubt the driver would take them along the Embankment, then over one of the bridges onto the south bank.

Pitt regarded Stoker with a new respect. He had not thought him capable of such human observation. It occurred to him, not for the first time, that he did not know Stoker very much at all. Outside his skill and intelligence in the job, and his well-proven loyalty, he was almost a stranger.

"So you don't think Rosalind Kynaston is having an affair?" he asked.

"That's right, sir. She looks like a woman who has very little to be happy about," Stoker agreed.

"Do you think she knows of Kynaston's affair?"

"Probably. In my experience people do know, especially women, even if they can't afford to admit to themselves that they do. Of course, when they're not in society, and there's not much money or a nice house to lose, there's not the same need to fix a smile on your face and pretend you've seen nothing. And I'll bet you anything you like," he added, "she's not the one who killed anyone and laid them out in the gravel pits—or slashed their faces to bits!"

Pitt shivered. "Quite. But you agree that whoever is doing it, the whole thing is connected with the Kynaston house?"

"No question," Stoker agreed. "I just don't know how! I've been turning it over and over, but nothing makes complete sense. For a start, why these mutilations? What kind of a person cuts the flesh on the face of someone who's already dead? The only reason I can think of is to disguise who it is. But we've got no idea, anyway."

"Or to draw our attention to it," Pitt said, thinking aloud.

"You mean two dead women dumped in a gravel pit isn't going to make us stop and think?" Stoker asked with heavy disbelief.

"Doesn't make as big a headline as two that are mutilated in exactly the same way," Pitt pointed out.

"What's the point of that?" Stoker was now looking at Pitt curiously, as if he expected an answer. He stared more intently. "You mean it's to draw our attention even more to Kynaston? Like the handkerchiefs?"

"Maybe."

"Why?" Stoker repeated.

"That's what I am struggling with," Pitt told him, trying to find words that were honest, and yet did not tell him about Somerset Carlisle. Not naming him would be easy, but Stoker would know he was evading giving an answer, and that was an insult he did not deserve. It would also damage the trust between them, which was one of Pitt's greatest assets. Without the trust of his men he was alone. He was increasingly aware of the lack of confidence from people like Talbot, and possibly others in the government. Even in Lisson Grove he had yet to earn the kind of respect they had had for Victor Narraway.

"It grows uglier, doesn't it? At least the possibilities do." He said this softly, barely heard above the noise of the traffic along Rotherhithe Street.

"It does. And nothing yet explains the four different women," Stoker answered.

Pitt was puzzled for a moment.

"Kitty Ryder, the first woman in the gravel pit, the second woman in the gravel pit, and the mistress," Stoker counted. "There's no way any two of those could be the same person."

"I can't think of anything that makes sense of that either," Pitt admitted. "And yet the two women in the gravel pit are linked by several circumstances: the place they were found, but not necessarily where they were killed; the fact they had been kept somewhere before being put in the gravel; the mutilations, which were hideous and seem to serve no purpose at all, because they were inflicted after death but were not effective in hiding their identity, because we don't know them anyway. They both appear to have been maids, but no one has come forward to claim them. Not to mention Kynaston's watch on one and his fob on the other."

Stoker nodded. "So what about it all being nothing to do with who the women are, but to do with Kynaston—to try to blackmail or coerce him into doing something? Or not doing something? Perhaps he's behaving so stupidly about this whole thing because he had some evidence that would ruin someone, and he's being blackmailed into silence?"

"Possible," Pitt agreed. It was possible indeed—and Somerset Carlisle did not fit into that story at all. That was why, much as he longed to believe it, Pitt did not.

"You got another idea, sir?" Stoker asked.

"Only a possibility," Pitt answered. He could not shut it out any longer. He was lying to Stoker, and to himself. Somerset Carlisle was as sharp as an open razor in his brain. But Carlisle would not kill—surely? What would he care about enough to do all this: the bodies stolen from somewhere, the mutilation, which must have been hideous, almost unbearable to him . . .

The only answer that fitted it all was something as serious as treason.

"Sir?" Stoker's voice broke through his thoughts.

"To force us to dig until we find the greater crime," Pitt answered.

"Greater than murder?" Stoker's tone was hard with anger and disbelief.

"Yes, worse than murder," Pitt answered levelly. "Treason."

Stoker sat rigid. He gulped. "Yes, sir. I never thought of that—not—not in all this . . ."

"Please God, you have no need to," Pitt said, staring straight ahead of him. "It's only an idea . . ."

"No, sir." Stoker turned to face the front also. "It's our job."

Whistler met them in his office in the morgue, a place that had become unpleasantly familiar to Pitt in the last few weeks. This time Whistler was busy and in no mood to offer the hospitality of tea.

"Newspapers got it," he said curtly. "Just want you to know it wasn't me." He glared at Pitt as if already Pitt had doubted him. "Like bloody dogs sniffing out the smell of death!" he said bitterly. "Don't know what the hell they'll make of this one—probably anything and everything." He started to shake his head, and ended up with his whole body shuddering, as if he had been dropped in cold water. "The mutilations were all after death. Told you that before. When I looked at them closely, so were the broken bones. Only a few made when she was alive, most importantly, the fracture of the skull. Bruises were made at the same time. Can't bruise after you're dead. No blood flow."

Pitt stared at him. "Was it the blow to the head that killed her?" He did not know what he wanted Whistler to say. It was a nightmare. All that would make it any better was to wake up.

"Blow," Whistler repeated the word, turning it over in his mind, examining it.

"Was it?" Pitt snapped.

"Large, flat object," Whistler said slowly. "Lot of bruises, can't define them exactly. Too long dead now. My opinion? She fell downstairs and cracked her head on the floor at the bottom. Nothing to think it wasn't accidental."

Pitt felt relief wash over him with an intensity that was close to the sort of pain you get when a frozen limb comes back to life. "So she wasn't murdered?"

"No reason to think she was," Whistler agreed. "But what bloody, God-awful lunatic then cut half her face off—that's another question— yours, not mine!"

Pitt thanked him with a nod, and they left.

First Pitt would go and speak with Somerset Carlisle. If he had per-petuated all this horror in order to force Pitt into investigating Kynaston, then it was time to face him and demand to know what crime he believed Kynaston guilty of.

He was undecided at first whether to warn Carlisle of his coming. Surprise had many advantages, and if he were to make it a formal appointment then he would have to state his reason for it. But if he did not, the chances were high of finding that Carlisle was not at home. And perhaps it would be a deceit that would only make him look absurd. He picked up the telephone and made the appointment. Carlisle made no argument at all; in fact he had sounded as if Pitt were welcome.

As it was, a soberly dressed manservant welcomed Pitt at the door and ushered him into a pleasant and very distinct sitting room where Carlisle spent the few evenings he had at home, in the winter by the fire now warming the whole room. For the summer there was a well-curtained French door.

"This must be important," Carlisle said with a wry smile. "It's a filthy night. What price spring, eh? Still, I suppose it will be the more welcome when it comes. Sit down." He indicated a whisky glass on a table beside the chair from which he had risen. "Whisky? Sherry?" He winced very slightly. "Tea?"

"Later, thank you," Pitt replied. "If you still feel like offering it." He found his throat tight and his mouth dry with the prospect of the unpleasantness to come, and a good whisky would have warmed him. Since he rose in rank, and income, he had learned the difference between good whisky and average. But he needed a clear head tonight. He could not afford to give Carlisle any advantage at all.

"That bad?" Carlisle indicated an armchair, then sat back down in the chair opposite. His keen face showed a similar tension to that which Pitt felt knotting inside him.

There was no point in being evasive. "I think so," he replied.

Carlisle smiled, as if they were playing some desperate parlor game. "And what is it that you think I can do? I know no one who murders women and leaves them in gravel pits. Believe me, if I did, I would already have told you."

"Actually, it is not so much that they died that concerns me at the moment," Pitt said, and smiled back. "It is what appears to be their connection with Dudley Kynaston." He glanced around the room with sharpening interest. He took time to notice the naval memorabilia more closely. The beauty of one of the paintings suggested a very fine artist, and was perhaps worth a great deal of money. If not, it had been chosen with some diligence. Maybe it was inherited from someone who had long loved the sea.

Carlisle was waiting for him to continue. How direct should he be?

"Kynaston's gold watch was found on the first body," he said, watching Carlisle's expression and seeing only the slightest change. "And the fob on the second woman. Among other, less concrete connections."

Carlisle hesitated. Quite clearly he was debating within himself whether to banter or to face the real battle. He must have decided on the latter because the amusement died out of his eyes and suddenly in the firelight and the softer glow of the gas brackets above him, the lines in his face seemed deeper. He was older than Pitt, perhaps into his fifties. It was his energy that occasionally made one forget that. Now the sun and windburn from his years of mountain climbing, the lines around his eyes that he had peered into far distances, marked his features.

"A very clear connection. How did he explain it?" Carlisle asked.

"That his watch was stolen by a pickpocket," Pitt replied.

"And you believe him?"

"I'm inclined to. It is not beyond your abilities to have had someone take it for you."

"Good heavens! Rather a backhanded compliment to my abilities. A dangerous undertaking, don't you think?"

"Extremely," Pitt agreed. "Therefore you had a very good reason. I cannot imagine any love affair he could have that would stir your anger or passion to the degree where you would use these women like this in order to draw me in."

"Not to love is to die by inches. Or perhaps it is worse than that,

Maybe it is to hesitate on the shore of life and never step into its waters. But the waters are dangerous as well—go too far, and one cannot only drown oneself but take others with them," Carlisle answered sharply, weighing his words. "He has at times allowed his heart to rule his head . . ."

"True," Pitt agreed. "But I believe you have something more specific in mind."

Carlisle's eyebrows rose in a sharp double-V shape. "Perhaps. But you are calling upon me, not I on you."

"Really?" Pitt said softly. "I had the idea that perhaps you were calling upon me, and that it was time I answered."

Carlisle hesitated barely a second. "Indeed? What gave you that idea, or are we past that particular point?"

"We are past it."

"I see. And your answer is?" Carlisle sat motionless, his whisky forgotten. In fact, he had not drunk more than a couple of sips. Its color reflected gold in the firelight; in the cut crystal it looked like a jewel.

"You have my attention," Pitt replied. "I am listening."

Carlisle did not answer.

"Come on!" Pitt said more sharply than he had intended. Carlisle was stretching his nerves. He could not afford to lose this game. Nothing in all of his experience with Carlisle suggested he had ever acted lightly or taken crazy risks that could cost him his freedom, even his life, unless the stakes were high enough to warrant it.

"I investigated Kynaston, and found nothing," Pitt continued. "Kitty Ryder is still alive, but she left at night, and without taking her belongings. She must have been very afraid of something. I can't see it as being the fact that apparently Kynaston has a mistress, unless she was an extraordinarily powerful man's wife." Even as he said it, he did not believe it.

"That's not worthy of you, Pitt." Carlisle sounded disappointed. "Why the hell should I care who Kynaston's in bed with?"

"You don't," Pitt agreed. "So I wonder what it is you do care about—sufficiently to step into this macabre farce. And it is a farce, isn't it?"

Carlisle's eyes did not leave Pitt's face. "Is it?" he whispered.

"If I don't find the truth of it, yes it is!" Pitt responded sharply, his own nerves taut.

He saw a flicker of fear in Carlisle's eyes, just for a moment, so brief he was not even certain he had seen it at all.

"I don't believe you killed either one of them," he added. "In fact you probably never saw them alive."

Carlisle breathed out slowly. Something within him eased, but only a fraction.

"And you put the pieces of the watch there as well," Pitt continued. He did not mention the mutilations; that was a hideous lacuna between them. "And probably the cupboard key. You must have been damn sure I wouldn't connect it up, and charge you!"

"You're the best detective I know," Carlisle replied, his voice a little hoarse, as if his lungs were starved, his throat tight.

"So what is it you want me to find?" Pitt leaned forward. "You left those women up there without a care for their bodies, or for who might find them! What matters that much to you, Carlisle? Murder? Multiple murders?" He shook his head. "Still not enough! It has to be treason!"

Carlisle took a long, deep breath. "Do you know Sir John Ransom?"

"Not personally. I know who he is."

"Precisely," Carlisle agreed. "It was a rhetorical question. If the head of Special Branch did not know the name of the man who leads scientific inventions regarding the navy, and naval warfare, then we have very deep problems indeed."

"What about Ransom?" Pitt asked.

"He is a friend of mine. A couple of years ahead of me at Cambridge," Carlisle replied.

Pitt allowed him to continue, knowing that this much preamble must be necessary. A log collapsed in the fire, sending up a shower of bright sparks, but Carlisle apparently did not notice it.

"He came to me two or three months ago," Carlisle resumed. "He had no proof at all, but he believed that certain highly sensitive facts regarding a new step forward in submarine warfare were being offered to another naval power. He did not say which because I believe he did not know."

"From the department where Kynaston works," Pitt concluded.

"Precisely. Ransom was very worried because he had little doubt in his own mind that it was occurring, but no idea who was responsible. But it rested between three men. The other two have since been exonerated . . ."

"Leaving Kynaston," Pitt said unhappily. "But there is no proof, or you would not be discussing it. You would simply have handed over the evidence to us."

"Yes. Without proof, allowing Kynaston to know that we are aware of what he is doing would only alert him, and perhaps make the matter worse," Carlisle agreed.

"So instead you make it appear that he murdered his wife's maid, over some real or imagined love affair, and hope that I will pull your chestnuts out of the fire!"

"That's about right," Carlisle admitted. "But you're damn slow about it!" He gave a harsh, twisted smile. "You like the man . . ."

"Yes, I do. But that has nothing to do with it," Pitt said angrily. "Whatever I think of him, I can't charge him with anything at all until I have evidence to prove something. And since Kitty Ryder was seen alive and well after the first body was found, and the second body doesn't even resemble her, I have no reason to accuse Kynaston of anything, really!"

"I slipped up there," Carlisle admitted, wincing at his own failure. "But I didn't know Kitty had been seen. Are you sure?"

"Yes. I have a highly diligent assistant . . ."

"Ah! The redoubtable Stoker. Yes. An excellent man." Carlisle smiled very slightly. "If he could actually find the woman, then she would testify as to what it was she saw, or heard, and why she ran away. Although it would be better to have something rather weightier than the word of a runaway lady's maid."

"I'll widen the search for her," Pitt promised. "Who else is involved?

He must be passing the information to someone? And why, for God's sake?" Even giving words to the question and speaking it aloud was painful. He had not thought Kynaston more than perhaps self-indulgent with his mistress, certainly not a man to betray his own country. He had become used to disillusion but this still hurt.

Carlisle pulled his mouth into a gesture of apology. "I have no idea. But I have no doubt he will have plenty of defenders simply because no one will wish to believe that he could have betrayed them, or that they could have let him! The prime minister will be displeased, to say the least of it!"

"I'm getting rather accustomed to displeasing the prime minister," Pitt said tartly. "It seems to be a function of the job. But catching Kynaston, even proving what he has done, is far from the end of the task . . ."

"Oh, I know that!" Carlisle agreed. "You need to know all of it! More than anything else, you need to know exactly how much information he has given, and to whom. Preferably, you also need to know how he came into such a position, and everyone else who is involved. And then, naturally, you need to deal with him so that as few people are aware of it as possible, in the circumstances. To have a trial and exposure would be almost as damaging as the act itself."

"Thank you, Carlisle! I am aware of that!" Pitt snapped. "I also would prefer not to be obliged to prosecute you! I accept that you did not kill either of the women, but you took their bodies from wherever they were kept—a morgue of some sort, I imagine—and you laid them out in the gravel pits. I prefer not to know that you also mutilated them in identical ways so we would be forced to conclude they were killed by the same person, and the link to Kynaston was too clear to ignore. Well, I have your message, and I understand it. You have succeeded."

Carlisle was pale, even in the firelight. "I am not proud of it," he said very quietly. "But Kynaston is betraying my country. He must be stopped."

"I will do all I can to stop him," Pitt promised. "And you will help me, if I can think of a way. And from now on you will do exactly what I tell you to . . . so I can find a reason not to charge you with body-snatching, mutilating the dead, and generally being a damn nuisance!"

"Would you—" Carlisle began.

Pitt glared at him. "Yes I would! And if you involve Lady Vespasia in this I'll see you pay for it with your seat in Parliament!"

"I believe you," Carlisle said very quietly indeed. "I give you my word I have not done so, and I will not."

"Thank you." Pitt stood up. "I thank you for at least this much truth. Now I wish I'd had the whisky!"

"It's still available . . ."

"No, thank you. I must go home. It's late, and I need to think how the hell I'm going to clear this up, starting tomorrow morning. By the way, where did you get the bodies? I assume you took them from some morgue?"

"Yes. But I'll see they are decently buried, when you've finished with them. As I promised in the first place," Carlisle replied.

Pitt stared at him for a moment, trying to find words for what lay between them, and failing. He turned and left.

Outside, the rain had stopped, but the wind was even colder. Pitt thought, seeing the hard, brittle glitter of the stars, that there could be a frost.

Walking briskly along the pavement he thought again of Carlisle. The man infuriated him, but he could not dislike him. And he could not believe that Carlisle had had any part in the deaths of either of the women—he had merely seized an opportunity. Pitt could imagine him carefully cutting the dead faces, women beyond indignity or pain, and apologizing for using them for what he believed was a greater and more desperate good. The man he had known in the past would never have killed anyone, even to expose treason.

But people can change. Unknown pressures can fall on them, old debts can need to be paid. Was that why Carlisle had rescued Pitt from the fury of Edom Talbot so fortuitously? And was it he who had created the situation in the first place, so Pitt would owe him a debt?

What debts did Carlisle owe, he wondered. And Kynaston? Was that the reason for his betrayal?

He looked up at the thin starlight; he could feel the ice on the wind, and he increased his pace.

14

CHARLOTTE HAD DELIBERATELY CHOSEN to spend more time with Emily, so when Emily invited her to go to a reception for a visiting Norwegian explorer, and to listen to his lecture, she accepted. She did it for Emily's sake, not because she was particularly interested in islands in the North Atlantic and whatever manner of birds might inhabit them. The thought of so much floating ice made her cold, even before she set out.

Had Pitt been at home it would have been a greater sacrifice, but he had been out many evenings recently, pursuing one aspect or another of the case of Kitty Ryder. He had said she was alive, but they still could not find her.

As Charlotte sat while Minnie Maude dressed her hair up, a skill she was rapidly developing, Charlotte thought more about the whole issue. She had not questioned Pitt further, because she knew from watching his face that he was deeply worried about the case and that it now concerned some other issue, which he could not tell her. That did not mean she was not free to try to discern it for herself.

She knew more of the personal lives of people like Dudley Kynaston than Pitt or Stoker could, because the Kynastons belonged to the level of society in which she had grown up, and to which Emily had belonged all her life. She and Pitt were now on the fringes of it, but to him it would always be alien, at least in some of its values, no matter how skilled he became at appearing to be comfortable.

When Emily arrived, Charlotte saw that she was dressed in pale green, the color that became her most. The gown itself was exquisite, and perfectly suited to the occasion. Charlotte recognized it as "battle dress" from the way it fitted, and the beauty of the subtle emerald and diamond earrings that Emily wore with it. When Charlotte kissed her quickly on the cheek, the opinion was confirmed by the perfume she detected, so subtle that she wanted to come closer again in order to catch it more definitely. It was nothing she could name, and no doubt very expensive. It was the sort of thing a woman buys herself if she does not have to count the cost of it.

As soon as they were seated in the carriage and had moved off from the curb into the roadway, Charlotte asked the question.

"Why are we going to a lecture on arctic exploration?"

Emily smiled. Even in the gathering dusk and the first glow of streetlamps, her satisfaction was visible. "Because Ailsa and Rosalind Kynaston are going to it," she replied. "I have been getting to know Rosalind a little better recently. It isn't difficult or odd in the circumstances. If Jack is going to be offered this position with Dudley Kynaston, then we shall possibly become friends."

"And is he?" Charlotte knew how another disappointment would affect Emily, and Jack himself. She couldn't keep the anxious edge from her voice.

"You don't want him to, do you!" There was a sudden edge of challenge in Emily's voice. "He's brilliant, you know. Or perhaps you don't know? It would be very interesting for Jack to work with him, and a promotion, of course. But you must know that, if you've thought about it at all!"

Charlotte forgot her resolve to be patient and gentle. "I want him to take it, as long as Kynaston's not guilty of anything," she said tartly. "If he was having an affair with his wife's maid I suppose that isn't very important, except to his wife, and perhaps to the maid. But if he has anything to do with those bodies found near his house, then I would very much rather Jack did not work with him. Until he is accused, of course, then I daresay he will be in jail, and there will be no possibility of anybody working with him."

"Jack will be pleased to know that you love him," Emily said icily. "Even if it does appear to infect your imagination with grotesque fantasies."

"Don't be so stupid!" Charlotte snapped. "It's you I love, and I like Jack, very much, but that will cease instantly if he hurts you."

"He isn't—" Emily began, but stopped equally quickly. When Charlotte turned to look at her she saw the tears brim over her eyes and down her cheeks. At another time she would have said something, even hugged her. Now the emotion between them was too brittle.

Charlotte sat in silence for several moments, allowing Emily time to regain her composure. When she thought it was long enough, she began another conversation. "What is Rosalind like?" she asked. She did not have to feign interest.

"Actually, I like her," Emily replied, her voice almost level again. "She is much more individual than she appears at first. She reads quite a lot, and she knows about all sorts of unusual things: adventures, explorers, the people who go to Mesopotamia, and Greece, and dig up tombs and find amazing things—artifacts and writings. And she has great knowledge of plants. I went to Kew Gardens with her, and she could tell me where dozens of the different trees and flowers came from, and who found them. I started paying attention to her out of courtesy, but quite quickly found I was genuinely interested. And she is nothing like as bland or easily misled as I used to suppose."

"Is that why she is going to this lecture?" Charlotte asked, surprised. She had thought Rosalind to be rather colorless when they met. Perhaps she was guilty of supposing that because her husband had a mistress, then she must be dull. Did all married women suppose that? If a man seeks another woman, then his wife must be cold, tedious, plain—something one could avoid being oneself, so it would never happen to you?

"I look forward to getting to know her better," she said.

EMILY MIGHT HAVE BEEN unhappy, but she had lost none of the social skills. She could still make careful planning look like complete chance, and soon she and Charlotte found themselves standing close to Rosalind and Ailsa Kynaston.

Rosalind was soberly dressed in a deep plum color, which looked gracious and expensive, yet lacked the flair that Emily could have achieved with far less.

Ailsa, on the other hand, had the advantage of height and the grace it gave her movement. There was a vitality in her face and a silver-pale gleam to her hair that attracted the eye, willingly or not. The somber blues of her gown were of no importance; if anything, they were a contrast that heightened her own energy.

They greeted each other with pleasure, as if it were good fortune that had placed them so closely. Both Ailsa and Rosalind remembered Charlotte and affected to be happy to see her again. If they connected her immediately with Pitt and the wretched business that had brought him into Rosalind's house, they were too polite to say so.

Conversation was easy and touched only on trivial things. Emily was at her best, being both interesting and amusing. Particularly she made Rosalind laugh, leaving Charlotte free merely to listen, and to watch the language of looks and gestures between Rosalind and Ailsa. Perhaps that was what Emily had intended. If she had, she could not have contrived it better.

"I am pleased so many people have come," Rosalind said, glancing around at the steadily increasing crowd. "I admit, I had feared there would be embarrassingly little support."

"We will all leave grateful that our spring, if chilly, is not nearly as harsh as it could be," Emily agreed.

Ailsa lifted her graceful shoulders a little. "The north has a clean beauty that many people admire," she said. She was not exactly contradicting Emily, but there was a coolness in her voice.

"Do you know the north well?" Emily asked with enthusiasm.

For a moment Ailsa hesitated, as though she were unprepared for the question.

"I have traveled north," she conceded. "It has great beauty, and one becomes acclimatized to the cold. Of course, summer is not cold at all, and brighter than here . . . quite often."

"So you will be familiar with places like the ones Dr. Arbuthnott will be mentioning," Emily concluded. She turned to Rosalind. "Have you been there also?"

Rosalind smiled. "Oh, no. I'm afraid I have never been farther north than Paris, which I find a marvelous city."

"Paris is south from here, my dear," Ailsa said gently.

Charlotte looked at her face. She was smiling, but there was no warmth in it, in spite of her tone. If she had liked Rosalind, Charlotte knew that she would not have made the observation at all.

Rosalind colored very slightly. "I know that. Perhaps I would have been clearer if I had said 'in Europe.'"

Several appropriate remarks occurred to Charlotte, which would have put Ailsa in her place, but she refrained from making them.

"I would love to travel," she said instead. "Perhaps one day I will. But I still find people more interesting than even the most marvelous cities. And I am grateful that there are men like Dr. Arbuthnott who will bring us photographs and magic lantern images to show the beauty of the places I will never visit."

"A lifetime's worth of them," Ailsa observed.

Charlotte pretended to misunderstand her. She was irritated at having her own life dismissed in such a way, but more offended for Rosalind, because to judge from her face, she felt the cut more keenly.

"Really? He did not look more than forty-five in the photographs. But perhaps they are not recent?"

Ailsa stared at her, then quite suddenly a flash of amusement lit her face, almost appreciation. Charlotte realized she respected someone who would fight back. She smiled at Ailsa with all the considerable charm she could call on when she wished, and saw the recognition of it, and a quick acknowledgment.

They took their seats and an expectant hush settled over the room. Dr. Arbuthnott appeared, to applause, and the lecture began.

Certainly what he had to say was interesting, and to Charlotte completely unfamiliar, but she could not afford to turn her attention to it fully. She and Emily had finally decided to take seats on the aisle immediately behind those of Ailsa and Rosalind. This gave her the opportunity to watch them both, while still appearing to be fully intent upon the lecturer.

Of course it would be ill-mannered to whisper to each other when Dr. Arbuthnott was actually speaking, but it seemed to Charlotte completely natural, and even expected, that at suitable moments one would speak to one's companion to remark on something of particular beauty or surprise. She did so to Emily without giving it thought.

Then she faced forward again, and began to study the two women in front of her. Both sat straight up, as governesses would have taught them. Beauty was a gift; deportment was acquired, as was graceful speech both in timbre and pronunciation. Having something of interest to say was, of course, quite another matter.

Rosalind inclined very slightly towards Ailsa, and murmured to her, but so quietly that Charlotte did not hear any of it.

Ailsa nodded, but did not reply. She did not lean her body towards Rosalind. A moment later she looked around the audience as discreetly as was possible, as if searching for someone she knew. Apparently she did not find them, because she did so again at the next opportunity, without being obvious about it. Charlotte was very curious as to who it might be.

She learned who later in the evening, after the lecture itself was finished and refreshments were offered. Many people congratulated Dr. Arbuthnott and asked him further questions about the power and beauty of the far northern oceans.

Emily was in close conversation with Rosalind, and Charlotte had decided to follow behind Ailsa as closely as she could without being obvious. She made herself appear to be looking for an acquaintance, and felt as if she were behaving like a complete eccentric. She hoped she would never have to meet any of those people again socially. Possibly if they thought she was peculiar enough, they would take trouble to avoid her?

She was abundantly rewarded. She had walked quite casually under an elaborate archway she had seen Ailsa disappear through, presumably seeking a little respite from the stuffiness and intense conversation of the room. It led to a side hall, a minor gallery that was beautifully proportioned, light pouring in from a large window.

Charlotte did not want a confrontation. It would be far too clumsy, and unmistakable that she had seen Ailsa go in and chosen to follow her. She dared not even go much farther, because there were several very fine mirrors on the wall, and her passing in front of one would catch anybody's eye.

But as she stopped abruptly, she realized she had inadvertently placed herself exactly where she could see Ailsa's reflection, in a mirror to her side, giving a clear profile angled in a farther mirror beyond Charlotte's line of sight. She could not take her eyes from it! Ailsa was standing quite still beside Edom Talbot. From their closeness to each other, and the look on Talbot's face, there was no one else in the room. He moved a little behind her so Charlotte could see only his arms as they gently curved around Ailsa's waist, and his shoulders above hers. She was tall, but he was several inches taller again. He was not a handsome man, but he was in a way distinguished, and quite unmistakable.

Ailsa did not move. She was smiling slightly, as though not only pleased but faintly amused.

Talbot's hands moved up a little from her waist, gradually inch by inch until he caressed her breasts. He did it with some confidence, as if he did not expect to be denied.

Charlotte studied Ailsa's face and saw her expression freeze. The gesture had not surprised her, but she found it distasteful. Charlotte could feel it as if it were her own body being touched. She saw the muscles in Ailsa's neck and throat clench as if she almost stopped breathing.

Charlotte's mind raced. Why did she endure it? She did not believe for an instant that Ailsa did not know how to deal completely effectively with such a thing. She had only to turn around sharply and confront him, or—even more simply than that—take a very carefully judged step back and put her heel on the instep of his foot, and then her weight. She was a handsomely built woman. The pain would be excruciating. She could pretend it was accidental, and they would both know it was entirely on purpose. And yet she did not.

Talbot bent his head and began to kiss her gently along the back of her neck and shoulder. She seemed to struggle to master her feelings. He could not see her face, only Charlotte could, and she read the revulsion in it as if it had been her own.

Then Ailsa turned and kissed him back quickly and pulled away. She said something, and Talbot smiled back. They began to move.

Charlotte dared stay no longer. There were too many mirrors. She could not afford to be caught staring. One meeting of the eyes and she would never be able to deny it.

Charlotte had no opportunity to tell Emily until they were in the carriage again on the way home, moving swiftly through the brightly lit traffic.

"What?" Emily said incredulously. "You must be mistaken! Are you sure it was Ailsa?"

"Yes, of course I am. Apart from her gown, which was quite individual, I could see her face!"

"Then maybe it wasn't Talbot! Could Dudley Kynaston have arrived, and we didn't see him?" Emily persisted.

"Dudley? She's the widow of the brother he adored!" Charlotte protested.

"Don't be naïve!" Emily said, more with disbelief than criticism. "Bennett is dead! What greater compliment could the devoted Dudley give him than to step into his shoes?"

"That's disgusting!" Charlotte retorted. "Would you be as quick into my shoes?"

Emily smiled. "Oh, I don't know. I think Thomas is rather sweet! And he'd never be boring! Would he?"

Charlotte realized she was being teased just in time to avoid making a fool of herself, and perhaps making a remark whose sting would linger far more than she intended.

"He snores," she said.

Emily looked crushed. "Does he?"

"No!"

Emily sighed. "Jack does. He looks quite beautiful asleep, with those eyelashes. But he does snore—sometimes."

Charlotte swiveled around. "Emily, were you serious that Ailsa could be the mistress that Dudley is so desperate to keep quiet about?"

Emily was immediately sober again. "Well, it would make sense, wouldn't it? It isn't that it's so terribly scandalous, so much as it is a desecration of his adored dead brother." She stopped. "Except that Rosalind told me Ailsa never really got over Bennett. She's still in love with him."

"Perhaps Dudley reminds her of him?" Charlotte thought aloud. "And in a weak moment, a lonely one, she slipped up?"

"What? And now she can't say no?" Emily asked incredulously. "Yes, she could. I'll wager Ailsa could say no to anyone—and mean it. If she's playing along, then there's something she wants."

"Except that this wasn't Dudley, it really wasn't," Charlotte insisted. "He was a similar height, but it was very definitely Edom Talbot. I saw his face. It was a reflection, but it was perfectly plain. She allowed him to touch her in a very intimate way, but she had to force herself to."

"Talbot," Emily said thoughtfully. For a little while she was silent. "There are so many possibilities," she said at last. "We need to discuss this. Come home with me and we'll talk. It's still early. I'll have the carriage take you home after. Please?"

"Of course," Charlotte said instantly. It did not matter whether it was really to discuss whatever they might have observed this evening, or simply because Emily did not want to go home alone—or even worse, to Jack being silent and withdrawn. Possibly he would even be tense about the situation with Kynaston, and therefore irritable. The very fact that he was not sharing his anxiety with Emily was the cause of hurt, whatever it was about. He probably thought he was protecting her. Men could be incredibly stupid sometimes, trip over the obvious, and still not see it.

But then Emily ought to know that by now, and not make an issue out of something that was not meant to be one.

Or on the other hand, perhaps Jack was drifting out of love, and a far bigger change was needed. And Charlotte was certainly not wise enough to answer that question. But she would go home with Emily and stay at least an hour, if Emily wished it.

"Do you think it really could be all about Bennett?" Charlotte asked when they were sitting beside the fire in Emily's drawing room, which perfectly reflected her tastes and character in its rich golds and pinks, the flashes of red, and the paintings on the walls.

"Why not?" Emily asked. "He seems to have been reasonable, from what Rosalind says. And actually very nice. He was the handsomer of the two brothers, and, at the time he died, he was considered the one with the greatest promise."

Charlotte thought for a minute, knowing Emily was watching her. "That sounds a little difficult to live with," she said at last. "I wouldn't entirely blame Dudley if his feelings about Bennett were a trifle mixed. Although Thomas did say he still keeps a portrait of Bennett in his study. He seemed to be devoted. He admired him enormously and in a way strove to be like him, even to finish some of the work Bennett began . . ." Charlotte shivered. "But to think that he wanted to complete it by having an affair with Bennett's widow?"

"Well, it's not impossible, is it?"

"No . . ."

"In fact it's not completely impossible that he started the affair before Bennett was dead!" Emily continued.

"But if Bennett were all that marvelous, why would Ailsa be willing to betray him, and with his own brother?" Charlotte argued.

Emily pulled her mouth into a grimace. "Not all men who seem handsome and clever and charming are all that interesting when you get to know them . . . well . . ."

"You mean in bed?"

"Of course I do." Then Emily laughed. "Oh dear! I'm not talking about Jack. That did sound a bit clumsy, didn't it?"

Charlotte was too relieved to argue. "Yes," she agreed. "It definitely did! But I accept your denial. Do you really think it could go that far back? That's . . . years! Poor Rosalind. No wonder she looks a bit . . . crumpled."

The shadow passed over Emily's face again. "She does, doesn't she?" She hesitated. "Do I?"

Charlotte had walked straight into a trap—perhaps not an intentional one, but very complete nonetheless. And Emily would see a lie, or an evasion instantly. She always had.

"Compared with the way you usually are, yes, you do," she said, hating each word as it came from her mouth. Had Emily wanted her to lie, even if neither of them believed it? It was too late now. She had to add something, retrieve hope from it. "Because you believe Jack has fallen out of love with you," she added. "That doesn't make it true! There are people who believe the world is flat! They even burned people for it, once."

"Actually several times," Emily said with an attempt at a smile.

"What's the point in burning anyone several times?" Charlotte asked without taking a breath. "Seems a little excessive, doesn't it?"

Emily laughed in spite of herself. "Are you trying to make me feel better?"

"I'm trying to make you see sense." Charlotte poured some tea for each of them. It was Earl Grey, very subtle, the exact opposite of the conversation.

"I've had another thought," Emily went on. "It's pretty awful! But what if Dudley and Ailsa really fell in love with each other way back when she was married to Bennett? And what if it's far worse than that? Are we absolutely certain that Bennett's death was natural? He was awfully young to die, when he wasn't fragile before."

Charlotte was stunned. "You mean that Dudley and Ailsa killed him? That was the secret that Kitty found out? How on earth would she?"

"I don't know! Ladies' maids find out all kinds of things. I'd hate even to imagine what mine knows about me. In some ways, more than Jack does. Even more than you do!"

Charlotte followed the thought. "Then why is Rosalind still alive and well? Or does she know, and has some kind of way of keeping herself safe? For heaven's sake, why bother? What on earth is a husband worth if he would so much rather be somewhere else?"

"Revenge? I don't know." Emily leaned forward. "Maybe they didn't kill Bennett. Maybe he found out and was so brokenhearted he committed suicide, and they covered it up? I'm sure a decent doctor could be persuaded to be discreet."

"And that's the scandal?" Charlotte thought about it for several moments. "That would be pretty awful, wouldn't it? What a betrayal! What a rotten tragedy. Dudley couldn't afford to let that be known. It's so . . . ugly!" She shut her eyes as if she could make the thought disappear. "I wonder if you go on loving someone after that, or if you end up hating them because every time you think of them, even see their face, you are reminded of what you have become because of your feeling for them. Don't you think a really good love should make you strive to be the very best you can? The noblest, the bravest, the gentlest?"

Emily stared at her. "Yes," she said very quietly. Slowly her shoulders eased as the tension slipped away from her. "Yes. I do." She smiled. "I'm glad you came this evening, and that you said what you did. I want to think about myself, for a little while, and what I need to do. We'll go on with the wretched Kynastons tomorrow, or the next day." She reached for the bell to ask the footman to fetch the carriage round to take Charlotte home.

15

Pitt had debated the issue briefly with himself as to whether he should repeat to Stoker the information he had received from Carlisle. Doing so would require that he also tell him all that he knew about Carlisle. That included the history between them, or as much of it as was required to have Stoker understand why Pitt trusted him, and the nature of the debt he felt towards him.

He realized the following morning that in fact the conflict in his mind was only as to how he would do it, what words he would use, and what he could leave out. It had begun with Carlisle owing a debt to Pitt for his silence in the Resurrection Row affair. Then, over the years, the balance had shifted the other way. Now, with the rescue from Talbot, the weight was on the other side: Pitt owed the greater debt.

It nagged at Pitt, whether Carlisle had orchestrated that rescue for that specific gain. Granted, it was unlike the man Pitt had known. He would have abhorred such manipulation. Then what for? It surely had to do with debt—and honor.

There was a sharp tap on the door. He had barely answered it when it opened and Stoker came in, closing it behind him. He looked scrubbed and eager, but there were dark lines of tiredness in his face, hollows around the eyes. He had pursued this case as if something he had learned about the missing woman had made her particularly real to him.

But then Stoker was a man who did not do anything in half-measure. If he would have denied caring about the woman and said it was simply the best way to do the job, he would have been wrong: it was both.

"Sir?" Stoker interrupted Pitt's thoughts, impatient to know why he had been sent for.

"Sit down," Pitt told him.

Stoker obeyed, not taking his eyes from Pitt's face.

Very briefly Pitt told him the history of events in Resurrection Row, the spectacular disinterment of corpses to expose murder and corruption, over a decade ago, and his first encounter with Somerset Carlisle.

Stoker stared at him with disbelief, laughter, and then amazement.

"Sorry, sir," he said, regaining a more sober expression. "You're not saying Carlisle's behind these bodies, are you? I could see why the other, but . . ." His eyes widened. "You are! Why? This is . . . grotesque . . ."

"So was the other, believe me," Pitt answered him. "And yes, I am sorry but I think he is behind these bodies, too. He has the ingenuity and the means—"

"Not without help, sir!" Stoker interrupted.

"I daresay his manservant is involved, and would probably die before admitting it. He's been with Carlisle for thirty years. I looked into that."

"But why?" Stoker demanded. Then he stopped abruptly, understanding flooding his face. "To force you to investigate Kynaston!" Stoker let out his breath in a sigh. "So we are talking treason, sir?"

"Yes, we are. Sir John Ransom suspects it, at least—but there is no evidence, no proof."

"That's . . . very ugly. Then we have to get him, whatever it costs. I'd like to meet this fellow, Carlisle. Shake his hand."

Pitt felt oddly elated. He had been afraid Stoker would resent Carlisle's interference and deplore his bizarre behavior. Stoker went up not only in his professional estimation but also in his personal regard. For all his outwardly dour demeanor and his lack of relationships or ordinary pastimes, his loyalties were unbreakable, and now it seemed that beneath the rigid exterior he had a powerful imagination.

"I'll see that it is arranged," Pitt promised. "If it doesn't occur anyway in the natural course of events."

"Thank you, sir," There was barely a flicker in Stoker's eyes, but for an instant his mouth twitched as if he were going to smile, perhaps within himself, even to laugh.

"Now we have to find Kitty Ryder," Pitt continued. "You may take two other men to help you, if you wish. It is no longer a matter of solving a murder already committed; it is preventing a continuing betrayal of our naval weaponry secrets. Do not repeat that. As far as anyone else is concerned, she is a witness in danger."

"Yes, sir. If Kynaston knows that, then won't he be looking for her as well?" Stoker's face was bleak with anxiety.

"That is the next thing I am going to do," Pitt replied. "Find out exactly what steps Kynaston has taken to find her."

Stoker stood up. "Who's he passing secrets through? We need to know that, sir. And make damn sure no one else does."

"I realize that, Stoker! He won't be in it all by himself."

Stoker frowned. "What the hell makes a man like Kynaston betray his country? It has to be for something more than money. No one in the world has enough money to buy your life, your decency, your home, your friends! Your sleep at night . . ."

"I don't know," Pitt admitted. "Perhaps love?"

"Infatuation!" Stoker said with disgust. "What kind of love can you offer anyone if you've sold your honor? And they certainly don't love you if they ask it!"

"I wasn't thinking of the love of men for women." Pitt was framing the thought as he spoke. "But perhaps your child's life? If we care about anything at all, we give hostages to fortune."

"Kynaston's children?" Stoker was clearly turning it over in his mind. "They're all adult, or almost. But I will get someone to check on them, if you think it's worth it?"

"Yes, do that, before you start off to look for Kitty again."

As Stoker left, Pitt turned his own attention to Kynaston. If Kitty had stumbled across dangerous information, and fled in fear for her life, then surely Kynaston would have attempted to find her himself? However frightened she was, there was always the possibility of her confiding in someone else, even if only for her own safety, or relief from the burden of carrying such knowledge alone.

Except that if she told anyone that Dudley Kynaston was a traitor to his country, who would believe her? It would inevitably create a stir and give away her whereabouts. If she was truly terrified, it would be far wiser to disappear and become as close to invisible as possible.

Would Kynaston then look for her? Or trust that she would be too frightened, and too wise, to repeat anything?

He would hardly go around the pubs and backstreets himself. A certain degree of inquiry for her would be natural. She was in his care and had disappeared from his house. A decent man would not need to explain why he had done such a thing. Perhaps it would be interesting to see his reaction to the question.

Pitt realized, as he set out to begin his own discreet inquiries as to whether it was Kynaston who was pursuing Kitty Ryder, that he still found it difficult to believe that Kynaston was a traitor and—given the right motive and opportunity—would also murder one of his servants, in order to protect himself.

Pitt could have given the job to one of his juniors. It was sufficiently important to move someone from one of the multitude of tasks that fell to Special Branch. But he did not wish any further men involved. He was not prepared to explain the reason to Talbot, or anyone else, should Kynaston hear of it and complain.

HE SPENT MOST OF the day doing the same kind of police work he had done in the past when investigating a murder. He went from place to place, asking openly about Kitty Ryder, obliquely about other inquiries for her.

In many accounts, he recognized Stoker as the questioner. But there were others in which the inquirer was fairly plainly Norton, Kynaston's butler.

"Yes, sir," the barman at the Pig and Whistle replied, shaking his head sadly. "Nice gent, Mr. Norton. All very proper, like wot you'd expect a butler to be, but right concerned 'e were, for sure." He wiped his hands on his apron. "Reckoned as she were sort of 'is family, like. I told 'im all I know'd, which weren't much. 'E thanked me nicely, good tip, but no matter 'ow much I'd 'a liked to, I couldn't 'elp 'im. I ain't got no idea where she went, nor why, for that matter."

"Did you ever ask?" Pitt pressed.

The man shook his head. "Well, there were Mrs. Kynaston's coachman, too. 'E pressed kind of 'ard, but like I told 'im, I can't tell you wot I don't know. 'E asked after young Dobson, an' I told 'im all I know about 'im, too."

Interesting, Pitt thought. So Rosalind had sent someone herself, apparently someone who took the issue a little further.

Pitt thanked the barman and went to look for other traces of Harry Dobson, to see if the coachman had followed up on the information. He was not surprised to find that he had, although it took Pitt the rest of the afternoon and all the following day to be certain of it. It seemed as if the coachman had been given the time and had used it with diligence and imagination, but no success. It spoke much for Stoker's skill that he had at least found Dobson, if not before Kitty had moved on.

Perhaps he should not have been surprised. Kitty had been Rosalind's maid. It appeared that the loyalty had run in both ways. Charlotte would have combed London to find Minnie Maude if she had disappeared, regardless of her own danger, never mind cost or inconvenience.

Pitt decided that, before speaking to Kynaston himself, he would find the coachman and ask him at what point he had given up. It was unlikely he had anything to add that would be helpful in finding Kitty now, but he should not overlook the chance.

"No, sir. I'm sorry, sir." The coachman looked puzzled. He stood in the stable just outside the loose boxes where the horses were peering curiously at Pitt. The groom was coming and going with hay.

Pitt enjoyed the familiar sensations that took him back to his childhood: hay and straw; clean leather; linseed oil; the sounds of horses themselves shifting from foot to foot, munching now and then, blowing air out through their nostrils.

"It's not something to apologize for," he told the man. "It's to your credit."

"I wish I 'ad, sir," the coachman assured him. "But I didn't. Ask Mr. Kynaston, sir. I were busy on 'is errands, or else taking the mistress to where she went."

"Wasn't it Mrs. Kynaston who asked you to look for Kitty?"

"No, sir. She were upset she'd gone, like, but she never asked me ter go lookin' for 'er. Reckon as she ran off with that carpenter fellow she were courtin'. Only Mr. Norton thought she might not 'ave. An' young Maisie." He smiled and tipped his head. "Too smart by 'alf for a scullery maid, that one. Either she'll make 'er fortune, or she'll come ter no good."

Pitt was puzzled. The barman had been sure of himself, and the information he had given Pitt had been correct. He had followed it and found the coachman's trail, until he, too, had given up.

"You were seen and identified," Pitt told him. "Why on earth deny it? It's a perfectly decent thing to do. I know exactly where you went."

"'Ceptin' I didn't," the man insisted. "Whoever said it were me were lyin'. You ask Mr. and Mrs. Kynaston. They'll tell you."

Pitt stared at the man, who looked back at him without a shadow of guile. Then suddenly a completely different thought occurred to him. Ailsa was also "Mrs. Kynaston." Was it possible she had offered her footman for the task, and this man was telling the truth?

Why would Ailsa do such a thing? As a favor to Rosalind, so her husband did not know? That answer was laden with several possibilities, the first to his mind was that Rosalind suspected her husband of some involvement in Kitty's disappearance and dared not have him know she was still pursuing it.

"It seems they were mistaken," Pitt conceded. "Perhaps they said what they thought I wanted to hear. Thank you." He turned and left, his mind racing through other scenes and ideas.

For example, was Ailsa looking for Kitty for Rosalind's sake, or for Kynaston's? Was she trying to prove him innocent, for all their sakes? If Kitty was alive, then there was no murder connected with the Kynaston house.

He walked to the areaway, weaving his path through the ash cans and coke scuttles, and went up the step to the scullery door.

He was still too early to see Kynaston himself, so he waited in the morning room. He would have preferred the kitchen, but Norton saw to it that he did not linger there. It was in the guise of hospitality, but Pitt had a strong feeling that it was actually to keep him from overhearing the servants' gossip.

By the time Kynaston appeared, Pitt had made up his mind. He would dislike forcing him to answer, but it would not be the first time a man he had personally liked had been guilty of appalling crimes.

Kynaston came in looking tired and cold, but his manner was as charming as ever.

"Good evening, Commander Pitt. How are you?" He held out his hand.

Pitt took it, something he would not normally do when interviewing someone he suspected. "Well, thank you," he replied. "I'm sorry to disturb you yet again, but this time I have happier news."

"Good. I'm delighted." Kynaston smiled and offered Pitt a seat beside the fire, and whisky if he wished it. Again Pitt declined. One did not accept hospitality in such circumstances.

Before he gave the news he mentioned his conversation with the coachman. Kynaston was bound to hear of it, and one did not speak to a man's servants without saying so to him, even if it was rather asking for permission after the event.

"I spoke to your coachman," he said casually. "We are still looking for Kitty Ryder, and in our search we've come across what seems to be evidence that he had looked for her also—possibly in his own hours, but more likely at your request . . ."

Kynaston looked baffled. "Hopgood? Are you certain? It was not at my request, I assure you. I'm surprised he had the time. Perhaps he had . . . an affection for her? She was a very handsome girl. I admit that had not occurred to me."

"So it was not at your request?" Pitt asked.

Kynaston's look did not waver. "No. I had Norton make a few inquiries, but that was some time ago. He was happy to do it, but he had no success. I began to accept that she ran off with her young man, in what I regret to say was a very callous manner. I would have expected her to have the courtesy to give notice, as one would normally do. My wife was distressed, as we all were. It was an uncharacteristically thoughtless thing to do."

"Hopgood assured me that he had not looked for her, either on his own or at your instruction," Pitt agreed. "I mention it only because no doubt you will come to hear of it, and possibly Mrs. Kynaston will also."

"Thank you." Kynaston still looked puzzled. He had taken whisky for himself and sat with the glass in his hand, its rich color made even warmer by the gas lamp now lit and the reflection of the fire.

"Possibly it was Mrs. Ailsa Kynaston's coachman?" Pitt suggested.

Kynaston's hand tightened on his glass so hard that the liquid spilled slightly with the change of position.

"Ailsa? I think that's . . . unlikely." He thought for a moment. "Unless Rosalind asked her to? Or she imagined she could help . . ." He left the idea unfinished.

"Perhaps the informants told us what they thought we wished to hear," Pitt said smoothly. "It happens sometimes. Anyway, it is of far less importance now, since we are sure beyond any question whatever that neither of the bodies in the gravel pits was that of Kitty Ryder. I don't know where she is, but you and your household are relieved of all suspicion in her disappearance. I'm sorry it had to touch you at all." He stared at Kynaston, watching every muscle in his face, his neck, his shoulders, one hand on his glass and the other on the arm of the chair. He saw the tension like a bowstring. Kynaston all but stopped breathing.

Pitt smiled blandly, as if he had not noticed, but he did not speak. The whole art was to leave Kynaston floundering, offer him nothing to reply to.

Finally Kynaston moved, with just an easing of his shoulders as he drew in a deep breath. He set the whisky glass down.

"That is a great relief. My wife will be delighted. It was a very poor way to behave, but thank God Kitty was not . . . killed." He pulled his face into an expression of revulsion. "Presumably you will no longer be wasting your time looking for her. A very good result all round, even if it was hard to reach. I cannot imagine what the stupid girl was thinking of! Still, it hardly matters now."

"Indeed," Pitt nodded. "Of course we still have to discover the identity of the two women who were found, but that will be a job for the local police."

Kynaston let out a long, slow breath, and his body slumped a little in the chair. "Thank you. It is most considerate of you to come and inform me personally, Commander." He stood up slowly, as if he were a little stiff. "I hope we shall meet again soon, in pleasanter circumstances."

"I hope so," Pitt agreed. "Good night, sir."

PITT ARRIVED HOME EARLIER than he had done for several evenings and was able to have dinner with Charlotte and both his children. He put Kynaston out of his mind and listened to their conversation, their news and their ideas. Daniel was full of his plan to play cricket in the coming summer and could think of little else. He talked about different strokes, catches, styles of bowling and batting, but to Pitt's pleasure and carefully concealed amusement, he also spoke of strategy. He explained it at some length over the first course and well into pudding, his face alight with enthusiasm. Various condiments were moved around the table to represent different ways of placing his fielders.

Jemima rolled her eyes, but listened patiently. Then, just to keep up her own position in showing off abilities that no one else understood, she spoke at length about medieval French history, smiling to herself as they pretended to be interested.

It was well into the evening before Charlotte and Pitt sat alone before the fire and she was able to tell him about her evening with Emily, which she was clearly eager to do.

Pitt had difficulty keeping his eyes open. The room was warm and extremely comfortable. The light was soft, only one gas lamp was lit. The fire flickered gently in the hearth and every so often settled lower as the wood collapsed. It was Charlotte who leaned forward and put on more fuel: old apple wood, sweet smelling.

Pitt made an effort to be interested.

"How is Emily?"

"Involved," she said immediately. "As I am. I think that's half her real problem—she's bored stiff!"

He tried to pay attention. "Involved in what? Didn't you say it was a lecture on Arctic exploring, or something? I can't imagine Emily caring even remotely about that."

"North Atlantic and North Sea," she corrected him. "And no, I don't think she cares about that any more than I do. Although some of his photographs were dazzlingly beautiful."

"You said involved . . . didn't you?" He must be half asleep. He was losing the thread.

She was smiling, leaning forward a little, her eyes bright.

"Fascinated. I saw Ailsa, almost accidentally—although I did follow her—in a most extraordinary affair."

"Affair?" She was speaking in stops and starts and he had lost the drift of it.

"Love affair, Thomas! Or perhaps it was more lust than love. Or maybe it was lust on his part, and something quite different on hers. I don't know what, not yet. But I mean to find out."

He sat up a little farther. "Why? What are you talking about? And how is it your concern? It isn't Jack . . . is it?"

"No! Of course it isn't Jack!" She was completely upright, her back like a ramrod. "Do you really think I'd be sitting here comfortably spinning it out if it were? I'd have brought you in here and told you before dinner!" she said indignantly.

"Oh. Yes, of course. Then why are you bothering with it?"

"Because it's Ailsa Kynaston and Edom Talbot!"

Now he sat upright, instantly wide awake. "What? Who did you say?"

"You heard me, Thomas. I was following her, and I saw her, reflected through two mirrors. He stood behind her and put his arms around her . . . intimately. I'd have broken the foot of anyone who did that to me, unless it were you."

"And she didn't mind?" he asked.

"Yes, she did mind, but she pretended not to. It took her a few seconds to master herself . . ."

"Are you sure? How do you know?"

"Because I could see her!" she said fiercely. "Then she turned round and kissed him. But she had to make herself do it! Doesn't that send a hundred questions racing around in your head?"

"A couple of dozen anyway," he agreed. "I'd begun to wonder if she were Kynaston's mistress. This makes it look very different."

"Not necessarily," she argued. "Maybe she's both?"

"Both?" he said incredulously. "Why would she allow Talbot to touch her, if she doesn't like him? Is that to mislead people that she's having an affair with him, and not with Kynaston?"

"Maybe," Charlotte conceded. "But it seems like a lot of trouble when no one seems to suspect it anyway. Unless, of course, Rosalind does?"

He was about to say something, but she rushed on. "But there are a whole lot of other possibilities, Thomas. What if they have been in love for a long time? Even when she was married to Bennett Kynaston?"

"With Talbot?" he said incredulously.

"No, of course not! With Dudley! Maybe that's why Bennett died so young?"

"Of what? People can't die of being betrayed, even by a wife and a brother. Or are you saying they killed him? Isn't that a bit—" He stopped. It was appalling, but then so was treason. Was it possible that the whole tragedy was both domestic and political?

"They might have," she answered. "That would be a terrible enough thing if Kitty Ryder found out. She'd run from that house, middle of the night or not! I would. And of course," she added, "the other possibility is that Rosalind found out, and she meant to kill them in revenge, or to expose them. That would be more effective—"

"You're letting your imagination run away with you," he told her sharply.

"No, I'm not!" she insisted. "You think just because Rosalind looks as if she hasn't the fire to break the skin on a rice pudding, she wouldn't hold that over their heads!"

"You don't break the skin on a rice pudding with fire, darling!"

"Don't be pedantic!" she said exasperatedly. "The flame inside her. There's something all twisted up going on there, Thomas. I'm only giving you a few possibilities. It's your job to find out which one is true."

He looked at her perched on the edge of the chair, her eyes bright, the firelight catching red and gold in her hair, her cheeks flushed. It was the last thing she would have thought about herself, but to him she was utterly beautiful.

"You have enough flame inside you to cook me rice pudding for the rest of my life," he said, keeping his tone light, for fear emotion swallowed him up.

"I didn't think you liked rice pudding!" she protested.

"I don't! But I like the flame!"

She laughed and moved forward off the seat and into his arms.

WHEN JACK RADLEY TELEPHONED Vespasia and asked if he might visit her in the afternoon, she was surprised, but she caught the edge of urgency in his voice.

"Of course," she said, as if it would cause no inconvenience at all. She had intended to visit an old friend and spend a leisurely time looking at an exhibition of art. They had not met recently, except at such functions as allowed no serious conversation. She had been looking forward to it. She would have her maid send a note, with profuse apologies. Perhaps she should send Mildred flowers tomorrow? A family crisis Mildred would understand. She had daughters herself, and now granddaughters as well.

Vespasia hesitated over offering tea. It was not a meal she imagined Jack to take, but it was an excuse to sit down and have an uninterrupted conversation. One never stopped until the full ritual had been observed. She believed that was what Jack wished for, even if a good stiff brandy would have been more to his taste.

He arrived punctually. For a man as busy as he was, it was a nice compliment to her that he had taken such care. But then, he had always had perfect manners. It dated from his years when he had lived on his charm. He had been the sort of handsome young man who had wit, poise, grace, and the intelligence never to overstay his welcome in any one place. He dressed perfectly, was graceful on the dance floor, had seen most of the latest plays, and, above all, never gossiped or carried tales from one household to the next, or spoke afterwards of the ladies he had accompanied to one function or another. He never drew comparisons, or made promises he did not keep. His ability to charm was deeper than a surface ease. There was a quality to his nature that was worthy of respect.

He came in now and greeted her warmly. The maid took his hat and coat, and he kissed Vespasia lightly on the cheek. He accepted her invitation to sit and assured her that he would be delighted to take tea with her.

The years had been kind to him. The touch of gray at the temples lent him a maturity, the few fine lines in his face deepened the sense of character, even gravity, rather than mere handsomeness. But in spite of his smile, she could see that he was worried.

"Please, my dear, don't waste time leading up gracefully to whatever it is that concerns you," she requested.

He smiled, relief easing out the worst of the tension in his body.

"Thank you. I daresay Emily has told you that I have the offer of a position working with Dudley Kynaston. It is something I would enjoy. He is an interesting man with a fine mind, and—more than that—I would be working on something specific rather than chasing many general subjects." He hesitated. "However, I know that Thomas has been investigating Kynaston because of the maid that went missing from his house, and then the body in the gravel pit nearby, which so resembled her. Somerset Carlisle was asking questions in the House, with the unspoken implication that there was a scandal about to break. That has not happened, but neither has the maid been found, or the bodies identified." He stopped, waiting for Vespasia to offer some reaction.

"Yes, I am aware of these things," she agreed. "You are concerned to make the right judgment?"

He looked embarrassed. "I can't afford to accept the position and then find it has disappeared. I know Emily has private means, but I have always refused to live on her first husband's estate, which is in trust for Edward, anyway. It is not pride, it is . . ."

"Honor," she said for him. "It is not pompous to say so. I understand, and respect you for it. Not only can you not afford to lose the income from an excellent additional position to that of member of Parliament, but you cannot afford the question of your judgment, should it transpire that Kynaston is involved in something uglier than unfaithfulness to his wife . . ."

Jack winced. "You say that easily, as if I might think the unfaithfulness acceptable . . ."

She smiled at him. "You are too sensitive, my dear. I was not thinking anything of the sort. Whom you knew, or how well you knew them before you married Emily is not of interest to me, nor do I believe is it to her. It is completely unacceptable to me to betray trust, but I am perfectly aware that it happens far more often than one would wish. You cannot afford to judge other men on that, when considering whether you wish to work with them or not. It is a luxury beyond most of us, so we all pretend we do not know. On the whole, it works very well."

"Not if you murder the maid and dump her body in a nearby gravel pit," Jack said unhappily and with a hint of bitterness.

"Have you asked Emily's opinion about it?" Vespasia asked, almost as if the idea had been an afterthought.

Jack shook his head. "I don't want to worry her with it. She shouldn't be asked to make this decision for me, nor carry the burden of it if I'm wrong."

"She may wish to," Vespasia replied.

"Emily doesn't like anxiety," he told her. "Especially when there is nothing she can do."

Vespasia smiled. "Do you mean there is nothing she can do, or that you would really rather that she did not attempt anything, and you are worried that if you tell her, she will try to help you?" It was a question so direct as to be blunt, but she knew how many misunderstandings were created by the use of euphemisms. One ended up being so oblique that nobody knew what on earth you were talking about.

He looked at her earnestly. "I'm trying to look after her! I want to make the right decision, and then present her with it. She's been unhappy lately. I don't know why, and she won't tell me. I think she's either bored with me, or she wants me to make a decision without having to be guided, but of course if she said that to me, it would be guidance in itself."

Vespasia sighed. "For all your charm, you don't know women very well, do you! Would you try that protective manner with Charlotte?"

He was startled.

"No . . . she'd hate it. But I'm not married to Charlotte. We would disagree about everything, and it wouldn't matter—" He stopped abruptly.

"My dear, you could disagree with Emily and it wouldn't matter," she assured him. "What you must not do is ignore her. If you continue with it much longer she will begin to think you are interested in some-one else . . ."

"She knows better than that." Now his voice was filled with emotion. "I adore her. In fact I dare not tell her so, because she hates growing older, but I think maturity suits her. She seems more . . . more earthy, more reachable. I don't feel as if she's infallible anymore, too confident, too ethereal to need my support, or protection . . ." He faltered to a stop, looking as if he had said more than he meant to. He bit his lip and looked away from Vespasia, down at the table. "I'm afraid she will resent being helped with anything, she is so self-sufficient . . ."

Vespasia reached across and touched his arm very lightly. "My dear Jack, one of the advantages of growing older is that we begin to accept that none of us can manage without friends, people to love and people who love us, even now and then a little help and a little criticism, if it is gently given. You may find that even Emily has learned some wisdom."

He looked at her with a flash of hope.

"My advice regarding Dudley Kynaston is not to commit yourself just yet," she continued. "Find some excuse to wait a week or so. Think of some other matters you wish to deal with, some other commitment you must conclude. And ask Emily's opinion, whether you actually take her advice or not."

He flashed her a bright, utterly charming smile. "I will do. May I have another jam tart? Suddenly I am hungry, and they are delicious."

"They are there for you," she replied. "You may have them all."

———

Vespasia had dinner with Victor Narraway. She had hesitated whether to accept his invitation or not. She could see Emily's situation so clearly, yet she was confused as to her own. She enjoyed Narraway's company more than that of anyone else she could recall. He had always been easy for her to talk to, to agree or disagree with. Yet lately she had felt a peculiar vulnerability in his company, as if somewhere during their friendship she had lost the emotional armor she had kept safely in place for so many years. She found herself caring if he called again, even allowing her imagination to wonder what he thought of her, and if their friendship was as valuable to him as it was to her.

She was older than he, a knowledge that came with a degree of pain. It had never been of the slightest importance before. Now, absurdly, it mattered. He seemed completely unaware of it, but then he was far too well mannered to allow such an ungallant thing to show. And it was clearly irrelevant. Of course it was. What was she allowing herself to think?

Because she could come up with no graceful way of declining, she accepted and found herself enjoying a late supper at one of her favorite restaurants.

However, they had barely finished their first course and were waiting for the second to arrive when he became very serious.

"There has been a development in Pitt's case," he said quietly, leaning a little forward across the table so as to be able to keep his voice very low, and yet be certain she could hear him. "It seems that the maid, Ryder, who left Dudley Kynaston's house in the middle of the night, has been seen alive and well since then, proving that it was not her body in the gravel pit."

She heard the urgency in his voice and did not interrupt. It was irrelevant that she knew this much already from Charlotte.

"The second body was not hers either," he continued. "It seems unavoidable now to conclude that they were both placed where they would be discovered in order to draw Pitt's attention to the Kynaston house." He was watching her closely, judging her reaction.

"And do you know the purpose for this?" she asked, her stomach knotting as she feared he was going to ask her the same question. Her loyalties were torn. She was not certain, but she believed that Somerset Carlisle had done this, and then deliberately raised the matter in Parliament when no one seemed to be taking it seriously enough. It had not required her to draw her own conclusion as to why.

Narraway was staring at her intently.

"Please don't play games with me, Vespasia," he said softly. "I am not asking you to betray anyone's confidence, even if it is no more than trust in a long friendship. I think you know who placed the bodies where they were, and why they did so."

"I can guess," she admitted. "But I have very carefully avoided asking." This was horribly difficult. She would not willingly refuse him anything, but she could not betray a trust—for anyone. "I . . . I will not ask him, Victor. I think he would tell me the truth, and then I would have to lie to you . . ."

He smiled, as if her answer had genuinely amused him, but there was also a look of pain in his eyes. She had hurt him, and the knowledge of it twisted inside her with a pain she could scarcely believe.

"Vespasia . . ." He reached across the white tablecloth and put his hand over hers, very gently, but with too much strength for her to pull away. "Did you really believe I was going to ask you? Please, give me credit for more sensitivity, and for caring for you more than that!"

She looked at him, and was furious with herself for the tightness in her throat, which made speech impossible. She would embarrass both of them.

"I am certain in my own mind who it was. And such a man would not do so macabre a thing unless he had a profound reason for it. My conclusion is that he did it to force Pitt to investigate Kynaston, because he believes that Kynaston is committing treason against his country. What I do not know is why. I do not think it likely to be anything so grubby as mere money. There is something far deeper, far more precious to him than that. Do you agree?"

She felt a tear slide down her cheek, and an overwhelming wave of relief.

"Yes, I agree," she answered. "It is very terrible to betray your country. I can hardly imagine anything worse, except perhaps betraying yourself."

The waiter arrived with the next course. They were silent until he was gone.

"Then we have something of a test before we decide what it is that Dudley Kynaston cares about even more than his country," Narraway said. "But perhaps not this evening. Thank you for listening. I very much wished to share my thoughts with you. You always make things seem clearer. Would you like some wine?"

Silently she held out her glass. "A debt that honor demands he must pay," she said quietly.

"What debt of honor could he owe greater than that to his country?" he asked.

"We must find out."

16

STOKER DREW IN THE help of two colleagues to help him rule out several of the places where Kitty Ryder might have been. But he was beginning to feel a flicker of desperation at how few possibilities there were left. Who was she so afraid of that she had run from Shooters Hill at night, and without taking any of her belongings? What had she seen or heard in the Kynaston house?

He had asked so many questions about her, heard so many bits of stories, that he felt as if he knew her. He knew the songs she liked, the jokes that made her laugh, that she loved roasted chestnuts, green apples, flaky pastry, although she wouldn't eat much because she did not want to lose her figure. She liked walking in the rain in the summer but hated it in the winter. She wanted to learn about the stars, and one day, if she ever had a house of her own, she would have a dog. He could imagine liking that, too. It reminded him of the dreams he had once had about Mary. It seemed like ages ago, and yet the emotion returned with a sharpness that took him aback. He realized how much he missed the friendship of a woman. There was a tenderness to it that was different from that of men.

Kitty loved the sea, not the beach or the cliffs, but the endless horizon and the great ships that sailed as if they had white wings spread in the wind. If he ever met her he would be able to tell her about some of the voyages he had taken, and the places he'd seen. She loved to watch the seabirds flying at sunset with the light on their wings, and dream about how it would feel. He had never been able to tell Mary, because she hated the sea. To her it meant loneliness, separation, an exclusion of all that she cared about. The sea's endless horizons were full of dreams, and Mary was practical.

Where had Kitty gone to? Was she still alive, or had someone else already found her and . . .

He refused to follow that thought.

Where could she go to hide, and yet still be able to see the things she loved? Water, ships. He needed to stop chasing every clue and use his intelligence. From what he knew of her, if she was frightened and lonely, where would she go for comfort, to gather her courage or make a decision?

Somewhere where she could see water, smell the salt tide, watch seabirds in the fading light. Let her dreams take wing also, just for a while.

Greenwich, down by the Royal Naval College? Except that was too close to Shooters Hill. What about the other side of the river, near the railway station, where she could stand on the shore and look across at where the sailing ships were riding at anchor? Somewhere like that. That is where he would go.

He had no better idea. It was close to dusk as he got off the train and walked down towards the river to watch the light die over the water in limpid silvers and grays. One brilliant bar blazed like a banner across the west, reflecting in the ripples of a barge's wake, as if each crest were burning with it. He stood in silence, pleasure touching him, the evening warming him with its untarnished beauty. Nothing could mar such loveliness; it was safe beyond the reach of human hands.

He waited until the very last of the light faded and his skin was cold. Then he turned and saw a woman a few yards away, her face still towards the horizon as if she could see some essence of sun left behind. She was tall, maybe only two or three inches shorter than he, and what he could see of her face in the fast gathering dusk had a beauty that held him from speech. He simply stared at her. She seemed as if she belonged here, in the evening and the wide, darkening sky where the only color left was an echo of the smoldering sun now slid below the west.

Then she became aware of him, and her eyes widened in fear.

"Don't be frightened!" he said quickly, taking a step towards her. Then he realized that only made it worse, and he stopped. "I'm not going to hurt you. I'm only watching the . . ." He nearly said "sunset," but it was not the color that held him, it was the quality of the light, the softness, the gentleness of the shadows. Did that sound ridiculous for a man to say?

She was staring at him. What had he to lose? She was a stranger he would never see again. "The way the light changes," he finished. "The darkness comes so softly . . ."

"Most people don't see that," she said with surprise. "They think it's all a kind of . . . dying. Are you an artist?"

He wanted to laugh; the idea was so absurd, so far from the truth, but actually it was also beautiful. A wave of longing washed over him. "No," he said quietly. "I wish I were. I'm just a kind of policeman . . ."

The fear was back in her face. He should not have said that.

"Not an ordinary policeman," he said quickly. "Just for spies and anarchists, people who want to change the whole country . . ."

"What are you doing down here?" she asked.

"Just taking time for myself," he said honestly. "I've been looking for someone for weeks and I haven't found her yet. I'm not giving up, I'm just . . . taking a little . . . peace. Maybe I'll get a new idea where to look."

"Is she a spy?" she asked curiously.

He laughed very slightly. "No! She's a witness, I think. But I know she's in danger. I want to protect her." He should be more honest. The twilight, the shared perception of the beauty of the sky over the river demanded it. "And I want to know what she saw or heard that made her run. She left everything behind, all her possessions, her friends, everything."

She stood without moving, not even to change her balance. "If you find her and she tells you—then what?"

"Then we'll know much better exactly what the treason is, and be able to stop it going on."

"What about her? Will you put her in prison, because she ran away?"

"Of course not! We'll make sure she is safe . . ."

"How are you going to do that? Won't they know you've found her? And why would anyone believe her?"

He stared at her. In the delicate gray half-light her face was beautiful, not just pretty but really beautiful. Her hair looked dark, but not black. In the sunlight it could have been any color, even auburn. And she was frightened, wanting to believe him but not able to.

"Kitty . . ." The moment the name was on his lips he felt ridiculous. He was letting this get to him, send his brain soft!

She froze, like an animal ready to run but knowing it was useless. She was caught by a predator far stronger and far swifter than she was. But she would fight; he could see that in her face, too.

He let out a sigh, but did not move at all. "I've been looking for you for weeks! We know Kynaston's betraying secrets, but we don't know why! Or how he's doing it. There's no point in just catching him, we need the people he's passing them on to as well."

She had not said anything—certainly not that she was Kitty Ryder, but he knew it as surely as if she had. It was there in her silence, and her fear. He understood that he should not take a step towards her.

"My name's Davey Stoker. I work for Special Branch. You don't need to run anymore. I'll take you somewhere you'll be safe . . ."

"Prison?" She shook her head sharply. Now she was shivering. "I won't be safe there! The people after me are bigger than you! You don't even know who all of them are!"

"No! Not prison. Why would I put you in prison? You haven't done anything." He knew exactly what he was going to do. "I'll take you on the train, now, to my sister's house. She'll look after you. No one else will know, then they can't tell anyone. You won't be locked in. You can run, if you want to . . ."

"Your sister? She in the police as well?"

He smiled. "No. She's married with four kids. She doesn't really know anything about Special Branch, except that I work there."

"You haven't got a wife? They'd know to look there?" she asked.

"I haven't got a wife. They wouldn't know about Gwen. And it won't be for long."

"Why would she do that? Take me in?"

"Because I asked her to," he said simply. "We're . . . close."

She stood silent for a moment, then she made the decision. "I'll come. But I haven't got money for a train . . . not more than a few stops."

"I have. How about supper first? I'm starving. Do you like fish and chips?"

"Yes . . . but . . ."

He understood. "It's not on me, it's on Special Branch." It was a lie, but he knew why she needed to believe it. She was probably quite hungry.

She nodded and started to walk very slowly back towards the street. He caught up with her quickly and they walked side by side, close, but not touching, keeping step with each other.

Gwen did not hesitate to welcome Kitty. She took one look at Stoker's face, and then at the fear and consciousness of obligation in the whole manner of the young woman with him, and opened the door wide.

"Come in," she said, looking directly at Kitty. "We'll have a cup of tea, then we'll sort out a room for you. It'll need a bit of juggling around, but it'll work. Don't stand on the doorstep, Davey! Come on inside!"

The warmth of the house wrapped around him immediately, and as he watched Kitty's face he saw her smile. Gwen took her up the stairs, calling back instructions to Stoker to put the kettle on.

An hour later, extra beds were made up for children to move in with each other, and they were told strictly not to sit up all night chattering. Gwen and her husband were sitting talking to each other in the kitchen, and Stoker sat with Kitty in the parlor, although it was chilly because the fire had only just been lit. It was a room used on special occasions, and it felt like it.

It was time for explanations.

"What did you learn that made you leave in the night, without any of your clothes, or even a hairbrush?" Stoker asked quietly, but with no allowance for evasion in his voice.

Kitty took a deep breath, stared down at her hands locked tightly in her lap, and began.

"I worked it out that Mr. Kynaston had a mistress. Once you think of it, it in't that hard to see. Just little things, you know?" She looked up quickly, then down again. "The way he explained where he was going, answering questions nobody asked, but not the ones they did, and you only realize it afterwards—"

"You noticed all that?" he interrupted.

"I did," she replied. "Most gentry forget that servants have ears. They get so used to seeing us around, and mostly not speaking, they don't reckon we can put anything together and understand. Or maybe they don't care. If we want to stay in service we aren't going to tell anyone. And it doesn't matter what we think of them. I don't think that's part of anything . . ."

He was puzzled. "So he has a mistress. It's not commendable, but it's not so unusual either. What did you learn that was so bad?"

"That his mistress was Mrs. Kynaston . . . not his wife, but Mrs. Kynaston as was the widow of his brother, the one whose picture hangs in the study, and he looks the way he does."

"Are you sure it wasn't that he was just taking care of her, because of his brother?"

She gave him the sort of glance Gwen did when he said something completely stupid.

"If anybody took it on themselves to 'take care of' me like that, I'd slap 'is face as hard as I could," she retorted. "Then I'd kick him as high up as my skirts'd let me."

"Oh . . ." For a moment he could not think of anything suitable to say. He felt foolishly embarrassed. "Did he know you saw, and think you would tell his wife?"

She gave a slight shrug. "Don't think so. I reckon as she pretty well knew for herself. An' either way, she wouldn't want to think I'd seen. Sometimes you've got to live with things, an' the only way to bear it hurting you so much is to pretend that no one else knows."

He studied her face in the firelight. He could see that she was frightened. She had told him only what she knew he would almost certainly have worked out for himself. It might be painful, immoral, but it was a common tragedy. Not even poets and dreamers imagined all marriages were happy, or faithful.

"Miss Ryder . . . I need to know," he insisted. "Who are you afraid of? Knowing that Mr. Kynaston was having an affair with his brother's widow was unfortunate, but—as you said before—servants know all kinds of things. Did you say something to him?"

Her eyes widened. "No! Wot do you think I am? A blackmailer?" She was angry, but she was also hurt.

He could have bitten his tongue. "No, that's not what I meant! I'm trying to get you to tell me why you ran away. Nothing you've said so far is more than a domestic unhappiness: deep, maybe, but nothing for Special Branch to care about, still less to threaten your life. What is it that makes that matter, Kitty?"

"She were Mr. Bennett's wife," she answered, staring at him almost without blinking. "But before that, she were someone else's wife . . . in Sweden."

He blinked. "Does that matter? Or are you saying she was still married to him? Then her marriage to Bennett would be bigamous. Is there money involved? Did she inherit from Bennett?"

She shook her head. "I don't know. She seems sort of . . . comfortable, but not rich."

"And Mr. Kynaston knew that you'd found that out? How did you find it out anyway?"

"She were staying a day or two with Mrs. Rosalind, like she did quite often. I had some cream for her, special made to keep ladies' hands white and soft. I'd made enough for both ladies, an' I took some to her." She was watching Stoker carefully, her eyes never leaving his face.

"She has this ring she always wears, sort of wide and a bit flat, with stones set in it, but not like usual. Just little stones, and she never takes it off. But she had to for this, 'cos the cream would get in it, maybe even not be good for it."

"Go on," he urged.

"I went in to turn the bed down, an' she was sitting there using the cream on her hands. The rings were on the table by the bedside. I moved them in case the bedcover flipped over them and knocked them off. I saw what was inside the special one."

"What was it?" His mind raced.

"'Anders and Ailsa, July 1881—and forever,'" she answered. "I must have froze, because I looked at the mirror on the dressing table where she was sitting, and I saw her staring back at me. I wanted to say something, but my tongue was stuck in my mouth and I felt the room was swaying round me like I was at sea. The look in her eyes, she would have killed me. Then I heard Mr. Kynaston coming up the top o' the stairs and along the landing. She changed all of a sudden like butter wouldn't melt in her mouth, and she were all sweet an' gentle with him. I went out past him and down the stairs into the kitchen."

"How was she next time you saw her?" Stoker asked.

Kitty's face was pale. "I only saw her once, going across the hall. I heard her tell Mr. Kynaston that there was something missing from the room, something valuable. I knew she was going to say as I took it." She closed her eyes, then opened them again suddenly, staring at him. "I did something stupid. I couldn't afford to lose my place, or my character either. Nobody's going to take on a maid who steals!" She gulped. "I stopped and I said to Mrs. Kynaston that I'd be happy to come with her and help her look for it. I looked straight at her when I said it, too. If what were written on that ring mattered that much, then let him see it, too! She knew exactly what I meant, and she changed her mind. Said to him that she probably hadn't brought it with her, and she was sorry for making a mistake. Then she looked daggers at me, and went on up to bed."

He admired her courage, if not her sense.

"Did you tell Mr. and Mrs. Kynaston about the ring?" he asked.

"No. I went to the kitchen and waited till everyone had gone to bed, then I just left." She hesitated for a moment. "I went out the back door and just kept walking. It wasn't that far to the pub, and I knew they'd put me up for the night, till I could get as far as Harry's the next day. I knew he'd look after me. But it weren't long before someone came asking questions, and I couldn't stay. Not fair to him neither, because I didn't want to marry him. I like him well enough, but not that much."

"And how did the blood and hair get onto the steps from the area-way to the street? And the broken glass?"

She looked down, clearly embarrassed.

"It doesn't make sense," he said quietly. "I have to know."

She raised her eyes. "I'm not lying! Everything I told you was true." She swallowed hard. "Mrs. Ailsa came after me into the kitchen. I knew she was 'oping to get me. She had a glass in her hand, and she was smiling. I ran for the back door, and she came after me. We fought on the steps. It was my hair she pulled out, but her blood . . . Just from her arm, where she knocked the glass. I didn't hurt her, I swear! I didn't even try—"

"I know," he said quickly. "Thank you. I don't know why it matters enough to come after you, but it must have something to do with what we suspect about treason. You stay here with Gwen. Don't tell anybody else about this—in fact don't talk to anyone at all until I tell you it's all right."

She looked at him. "What happens if you don't catch them?"

"I will catch them," he said a little rashly. "I always catch them. But I'm not alone. There are lots of us. Just stay safe here." He stood up. "Gwen'll look after you until I come back again. I may not do that for a little while. I'll be busy, and . . . and you'll be safe if no one knows you are here. Gwen's name's different from mine. No one will automatically connect her with me. Please . . . do as I say!"

She nodded, her eyes suddenly filling with tears as she realized that for a little while, at least, she was safe.

He said good night to Gwen and her husband in the kitchen, and thanked her again. Then he went out into the night smiling to himself, his step light, the ground easy under his feet.

Pitt telephoned Narraway at home and was told that he had gone to the House of Lords. An hour later he had received a message from Narraway, in answer to his request. They met on the Embankment. It was still only a little past ten in the morning and the March wind had a new softness to it. It was easy to believe that spring would begin in a day or two.

Briefly Pitt told Narraway what Stoker had told him when he had arrived at Keppel Street a minute or two after seven. Narraway listened as they walked, without interrupting.

"Then it seems inescapable that Ailsa Kynaston is the force behind Dudley's betrayal of his country," Narraway said when Pitt had finished. "The questions are why, and to whom is he giving the secrets of our naval submarine plans, which possibly cover the whole area of weapons, on which our survival might depend! We need to know a hell of a lot more about her!"

"And Bennett," Pitt added. "I feel his death more than likely has something to do with all this."

Narraway gave a brief, tight smile. "I hadn't thought you were telling me simply to satisfy my curiosity. That would have done over dinner, when you had the solution."

Pitt made no excuses. "You have connections I don't, people you know who won't trust me yet. I'm going to speak to Sir John Ransom and find out exactly what Kynaston has knowledge of, and see what I can learn from him. I've got to discover where the information is going, and through whom. What a mess!"

"Be careful what you say to Ransom," Narraway warned. "The whole Kynaston family has been highly respected for several generations." His face pinched as he said it, imagining the grief, the refusal to accept what would in the end prove to be unavoidable.

"He already has a good idea of it," Pitt replied, remembering Carlisle's account and his sadness for a friend betrayed. He turned and smiled at Narraway, a mirthless means of communicating that he had no intention of telling him how he knew. It was not that he did not trust Narraway, but that he did not want to place on him the burden of keeping it from Vespasia. Neither of them yet knew where this was going to lead.

Narraway did not press him.

Pitt came to a stop along the path. The wind off the river was still cool, the bright sun on the water deceptive. He suddenly recalled Kynaston's study and the paintings he had said were of Sweden, several of them clearly attached to memories. He mentioned them to Narraway, given that Bennett had spent time in Sweden. Then he turned to walk back to Westminster Bridge. He was not looking forward to having to tell Ransom what he now knew, but since it was unavoidable, the sooner it was done, the better. This was his job, one of the darkest sides of it.

RANSOM RECEIVED HIM IMMEDIATELY. He was a quiet man, tall and thin with gray hair receding from a high brow.

"I hoped you would not come," he said, shaking his head a little. They were in his office, a large space, which he had managed to fill with books and papers. They were jammed in together on the shelves that lined three of the walls, and still they spilled over into piles on odd chairs, and even onto the floor. Pitt wondered how much he lost, or if actually he knew what every pile contained. From the steady eyes of the man and his gentle, precise voice, he imagined the latter.

"I hoped so, too," Pitt replied. They were both still standing. Somehow it did not seem the occasion to sit. "I'm afraid it is now necessary."

"Kynaston?" Ransom asked. "Or am I preempting what you have to say?"

"No, you are actually making it easier," Pitt said truthfully. "It is not yet proved, but I can see no alternative explanation for what I know."

Ransom was pale. "It appears I was denying what, if I was honest, I had already accepted was true. But I thank you for coming. Are you arresting him?"

Pitt shook his head. "Not yet. I need proof before I blacken a man's name. I don't need to tell you that you should not allow him access to any further new material. And I need to have you tell the government of the information he could have passed to our enemies—or even our friends, for that matter."

Ransom smiled sadly. "When it comes to weapons of war, it is not always so easy to tell the difference. I have not had such a thing happen since I have been in charge here. Of course I have thought of it—one has to—but somehow the reality hurts more than I had foreseen. I like the man. What in God's name can have made him do it?"

"I don't know yet," Pitt answered. "We may never know."

Ransom looked at him, frowning, his face filled with misery. "I suppose you find this sort of thing again and again, in your profession. How do you go on trusting anyone? Or don't you?" He stopped, searching to defend his idea in words. "Do you learn whom to trust? Is there some sense, some formula that you use? How do you know when a man you have liked and believed in for years is actually heart and mind serving someone else, something else, different sorts of ideals and beliefs altogether? Do you then doubt everyone else as well?"

"No," Pitt answered before he allowed himself to think of it. "Then you are allowing them to destroy you, as well as themselves. Over time and experience you make enemies, for lots of reasons, but you also make friends. People who will disagree with you openly, but never betray you to another, even when you are wrong."

Ransom said nothing.

"Actually I like Kynaston, too," Pitt added. "You might be pleased to know that Kitty Ryder, the maid who disappeared, is alive and well. I would prefer it that you did not make that public, for her safety."

Ransom sighed and rubbed the heel of his hand over his forehead. "That's something. Although it means some other poor woman is dead, whoever she is."

"We'll give her a decent burial," Pitt promised. "Both of them. Thank you for your time, sir."

Ransom shook his hand and Pitt left to begin the next step.

NARRAWAY THOUGHT LONG AND hard about whom he should approach regarding the death of Bennett Kynaston, and the relationship he had had with his brother. Certain records were easy enough to find: birth, schooling, and university. He checked them, but it confirmed only what he already knew. The Kynaston brothers were wealthy, privileged in society, extremely well educated, and both of them of well above average intellect. Dudley was slightly the more serious of them; Bennett had the charm and was the one from whom all had expected great success. Nothing suggested tragedy to come.

Nobody was going to be willing to give away secrets. Narraway knew from the beginning that he would have to find someone who owed him a debt the payment of which they could not afford to back out of. He found it distasteful to collect on a debt of help that had been freely given. Yet the only alternative was worse. The choice between good and bad was simple; anyone could make it without a moment's hesitation. It was the choice between bad and what might or might not be worse that tested the judgment.

And yet Narraway barely hesitated. He debated with himself all the way to see Pardoe, the man whose debt he was about to call in, but he did not digress from the path. A long time ago he and Pardoe had been in the army together. Pardoe had made a bad error. It was an honest mistake, but it would have looked like cowardice, and that would have ruined not only his army career, which he had not cared about so much, but his social career as well. "Coward" was a word that closed all doors irrevocably. Narraway had covered for him, at some risk to himself, although in the end he had not suffered any consequences. But since he had put himself at risk, the debt existed.

He went to the offices in Whitehall where Pardoe worked and left him a brief, sealed message. Two hours later he and Pardoe sat down to dinner at Narraway's club.

Narraway approached the subject immediately. There was too little time to waste, and to begin with pleasantries would be almost insulting.

"I need a little help from you," Narraway began. "I wouldn't ask if it were not of the utmost importance."

"Of course," Pardoe responded, but already the shadow was across his face. He knew Narraway too well to imagine he was going to be given an alternative. Narraway had never asked anything of him before, and now the debt was due. Pardoe cleared his throat. "What can I do to help?"

"Tell me about Bennett, Ailsa, and Dudley Kynaston," Narraway replied.

"What about them?" Pardoe was confused. "Bennett's been dead for years. I think Dudley looks after her to some extent, for Bennett's sake. He was devoted to him. But I'm sure you know that. It's hardly a secret."

"Let's start with how Ailsa and Bennett met. Was it through Dudley?"

"Good heavens, no!" Pardoe was clearly surprised. "It was by chance, in Stafford, I think. Ailsa was over on holiday."

"Over? From where?"

Pardoe was slightly surprised. "Sweden. Ailsa is Swedish. I think originally her name was Ilsa, and she changed it to the more Scottish-sounding name. I think she did not wish him to know she was Swedish."

"Why not?" Narraway was puzzled. "I thought both Bennett and Dudley loved Sweden?"

"They did, until . . ." Pardoe was obviously embarrassed.

Narraway could not afford to ignore anything. "Until what, Pardoe? I haven't time for delicate answers."

Pardoe clenched his jaw, and there was a small muscle beating in his temple. He looked wretched.

"Look, Narraway, this is all a long time ago, and a private tragedy. It happened when Bennett was on a trip to Sweden, and it can't have anything to do with whatever you're looking for. It wasn't his fault. It could happen to anybody. You of all people should know that!"

Narraway was surprised. "I should! Why?"

"You've sown a few wild oats, and certainly used your charm to extricate yourself a few times." There was an edge of bitterness in Pardoe's voice.

"Pardoe!" Narraway said sharply. He hated having to do this, but he was too good at it to find it difficult. "Stop mincing around and tell me the story."

Pardoe gave in. The weight of his obligation was something he could never have denied. He might have told any other man to go to hell, but not Narraway. Their relationship was old and deep.

"Bennett was very charming," Pardoe said quietly. "It was perfectly natural, not an act or something he turned on and off. He went for a long break, several months, to Sweden. He stayed with a family called Halversen. They all got along well, except that their younger daughter, Ingrid, was about fifteen. Lovely young girl, but a bit of a dreamer, very intense. I daresay we all are, at that age." His face grew tighter, the muscles in his back strained.

"Go on," Narraway prompted.

Pardoe resumed reluctantly. "Ingrid fell in love with Bennett, and wrote him love letters that she never sent. He had no idea. When he finally found out, he was horrified. He had no intention of having anything but the occasional friendly conversation with a girl that age. He was about thirty at the time. Perhaps he wasn't as gentle as he could have been, or maybe he was! Regardless, the result was that she felt rejected, humiliated, even deceived. She took her own life, rather dramatically. Drowned in a stream near the house, but it was definitely suicide. The family blamed Bennett and read her letters to mean that he had seduced and deflowered her, and she died of misery and shame."

"What a wretched tragedy," Narraway said quietly, trying to imagine the pain of it, the misunderstanding, the hysteria of youth. "Is that why Bennett couldn't go back to Sweden?" He was disappointed. It didn't seem to be relevant to Dudley's treason, but he could not tell Pardoe that.

"Good God, no!" Pardoe gave a grating laugh. "The . . . family regarded him as a rapist and had him charged. The whole town was up in arms, and he was arrested pretty much for his own safety. The father was a man of some influence. Gradually he prevailed on the local authorities to make the charge stick, and bring Bennett to trial. He was painted as an arrogant foreigner who went around seducing young girls too decent and too innocent not to be taken in. Abuse of hospitality is one of the most morally repellent of crimes in a lot of cultures. It's a betrayal of all that's basically good. It's practically a denial of God to some people—"

"I know that!" Narraway cut across him. "What happened? Bennett died in England, didn't he, so he must've made it back."

"Yes . . . yes. When Dudley heard of it he was frantic. He went to Sweden to do anything and everything he could to rescue the brother he adored."

"And succeeded?"

"Yes. But at some cost. It turned into a very ugly battle, and Dudley finally found the help of a man called Harold Sundstrom, who had a great deal of influence. Sundstrom used all his power to get Bennett out on bail, and then helped him to escape out of the country altogether, and home to England. Then he persuaded the Swedish authorities to let the matter drop. He pointed out how much better it would be for the family's reputation, especially that of poor Ingrid. He paid the local coroner, or whatever they're called in Sweden, to say the death was accidental, and let the girl be buried in peace, without the stain of suicide."

"I see," Narraway responded. What he saw was that Dudley Kynaston had saved the reputation, and possibly the life, of the brother he loved, and incurred a debt towards Harold Sundstrom that he would never be able to pay for the rest of his life—except by installments of treason, an inch at a time.

Pardoe said nothing, but the answering emotion was in his face.

17

EARLY NEXT MORNING, PITT was sitting in his own kitchen with a cup of hot tea and fresh toast, butter, and marmalade. With him were Stoker, Narraway, Vespasia, and, of course, Charlotte. Minnie Maude was busy making more toast, holding the slices of bread on the toasting fork as close as she could to the open door of the stove where the coals were hottest.

Narraway had already told them what he had learned about Ingrid's death and the accusation against Bennett Kynaston, and how Dudley gained such a debt of honor by having Harold Sundstrom rescue him, possibly from death.

"And Ailsa was the wife, and then widow, of Anders Sundstrom?" Charlotte said as it became clear to her. "So she is collecting Harold's debt from Dudley?" She frowned. "Is Harold dead?"

"No," Narraway replied. "I've been up half the night checking various details with people I know. Harold Sundstrom is quite an important man. He was certainly alive and well a few days ago. He has a position in naval research . . ." He let that last sentence hang in the air, its implication clear.

Pitt sat silently for a few minutes, turning over the pieces in his mind. "And Ailsa manipulated her dead husband's brother into betraying his own country because she is a loyal Swede?" he asked thoughtfully. "Or to help her first husband's father? That seems an odd division of loyalties."

"And a betrayal of Bennett as well," Charlotte added. "Rosalind said that Ailsa was still so in love with him that she can't consider marrying anyone else . . . but she is still having a sort of an affair with Edom Talbot."

Vespasia's eyebrows shot up. "Edom Talbot? For heaven's sake why? She's a beautiful woman, certainly very striking. She could easily find someone of her own social class. And I think that would matter to her."

"Perhaps she loves him?" Narraway suggested.

"No . . . she doesn't!" Charlotte said quickly. "She finds him . . ." She struggled for a word that was exactly right.

"Distasteful," Pitt supplied it for her, remembering her description of the scene she had observed.

Stoker looked puzzled, and with some embarrassment Charlotte told him what she had seen reflected in the mirrors.

Instead of disapproval, which Pitt knew she had expected, Stoker's face reflected a degree of admiration. "So she is still in love with Bennett Kynaston, her late husband; she is daughter-in-law of this Swedish chap in their naval department; and she is using Edom Talbot, who is close to our prime minister, and sometimes Dudley Kynaston, who is giving away our naval secrets to the Swedes," he observed with incredulity. "It doesn't make sense. Especially added to the fact that she was the one who was trying to hunt down Kitty Ryder. We've missed something."

"Rather a lot," Narraway said bleakly.

"Did Ailsa know anything about the connection between Bennett and Ingrid's death?" Vespasia asked.

"She had to," Pitt replied. "It was her father-in-law at the time who rescued him, at some considerable labor and cost to himself."

Vespasia looked at him, her brow puckered in thought. "What was Ailsa's surname before she married Anders Sundstrom?"

Narraway pushed his chair back and stood up. "I shall find out. She is still a Swedish national, living here in Britain. It will be a matter of record. May I use your telephone, Pitt?"

"Of course," Pitt replied quickly. "It's in the hall."

Narraway nodded and went out immediately. They heard his footsteps along the linoleum in the passage.

No one spoke until he returned. Minnie Maude silently made another piece of toast and refilled the teapot with boiling water, the patter of Uffie's claws on the floor behind her the only sound.

When Narraway returned, the tension in his body and the look in his face gave him away.

"Revenge," he said simply. "Ingrid Halversen was her sister. She probably married Bennett Kynaston for the purpose of revenge, only before she could ruin him he died of what seems to have been natural causes. She carried her vengeance on to Dudley. After all, he was the one who rescued Bennett from what she saw as justice the first time."

No one argued, in fact no one said anything. It all made perfect sense now.

Charlotte was the first to speak. "So she wanted to have an exquisite revenge, the disgrace as well as the ruin," she said slowly. "I suppose she meant to get Dudley in beyond any way of extricating himself, and then she would have exposed him?"

"Would have?" Vespasia said quickly. "Surely she still will do?"

"We must prevent that!" Pitt responded. "It would do immeasurable damage to us. We would lose all respect, or credibility. Even our own navy would have no belief in us. Our allies, enemies—"

"We understand," Narraway cut him off. "She is having an affair with Talbot, but does not like him. Therefore she has another reason for it. Does it have anything to do with the information going from Kynaston to Sundstrom?"

"What do we know about Talbot?" Pitt asked, speaking to himself as much as anyone else. He tried to put his personal dislike of the man out of his mind; his feelings were irrelevant, as was the fact that Talbot disliked him. He was surprised that it was Vespasia who answered.

"An ambitious man, who desires to belong to society, which will always see him as an outsider. Unfortunately he has allowed it to make him bitter . . ."

Stoker looked at her quickly, but was too aware of his own status to make any remark. Pitt knew he was seeing her as someone exquisitely privileged who had never known exclusion from anything, let alone society itself.

She caught his glance. "I am not approving of it, Mr. Stoker, merely observing it as possibly relevant to Mr. Talbot's behavior. It may not be something you have thought of, but most women understand society's exclusions. Some of us even wish to have a vote as to which govern- ment we live under, but that possibility does not seem to lie in the near future, regardless of our means, or intelligence."

She had spoken quite gently, but Stoker blushed scarlet. Clearly he had never given the matter any thought; it was simply a part of life, and had always been so. He lifted his chin a little higher and swallowed hard.

"I'm sorry," he said, looking directly at her. "You are right. I never thought of that."

She smiled back at him. "At least since the Married Women's Prop- erty Act, I may own my own clothes."

He stared at her in amazement.

She gave a wry, slight laugh. "You are too young to remember. I mention it only to persuade you that I do understand the anger at what one perceives to be totally unfair. I have some sympathy with Mr. Tal- bot. He is probably more intelligent and more able than many who will always be his superiors not because of ability or honor, but the circum- stances of both. The tragedy is that he may have allowed that resent- ment to rob him of the positions within his reach. No matter how understandable it is, anger is still a poison, albeit one that works slowly, eating away at the judgment, at mercy, and eventually at life." She suddenly became aware that everyone was looking at her, and she colored very faintly.

Pitt was the first to speak, in order to fill in the silence. He saw Vespasia in a new light, perhaps more vulnerable than she had ever allowed herself to appear before. He had taken it for granted that all doors were open to her. Now that he considered it, clearly they were not. She was well born and wealthy, perhaps. She was truly beautiful. But she was still a woman. His admiration for her, even love, had allowed him to forget that. But it would be tactless to say so now.

"Then it seems extremely likely that Talbot is the one also seeking a kind of revenge by selling the secrets of the establishment that has denied him, on a prejudice he finds intolerable," he observed.

Charlotte drew in her breath as if to speak, then let it out again in silence.

"Do you disagree?" Pitt asked.

They all looked at her, waiting.

Now she had no choice. "I agree that it is almost certainly Talbot," she answered. "But I think revenge could have waited, and it will satisfy him little. To succeed would have been far better. I think his more urgent motive may have been money."

"Money?" Narraway repeated. "Do you know something of his affairs?"

She smiled at him. "I've seen how he dresses, and I know what such suits cost Thomas. And shirts! Talbot has gold cuff links. I've noticed several different pairs. And shoes. And I've seen where he dines. I could feed my family for a week on the cost of one of his cigars. And I daresay some of the nice little trinkets that Ailsa wears were gifts from him. Whatever other arrangements lie between them, he desires her physically, and to court a woman like her, one needs to give gifts, flowers, to ride in carriages, dine at the nicest and most fashionable places. Possibly he has to compete with Dudley Kynaston, who has wealth, position, and considerable good looks. He is also charming, and socially at ease. In fact his only disadvantage is that he is already married. And, since she does not love him—in fact she hates him—that is no disadvantage at all to her."

Stoker stared at her, then at Pitt, then lowered his eyes.

"I think you are perfectly right," Vespasia agreed. "The question is, what are we going to do about it? And I believe we may not have an unlimited amount of time in which to decide."

"We need proof, sir." Stoker looked at Pitt. "If he did it for revenge, I don't know what proof there would be of that. But if Mrs. Pitt is right, and it was at least partly for money, then there will be proof. Once you know what you're looking for, there are always tracks of money changing hands, especially if it comes from another country. And if he's spent anything above what he earns, we can find it."

"He would likely imply he'd inherited the money, if anyone asked," Pitt said, thinking about conversations with Talbot in Downing Street, trying to remember if money had ever been mentioned.

"We can check that, too, sir," Stoker said quickly. "I'll do it straightaway, if you wish."

"Yes," Pitt agreed, looking around the table, first to Narraway, then to Vespasia. A flicker of amusement crossed his mind at the fact that she held no office at all, official or otherwise, and yet he quite naturally sought her opinion, even in front of Narraway, who was his most trusted adviser.

He thought he saw an answering flash in her silver-gray eyes, but it was so quick he was not sure.

Narraway nodded and stood up. "I will look more closely at Ailsa Kynaston and her past, and other possible connections, consulting the friend I spoke to earlier. Pitt, I don't doubt you will follow up on Dudley Kynaston and his associates, on the small possibility that we are wrong. Mr. Stoker . . ."

"Yes, sir?"

"I would rather you did not give us details, but I trust you have Miss Ryder somewhere very safe indeed?"

Stoker blushed. "Yes, sir!"

"And her statement in writing, and signed?"

"Yes, sir."

"Witnessed?"

There was a short hesitation, less than a second. "Yes, sir."

Narraway caught it. "But you are not sure if the witness is . . . unbiased?"

Stoker gulped. "Yes . . . sir." He had forgotten how quick Narraway was. He had worked with him for years, but had adapted his thoughts now to working with Pitt. Already Narraway belonged to the past.

Pitt felt vaguely uncomfortable for it, but there was no time to indulge emotions. Stoker had hesitated because no doubt the witness was one of his own family, his sister or her husband. He found himself smiling, but at how much care Stoker had taken, and at his rigid honesty, not at any lapse of judgment.

Narraway must have seen Pitt's face, because he did not pursue it. They parted company, each to set about their own task.

Vespasia arrived home with her mind in turmoil. As soon as she was through the door and into the hallway, where the long window at the top of the stairs shed sunlight like a pathway upward, she was met by her maid.

"M'lady, Mr. Carlisle called to see you. He seemed to feel it was urgent." She took a breath, uncertainty in her eyes. "I told him I didn't know when you'd be back. It could be hours, or even all day, but he was determined to wait. So I asked him to make himself comfortable in the sitting room. I hope I didn't overstep myself . . ."

Vespasia glanced at the longcase clock to her right. "You did exactly the right thing, thank you," she said. "It is rather too early for tea; perhaps he would like something else. If so I shall ring for you. Otherwise I would prefer not to be disturbed."

"Yes, m'lady." Relieved not to have been told she was mistaken, the girl hurried away.

Vespasia went into the sitting room, her mind racing as to what she should say to Carlisle.

Carlisle stood up. He was immaculately dressed as usual, but he looked anxious, even distressed, and as if he had not slept.

"I apologize for troubling you," he began, "especially at this hour in the morning, but I think the matter is urgent."

"Then you are probably right," she agreed, reasserting the composure for which she was so much respected, sometimes even held in awe. "In all the years we have known each other, I have not seen you panic." She sat down, so that he might also. "What has happened?"

His quirky face still held its usual humor, but also a shadow of pain. "I have had time to think very hard about what I have done in my outrage at Kynaston's treason," he replied. "And I realize that part of my reaction was fear. We have not so very long to go before the turn of the century. Much will change. The queen is old and, I believe, very tired." His own voice sounded weary as he said it. "She has been alone for too many years. Because it has been so long in coming, I think the new reign will be very different."

She did not interrupt him. She had had these thoughts herself.

"Powers are shifting," he went on. "I see shadows in many directions. Perhaps it is just such shadows that are frightening me, but I don't think so. We cannot afford treason now. The world political situation is growing more tense. Nevertheless, I acted . . ." He looked for the right word. "I acted without foreseeing some of the results of what I was doing, or how they might affect others. Pitt did not charge me, and he easily could have." He looked very directly at her, his eyes deeply troubled. "I owe him a debt now that I need to repay."

She wished very much to help him, but there were bounds she could not cross. "If you are looking for information, my dear, I cannot help you," she told him. Her voice was gentle, but there was steel in it. She could not allow him to think that she would relent.

Amusement flickered across his face and vanished. "If you did, I would hate it more than you can imagine," he replied. "You are a fixed part in a constantly eroding universe. We have to have a polestar, one true north."

She blinked rapidly to hide the tears that sprang suddenly to her eyes. "That is quite the oddest compliment I have ever received," she said a little huskily. "But unquestionably one of the best. What is it that I can help you with, if not information?"

"Tell me of something I can do to help," he replied.

"What could you do that they are not already doing?" She was puzzled. Did he have something in mind, or was he searching as discreetly as it seemed?

"Many things," he said with a gesture of his hands as if to encompass a vast space. "I am not restricted by the law. I know it quite well, but there are areas of it for which I have little regard. And if I can take risks when it suits me, I can make it suit me now."

She looked at his face, the desperation in his eyes, and believed him. "Please do not steal any more corpses and put them in dramatic and important places," she said wryly. "There are other ways of attracting people's attention."

He gave a very little smile. "You must admit, there are very few that work as well!"

"I do admit it, but I doubt any judge would dare to, whatever he actually thought. Not many of them have a lively sense of the absurd. How could they? But regardless of that," she continued before he could answer, "it will not work again for some time!"

"Please?" he begged. "Something . . ."

What could she tell him, without breaking Pitt's trust?

Carlisle leaned forward a little in his chair, his face grave. "Kynaston is selling our country's secrets, and God knows to whom they will go. Lady Vespasia, it matters too much to indulge in emotional self-protection. I don't know why he is doing it! But I do know he is. I suspect that perhaps his sister-in-law is involved, and maybe that rather rough lover of hers, Talbot. Although I have no idea whose side he is on. Possibly his banker's. And I apologize if I malign the man."

"Do you think so?" she asked quickly. "That he lives beyond his means? A judgment, not merely an impression."

He looked at her very steadily, unblinking. "Would you like to know? More than just out of . . . curiosity?"

She knew what he was asking. She hesitated only an instant. It was like jumping off a cliff into an ice-cold sea, far below you. If you hesitated, actually looked down, you would never do it.

"Yes. I think I might like to know that very much," she replied. "I do mean know, not suppose. I suppose it already."

He leaned forward and kissed her gently on the cheek. It was a touch of the lips, an impression of warmth, no more. Then he stood up and left. She heard his voice saying good-bye to the maid in the hallway, and thanking her for allowing him to wait for Vespasia, then the sound of the front door closing.

She sat quite still for half an hour. She watched it on the mantel clock. Then she rose and went to the telephone to call Pitt. She did not panic until she found that she could not reach him.

What danger had she pushed Carlisle into? This was not some game; it was treason. If not yet murder, it could be any day. They hanged people for murder, piracy—and treason. If he was guilty, then Talbot had nothing to lose by killing him.

She must steady herself. She had prompted Carlisle to go after proof of Talbot's involvement. It was her responsibility to take care of him now. Since she could not reach Pitt, she had to call Narraway. What he thought of her was irrelevant, however much it might hurt. And it would. Now, when she might be about to lose it, she realized his good opinion of her mattered more than that of anyone else, and in a different kind of way. She understood with an amazing degree of pain that she loved him.

One did not fall in love at her age. It was undignified and absurd! And yet it was also as real as the passions of youth, and deeper. There was all the past hunger and laughter and experience to add to it, as well as her experiences of pain, and the infinite sweetness, of life.

She picked up the telephone and asked for Narraway's number, her hands shaking. It seemed like minutes before she heard his voice at the other end, but it was actually barely a few seconds.

She began immediately. "Victor, when I arrived home I found Somerset Carlisle waiting for me, in a state of some distress . . ."

"What has happened?" he interrupted. "Are you all right?"

She sounded panicky. She must control it. "Yes, thank you, I am perfectly all right. It is not myself I am concerned for. Please listen to me." She could not allow him to think of her comfort now—it would make it impossible to tell him about Carlisle's danger.

"He cares desperately about the treason," she continued more levelly. "He sees a darkness coming, more than just a change. He is afraid for the future for all of us. The turn of the century will bring much that is new, shifts of power in Europe . . ." Her voice was rising and beginning to sound panicky again.

She took a breath and resumed, more calmly, "He is afraid that time is short to stop Kynaston, and that if we delay he may escape, or whomever he is giving the secrets to may find other ways to continue."

"I know that, my dear," Narraway cut across her. "Time is very short. But if we do not find proof of Talbot's involvement, there is nothing we can do. And to arrest Kynaston and not Talbot, if he is our go-between, is only half a result . . ."

"Victor! Please . . . Carlisle seems to know that Talbot is involved. It all fits together too well for him not to. He has gone to try to find proof that Talbot has money he has not earned . . ."

"Gone where?" Narraway said with surprising calm; there was barely an edge to his voice.

"I don't know. I imagine to Talbot's house, or wherever he might hope to find proof of his income . . ."

"Have you told Pitt?"

"I can't reach him. He doesn't answer his telephone."

"You said Carlisle has gone to find proof of Talbot being paid fairly large sums of money that he can't account for?" he repeated carefully.

"Yes." She sounded steadier. "He knew Talbot was involved. I told him nothing." She hesitated. She must explain before he asked. It was acutely painful that she had behaved with such little discretion, even more so since she knew she might well do so again. Her pity for Carlisle, and her understanding of exactly what he felt, was too powerful to ignore.

"Vespasia?" Narraway prompted urgently.

"Yes. I . . . Carlisle felt a terrible guilt over the way in which he drew Pitt into the investigation. He wants to redeem that debt, regardless of the cost to himself."

"We'll deal with that later," he told her. "Right now we must consider where he may have gone. As you fear, if he is caught by Talbot himself, he will suffer nothing as simple as being arrested in the act of burglary. And worse than that, Talbot will know that we are after him. At best he will disappear, possibly to Sweden where we will not be able to reach him, and taking with him whatever else he knows. At worst, he may kill Carlisle . . ."

Vespasia felt herself freeze inside. She could have stopped him. She should have, however much it hurt or seemed a rebuff.

Narraway was silent on the other end of the telephone line.

She seemed to wait for ages. The ticking of the longcase clock was counting into eternity.

"There's less likely to be anything damning in the house," Narraway said at last. "Far more likely to be in his bank. I wonder if Carlisle will have thought of that."

"But we can't gain access to anything in his bank," she said reluctantly. "I don't even know if Thomas could."

"Not easily," he replied. "Probably not at all, unless he thought of a really imaginative lie . . . but then that seems to be what Carlisle is rather gifted at." There was a slight trace of amusement in his voice, not just anger. "We must find out where Talbot banks. That may take a little while, but it will have to for Carlisle as well. Please stay—"

She cut across him, something she would never ordinarily do. "Victor, he is a social climber. It is intensely important to him to belong. He will be at the most exclusive bank there is." Vespasia named her own bank.

She heard his sigh of relief. "Yes, of course he will. Thank you. Do you think Carlisle will have thought of that?"

"Yes." She had no doubt at all. It was a deep, instinctive knowledge Carlisle would share. "I'll meet you there," she added.

"No! Vespasia!" His voice was sharp. "It could be unpleasant . . ."

"I don't doubt it," she agreed. "But Carlisle will listen to me more than to you." And, before he could argue any further, she replaced the earpiece on its hook, cutting the connection.

NEARLY AN HOUR LATER she and Narraway stood in the manager's office of the most prestigious bank in London. Vespasia was, of course, known and respected there. Narraway was not, but because of his previous position as head of Special Branch, and now a member of the House of Lords, he was known by repute.

The manager was an exquisitely dressed, aquiline-faced man in his early sixties. He concealed his nervousness behind a mask of propriety, but Vespasia could see that he was trying desperately to salvage the bank's reputation out of a disaster he could barely comprehend.

"But he was a member of Parliament!" he said yet again. "He said it was state business of the utmost importance. A constituent of his was involved in a financial transaction that could start a war, if it were not dealt with immediately. He proved his identity to me, beyond any doubt. And, apart from that, I know him by sight anyway. He banks with us! Has done for years. You must be . . . mistaken, my lady."

Narraway glanced at the manager, then at Vespasia, but did not interrupt.

"Permit me to guess, Sir William," she said with a very faint smile. "Mr. Carlisle wished to know if Mr. Edom Talbot had received regular and very substantial payments from Sweden over the last year or so."

His eyebrows shot up.

"Yes! Yes, indeed. He said they were fraudulent and could involve Mr. Talbot, and even the prime minister himself, in an appalling scandal, if his fears were well founded. I assured him they were perfectly legitimate, and the funds were all accounted for."

"But spent," she said drily.

"Of course." His face was bleak. "It was his money, quite legally obtained. All the paperwork was in order, I assure you. The money was transferred in the usual way . . ."

"From a Mr. Harold Sundstrom?" she asked.

Sir William paled. "Yes, although perhaps I should not disclose that, except that Mr. Sundstrom is a reputable gentleman in the Swedish naval establishment. We checked. There was nothing questionable about any part of the transactions. Were it anyone other than a man of Mr. Carlisle's position, I should have discounted his fear entirely."

"But you didn't," Narraway spoke at last. "Did you show him the proof he asked for?"

"I did not. I merely gave him my word that all the papers were in order, and that the amounts were roughly what he estimated," Sir William said stiffly. "He wished to see them, but he accepted my assurance."

Narraway's face was grim, his jaw tight. "And you informed Mr. Talbot that the inquiry had been made?"

"Of course. I telephoned him at Downing Street. He was extremely distressed. Which made me conclude that he was afraid Mr. Carlisle's fears were well grounded. Mr. Talbot has somehow been the victim of an international fraud. I have no idea what it is, but—"

"I have," Narraway said instantly. "If you do not wish to have the bank complicit in treason, Sir William, you will keep all these papers in your safe and allow no one else to see or touch them. And I mean no one! *Including* Mr. Talbot. Special Branch will come for them as soon as they can obtain the appropriate warrants. Do you understand me?"

"Yes, sir, of course I do!" Sir William said stiffly.

Narraway smiled. "Thank you. The nation will be obliged to you, although very possibly they will never know it. But I will make it my business to see that the prime minister does." He took Vespasia by the arm. "Good day, sir."

Outside on the pavement in the wind and the sun, Vespasia let out a sigh of relief, and turned to Narraway.

He was smiling. "Thank you," he said quietly. "Thank God for Talbot's social aspirations, poor devil." Then his face shadowed again. "But I wish Sir William had not told him. I suppose it was inevitable. We had better try Pitt again. Talbot may well run, and I have no means to stop him." He took her by the arm and began to walk quickly. "We had better find a telephone."

She hated to say it, but honesty prevailed. "You will move faster without me, Victor. Please go . . . Talbot will not only escape, he may take Ailsa with him, and leave Kynaston to take all the blame."

"Which would be a hell of a mess," he agreed without slackening his pace at all. "Or worse than that, he could stop them himself, even kill them if necessary, and emerge as the hero."

"How on earth could he do that, with the money in his name?" she asked. She had to run a step or two to keep up, although he still had her by the arm, and it was more than a trifle undignified.

"Say that it was part of a plan to stop Kynaston," he answered.

"What about Ailsa? She doesn't love him!" she protested.

"Then he might very well have to get rid of her, too," he agreed. "Perhaps that is what he has gone to do, rather than to the bank, whether he now knows we are on to Ailsa or not. Then it is only his word against Kynaston's, and it is Kynaston who stole the secrets."

She was too out of breath to argue, even if she had had something useful to say.

They swung round a corner, and, after glancing in both directions, he started across the street, still holding her arm. They had reached the discreet entrance to a gentleman's club, and he stopped abruptly, forcing her to halt.

"They won't let me in," she told him. "Don't waste time arguing with them, use the telephone and call Thomas. If you can't get him, then try Stoker."

He hesitated.

"For heaven's sake, Victor, get on with it!" she ordered him.

Without any warning at all he put both arms around her and kissed her firmly on the lips, with intense gentleness, as if he would have made it longer and deeper had time allowed. Then he turned and strode up the steps and in through the door, allowing it to slam after him.

Vespasia stood on the steps, stunned and burning with a sudden and completely overwhelming warmth, her imagination soaring.

He returned ten minutes later, his step light, his face shining with relief.

"You spoke to Thomas?" she said, moving towards him. "He will go after Talbot?"

"Yes, with Stoker." He put his hands on her arms, holding her so that she faced him. "It was very good advice—'get on with it!'" He repeated her words in exactly the tone that she had used earlier. "One should have the courage of one's convictions, win or lose. Vespasia, will you marry me?"

She was speechless. They were standing in the middle of the street. It was as unromantic as it was possible to be. And yet she had no doubts at all. They should be thinking of Talbot, and whether he would kill Ailsa or not, of Kynaston's treason and the appalling damage a trial would do. Yet she knew without hesitation that the most important thing in her life was that Narraway loved her, not only as a friend but in the same intense and passionate way that she loved him.

"Yes, I will," she replied. "But quietly, if you please. Not in the middle of the street."

Such an intense happiness filled his face that two men passing by hesitated and looked at him, then at each other, but Narraway was completely unaware of it.

"I shall live the rest of my life so that you never regret it," he said earnestly.

"I had not considered the possibility," she replied with a smile. "Time is sweet enough not to waste any of it in less than the very best way." She touched the side of his cheek with her fingers, a tender and intimate gesture. "Now may we please get out of the public thoroughfare, where we are causing something of a spectacle?"

18

Pɪᴛᴛ ʜᴜɴɢ ᴜᴘ ᴛʜᴇ telephone and turned to Stoker. He had requested the police to go to both Talbot's house and his office at Downing Street, but it was merely a precaution. He did not think for a moment that the man would return to either place. He agreed with Narraway that Talbot would make an attempt to silence Ailsa, the only witness who knew exactly what he had done. Without her he could still twist the truth until he emerged the hero who had discovered Kynaston's treason and deliberately trapped him. Since he had worked so closely with the government, the prime minister in particular, there would be many happy to accept that answer. It would be the perfect way to avoid a scandal, which Talbot would know.

Pitt had just telephoned the Kynastons' home first, in case Ailsa was there. The butler had told him that she was on her way to luncheon. He could not say with whom, but it was in a restaurant just across Tower Bridge. Apparently the walkway across the great span from the height of one tower to that of the other was a marvelous experience. Pitt had thanked him.

"Tower Bridge," he told Stoker. "Restaurant's just below. We'll get a hansom. Come on!"

"How long ago did she leave?" Stoker asked, following Pitt out onto the street and striding along towards the nearest corner to find a cab.

"Half an hour," Pitt replied, charging out into the roadway and waving his arms as a hansom approached.

The horse drew to a startled halt, steering the cab sideways.

"Tower Bridge!" Pitt called out as he swung up into the cab. Stoker charged round the other side to climb in beside him. "Fast as you can!" Pitt shouted. "Double the fare if you make it in time!"

"Time for what?" the cabby demanded. "Damn lunatic."

"To save a woman's life," Pitt replied. "Get on with it!"

The cab lurched forward and rapidly picked up speed until they were driving as if their own lives depended on it. They swerved round corners on two wheels and thundered along straight roads, the driver cracking his whip in the air and other traffic scattering before them.

Pitt and Stoker clung on to their seat, and by now Stoker had his eyes shut. Pitt lost track of where they were. They avoided the main thoroughfare, very wisely.

Pitt had two main anxieties ahead of all the others, ahead even of being too late to stop Talbot from possibly killing Ailsa. The lesser thing he feared was that they would succeed in getting there on time, and he would owe the driver far more than he could afford to pay. The greater was that he had misjudged the whole affair, and they would arrive to find neither Talbot nor Ailsa anywhere near Tower Bridge.

He sat with hands clenched, not only to keep himself from being hurled from side to side and cracking his head against the interior walls of the cab, but to try to stop his imagination from building in his mind a sense of total humiliation. He had abandoned the rules he had lived by all his life, taken decisions he had no right to. His initial instinct had been right—he was not fit for this job. He had not the wisdom nor the steel in his soul. He was guessing frantically, and he was going to let everyone down.

They were now careering along the Embankment. If it were possible to look outside without risking breaking his neck, he might see the magnificent outline of Tower Bridge like twin battlements black against the sky.

Stoker was sitting rigid in his seat, eyes still closed. He would have nightmares about this. It was a pity. Pitt wondered idly if Kitty Ryder had lived up to Stoker's vision of her. Everything in Stoker's smile, and his silence on the subject, made him think that perhaps she had. He was pleased. If this turned out to be a complete fiasco, it would not be Stoker's fault. He should escape the blame.

They came to a shuddering halt. Stoker all but fell out onto the pavement. Pitt climbed out more stiffly, straightening up as if he had been cramped for hours instead of less than one.

"There y'are, sir," the driver said in triumph. He strained his neck up at the towers soaring into the air. "She's a fine-looking bridge, in't she? Won't see the like o' that nowhere else. That's London, that is." He gave Pitt a gap-toothed smile of pride. "That'll be nine shillings and sixpence, sir."

Expensive. Practically half a constable's weekly pay, and—since he had promised to double it—it was pretty well the whole of it. He fished in his pocket: thirty shillings altogether. He offered the man twenty. "Thank you," he said sincerely.

The man looked at the twenty shillings, then heaved a deep sigh. "Ten'll do it, sir. Enjoyed myself. Old Bessie 'ere in't had a gallop like that in years. Put the fear o' God into some o' them along the way, didn't we, eh?" He grinned.

"Take the twenty," Pitt said graciously. "Give Bessie a treat. She's more than earned it!"

"Thank you, sir. I'll do that." He picked all the shillings out of Pitt's hand and put them into his pocket. "Good day, sir." And he urged the horse on in a slow, steady walk.

It took them ten minutes to find the restaurant. It was now very late for luncheon, and there were few diners left.

Suddenly Stoker gripped Pitt's arm so hard his fingers bit into the flesh.

Pitt froze, then turned slowly to follow the line of Stoker's gaze. Ailsa Kynaston and Edom Talbot were walking, arm in arm, towards the way out that led towards the steps up to the north tower of the bridge. They were close to each other, as if lovers. She walked with her head up, gracefully, proud of her height. He seemed protective, as though he would guard her, even though he was actually taking her out into the first heavy spots of rain.

Stoker shot a questioning glance at Pitt.

It was too late to back out now. He had made this decision. He must live with it.

Together they followed, at a distance just great enough to make it look like chance, but careful not to lose sight of them.

They were going to walk across the top, the already famous path between the two towers that spanned the entire river, so that they would have one of the most spectacular views in London. Perhaps getting wet was a very small price to pay. Considering the now torrential rain, they might even have the place to themselves.

To themselves! Suddenly the significance of that shot through Pitt as if he had been physically struck. He started to race up the steps two at a time, Stoker behind him. They burst through the doors onto the walkway high above the river. The first drops had now turned into a blinding deluge, and they could hardly see it. They could just make out two figures standing near the rail looking over.

They started to run towards them, but they were slipping in the streaming rain, half blinded by it, hearing nothing but the beat of water and the splashing of their feet.

Talbot was extraordinarily strong. He caught her from behind and threw his weight into lifting her. She went over the edge, hesitated for a moment, struggling, then plunged into the void. In the thunder of the rain they did not even hear her scream, or strike the river below. But he knew that within moments the swift and icy current would drown her.

Talbot stared for a moment, then turned to see Pitt only feet away from him, Stoker almost level with him.

Pitt smiled, or perhaps it was more a baring of the teeth.

Talbot smiled back. "Terrible accident," he said a little hoarsely. "Or perhaps it was suicide. I was pursuing her. Not really my job, more yours, but you seem a little slow." His voice was raised above the noise, but perfectly steady. "She was passing secret information on to a foreign power, or maybe you hadn't worked that out yet. Better this way, perhaps? We can't afford a public trial. Make us look like fools. Make our enemies rejoice and our allies despair of us. Do more harm than the information itself."

"Quite," Pitt agreed, taking a deep breath to try to stop himself from shaking. "Treason trials are extremely embarrassing. I always do what I can to avoid them. Trials for murder, on the other hand, are a completely different thing."

Talbot froze as a terrible realization struck him.

Pitt smiled again. "Edom Talbot, I am arresting you on a charge of murdering Ailsa Kynaston. Lovers' quarrel, I imagine. That's what it looked like, don't you think, Stoker? Citizen's arrest, of course, but it'll stand. As you say, nobody wants trials for treason. Makes us look incompetent."

"Definitely, sir," Stoker agreed. "Seems the lady rebuffed him. Very hard thing to take, sir, women laughing at you, scorning you like that. Saw it myself. Damn silly place to tell a short-tempered man that you're finished with him."

Talbot gave him a shriveling look. Stoker smiled back at him, as calm as the sun, which was reappearing through the wind-torn clouds.

———

Pᴉᴛᴛ ᴡᴇɴᴛ ʙᴀᴄᴋ ᴜᴘ the river straight to the House of Commons and sent a message inside that he required to speak with Jack Radley immediately, on a matter of state.

He waited twenty minutes before Jack came out of the chamber into the hall, treading softly in the echoing vault of it. He looked very pale.

"What is it?" he said in a hushed tone, just audible over the murmur and the soft shuffling of feet as others met and parted, or entered the chamber he had just left. "What's happened?"

Very briefly Pitt told him.

"I called you out to ask you to accept the position to work with Kynaston—" he began.

"But you've just said he's guilty of treason!" Jack all but snarled the words.

"Exactly," Pitt agreed, grasping Jack's arm. He held it so hard that Jack pulled back, using all his weight, but it made no difference. "He has sent real and important information to the Swedes, and thus God knows who else, in order to settle a debt of honor owed by his dead brother. I am going to have him now send them false information to settle his own debt—to us. If you agree, you will work for him, and oversee it . . ."

Jack's eyes widened, and he stopped pulling away, forcing Pitt to adjust his balance rather quickly.

"Will you?" Pitt asked.

Jack gripped his hand hard, and Pitt winced. "I will!" he said fiercely. "You'll never regret it, Thomas!"

"I know," Pitt answered, returning the grip. "Now I'd better go and inform Kynaston!"

Pᴉᴛᴛ ᴡᴇɴᴛ ᴛᴏ ꜱᴇᴇ Dudley Kynaston that evening. He found him alone in his study, sitting beneath the portrait of Bennett. He looked pale but composed.

"I know Ailsa is dead," he said quietly as Pitt closed the door. "Did she speak to you?"

"No," Pitt replied. "But it wasn't necessary. I know why Talbot killed her. I tried to save her, but I was too late. But probably it is better this way." He remained standing with Kynaston looking up at him, his face white, eyes hollow.

"You know . . ." Kynaston said huskily.

"Yes. Probably more than you do," Pitt replied. "I know that she was Ingrid's sister and she never forgave Bennett for her death . . ."

Kynaston stood up from the chair. "It wasn't Bennett's fault, for God's sake! She was infatuated with him! He never gave her . . . Ingrid's sister? Are you . . . sure?"

"Yes, of course I am! And it doesn't matter now what the truth of it was," Pitt said gently. "It probably was no more than a tragedy, but Ailsa blamed Bennett for it. She could not accept that the sister she adored was mentally fragile, obsessed with a man who did not love her. It was Harold Sundstrom who rescued Bennett for you, so you owed him a debt you could never repay: Bennett's debt. I understand that. But it is still treason."

"I know," Kynaston admitted quietly. "I suppose if I had been thinking clearly I would always have known. It began in such a small way! Just a simple question answered. It seemed almost harmless, just interest."

"And you were in love with Ailsa . . ."

"Infatuated," Kynaston amended. "Ingrid was fifteen, you know! God! How could I blame her when I have no more sense myself? Then it was too late . . . I was terrified when they found that body in the gravel pit. I was so afraid it was poor Kitty. I thought they'd killed her to warn me!"

"Kitty is alive and well," Pitt assured him. It was absurd to feel sorry for him, and yet he did.

"I'm glad. Whatever will happen to Rosalind? She doesn't deserve this either . . ."

Pitt's decision was already complete, and he intended to carry it through. Once committed to, it would be impossible to reverse without acute embarrassment to the government.

"Nothing will happen to her," he said firmly. "I have no intention of arresting you. That's not what I've come here for. I know you have been passing secret information to Ailsa, which she then passed on to Edom Talbot, who sold it to Sundstrom, incidentally the father of Ailsa's first husband. Perhaps you don't know that?"

Kynaston stared at him, eyes hollow. He gave a minute shake of his head.

"You are going to go on passing naval information to Sundstrom," Pitt continued. "We will find a way for you to do it. Clearly he will know that Ailsa has died, but we will say that Edom Talbot killed her in a lovers' quarrel. Seems she rejected him, and he couldn't cope with it. He will be tried for murder and found guilty."

"But . . ." Kynaston stammered.

Pitt smiled at him. "Sir John Ransom will give you the information we wish pass on, and you will be given a new contact, now that Ailsa is no longer available. It will come through Jack Radley. I know that he shall accept the position you offered him after all, because I have seen to it."

"But he's totally loyal!" Kynaston protested. "He wouldn't—"

"Yes, he will, if instructed to," Pitt told him. "I know him very well. He's my brother-in-law, remember. He'll make a very good job of sending all kinds of information to Sundstrom."

Kynaston blinked. "You mean misinformation?"

"Precisely. You have done much damage. You will now do much good. That is how you will repay your debt."

Kynaston sat back in his chair, tears filling his eyes. "Thank you," he said so hoarsely the words were hardly distinguishable. "Thank you, Pitt."

For more high-stakes murder and mystery on the streets of
Victorian England, turn the page to sample

THE ANGEL COURT AFFAIR

The newest Charlotte and Thomas Pitt novel
from Anne Perry

1

Pᴵᴛᴛ sᴛᴀʀᴇᴅ ᴀᴛ ᴛʜᴇ Home Office minister with disbelief. They were standing in a quiet, sunlit room in Whitehall, the traffic outside inaudible.

"A Spanish saint?" he said, struggling to keep his voice more or less level.

"She's not Spanish, she's English," Sir Walter replied patiently. "She merely lives in Spain. Toledo, I'm told. She is here to visit her family."

"And what is this to do with Special Branch, sir?" Pitt asked. Special Branch had been created initially to deal with the Irish Problem, and now in the spring of 1898, its remit had broadened greatly to address anything that was considered to be a threat to the security of the nation.

All Europe was in turmoil as the century drew toward its close. Unrest was escalating and becoming more open. Anarchist bombings occurred in one place or another every few weeks. In France the Dreyfus affair was raging on toward a climax no one could predict. There were even rumors that the government might fall.

Addressing the threat of assassination to a dignitary visiting England was among the duties of Special Branch—but seeing to the needs of a touring nun, or whatever she was, was certainly not. Pitt opened his mouth to point this out, but Sir Walter spoke first.

"There have been letters containing threats against her life," Sir Walter said, his face completely expressionless. "Her opinions have caused some concern and . . . anger. Unfortunately she has been rather too free in expressing them."

"It's a police problem," Pitt said tersely. "I doubt anyone here will care enough to argue with her, let alone cause a nuisance. But if they do, then the local police can take care of it."

Sir Walter sighed, as if this was a tedious argument. "Pitt, this is not a suggestion. You may think that many people are apathetic as to the exact details of religious doctrine, and only deeply committed Christians will argue with her—and even if they do, you trust that they at least know how to behave within the law." He raised white eyebrows. "If so, you are a fool. Some men will argue more passionately about religion than anything else on earth. To many, religion represents order, sanity, the inevitable victory of good over evil. It confirms to them their place in creation." He smiled bleakly. "Somewhere near the top. The appearance of modesty forbids the very top. Something has to be held back for God." His smile faded and his eyes were grim. "But say something to threaten that place near the top, and you threaten everything."

He shook his head. "For God's sake, man, look at how religion has torn us apart throughout history. Start with the Crusades, and the Inquisition in Spain, the persecution of the Cathars and Waldenses in the rest of Europe, the massacres of the Huguenots in France. We've burned both Catholics and Protestants ourselves. You think it couldn't happen again? If Dreyfus were not a Jew, do you think this whole monstrous affair would ever have started, never mind reached this proportion?"

Pitt drew breath to argue, and found the words frozen on his tongue.

It was barely the end of April. Earlier in the month President McKinley had asked the U.S. Congress for a declaration of war against Spain. Cuba had been seeking independence from Spain for many years, and the United States had begun to intervene in the dispute, seeing an opportunity to gain power and position. When the battleship USS *Maine* had been mysteriously blown up in Havana harbor, the powerful U.S. press openly blamed Spain. On 21 April Congress had ordered a naval blockade of all Cuban harbors, demanding that Spain surrender control of Cuba. On 25 April, four days ago, America had declared war. It was the first time they had done such a thing in their brief, idealistic existence. They had focused on internal expansion, had settled the land, built, explored and developed industry. Now suddenly the country was increasing the size of its armies and its navy and looking for possessions overseas, as far away as Hawaii, and the Philippines.

This new desire for outward expansion could grow to involve other naval powers, even Britain, if America chose to make it so. If anything went wrong with this Spanish woman's visit, it could easily be misconstrued by Spain. A chilling thought given the state of affairs across Europe. President Carnot of France had been assassinated four years ago. Last year it had been Prime Minister Cánovas del Castillo in Spain, where the violence had reached new abominations.

"She is bringing half a dozen or so of her . . . acolytes," Sir Walter went on, as if he had not noticed Pitt's absence of attention.

"God only knows what sort of people they are, but we don't want any of them killed on our soil. I'm sure you understand the embarrassment that would be to Her Majesty's Government. Especially in light of our history with Spain. We don't want to give them any excuses for war with us as well." He looked at Pitt carefully, as if possibly he had overestimated him and would be obliged to reconsider his opinion.

"Yes, sir," Pitt replied. "Of course I understand. Is it even remotely likely that she would be attacked here?" He asked the question not in a spirit of incredulity, but hoping for some assurance that it was not so.

Sir Walter's expression eased a little, the deep lines about his mouth less severe. "Probably not," he replied with the ghost of a smile. "But apparently this woman's English family do not approve of her at all. She left in the first place over some quarrel of principle, so I hear. Families can be the devil!" There was some sympathy in his voice.

Pitt made a last effort to avoid the task. "I would point out that domestic violence is also police work, sir, not Special Branch's. We have a big case of industrial sabotage at the moment that looks as if it is foreign inspired. It's getting worse and has to be stopped."

Sir Walter's eyes were bright and sharp. "I am well aware of Special Branch's concerns. I will remind you that it is the effect on the nation that determines whose problem it is, Pitt, and you know that as well as I do. If you didn't, believe me, you would not be long in your position."

Pitt cleared his throat, and spoke quietly.

"Do we know the nature of this quarrel within the woman's family, sir?"

Sir Walter gave a slight shrug. If he noticed the change in Pitt's tone, he was sophisticated enough not to show it.

"The usual sort of thing with willful daughters, I believe," he replied, the smile back on his face. "She declined to marry the young man of excellent breeding and fortune, and tedious habits, they had selected for her."

Pitt remembered that Sir Walter had three daughters.

"And ran off to Spain and married some Spanish man of unknown character and probably unknown ancestry, at least to Sofia's parents," Sir Walter added. "I imagine it was embarrassing to them."

"How long ago was this?" Pitt asked, keeping his face as expressionless as he could. His own daughter, Jemima, was fast approaching marriageable age. He didn't like to think about it.

"Oh, it has been some time," Sir Walter replied ruefully. "I think it is her religious views that have now compounded the problem. It wouldn't matter so much if she kept them to herself. But she has formed something of a sect. Has her acolytes, as I mentioned."

"Roman Catholic?" Pitt imagined a cult to do with the Virgin Mary, perhaps, causing old persecutions to be remembered.

"Apparently not." Sir Walter lifted one elegant shoulder. "It hardly matters. Just see that no one attacks her while she is in England. The sooner she leaves the better, but alive and well, if you please."

Pitt straightened to attention. "Yes, sir."

"SOFIA DELACRUZ?" CHARLOTTE SAID with a sudden sharpening of interest. She and Pitt were sitting by a low fire in the parlor, the curtains drawn across the French windows onto the garden. Almost all the light was gone from the cool spring sky and there was a definite chill in the air. Sixteen-year-old Jemima and thirteen-year-old Daniel were both upstairs in their rooms. Jemima would be daydreaming, or writing letters to her friends. Daniel would be deep in the adventures of the latest *Boy's Own Paper*.

Pitt leaned forward and put another log on the fire. It gave less heat than coal, but he liked the smell of the apple wood.

"Have you heard of her?" he asked with surprise.

Charlotte smiled slightly self-consciously. "Yes, a bit."

He remembered Sir Walter's reference to a scandal in the past; he knew how Charlotte loathed gossip, even when it was the lifeblood of investigation. She listened to it, but with guilt, and a thread of fear. She had seen too many of its victims firsthand to take pleasure in it.

"What did you hear?" he said gravely. "She may be in danger. I need to know."

Charlotte did not argue, which in itself was indicative of a different kind of interest. He detected concern in her eyes. She put down the sewing she had been doing.

"You are going to protect her?" she asked curiously.

"I've assigned Brundage to it," he replied.

"Not Stoker?" She was puzzled.

"Stoker's quite senior now," he pointed out. He did not want to be sharp and set a division between them. This quiet evening alone with her was the best part of his day. Its peace mattered intensely to him. "He has other responsibilities. Brundage is a good man."

"I've heard Sofia's ideas are pretty radical." She was gazing at him steadily.

"For example?"

"I don't know," she admitted, pushing the sewing away entirely and leaning forward a little. "Perhaps I'll go and listen to what she has to say when she arrives. She has to have more fire than our local minister." Charlotte went to church on most Sundays because she took the children. It was a natural part of belonging to the community and of being accepted. It was also the best place for Jemima and Daniel to meet other youths whose families Charlotte knew in a somewhat substantial way.

More often than not, Pitt discovered some pressing duty elsewhere on Sundays.

Pitt nodded agreement, but he was far more conscious of a sharp memory stirring in his mind. His mother had taken him to the parish church on the edge of the estate every Sunday of his childhood. He could still picture the shafts of colored light slanting downward from the stained-glass windows; smell the stone and faint odor of dust. There were shuffles of movement, a creaking of stays, and the dry riffle of pages being turned. Very seldom had he actually listened to the sermons. Some of the stories from the Old Testament were good, but they were isolated, forming no consistent history of God and man. To him the Bible seemed to be more a series of errors and corrections, well-earned disasters and then heroic rescues. A lot of the rest of it was lists of names, or wonderfully poetic prophecies of desolation to come.

Had he believed any of it? And even if he had, did it matter? If he were honest, the stories from his borrowed copies of *Boy's Own* had stirred his heart far more, with their tales of adventure, of heroes any boy would want to copy. He smiled now with quiet pleasure; he felt a sense of identity with his son when he saw Daniel reading. The magazine now had a new name, the stories had different settings, but the spirit was the same.

So what was it that still clung to him so sharply about those old memories of church? The companionship of his mother, the rare sense of peace within her when she was there, as if she were at last safe, loved and completely unafraid? He had thought at the time that her faith was simple and certain. While he was glad for her, because he knew it comforted some of her fears that he could not, he had no desire to be the same way. It was a subject they had never spoken about, out of choice on both of their parts.

He wondered now if perhaps it had not been nearly as easy for her to keep faith as he had supposed, that she had led him to think it was because it took a certain burden from him. It was one area in which he could be a child. She had allowed him that, as she had so many other things of which he had been unaware at the time. She had died without ever telling him she was ill. She had sent him away so he would not notice, not suffer with her.

Charlotte was watching him, waiting. Was she aware of the thoughts inside him?

"You truly want to go and listen to her?" Pitt said, breaking the silence at last.

"Yes," she said immediately. "As I said, I've heard she is outrageous, even blasphemous in her ideas. I'd love to know what they are."

He realized how little he and Charlotte had ever spoken of their beliefs when it came to matters of religion. And yet he knew everything else about her. He knew what hurt her, made her angry, and made her laugh or cry, who she liked and what she thought of them, and what she thought of herself. Often he would read her emotions by her expression. At other times it was in far smaller things: a sudden silence, an unexplained kindness, the letting slip an old grudge someone else could have held on to, and through these small actions he knew she had understood a shadow, or a pain.

"Does it matter to you?" he asked. "If she is blasphemous."

She looked at him with surprise. At first he thought it was because he had asked. Then he realized that she was surprised to not have a ready answer.

"I have no idea," she confessed. "Perhaps that is why I want to go. I'm not sure I even know what blasphemy is. Cursing, or the desecration of a shrine, I understand. But what is an idea that is blasphemous?"

"Darwin's *On the Origin of Species*," he answered immediately. "The suggestion that we evolved from something lesser rather than descended from something greater. It threatens our entire concept of ourselves." He smiled ruefully.

"Well, if that is what she has come to talk about, she is a little late to cause trouble with it," Charlotte said drily. "We've been fighting about that one already for the last thirty some years! It isn't even interesting anymore."

"So you're not coming, then?" He tried to keep his face straight, as if he were not deliberately teasing her.

"Of course I'm coming!" she said instantly, then realized what he was doing and smiled. "I've never seen a woman blasphemer. Do you suppose there will be a riot?"

He did not satisfy her by answering.

PHOTO: © DIANE M. HINDS

ANNE PERRY is the bestselling author of two acclaimed series set in Victorian England: the Charlotte and Thomas Pitt novels, including *The Angel Court Affair* and *Death on Blackheath,* and the William Monk novels, including *Blood on the Water* and *Blind Justice*. She is also the author of a series of five World War I novels, as well as twelve holiday novels, most recently *A New York Christmas,* and a historical novel, *The Sheen on the Silk,* set in the Ottoman Empire. Anne Perry lives in Scotland.

WWW.ANNEPERRY.CO.UK

To inquire about booking Anne Perry for a speaking engagement, please contact the Penguin Random House Speakers Bureau at speakers@penguinrandomhouse.com.

ABOUT THE TYPE

The book was set in Goudy Old Style, a typeface designed by Frederic William Goudy (1865–1947). Goudy began his career as a bookkeeper, but devoted the rest of his life in pursuit of "recognized quality" in a printing type. Goudy Old Style was produced in 1914 and was an instant bestseller for the foundry. It has generous curves and smooth, even color. It is regarded as one of Goudy's finest achievements.